VIKING

75 years

IN MY
BROTHER'S IMAGE

❖

IN MY BROTHER'S IMAGE

❖

Twin Brothers Separated by
Faith After the Holocaust

Eugene Pogany

VIKING

VIKING
Published by the Penguin Group
Penguin Putnam Inc., 375 Hudson Street,
New York, New York 10014, U.S.A.
Penguin Books Ltd, 27 Wrights Lane, London W8 51Z, England
Penguin Books Australia Ltd, Ringwood, Victoria, Australia
Penguin Books Canada Ltd, 10 Alcorn Avenue,
Toronto, Ontario, Canada M4V 3B2
Penguin Books (N.Z.) Ltd, 182–190 Wairau Road,
Auckland 10, New Zealand

Penguin Books Ltd, Registered Offices:
Harmondsworth, Middlesex, England

First published in 2000 by Viking Penguin,
a member of Penguin Putnam Inc.

1   3   5   7   9   10   8   6   4   2

A portion of this work first appeared in *Crosscurrents*.

Photographs are from the private collection of the author.

LIBRARY OF CONGRESS CATALOGING-IN-PUBLICATION DATA
Pogany, Eugene.
In my brother's image / Eugene Pogany.
p.   cm.
ISBN 0-670-88538-X
1. Pogany, Nicholas, 1912–   2. Pogany, George, 1912–1993.   3. Jews—Hungary—
Biography   4. Jewish converts from Christianity—United States—Biography   5. Priests—
Hungary—Biography.   6. Holocaust, Jewish (1939–1945)—Hungary—Biography
7. Holocaust survivors—Biography.   8. Hungary—Biography.   9. United States—Biography.
I. Title.

DS135.H93   A163   2000
909'.04924082'0922—dc21
[B]   99-053358

This book is printed on acid-free paper.
∞

Printed in the United States of America
Set in Fairfield
Designed by Kathryn Parise

And still it is not yet enough to have memories. One must be able to forget them when they are many and one must have the great patience to wait until they come again. For it is not yet the memories themselves. Not till they have turned to blood within us, to glance and gesture, nameless and no longer to be distinguished from ourselves—not till then can it happen that in a most rare hour the first word of a verse arises in their midst and goes forth from them.

RAINER MARIA RILKE
The Notebooks of Malte Laurids Brigge

CONTENTS

ACKNOWLEDGMENTS

❖

"The moment one definitely commits oneself," wrote Goethe, "all sorts of things occur, raising in one's favor all manner of unforeseen incidents and meetings and material assistance which no man could have dreamed would have come his way." In addition to those individuals mentioned in the Author's Note who helped with the factual content of this book, there are numerous others whose assistance and goodwill were invaluable in making it a reality. I wish to express my gratitude to Nancy Malone, O.S.U., the tireless and visionary former editor of *Cross Currents: The Journal of the Association for Religion and Intellectual Life*. Along with her discerning coeditors, Joseph Cunneen and William Birmingham, Nancy introduced this story to the journal's interfaith readership by featuring my essay, "In Each Other's Likeness," in its Spring 1995 issue (Vol. 45, No. 1). I have quoted briefly here from both that essay and my later piece, "Exile and Memory: Reflections on Tisha B'Av," which appeared in the Winter 1995–96 issue of *Cross Currents* (Vol. 45, No. 4).

My friend Jürgen Manemann, of Westfälische Wilhelms University, Münster, Germany, further advanced the telling of the story by translating "In Each Other's Likeness" into German and facilitating its publication in the Swiss Catholic periodical *Orientierung*, where it appeared in August 1997 (Volume 6, Number 15/16). Similarly, I wish to thank Professor Randolph L. Braham, preeminent scholar of the Hungarian Holocaust, who graciously recommended my essay to the distinguished Budapest Jewish quarterly, *Múlt és Jövő* [*Past and Future*], where it appeared in its 1997/2 issue.

From the very inception of this book project, I have been especially grateful for the friendship of Beverly Coyle. Her support and goodwill have helped to open doors, and her timely advice has familiarized me with the publishing world. My agent, Helen Rees, believed in this story and convinced me of its viability as a book, and her endless enthusiasm helped find the book a home with Viking. My editor at Viking, Jane von Mehren, steadily and decisively stewarded this project through the entire editorial process, from the initial board meeting to the crafting and shaping of the book through its various stages. I was blessed throughout by her skill, sensitivity, and unflagging good judgment, as well as by her gracious support. Jane's assistant, Jessica Kipp, provided a literary ear and thorough professionalism well beyond her youthful years. Copy editor Carole McCurdy's meticulous attention to detail and style, as well as her profound sensitivity to the story, helped to make this a better book than it otherwise would have been.

Abundant thanks, as well, to Joan Leegant and Ronnie Friedland for their generous editorial counsel during the early stages, and to Don Gropman and Sandi Gelles-Cole for their seasoned advice and adept assistance on the book proposal. My good friend Jeff Baker brought a keen and sophisticated sensibility to his reading of a first, voluminous draft of the manuscript. Charlie Puccia unselfishly did everything from arranging my travel to Italy to translating my uncle's Italian letters.

I extend my appreciation to Professor John Clabeaux of St. John's Seminary, in Brighton, Massachusetts, and Father Tom Kane, S.J., of the Weston Jesuit School of Theology, in Cambridge, both of whom refined my understanding of Catholic ritual, liturgical practices, and Scriptural interpretation. I am responsible for whatever errors remain in the text.

I also wish to acknowledge the dear members of the Boston One Generation After writers' group, in whose warm and supportive company I thought and wrote, read, and listened for more years than I have worked on this book. Special thanks also to Cynthia Ozick, whose incisive correspondence alternately blessed my efforts and impelled me to think deeply and clearly about the painful history between Catholics and Jews.

I am immensely grateful to Katharina Lamping for the many hours during which she shared stories and vignettes with me of her seventeen years of service to my uncle and his parish church. My brother, Peter, and sister, Ellen, were always in my thoughts, especially when I wrote of our early years together. Although people's recollections of the same events can often vary widely, my siblings naturally served me as touchstones for those times. Thanks, as well, to Bob Buday, our long-lost relative, who also helped get this book off the ground. The excitement and love of the many extended-family members and personal friends who have watched me bring this story to life over the years, often in relative isolation, have been a source of ongoing comfort.

Although my father and mother are noted in numerous other places for the contributions they made to informing the content of this book, there is insufficient room to adequately thank them. I was initially afraid that they would tire of the many hours they spent with me during the past several years being recorded on audio, video, and notepad. I can only hope that they have been as enlivened by our encounters as I have been. I can now more confidently say that I truly know my parents—what they have lived and suffered and how their lives have influenced the person I have become. May what my father and mother learn about their son for his efforts at portraying them prove equally as precious to them.

Finally, my dear wife, Judy, prolific reader and no-nonsense critic, gave timely and insightful feedback and showed immense patience and forbearance as wife and mother throughout the years of this project. This book would not have been conceivable without her abiding and loving presence. Last but not least, our sons, Ben and Elias, must often have wondered what this complex story was all about and when it would actually be completed. Now that I can place the book into their hands, may the silences that pervaded our family's life during my own childhood begin to be dispelled in theirs. I dedicate this book to them.

AUTHOR'S NOTE

❖

I began work on this book a few weeks after the death of my uncle, Monsignor George Pogany, in July 1993. It is a sad irony that I could not begin to tell the story of my Jewish father and his Catholic twin brother until after they were separated by death. When my uncle came to the United States in 1956, he promised my father that he would not bring up religious differences with his brother's children. In the aftermath of the brothers' nearly two-decades-long separation, however, they seemed to have little ability or willingness to discuss with each other the agonizing matters of grief, disappointment, and recrimination surrounding their mutual losses in the war and my formerly devout Catholic father's return to Judaism after the Holocaust. Consequently, there was much silence growing up in their midst, interrupted by sometimes tense conversations about themselves and their family. Their sister's only visit from Australia, in 1984, generated discussions among the three siblings that helped familiarize me with virtually all of the people in earlier generations of our family, as well as with some of the more poignant themes in their lives.

When my uncle died, my father broke the brothers' vow of silence about religion and the war. In the process, he revealed a truly astounding memory for details, going back to the beginning of their lives. He shared facts, conversations, and impressions of the various characters, as well as hunches about their inner lives and motivations. We took two trips to Hungary together, which liberated his memory and immensely enhanced my understanding of my father's origins.

As work on the book proceeded, my mother became equally engrossed in the project. She had always told dramatic and heart-wrenching tales of suffering, loss, and survival. Now, she provided necessary and gripping details, and courageously touched on closely guarded, painful stories of how her identity as a Jew had been threatened. These accounts only affirmed for me the resilience of the Jewish spirit, even after the Holocaust, and heightened my appreciation for my mother having so thoroughly instilled in her children a love of belonging to the Jewish people.

Partly through my uncle's lifelong love and solicitude toward me as his nephew, I gained a realistic and direct sense of him as a person. After his death, Katharina Lamping, George's devoted parish assistant and housekeeper of many years, provided invaluable insight into my uncle's faith and religious vocation. Katharina's reminiscences, coupled with the survival of a sizable collection of his homilies, as well as what my father eventually shared with me, helped me to form a picture of Father George's life as a singularly devoted Roman Catholic priest. Although the conversations I recount between him and Katharina occurred more in my imagination than in actuality, they are based on everything I have learned about the relationship between them, on actual events in George's life and statements he made, as well as on his psychological and spiritual sensibilities as evident in these sources.

In regard to my uncle's life with Padre Pio, in Rome I met with Padre Pio Abresch, George's former boyhood student of Greek (and chess) in San Giovanni Rotondo. Soon after, I journeyed to that town to visit the Our Lady of Grace friary, where I was graciously guided by Padre Joseph Pius Martin. Both of these very kind padres helped me gain a vivid appreciation of the years George spent in the service of the saintly Padre Pio of Pietrelcina.

In addition, the Reverend C. Bernard Ruffin was exceedingly helpful for his superlative biography of Padre Pio, which includes an invaluable interview with my uncle. The Reverend Mr. Ruffin's encouraging correspondence and phone conversation were also extremely informative. The most gentle and generous Father John A. Schug, Cap., who is also an eminent biographer of Padre Pio, shared with me the correspondence of Father Dominic Meyer, English and German secretary to Padre Pio from 1947 to 1959, relating to my uncle's life among the Capuchian fathers of Our Lady of Grace. Mrs. Anna Zegna of Biella, Italy, wife of the late Albino Zegna, was also helpful in this area. Both husband and wife had been close personal friends of my uncle and devoted followers of Padre Pio. Mrs. Zegna, along with her daughter and son-in-law, Gianna and Roberto Borsetti, provided valuable correspondence—including many of my uncle's letters—and precious insight into the nature of the lifesaving sanctuary Padre Pio offered my uncle as a Jewish-born Catholic priest in San Giovanni Rotondo during the years of the war. Ms. Maria Callandra, of the National Center for Padre Pio, in Barto, Pennsylvania, forthrightly shared her understanding of the inviolability of Padre Pio's spiritual purity in the midst of danger to innocent life during World War II. I wrestled greatly with her comments.

Events occurring among family members, as narrated here, are based on history that I witnessed or that was personally conveyed to me. They are honest attempts at capturing the spirit and content of interactions, many of which I know to have taken place but for which I could not have actually been present. They serve to establish a more vividly realistic and textured portrayal of social and historical circumstances.

I especially agonized over interactions among members of my family and historical individuals, such as those between my father and Bishop Vilmos Apor, a singularly courageous opponent of the Nazi designs on Hungarian Jews. My father's distant memories of the content and spirit of Father Apor's sermons while he was a pastor in Gyula, Hungary, helped to inform the statements I attribute to him. I was equally concerned with the credibility of discussions between my uncle and Padre Pio. My uncle had spoken with me and others about the nature and content of personal conversations with the padre. While no one still living knows precisely what warnings Padre Pio gave George about the potential dangers to him during the war had he left San Giovanni Rotondo, I have relied both on secondhand reports of individuals familiar with the two men (referenced in the Notes) and on inferences drawn from what I know of my uncle's circumstances during those years. The nature of their discussion about my father's turning away from Catholicism is also referenced in the Notes.

My efforts, then, to reconstruct interactions among my ancestors and to elaborate the nuances of their beings—their feelings, inner dialogues, points of view—spanning nearly an entire century, represent an attempt to enter and participate in the lives of those to whom I am admittedly connected, through my own longings and imagination as much as through the historical record, personal reports, and my own life experience. My relatives speak through me about themselves, and I boldly speak for them in order to illuminate a religiously and historically turbulent landscape of Jews and Christians in the century of the Holocaust.

All of the larger historical events narrated here are as accurate as a nonhistorian's research would allow them to be. The seminal works of Randolph L. Braham, Eugene Levai, Moshe Y. Herczl, and Raphael Patai—among a host of other resources referenced in the Notes—provided the backbone of Jewish and interfaith cultural history and Holocaust political history to which I can only hope I have done justice. In a few cases, names have been changed, abbreviated, or omitted in deference to the dead, in respect for the living, or in the spirit of not unnecessarily invoking the various names of Amalek, the namesake of those who have been committed throughout history to the destruction of the Jewish people.

Now, at the end of the millennium and the beginning of the next, much progress has been made among Jews and Christians in coming to some mutual understanding of their respective roles in the spiritual unfolding of history, and in the Catholic Church's increasing willingness to take responsibility for the atmosphere of hatred that fostered the Holocaust. I know that many people—perhaps my father among them—remain skeptical about the possibility of a complete healing between the Jewish and Christian communities of faith in the aftermath of the Shoah. But even in deference to those whose life experience I must honor, I believe that if there is one singular and preeminent purpose for telling this story, it is to envision that Jewish and Christian brothers might someday stand—although my father and uncle could not—at the gates of Jerusalem and embody the spirit of Isaiah 52:8: "Together they shall sing, for eye to eye they shall see when the Lord returns to Zion."

In My Brother's Image

❖

PROLOGUE

❖

Sorrow in Search
of Memory

How goodly are thy tents, O Jacob!
How beautiful your sanctuaries, O Israel!
NUMBERS 24:5

A seminal fragment of my family's lore: on a sweltering afternoon in the summer of 1918, two five-year-old boys named Gyuri and Miklós scurry across the vast cobblestone courtyard of St. Stephen's Basilica in Budapest. They climb the two long tiers of granite steps to Hungary's largest cathedral, located only a few blocks from the banks of the Danube, the fabled river that divides the nineteenth-century half of the city from its thousand-year-old counterpart. The boys look more alike than brothers. In fact, they are identical twins, indistinguishable in the smooth innocence of their faces, their wide brown eyes, and their shorn hair, nearly shaven to their scalps to thwart the summer heat. They are dressed alike—in white, short-sleeve summer shirts and light blue short pants with attached suspenders of the same material, crossed in the back and buttoned in the front. Their cumbersome, high black shoes rise halfway up their calves. Most of the time, from the day of their birth, it has been difficult for almost everyone to tell them apart. The brothers know each other as only identical twins can.

At the entrance to the grand church, the boys surreptitiously slip through the six-inch-wide opening of the formidable oak middle door, with its inlaid bronze bas-relief portraits of the Hungarian kings. They giggle gleefully and a bit nervously as they peer into the dimly lit chamber, which feels refreshingly cool in contrast to the scorching afternoon sun they have just escaped. In mannerism and impulse, the twins mimic and build on each other's playful daring. Even their spirited laughter is identical, punctuated by squeals of delight.

The awe-inspiring sanctuary, sheathed in red marble and gilt, is lined with magnificent statues of saints, angels, and kings, larger-than-life somber paintings of the crucified Christ, and four enormous central columns supporting a domed cupola that rises to where heaven meets earth. What natural light enters the sanctuary filters through a number of oblong windows at the base of the dome, interspersed evenly among painted friezes of celestial beings. There is also a circular window at the very height of a second dome above the apse, directly over the altar. It illumines the guilded paintings of archangels along the dome's curved walls.

At the moment the boys enter, only a few people occupy the unending rows of delicately carved mahogany pews that fill the nave of the church. An elderly woman with deep creases crisscrossing her face, wearing a plain black dress and a red flower print babushka covering her head, is seated in the last row on the right side of the central aisle as the boys tiptoe in, still giggling. When they realize that she is there for her own purposes, and is not about to tell them to leave or behave themselves, their anxiety abates as they stride in a make-believe processional up the aisle with the imagined solemnity of priests and the exaggeratedly stiff gait of soldiers.

An old man in a coarse brown shirt, workman's trousers, and well-worn cavalry boots, hat in hand and his head bent over onto his chest, is seated on the opposite side of the aisle, in the front section of pews, just beyond the first two giant columns. The boys pay him no mind as they high-step past him with an air of impunity, making their way toward the imposing altar. Their solemn march dissolves, and they trot, then dash toward the front row of seats. Suddenly, the boys stop in their tracks and their attention becomes sharply focused. They stand transfixed, frozen and inert, gazing impassively at a brightly painted statue of a thinly clad man suspended on a cross, with drops of blood flowing from his hands and feet. As they stare at the figure, they instantly imagine the agony he must feel. Then the moment is over, as suddenly as it began, and the boys proceed to play at genuflecting, crossing themselves and mumbling imitations of incomprehensible Latin liturgy.

These children have never been to a church service before. In fact, they have never been inside a church sanctuary. But on numerous Sunday mornings they have overheard the Latin chants issuing from the open doors of their neighborhood church, less than a block from their family's apartment on Tölgyfa, or Oak Street, in Buda, near the foot of the Margit Bridge. Some of their Christian playmates have told them about crossing oneself and bending one's knees to pray in church, so they have a vague notion of Christian ritual.

Now, standing in front of the altar, they pretend to chant, interspersing familiar names or Hungarian words: "Domino, pomino, Jesus, Maria, Isten öriz . . . "

"Let's go find his hand," says Gyuri, with an irreverent laugh.

"What?! What are you talking about?" asks his brother.

"St. Stephen's hand. The king who made the Hungarians Catholic. That's his statue over there," he says, pointing to a shiny and colorful icon in the middle of the altar. "I heard that his hand is kept in a golden box behind the altar somewhere. Let's go find it, Miki," Gyuri continues, with a look of mischievous relish.

"No!" Miklós blurts out. "We're not supposed to go back there," he says, with a reverence in his voice that borders on fear and panic. Then a laugh breaks his momentarily stiff mood. "But that's the craziest thing I ever heard—a king's hand inside a box in a church. He must have been pretty mad when they cut his hand off."

Gyuri laughs and gives his brother a gently dismissive shove on his shoulder.

Earlier that afternoon, the boys had become bored in their summer villa in Rákosszentmilhály, on the outskirts of Budapest. Their mother was ill in bed and their step-grandmother was not the most engaging of caretakers, especially when she needed to look after their baby sister. The twins roamed briefly and impatiently in the large garden of the villa, then decided on impulse to climb the lone mulberry tree at its edge, up over the high wooden fence surrounding it. They walked along the tram tracks toward the station, which they knew would surely guide them into the city. Then, acting on another sudden impulse, they decided that their destination would be the basilica, where they would go to "pray." The boys' father had been away at war for nearly four years, serving as a captain in the Austro-Hungarian Army, and they knew he had become Christian before his departure. Their impetuous pilgrimage may have been partially an impulse to be closer to him, the father they hardly knew.

When the local tram conductor, who was familiar with the boys, saw them walking on the tracks, he stopped to pick them up. They told him they were going to pray at the basilica, and he offered to take them there. At least he would take them to another tram that would drop them within walking distance of the church. The boys didn't hesitate for an instant. If walking into the city was a feasible project, how much better to get a free ride on the tram. They even handled the transfer onto the next tram with confidence, sure that grown-ups would naturally take care of them.

On their foray into the church, the boys were acting out an assimilationist impulse all-too-common among many Hungarian Jewish families, some of whom they were acquainted with. They had rarely seen Orthodox Jews in their neighborhood and had only heard stories of old men with beards, dressed in black, who spent their days in prayer and lived far away in the countryside, or at least in the Jewish quarter of Pest, somewhere on the other side of the river. None of their Jewish relatives or family friends gave them any idea of what being Jewish meant: these Jews observed the Christian holidays as national days of celebration and gift-giving. Today Gyuri and Miklós were Jews merely playing at being Christians, but, their own Jewishness notwithstanding, they knew more about Christianity for their visit to the basilica than they had ever learned about Judaism.

The boys continue standing before the altar of the basilica for several minutes. It is a struggle for Gyuri to tear his gaze from the awe-inspiring figure suspended on the cross directly above him. He finds the image strangely comforting. He imagines that even a god as powerful and revered as this one is also human and tangible and can feel pain and suffering. The child studies the pierced hands of this suffering Lord and feels sad and sorry for Him. For reasons he cannot begin to understand, this sorrow comforts Gyuri and helps him feel less alone in his private melancholy, for his mother is often sad and sick, and he misses his father terribly, fearing that he will never see him again.

While Gyuri remains entranced, Miklós turns away from the wounded god on the cross. Though just as enraptured as his brother, on this hot summer day he is more aware of how refreshed and revived he feels in the cool and mysterious sanctuary. Here in this marvelous chamber, Miklós feels, if only momentarily, welcome and at home.

✤

Well before dawn on an autumn night in 1992, seventy-four years later, the city was darkly quiet. Directly outside our hotel, the Chain Bridge connecting Buda and Pest was still partially illuminated, as were the facades of palaces and other imperial buildings overlooking the Danube. Budapest was undeniably beautiful, yet its predawn serenity felt as tenuous and fragile as the momentarily quiet surface of the river that flowed through its heart. I sensed a subtle but grinding tension just below the surface, and below that a deeper current of sorrow—silent, unclaimed, and unredeemed.

My family had arrived from New York the previous afternoon. There were fourteen of us scattered throughout the Budapest Hyatt. My brother, sister, and I had come with our respective families to accompany our parents back to the country of their origin on the occasion of our father's eightieth birthday. Among all the members of our immediate family, only my uncle George was missing.

George had not ignored the importance of this landmark occasion, for as my father's twin it was his birthday, too. But the country of their birth had come to possess painfully different and seemingly unbridgeable meanings for them. Neither had left it with pleasant memories, but the nature of their earlier choices and the timing of their departures colored how each felt about coming back.

My wife lay asleep beside me as I listened to her breathing and that of my two young sons in the adjoining room of our suite. I lay still, gazing at the faintly illuminated city through the gossamer curtains of our hotel window. I could hear the occasional rumble of a car or taxi disturb the stillness of Roosevelt Square, by day a bustling thoroughfare to the Chain Bridge.

A shrill, high-pitched ring cut through my unfocused consciousness. I grabbed for the telephone.

"Good morning," said a man's monotone voice in Hungarian-accented English. "This is your wake-up call."

"Thank you," I said, and hung up. I glanced at the digital clock on the nightstand as I replaced the receiver. It read 5:30.

I arose without hesitation, reached half-blindly in the unlit room for some clothes that still lay packed in open suitcases on the floor, and proceeded to wash and dress without disturbing my wife and children. I then put on my hooded green woolen coat to meet the cool air of the city that was born—according to Gyula Krudy, a turn-of-the-century Hungarian novelist—of the same mother as autumn. Almost surreptitiously, though no one was watching, I stuffed two satin-lined velvet pouches, one blue and the other gray, each decorated with colorful and arcane embroidery, into my coat pockets. I vaguely feared that on the streets of Budapest someone might take them for implements of sorcery or black magic. I carefully made my way past the cots on which my seven- and three-year-old sons slept, opened the door to the suite, and quietly pulled it closed behind me. I walked down the stairwell to the main lobby, where I signaled the young Magyar doorman to hail me a taxicab.

As he opened the door to the cab, which had been parked at the head of a short row of taxis directly in front of the hotel, the doorman asked me in Hungarian where I wished to go.

"*Wesselényi Utca*" (Wesselényi Street), I answered.

"*Milyen cim?*" (What address?), the cabbie continued in Hungarian, overhearing my response to the doorman.

"*Hét*" (Seven), I replied. In childhood, this language had rolled smoothly from my tongue, but now speaking even these few words felt thick and wooden.

The cabbie smiled, instantly recognizing my halting accent, and seemed to humor me by saying in Hungarian, "So, good, I think I know where it is. Come, please get in. We'll find it."

Driving through the still-darkened streets of Pest toward the former Jewish ghetto, the cabbie, a good-natured man in his fifties, asked in carefully measured Hungarian, "You are American?"

"Yes, and aren't you Hungarian?"

"No, I am Greek. I have been here for five years."

Then he took the opportunity as a non-native worker to express his concern over how difficult life had become since the fall of Communism—not because he bemoaned its fall, but simply because life was harder and less predictable than many people had hoped it would be.

"Now where is this 7 Wesselényi Street? What's there, an office?" he asked, changing the subject, as if my hesitation had made him doubt my comprehension.

"No, a small synagogue, next to a large one, I think near Dohány Street. I am going there to dream."

The driver looked puzzled, but still he humored me in a helpful, nonpatronizing way. "You are going to dream? A person dreams when he sleeps. Now, aren't there those who do go to church to sleep and dream? But maybe you are thinking of *worship* because it sounds like the word *dream*. Perhaps what you really want to say is *pray*. You are going to the synagogue to pray."

So the kind man finished the first of the many impromptu language lessons I was to receive that week. But, unwittingly, in my initial attempt at reviving the language of my childhood, I stumbled upon the fluid boundaries between dreaming and praying, memory and longing.

Now realizing that I was an American Jew, the cabbie returned momentarily to his more serious tone and shared with me his sense that the life of Jews in Hungary seemed once again uncertain and even threatened. "Not good," he said. "It's not good for Jews now. Even people in Parliament speak against them. Such a shame. Do people never learn, especially after what happened?"

Heading down the street, the driver pointed out the magnificent Moorish-style building of the Dohány Street Synagogue, the largest in Europe. It was surrounded by scaffolding and was, like its attendant Hungarian Jewish community, in the process of being rebuilt after nearly a half-century of neglect by its Soviet oppressors. Driving past the synagogue to the end of the block, the driver turned left, then left again onto Wesselényi Street, before stopping in front of a nondescript city building that housed the synagogue I was seeking.

I thanked the driver warmly and gave no thought to earlier warnings I had received about the gouging tactics of Budapest's cabdrivers. I gladly paid his fee and gave him hundreds more forints of the still unfamiliar Hungarian currency for his friendly language lesson and introduction to the city.

Once inside the musty Orthodox shul, I took a black linen yarmulke out of my coat pocket and placed it on my head. A slightly surprised and nervous-looking middle-aged man dressed in a drab gray suit and a wide striped tie approached me as I stepped into the central hall. With my arrival, he was apparently relieved that he was now one person closer to reaching a minyan, the quorum of ten men required to conduct a Jewish prayer service. He graciously shook my hand and took me by the arm, escorting me down the hallway to the sanctuary, which looked like a large yeshiva classroom.

As I looked around the room, three old men, somewhat crusty and embittered-looking, gave receptive nods as my eyes met theirs. They offered garbled and terse salutations in Hungarian with a mixture of warmth and mild distrust. Two or three young men, in their twenties or early thirties, in threadbare suits or faded trousers and well-worn shirts, also appeared reserved, but they were friendlier. While neither I nor members of my family had ever practiced Judaism with the devotion of these Orthodox Jews, I had the uncanny feeling of being deeply connected to the members of this remnant community. To be praying now as a Jew in Hungary was for me a way of binding my fate to theirs. I felt I had come home.

All those present were in the process of wrapping tefillin, or phylacteries, to their arms and foreheads. Tefillin consist of thin black leather straps attached to small leather boxes housing parchments inscribed with the *Sh'ma Israel*. Jews had been commanded thousands of years before to bind the words proclaiming the oneness of God as "a sign upon your hands and for frontlets between your eyes." I walked to the back of the room and drew my blue and gray pouches from my coat pockets. I took off my coat and placed it on the wooden school chair behind me. I then took my long white-and-black-striped tallis, or prayer shawl, from the blue embroidered bag and draped it around my shoulders. Next, I withdrew my tefillin from their gray pouch and, while reciting the appropriate blessings, wrapped them according to the ancient custom. I had learned the technique and correct sequence in my youth, but I had fully mastered it only a few weeks earlier and still felt self-conscious about binding my religion to my head, my arm, and my hand. But it was at that moment of draping and binding Jewish law to my own body that I truly entered the sacred space in which observant Jews have, for countless generations, offered their daily words of worship and prayer to their one living God. The space inside one's own head and body, wrapped in the tefillin and the soft, soothing cloth of the tallis, was the ancient inner sanctum of Jews.

By now there were twelve or thirteen men in the room. Without prior notice, a grim and brittle-looking leader, in his late sixties or early seventies, launched unceremoniously into the daily liturgy. He prayed with what seemed to be perfunctory speed and precision, in driven tones that rose, nonetheless, from a source much deeper than his mouth or throat. I imagined that his words emerged remotely, from grooves and scars embedded in the recesses of his heart. Had those scars been present, I wondered, ever since he returned from his own hell in Poland or Germany to this—its local, Hungarian antechamber?

Early in the prescribed sequence of prayers, the cantor rapped his knuckles on the wooden *bema* on which his prayer book rested, standing directly in front of the makeshift ark housing two Torah scrolls. In that same instant, he issued a piercing signal for the mourner's prayer, "Kaddish!"

Except for the cantor, we were all seated. At his signal, I sprang to my feet with four or five others and began to utter the ancient words extolling the greatness of God and the inscrutability of His will, even in the shadow of the death of loved ones. I spoke these words that I had only recently begun to speak among members of my home congregation in Boston, but which were so familiar to me I could almost recite them in my sleep. The words rose from an unknown and perplexing source of pain inside me, drawing now choked and halting, then sure and robust sounds from my voice. The Kaddish illuminated that usually dim and distant region of my mind where I unconsciously carried the collective memory of my ancestors, a chamber beyond my own life's memories where fantasy, dream, and longing reside:

"Yit-ga-dol v'yit-ka-dash shmei rabba."
"Exalted and sanctified be the name of God in this world of His creation."
A run-down, dilapidated factory building on the margin of a quaint Hungarian town.

"May His will be fulfilled,"
A beautiful spring dawn; the grass is green, flowers bloom in the fields and gardens of nearby houses and cottages.

"and His sovereignty be revealed in the days of your lifetime,"
Birds are singing, but their songs are barely audible over the chaos in front of the factory.

"and in the days of the life of the house of Israel,
speedily and soon, and say amen."
Surrounded by a few onlookers, armed gendarmes are herding the Jews of the village out of the front entrance of the provisional factory ghetto. The Jews are terrified as they are prodded onto horse-drawn wagons. Their muffled cries of panic and terror have quieted the cock, as if it has postponed its call.

"Be His great name blessed forever, to all eternity."
One by one, at riflepoint, hundreds of Jews, young and old alike, are forced onto the wooden wagons.

"May the most holy One be blessed,"
The faces of the onlookers wear veiled expressions

"and praised,"

of malicious joy,

"honored,"

of composure,

"extolled,"

or resignation.

"and glorified."
They are standing frozen and inert

"Adored and exalted supremely"
while others peer from behind their drawn curtains.

"be the name of the most holy One blessed"
Like many in the crowd, one heavyset middle-aged woman, with graying hair and swollen hands, struggles with a small suitcase. Her other hand is closed around an unseen object.

"beyond all blessings and hymns,"
As she exits the factory, two gendarmes, acting as if they were waiting specifically for her, separate her from the others. They escort her to a waiting cart, relieve her of her suitcase and sheepishly help her board; then one of them places her suitcase beside her. She peers with bewilderment and anguish at their faces,

which she seems to recognize. Her own face possesses the look of one who has been utterly betrayed.

"beyond all praises and consolations that may be uttered in this world,
and say amen."
Leaning against the side of the cart, she lowers her head and places her closed hand on her breast. Her hand opens and the object is revealed: a small wooden crucifix bearing the image of her Lord. She is being deported with the Jews of her village because she was born a Jew and is considered a Jew even though she has lived for decades as a pious and devout Christian. She will be carted away with the hundreds of others of her community to the train station, where she will board a cattle car and never return.

"May He who creates peace in the heavens
create peace for us and for all Israel, and say amen."
The devoted mother of twin boys and a young girl, my father's beloved mother, the grandmother I never knew, was taken away to be killed in an Auschwitz gas chamber. And, it was as if then, and only then, that the cock crowed and the sheep were scattered and . . .
Kaddish ended.

❖

As their afternoon reverie winds down, the twins leave the coolness of the basilica more subdued, with less ceremonial fanfare. Once past the outer doors, they leave each other's side for a moment. Gyuri quickly moves out of the midafternoon shadow of the church. He flies down the stone stairs and follows the sun in its path of retreat above the rooftops ahead of him, in the direction of the river.

Already young Gyuri feels the strangely liberating sorrow of the captivating figure hanging on the cross above the altar of the basilica. He experiences a peculiarly reassuring feeling that it is all right to be alive, despite anything he does or deserves—that he is loved, deeply, in his soul, regardless of his continual misbehavior and ever-faltering degree of virtue.

Standing completely alone in the middle of the square, Gyuri cocks his head back on his neck, closes his eyes, and feels rapturously caressed and comforted by the warmth and light. He is pleased by the tranquillity of the vast and vacant courtyard. What a fitting end it is to his first encounter with the figure on the cross.

For Miklós, the immense courtyard of the basilica seems frighteningly empty and abandoned. Though he sees his brother below him, he feels isolated and exposed. Miklós squints and averts his gaze from the still intense midafternoon sunlight and steps back into the sheltering shadow of the basilica's entryway. He feels oddly distanced from the feelings he has just experienced in the sanctuary, where, only moments before, he fleetingly felt reassured and embraced. How peculiarly estranged Miklós now feels from the church's cool and sublime sanctuary, which had, only moments before— if ever so fleetingly—drawn him and his brother to her bosom with such exquisite enchantment.

And so they stood, these identical twin brothers, one in sunlight, the other in shadow. They were as alike as two human beings can be, but on this sweltering afternoon in the wartime summer of 1918 neither they nor anyone else could possibly imagine the totally different lives they would lead. Nor would it have occurred to anyone that, nearly eight decades later, I, the son of the twin standing in shadow, would strive beyond my own memory to tell their story.

✤ **CHAPTER 1** ✤

Departing

Salus extra ecclesiam non est.
(Outside the Church there is no salvation.)
St. Cyprian

On a fine spring day in Budapest, in 1914, Béla Pogány (né Popper), a recently trained veterinarian, knelt before a Roman Catholic priest at the Regnum Marianum Church to receive entry into the Catholic faith through the rite of baptism. The priest drew water from the baptismal font and poured it freely over the forehead of this short, stout man with brown, careworn Jewish eyes and high cheekbones like a Magyar's.

As the celebrant chanted, *"In nomine Patris et Filii et Spiritus Sancti,"* Béla's thoughts wandered from the Lord he was about to accept into his heart to his beloved wife, Gabriella, and their two-year-old twin boys. Béla was a practical man not given to religious reverie or philosophical reflection. But I am willing to imagine that by the power of this solemn and mysterious ceremony, his life passed before his eyes as if he were about to die, as he presumably was—from the life of the body—to be born again to the life of the spirit in his new Lord.

Béla's background provides only an incomplete picture of how he had come to such a pivotal juncture in his life. He had been brought up by professed but less-than-perfunctory Jewish parents in Galgocz, a small town in the northwestern, Slovakian region of the Austro-Hungarian Empire. His birth was recognized by the Jewish community, his birth certificate signed by the rabbi of the town. On the document, biblical names of his family members, such as David and Isak, appeared alongside appropriated German ones, like his grandfather's, Adolf. Slovak and German were spoken at home even more freely and fluently than Hungarian. The family knew only fragments of Yiddish and even less Hebrew. But for those few socially obligatory occasions when they might have attended synagogue services or spent holiday evenings at friends or neighbors, they were not at all religious. As a family, they observed none of the Jewish holidays or ritual practices. Béla's father had no interest in religion. His mother, Regina, was independent, intelligent, and completely secularized. She would have stayed working at her sewing machine on Yom Kippur had her family members not restrained her.

Jewishness for my grandfather's family was a fact of social life, not of religious identity or practice. The family's four children received no religious education—no bar mitzvahs for the sons or training for the daughter in setting a Sabbath table or keeping a Jewish home. The boys, however, were circumcised. For Jews of any inclination in Hungary at the time, it was a foregone conclusion that their male children would receive the B'rit Milah of circumcision, thereby bringing them into the Hebrew covenant. To do otherwise would have surely antagonized the small, closely knit, even if not uniformly religious Jewish community of the town in which they lived and did business. For practical reasons, they could not afford to perturb that community because the success of the family's brewery was as dependent on the area's Jews as it was on non-Jews, despite the reputation of the former as nondrinkers.

Béla's motivation to become a Christian probably stemmed from his years in Budapest, where he had arrived in the autumn of 1901 at the age of eighteen. He entered a five-year course of training at the Veterinary University, which would enable him to attain his supposedly lifelong ambition of being an animal doctor. The uninspired manner with which he pursued those studies over more than a decade would suggest that his ambition was less than fierce. The coffeehouses that lined the inner city of Pest had a much more magnetic allure to such occasional students than the lecture halls and laboratories of the university. And Béla's family didn't seem to mind indulging his protracted student life.

In Budapest, Béla circulated in a predominantly Jewish, bourgeois culture. Yet he was at best only ambivalently tied to that culture and almost completely disconnected from its religion and tradition. He never fully recognized the matter-of-fact sustenance he received from the familiarity of his Jewish brethren, much as a fish never recognizes the water in which it swims. Instead, like the other Jews with whom he associated, he acted as if Jewishness and Judaism were merely a part of his ancestral identity that only minimally figured into who he was and how he saw himself. As a result, he lived along the surface of that culture, never exploring its depths and never taking into account the buoyancy he gained from living in what was certainly a prosperous and creative era for Jews in Hungary.

At some point, however, the realization of his Jewishness did break into Béla's awareness, with an event that became part of family lore. It supposedly took place on a blustery winter afternoon as he sat with some friends huddled over steaming coffee at a favorite café near the university. In the midst of this subdued atmosphere, a disheveled and wild-looking patron, who had earlier been sitting glumly in a corner averting anyone's gaze, suddenly shot to his feet and accused the café owner of cheating him on his change and pandering to the Jews. Reaching across the counter and grabbing the terrified proprietor by his shirt, the enraged customer howled, "What kind of Jew nest is this? You rob me and treat me like I'm inferior to these swine." Slamming the owner against the rear wall and knocking him senseless, he glared at Béla and his friends, screaming, "You dirty Jews. You think you own this city. You drink our blood and act like innocent lambs. We'll have our revenge some day. Our Lord's blood be upon you and upon your children." Then he stormed out, leaving the other patrons to stare after him in shock and disbelief.

Until then, Béla had not been keenly aware of the ages of discord between Christians and Jews in his native Hungary. In his own personal experience, he had known only indirectly of anti-Jewish sentiment and agitation. A year before his birth, there had been a notorious case that revived the age-old "blood libel" against the Jews that had stained the European landscape since the Middle Ages. A Jewish man, a ritual slaughterer in the distant town of Tisza-Eszlár, had been accused of killing a Christian girl and using her blood to make matzahs for Passover. The Jew had eventually been acquitted after a highly publicized and lengthy trial, but Béla always remembered how his family talked for years about the rioting that had taken place in the wake of the verdict, as close by as the city of Pozsony, only thirty miles from his family's home. The story had planted a small but enduring seed of fear in his own heart and the hearts of many Jews who otherwise enjoyed a privileged and protected life in the Hungarian kingdom.

After the enraged patron exited the café, Béla turned to his friends, and, with a mixture of naiveté and denial, asked, "*Whose* blood be upon *whom?*

What's this crazy man saying?" But even as he spoke those words, he felt the stirring in his gut of a mysterious and ancient terror that awakened memories, not in his mind but in his bones—memories of being hated and hurt. Béla wondered if these were real memories from his childhood or residual fantasies of what it meant to be a Jew. And were they his alone or were they shared by all Jews? He wanted to forget the whole incident, but he couldn't. Where had this poisonous hatred come from and where would it end?

In truth, even after that day, Béla was still far from the baptismal font. He did not care enough about Judaism to embrace it, but neither did any other religion interest him. And he didn't feel sufficiently threatened by these occasional moments of fear to want to run away from his Jewish identity. He was content enough to live as a nominal Jew in a culture and a nation that had been, for the most part, immensely hospitable to Jews.

This would change after Béla met his future wife, Gabriella Groszman. On a late spring day in 1907, he stopped into the B. Fehér tailoring house, an elegant shop in the fashionable inner city of Pest, to purchase a suit of clothes. By chance, Béla happened upon a young woman who worked there as a bookkeeper and office manager. He was immediately drawn to her beauty and vibrancy. Perhaps it was an attraction of opposites, for her focused energy was in sharp contrast to his casual manner. Yet her vitality seemed balanced by a subtle reserve. Her smile was warm but reluctant. It needed gentle and whimsical coaxing. And beneath the sparkle in her eyes he sensed a hint of deeper sadness and remoteness—not aloofness, but rather fragility and vulnerability—which made Béla feel safe.

Acting on the impulse of the moment, he invited Gabriella for coffee when she was free. They met at an outdoor café one warm spring afternoon. Custom demanded that they be accompanied by a chaperone, so Mrs. Ledényi, an older woman with whom Gabriella worked, went along with her. As soon as the couple, undeterred by their lack of privacy, began to share bits and pieces about themselves, they immediately if tacitly recognized the differences in their respective stations in life. His family was well-to-do, hers was poor. But there was an instant rapport between them. He was thrilled by her intelligence, by her eloquence in Hungarian and fluency in German, which she had, like most Hungarian Jews, learned at home (in her case, aided by her father's long stint in the emperor's army). She had read novelists and poets in both languages, writers with whom Béla himself had only passing familiarity. For her part, Gabriella was amused to find that such a bright, well-bred, and seemingly ambitious man knew more about the interior of various coffeehouses in Pest than about the anatomies or breeding practices of

the animals he was supposedly studying and about which he could speak so
glibly. He was drawn by her intensity; she was taken by his affability, by his
gentle, ingenuous manner. He was easy to like.

They saw each other again, at first, not too frequently. As months passed,
they began a more serious courtship, as much as Béla was capable of anything serious or sustained. His comfort in her presence never vanished, and
he became assured, as she did, of the growing inevitability of their union. But
that union was not a foregone conclusion. Béla's family opposed it from the
start.

✤

The need and the occasion for converting to Catholicism would not come
until later. But a fatefully overheard comment and a clash of sensibilities
added to its eventual desirability. It may have crystallized in one day, at a family Passover seder in 1911, four years after my grandparents met and three
years before my grandfather actually converted. The seder, if it could be
called that, might just as well have been an Easter celebration, for there was
no ritual observance of the Jewish holiday. As far as Béla was concerned, the
overriding purpose for the occasion was to allow his stuffy relatives to meet
and evaluate Gabriella. Some of them had already met her, but so far the response was not encouraging: they simply didn't think she was good enough to
marry into their family. So when Béla received the invitation from his sister,
Laura, he considered the option of declining it. He didn't realistically believe
that his convention-bound family members would warm up to Gabriella, but
since he foresaw no particular danger, he couldn't very well refuse the invitation. He accepted.

As Béla and Gabriella got off at the tram stop and walked down Damjanich Street toward his sister's well-appointed, sumptuous flat in the predominantly Jewish area of Pest, they were a modest-looking couple. Their plain
attire contrasted with that of many of the other more fashionable passersby, as
well as with the atmosphere set by the ornate marble facades and elaborately
carved friezes of the buildings lining this street in the Seventh, or Elizabeth
District of Pest. Gabriella's cloth coat was handsome but unpretentious. Béla,
who could easily afford to dress more lavishly, wore one of his two dark
woolen suits with a brown tie. But his mind was not on clothing fashions or
architecture. All he could think of was his family. He was already imagining
the persistent rumblings going on inside his sister's apartment about the couple who were supposed to be the guests of honor.

Béla had visited his sister and her family many times and thought he
knew precisely what he was walking into. In his mind's eye, he saw the spa-

cious apartment with its high-bourgeois decoration—the Austrian crystal chandelier over the massive, distinctively Hungarian mahogany dinner table, the heavy plush drapes over the windows, the rich Persian rugs on the floors, the lavish French tapestry on the wall. He had little use for this ostentatious display of wealth. His own tastes were simpler, and he usually found his sister's apartment stuffy and oppressive.

He squeezed Gabriella's hand as he thought of their host, his brother-in-law Károly (Karl) Schneider, the unquestioned patriarch of the family. Karl's marriage to Laura seemed an unlikely coupling, as it had little to do with love; she had been a stunning young beauty and he was twenty-five years her senior. But Karl was such a wealthy and successful man that Laura's parents couldn't imagine refusing when he asked for her hand in marriage. Now he was a heavyset, overbearing man in his sixties, smug, self-satisfied, and always convinced that he knew best.

Béla imagined Karl impeccably dressed in his customary formal black suit, high-collared white shirt, and crimson silk tie. He envisioned him in his drawing room, sitting in a Queen Anne armchair upholstered in green and gold brocade, holding forth for his guests, passing judgment. One hand would be raised to underline a point, the other holding a cordial glass of Tokay from his vineyard in Mád, wine that he had presented at the courts of the emperor and czar. "But she's just an office girl," Karl would proclaim in his commanding bass voice. "How could a young man with such a promising future and a family of such means marry an office girl?"

One entire wall of the drawing room was covered, from floor to ceiling, with a pastoral landscape. It had been painted by a local artist of growing renown and Karl took great pride in it. Béla could readily envision his brother-in-law rising from his chair to pose in front of the prized canvas, the very image of a wealthy, strutting Budapesti Jew, as if Karl were patronizing the humble peasants in the painting. Karl would shake his head with mock pity and say, "Yes, just a poor Jewish girl . . ."

Béla had heard this refrain before, but as it played in his mind he could feel the muscles of his stomach tighten. He longed for an ally in the group, someone in the family who would take his side. Perhaps it would be his recently widowed mother, Regina, who had come from their village of Galgocz to live with Karl and Laura after Béla's father died. He had reason to hope. During a number of family discussions about Gabriella, Regina had said, "So she's poor and doesn't have a dowry. So what?" Regina herself had become a prosperous woman who knew all too well the importance of wealth and social standing for her children's well-being. But neither had she, Béla realized, forgotten her own humble origins. Béla had heard her say many times, "We didn't exactly come here from the court of Maria Theresa."

In his need to find comfort, and to ease his growing sense of dread, Béla imagined his mother defending Gabriella. Karl needed to be deflated, and perhaps only Regina had the sass to do it—if not in reality, then at least in Béla's wistful reverie. "It's not as if she's some Hasidic girl," Béla imagined his mother saying, "who just got off the train from Galicia and had to have her marriage arranged by her family." The subtle dig at Karl would, of course, be inadvertent. "She has only a stepmother who is gracious and proper and not in the least anxious about marrying her off." What relish Béla took in these private mental conversations. "Let her be," Béla longingly fantasized his loving mother saying. "She may seem unapproachable, but she's quiet and reserved, very modern, and better read than you or I. She's simply more nervous and frightened of all of you than unfriendly. And Béla adores her. Don't dare hurt their feelings."

Although he'd fantasized them out of whole cloth, his mother's imaginary words offered Béla some comfort as he and Gabriella, still holding hands, walked up the two flights of stairs to Laura and Karl's apartment. They paused on the landing. Béla gazed at Gabriella. He loved the way she looked—her sculptured face, her sad eyes, her modest, unpretentious appearance. He squeezed her hand again and said softly, "Remember what I told you about my family, especially Karl. He doesn't have much good to say of anyone." She nodded and returned a faint smile, as if everything was all right. But her hand was cold and he saw apprehension in her eyes. He swallowed hard, wiped his sweaty palms against his trousers, and pulled the bell cord.

The chatter in Karl's drawing room muffled the sound of the bell. Laura had been in the kitchen and, not listening to the shrill commotion, opened the door herself and welcomed the couple. As she waved Béla and Gabriella over the threshold and into the foyer, Karl was obliviously disparaging Gabriella with precisely the same tone that Béla had imagined: "But we all know what secretaries and office girls are *really* hired for."

Béla was stunned. The words struck him like a slap across the face. Then he heard Gabriella's audible gasp and saw the fleeting look of pain in her eyes. He saw her try to regain her composure as he himself tried to will away the blood that quickly rose to his flushed cheeks. He leaned closer to her and promptly whispered, "Remember what I said about Karl. He envies our happiness and makes a fool of himself."

Karl's words still hung in the air as the couple entered the drawing room.

At the sight of them, a mortified silence fell upon the scene, for the others were certain that the newly arrived guests of honor had overheard Karl's remark. They were also certain that the two had understood its meaning and intent.

Béla would not look at Karl. He coughed to clear his throat, as if to signal his defiance of the atmosphere in the room and his disdain for the words that had caused it. But the insult had struck home. Gabriella had succeeded in masking her humiliation, and Béla was more or less able to conceal his shame and outrage. The moment would pass quickly. But neither of them would ever forget it.

Béla resolutely introduced his fiancée to the others. They had little to say in their embarrassment and humiliation, but they awkwardly tried to be gracious. Then it was time to gather around the dinner table.

The impromptu and now subdued festival meal went ahead without further incident. Fine domestic wine from Karl's vineyard had been readied for the occasion. No one cared that it was hardly appropriate for ritual purposes. Nor was there a proper seder plate on the table; separate dishes of parsley and minced apples and walnuts, sitting in isolation, were all anyone could remember of the symbolic Passover foods. Someone had brought matzah, almost for novelty's sake and because it was so readily available among the city's large Jewish population. These few vestiges of Jewish tradition, however, did not prevent Laura from baking the breads—forbidden on Passover—and cooking the nonkosher Hungarian creamed meat dishes that were the family favorites. Despite some brief and satirical commentary on the liberation of the ancient Hebrews from enslavement in Egypt, there was an undercurrent of collective embarrassment and unease among the Schneiders and Poppers, these modern, middle-class, and affluent Budapestis who somehow still referred to themselves as Jews. Feeling set apart from the others by the incident, Béla more than anyone noticed the farcical quality of the ceremony.

Now Karl spoke up for the first time since his hateful insult. "Isn't it curious how we still call ourselves Jews when all this means so little to us?" Nobody answered, but Karl's question was merely rhetorical and he was prepared with an answer. "But there's more to being Jewish than these ridiculous rituals," he said, his tone growing more self-assertive as he spoke. "We live in the Golden Age of Hungarian Jewry, but I assure you it's not because we are such a religious people."

"Why then?" one of the wives asked.

Karl cleared his throat and answered. As he began, his voice was uncharacteristically subdued. "Because we are brilliant and talented and have become gloriously prosperous in this wonderfully hospitable country of ours, and all within the past fifty years. This city has been built with Jewish genius." With each word, Karl was regaining his earlier self-inflation.

Gabriella, who had been silent and remote, raised her eyes to meet Karl's. At the same time, she raised one of her hands from her lap and placed it, with symbolic defiance, onto the table next to her plate. Her voice was steady and calm. "But in the meantime," she asked, "what has become of the soul of this city?"

"My dear Gabriella," Karl said, as deferentially as he could muster, "Budapest gets its soul from the Christians. There are enough priests and churches to save the city for another thousand years. We have inspired its mind and heart. We have enriched this city and made it a jewel in Europe." He emphasized his words with a wave of the piece of matzah he held in his hand. "Look at the banks, the universities and professions, and the artists and writers. You're no doubt well acquainted with them. And Jewish journalists love and defend this country more than the Hungarians do."

Karl was irrepressible, Béla thought, and on this subject he seemed especially impossible to argue with, as much as several among them would have liked to. For his imperious tone, Karl drew silent scorn, but his words were weighty. Gabriella bravely pressed on. "Why do you so willingly leave the domain of soul and spirit to the monopoly of Christians?" she asked.

"Because they need it more than we do. The Christian spirit has always been the thread binding the Magyar masses to civilization. There are fewer of us, so in their enlightened state, they have emancipated us, so to speak, and have even made our religion virtually equal to theirs. We are as Hungarian as they are. We've shared the same history and have been here since the beginning. It's a beautiful partnership. I'm not terribly interested in their religion and they don't seem particularly worried about ours. What's more, I don't need to be involved in the Jewish religion in order to be quite content with being a Jew in this most extraordinary city and country."

"But you must admit," said Béla, "they've also used that Christian spirit to keep us at arm's length. We don't accept their savior, and we've paid for that throughout what you call our beautiful thousand-year partnership. For all we've done for this country, we're still seen as a self-interested foreign element that panders to the aristocracy. We're as liberal and patriotic as it suits our need to get ahead. We're resented for it and we've periodically paid for it. I'm not so sure we have seen the end of it."

There was some truth in what Béla was saying, but he had never until that moment acknowledged such acute awareness as to the status and fate of the Jews. He was drawing on his own admittedly thin personal experience with anti-Semitism and his even more flimsy political understanding. In truth, he was simply taking a swipe at Karl, at this stereotypical bourgeois Jewish admirer of the ruling Hungarian aristocracy.

"You know, Béla, in all the time I spent in America," said his brother, Louie, reclining in his chair and twirling his wineglass between his thumb and forefinger, "I never thought you'd become such a keen observer of our Jewish culture." Louie had spent fifteen years in America, where he became a bookbinder, and had returned to Budapest following his father's death. "And this from my little brother who was always more content to be playing with animals than becoming politically educated."

"I don't have to be such a keen observer to see the obvious. Look at how people feel about Jews in spite of how we've helped build this country. You watch: as the emperor and empire grow old, we haven't seen the end of Christian hatred of Jews." Béla himself was startled by the raw feelings that were welling up in him.

"What are you so afraid of?" asked Karl, with a subtly dismissive wave of his hand. "You've never suffered as a Jew. And you'll probably do just fine in life with such a generous family, a good profession, and of course your lovely and devoted wife-to-be." At that, Gabriella reached her hand over to Béla's lap and clutched his wrist as if to beg him not to respond to Karl's sarcasm.

Karl's insinuations were once again offensive, but Béla was still preoccupied with his own thoughts. And his eyes were opening. No, he wasn't terribly afraid of suffering as a Jew. But he was terrified at the prospect of having to try to make a life for himself and Gabriella in the midst of the kind of culture that Karl represented. Béla deferred to Gabriella; he did not respond. Karl had succeeded in effectively silencing both of them.

Béla looked around the table. He glanced at his poor sister, who had done so well by wedding this pompous ass. She looked beaten down and servile. She had lost some of her former beauty, but she would be well taken care of materially for her dutiful solicitude. Béla then looked at his mother, sitting next to Laura. She was always a loving and devoted matriarch. He admired and appreciated her. He could not have survived all those years as a university student without her generosity. But this was also the same mother who, terrified for her children's welfare, had forced her daughter back into her unhappy marriage with Karl when she wanted to leave him. What made it worse, Béla knew, was that his mother privately detested Karl even while she kowtowed to his wealth and position. Béla felt blessed to have found someone in life whom he loved and who loved him in return.

As the dinner proceeded, these frontal assaults and subtler attacks at the flanks were suspended. But, to add to their earlier wounds, the couple increasingly felt quietly but painfully excluded. Karl's bombast eventually died down, partly because of the watchful eyes of his otherwise submissive relatives. Béla sensed the tacit scorn in their pursed lips and slightly raised brows, in the hesitant, guarded questions directed at Gabriella. Somehow, she represented happiness, a rarer, unarranged, and more fateful happiness than these striving, insecure relatives were used to.

Béla turned to Gabriella and saw her looking defeated and unable to resume eye contact with anyone at the table. With her downcast eyes, she seemed disappointed and empty. There was always so much he could tell from her eyes. He wasn't certain if she still suffered from the earlier humiliation or from the discomforting conversation at the table. But he also wondered if these religious occasions evoked a deeper and more elusive longing in her. He had noticed it before, but it had barely been talked about. He never knew what to say or think about it.

By all outward appearances, Béla and Gabriella had survived the evening. But they were permanently wounded. On leaving Karl and Laura's home, they glanced over at each other with a combined look of relief and exasperation, as if they had been forced to hold their breath for three painfully long hours and could now once again freely draw air. They stood silent for a moment in the soft glow of the gaslight street lamp in front of the apartment. Béla spoke first. "You know we can't go on living among them."

"I know," Gabriella said, as the pent-up tears streamed down her face. "They expect too much of me, and their disappointment is painfully obvious. They treat me like I'm a gold digger. I don't think they ever really wanted us together."

As Gabriella spoke, Béla sighed and sputtered with indignation, "They're jealous, especially Karl, that our marriage will not be engineered by our families. My poor sister has suffered all these years from her supposedly successful marriage. She's never found happiness, but even she is infected by the scorn."

They walked down the street arm in arm. The district was alive on this cool spring night with the murmurs of Jewish families conducting seders in their homes. From the open windows of the more religious Jews they heard Hebrew songs and blessings drift out on the night air.

"You're hurt over the seder?" asked Gabriella.

"No, I only wish I were more so. It means less to me than I want to believe." Béla had never truly found any sustaining warmth or light in his religious tradition. For that matter, he had never sought any protection from the cold or dark, neither of which he particularly feared. The cold was as familiar as the chill in the spring air. And the dark was tolerable, for he was a practical man not given to much soul-searching. As for the darkness inside others, it had only touched his life on rare occasions and not inspired any need to hide or flee. "What bothers me intolerably," Béla continued, looking straight ahead, feeling too embarrassed to look at Gabriella, "is the haughtiness and divisiveness of my Jewish family. I need to get away from them. I think we both do if we are ever going to survive."

"It bothers me as well," said Gabriella, "terribly, especially the emptiness that you mentioned at religious occasions like this. I know God speaks to us through the stories of his chosen people. But people don't see it." Béla was coming to understand that Gabriella feared the emptiness, the hollowness of a life that didn't speak to her soul. Unlike himself, she needed warmth and light, and was disheartened not to find it in Béla's family's Passover celebration that night, nor in their common religious tradition or culture. Béla needed to depart, Gabriella to arrive. But they hadn't yet found a common path, nor was the time ripe.

✦

On a cold January day, soon after the New Year of 1912, Béla and Gabriella were huddled next to each other on a wooden bench in the hallway of a drab Budapest courthouse. They were waiting outside the chamber of a justice of the peace who would marry them. Four or five offices with wooden doors and opaque glass windows bearing the names and titles of their occupants lined the narrow corridor. The air was stale from the tobacco smoke that wafted endlessly through the stark public hallway.

"I'm so relieved we can do this in a civil ceremony," said Béla, "rather than go through the ordeal of a religious one with our families involved."

"Yes, I suppose we're reaping the benefit of the enlightened ruler of this holy empire," said Gabriella, exaggeratedly inhaling the musty air as she began to be warmed by the heat of the building's clanking radiators. "He's even provided a hearth and sweet incense to adorn our ceremony. May God bless him." Not many years before, Emperor Franz Josef had invoked the institution of civil marriage. Hundreds, even thousands of Hungarian couples had since exercised the option, much to the chagrin of the various Christian churches as well as the rabbinic leaders of the country.

Béla quickly felt Gabriella's sarcasm and consternation. "You obviously are not very happy with this."

"I'm sorry. I don't mean to be so harsh." Gabriella's tone softened and she reached for and tenderly held Béla's hand. "You know that I am very happy. I have always loved you and I'm certain that you love me." After a pause, she continued, "But I wanted to be married in the presence of God, not just in the presence of official witnesses in a court of law, in the dead of winter. And I wanted to do it with our families' blessing, without feeling that we were going behind their backs." She was still shivering slightly from the cold outside, her teeth clenched together so that they wouldn't chatter. But there was a sweetness to her voice.

"Of course, my dear one, I love you, and I would like the same thing." He hesitated, then continued, "But that's not reality." His smile stiffened. "My family would have come, begrudgingly, but we would have felt their disdain. Look, I've made my choices. We're not going to live the way they do. And," he added as an afterthought, "I can't imagine you'd want to have your stepmother present."

"I know, we've been through this already. But she's happy for me, and don't forget she likes you very much—not because of the life you can provide me, but for who you are. I felt bad that I couldn't invite her, or even my aunt Bertha and cousin Elza. Having Bertha here would have been as close as I could come to my dear mother being present. And Elza's my best friend. But I accept that we couldn't have family here—not yours, not mine." Gabriella's words trailed off on a note of resignation.

Béla went on disjointedly, without fully acknowledging Gabriella's feelings. "And what kind of religious ceremony would have been more meaningful than the uninspiring Jewish ones to which we've been such strangers?" There was a pause. Béla knew that Gabriella was not disagreeing with him. But her eyes evaded his. He knew something was missing for her and he had come to believe that, indeed, it was a spiritual and religious matter. But he still didn't know how to address it.

Neither of them spoke for a minute. "I know we'll find our way and I'm not any less happy for this moment," Gabriella finally said, trying to reassure Béla. He didn't believe her but felt comforted nonetheless. Béla knew that Gabriella would never complain, but in the back of his mind he reminded himself that the woman who was about to become his wife was searching for something more than material sustenance and comfort, and that her life would not be complete without it. Even though their marriage would not be religiously sanctified, they both knew what a triumphant achievement it was. It was not only a public tribute to their love but also a monument to their strength and will to separate themselves from a commanding family and a binding culture. And it had taken them almost five years from the time they met to finally get to this musty, cold hallway outside the office of the justice of the peace.

A few days after the wedding, Gabriella moved from her family's flat in Buda to Béla's apartment in Pest, near the university. By that spring, Béla was preoccupied with preparing for his final examinations and the completion of his studies, after more than ten years as a habitual student. Following his marriage, he had instantly become serious and focused about his work. His mentor at the university kept Béla on as a veterinary assistant and part-time instructor, which helped the couple make ends meet.

Virtually within weeks, Gabriella was blessed with a pregnancy. In early autumn, she gave birth to identical twin boys, György (who would always be called Gyuri, or Georgy) and Miklós. Family lore suggests they were each born in a caul—an unbroken amniotic sack—which, according to legend, is a sign of individuals who will fulfill lives of destiny. The boys were small and dark, with the high cheekbones of their father and the large, brown, sad eyes of their mother. From the moment of their birth, it was difficult for almost anyone to tell them apart.

Béla's family, unmindful of the aloofness he and Gabriella had put between them, descended on the couple after the children were born. Regina was thrilled that her youngest son was now the father of two boys. Laura, who had four children of her own, seemed ready to moderate the distance at which Gabriella was kept by the family, in deference to the newborn sons. The fact that the boys were, in the natural course of events, circumcised according to Jewish ritual had nothing to do with the influence of either of the couple's families, nor was it a sign of the parents' determination to perpetuate the Hebrew covenant. Just as with their father before them, it was unthinkable for these Jewish boys not to be ritually circumcised. The rabbi insisted on it and carried out the B'rit Milah with both boys at the couple's home. That Béla and Gabriella agreed to this, even without much devotion or fanfare, was, nevertheless, a significant event. Gabriella, more than Béla, was concerned with giving her children more of a religious heritage than either of their parents had received. Beyond that, she may also have overestimated the importance to Béla's family of this Jewish ceremony. Frequently solicitous of them, she was unwilling to disturb their supposed Jewish sensibilities, especially regarding as ancient a tradition as circumcision. The children's subsequent exposure to Jewish ways, however, would not exceed that which their parents had themselves experienced.

❖

It was a brisk day toward the end of March in 1914. Gabriella was in the third month of her second pregnancy. Her active two-year-old boys were momentarily occupied by their step-grandmother, who was visiting and helping mind the twins, whom she adored. Béla had just finished teaching an anatomy class at the university. On his arrival home, he hurriedly coaxed Gabriella to sit down in the drawing room. He took the soft velvet armchair and she sat on the Victorian sofa to his side.

"After class, I met with Professor Nagy and he offered to submit my name for a civil service job as the animal doctor of a small village called Báránd, not far from Debrecen and next to Püspökladány." Speaking in one breath, Béla could hardly get the last few words out.

Gabriella could barely respond. She was as dumbstruck as he had initially been. "What?" she finally managed to utter. "That's . . . marvelous!"

"Of course, it's a big decision. Life would be harder and I'll never get wealthy as a civil servant. You know that the civil service is called the 'mule's steppingstone.'"

"Well, you're obviously no mule," Gabriella managed to inject. "At least not anymore," she said, poking fun at her husband. "But we've always lived modestly. We'd manage."

"And I've always believed rural life would be our natural element." His hands moved to the quick tempo of his words. Barely managing to stay seated on the edge of his chair, he went on impetuously, without giving his wife another chance to respond.

"But there is something further I have to tell you about this," he said, rising from his armchair and trying to check his excitement by clasping his flailing hands together and holding them still under his chin. "It's an important matter we'll have to give much thought to."

"How much more important could it be than what you just told me?" Gabriella teased with a smile, raising an open hand in a gesture of playful naiveté. "So, end the suspense and tell me what it is."

"You know Nagy wouldn't do this if he didn't like me. And you know his feelings about Jews."

Gabriella looked puzzled. "Yes, it's always been peculiar, but it's not news. He's done well by you, and you by him. But what of it? Don't keep leading me on this way."

"Well, he seemed to have my best interests at heart when he told me." Béla was still hedging, but then he blurted it out. "You know how difficult it is for Jews to be appointed to the civil service. Nagy suggested that we Christianize our surname and cross over to Christianity. It might be our only chance, and it would be a way of blending in with the community and not becoming too isolated in a place with only a small number of Jews living there."

Gabriella appeared not to hear any of the words after "Christianity." She turned her head slightly away from Béla and gazed off into space, looking

through things, not really at them. He recognized that she had turned inward, toward her private thoughts and feelings. "That sounds like a good
idea," she said in a measured, understated way. "We'll truly be making a new
home—won't we?—with a new faith and a new community." Béla thought he
could detect a tone of peace and contentment that he had hardly heard before.

He himself could not have thought of a better way to accomplish all that
he wanted to in regard to his hovering and hostile family. Leaving Budapest
would separate him from them and allow him to live by his and Gabriella's
own standards and values, which were so different from theirs. He had never
wanted to be a visible and wealthy Budapesti Jew. He just wanted a simple
life as a country veterinarian. And Catholicism, what a brilliant way, he
thought to himself, of loosening his emotional ties to his family and his culture. He didn't much expect Catholicism to save his soul. But maybe it would
give him a livelihood and free his spirit so that he could live a life of his own
choosing.

Béla felt exhilarated. He laughed. "Then we'll go. We'll tell the children
and our families, and we'll go. We'll work out the details, but for now I may
have to proceed faster than you and the children need to, at least as far as our
name and our professed religion." As far as Béla was concerned, the religious
matter didn't really require as much thought as he had let on. And he was instantly encouraged by Gabriella's apparent euphoria. The children and their
grandmother Rosa had entered the room and they shared in the excitement
and anticipation.

In subsequent days, Béla informed his family of his decision to accept the
position in Báránd. They were shocked at first and became increasingly forlorn that they'd be losing contact with him and his family, especially at such
a tender time in his children's lives. But they realized soon enough that Béla
could not go on indefinitely working as an assistant at the university. His
mother had hoped for a university appointment for him, but in two years it
had not materialized. When he told them of their decision to convert to
Catholicism, his family seemed indifferent in their response. Indeed, they
recognized that it would be prudent for them to blend in with the local population. Appearing in their new rural home as worldly and bourgeois Jews
from Budapest was simply unwise. They all seemed to accept Béla's decision
matter-of-factly.

Shortly before he was baptized, Béla decided to proceed with changing
his family's name and "Hungarianizing" it. Most Jews, even religiously observant ones, had already taken on Hungarian names soon after the turn of the
century. It was not in the least unusual to alter the country's "motherbook" of

the names of its citizens, thereby making Jewish Hungarians indistinguishable from Christian ones. Béla chose to change his surname from Popper, a name fairly common among Jews with German or Austrian roots, to Pogány, a Hungarian name equally unexceptional except for the fact that the word means "pagan," that is, one who is neither Jew nor Christian. By choosing it, Béla was not proclaiming himself a heathen. The name signaled that he was neither embracing Christianity nor necessarily forgetting his background as a Jew. He may have been simply indicating the utilitarian nature of his new identity.

The couple decided that Béla would be baptized first, before Gabriella and the children, because he had to proceed quickly, and it enabled them to keep up the appearance that conversion was nothing more than a practical consideration. In a month or two, Gabriella and the boys would follow Béla into the church and then to their new village, where he was to begin working that summer.

❖

By his solemn Latin incantation, the priest announced Béla's spiritual rebirth, such as it was. *"God the Father of our Lord Jesus Christ has freed you from sin . . . so may you live always as a member of his body, sharing everlasting life."* At the very end of the ceremony, the priest placed salt on Béla's tongue, an ancient part of the baptismal rite indicating the likelihood that members of the fledgling church would be persecuted. "Everyone," says the Gospel of Mark, "shall be salted with fire." Ironically, the book of Leviticus in the Jewish Bible is the source for this institutionalized anticipation of victimization. There it is instructed that all sacrifices offered up to God are first to be salted. It is a symbol of the everlasting covenant between God and the Jewish people.

It is difficult to imagine exactly what Béla felt about his Jewish past at this moment of conversion. Was this like the forced "convert or die" apostasy of a Marrano during the Spanish Inquisition? Was there a burning stake awaiting Jews if they felt they couldn't publicly renounce the error of their ancestors' ways? Hardly. But even Béla had an obscure sense of the scandals and threats to which Jews were continually exposed throughout his nation's history. Was he naive enough to think that he could ultimately escape the fate of Jews? Or might he have heard a small voice in the back of his mind telling him he'd never escape it, whatever that fate might turn out to be? A practical man, not given to soul-searching or philosophical contemplation, Béla's recognition of his Jewish soul would remain private, as matter-of-fact as his Christian exterior.

At the completion of the ceremony, Béla rose to his feet, the taste of salt still on his tongue, his hands clasped prayerfully in front of his heart. He bowed respectfully to the anointing priest, then turned and slowly walked to the front pew, where he was greeted by the neighbor who had sponsored his baptism and a few other congratulatory friends and parishioners who had accompanied him.

Outside the church, Béla took leave of his new fellow parishioners and walked the few short blocks to his apartment alone. Gabriella was in her last months of pregnancy and had been home resting with the twins. She was on the couch when he entered. She looked up, and Béla casually but proudly announced: "I am now a Catholic." He sat on the edge of the couch, and as Gabriella embraced him she felt tears of joy fill her soul, for she herself was now a step closer to their common goal.

✤ CHAPTER 2 ✤

Crossing Over

All holy men and women pray for us.
Roman Catholic baptismal rite

A few weeks after Béla's baptism, Archduke Franz Ferdinand was assassinated. One month after that, in July 1914, Austria-Hungary declared war on Serbia. With the postponement of civil service appointments, Béla was temporarily without a future. Gabriella and the children's baptism would also have to wait. But Béla would be well served by his Christian confession and Hungarian name. He was promptly called up for military service and, instead of becoming a country animal doctor, he became a soldier in the emperor's army.

From early on in the war, Gabriella tried to find reassurance from one-sidedly encouraging reports in the newspapers. Béla's infrequent letters, though, were more sobering. The battles were unrelenting and unspeakably costly in lives and resources. Hungarian men and boys fought with great courage, but with antiquated formations and outmoded equipment. Like many devoted soldiers, Béla doubted whether usurping Bosnia from under the noses of the Serbs had been worth the terrible price the Austro-Hungarians were paying. Gabriella took only small comfort in the fact that her husband was relatively safe since, as captain responsible for the health of the horses, he did not see direct combat. She readily imagined that he could not desist from helping the wounded and bloodied soldiers close to the front lines. But she refused to be discouraged by her own anxiety, and persisted in her prayers for Béla's safe return. Because his furloughs were infrequent, Gabriella feared that her twins would grow up into men without him, and that her baby daughter, Klari, who arrived only months after Béla's departure, would barely know what it meant to have a father.

Gabriella was used to managing on very little physical and emotional sustenance. When she was four, her mother died. Her father, Morris Groszman, soon remarried to a self-possessed beauty from the city of Tata who never formed a genuine emotional attachment with her shy and retiring stepdaughter. Morris was a tailor of modest means, but he might as well have been a professional soldier. He served in the Austro-Hungarian Army for a dozen years. Even years before Gabriella was born, Morris's army commission was extended when the emperor's forces occupied the Turkish provinces of Bosnia and Herzegovina in order to keep order among their unwilling hosts. Serving all that time, Morris barely knew his daughter for the first several years of her life.

During much of her father's absence, Gabriella lived in the same apartment house as her aunt Bertha, her mother's sister, in a small flat on Lipthay Street in Buda. Bertha was a kind and wise woman who was consulted by everyone who knew her for her sensible and insightful advice on virtually any problem or dilemma. Even though Bertha had five children of her own, she became especially dear to Gabriella after her mother died. She was Gabriella's closest connection to her mother, of whom a cameo photo in a gold locket was her only remaining keepsake. Gabriella also grew especially close to her cousin Elizabeth, called Elza, one of Bertha's children. Although she was seven years older than Elza, they were very fond of each other from the start and eventually became each other's best friend.

In her adult years, after her father died abruptly at the age of fifty-two, Gabriella was compelled to work for the Fehér tailoring house in Pest, where she was a competent and well-respected bookkeeper and office manager. When she married in 1912, at the age of twenty-six, she was already considered to be beyond prime marriageable age. Now she was the mother of three young children while her husband was away at war. She felt as if most of her life had been spent in waiting.

By the autumn of 1918, no one spoke much about the war. Budapest had grown grayer and people had become accustomed to each other's evasiveness. It was as if they were protecting their last shreds of hope from the penetrating gaze of their fellow countrymen. Everyone tried to put on a confident face, but despair and anger lay just beneath the surface and were difficult to hide.

The twins and their baby sister were not truly aware of the cataclysmic events that had occurred, but they saw the gloom in the faces of the adults around them. They did not yet comprehend that their nation's defeat was at hand or what it would mean. But they saw that their mother was often sick and that, despite her efforts to hide it from them, she cried whenever she got news of the war—from the newspapers, from neighbors who also had men at the various fronts, and especially when she received a rare letter from their father, whom they had seen only two or three times in four years.

✤

It was an early November afternoon in 1918. Gyuri and Miklós, now six years old, were playing in front of their apartment house on Tölgyfa Street. They had moved back to their mother's former neighborhood shortly after their father went to war. Their hair, close-cropped the summer before, had grown out wavy and black. The red and gold leaves on the oak and acacia trees in the small park near the river, around the corner from their home, had turned brown early and had already begun to fall. This year the colors of the foliage seemed less vivid, although few people seemed to notice. The children's street had been named for the oak trees covering the hills just beyond their neighborhood. Many people consider the oak to be an enchanted and auspicious tree, but, ironically enough, there were no oaks growing on this Oak Street. In place of these majestic, sheltering trees, this barren street was lined with gray, long-neglected apartment buildings. The family could not endure much longer in this hapless place.

On this day, as the glow of the setting sun reddened the wispy clouds hanging over the river, there was a stirring in the crisp autumn air. Gyuri and Miklós were playing tag, running from one drab apartment building to the next. Since school had been canceled as the war drew to a close, they had been cooped up for weeks in their flat, and were greatly relieved to be outdoors.

As they rested for a moment on the step of the building next to theirs, one of the twins pointed to a soldier who was crossing to their side of the street, most likely on his way from the tram stop near the foot of the Margit Bridge. He had a large canvas knapsack slung over one shoulder and was wearing the familiar grayish-blue uniform of the Austro-Hungarian Army, although in the fading daylight it was difficult to make out its color. Nor could either boy recognize the uniform's distinguishing epaulets. They only knew that this soldier looked familiar enough to inspire their curiosity and cause an inexplicable excitement to rise in their chests.

As he approached, Gyuri pulled at Miklós's coat sleeve, signaling to follow him quickly into the doorway of their apartment house. The boys bounded in unison up the few steps and were in their first-floor flat in a matter of seconds. With absolute certainty, Gyuri bellowed that a "soldier man" was coming to their house. His mother knew immediately what he meant. At the sound of his words, her suppressed hope and longing welled up and flooded her eyes. Just as she held her breath and swallowed hard to hold back the tears, the tarnished bronze doorknob quietly turned, the door opened slowly, and there stood Béla.

Time seemed to stop as he stood framed in the doorway, one hand on the knob and the other on the strap of the knapsack still slung over his shoulder. The twins and their little sister, Klari, stood motionless alongside their grandmother Rosa, who had tactfully stationed herself on the other side of the room. Anna, the young Swabian fräulein who was the live-in housekeeper and German tutor for the children, stood back even further. Though it seemed like an eternity, in reality only a few seconds passed before Gabriella lunged forward, threw her arms around her husband, and buried her face in the coarse woolen jacket of his uniform. Locked in his tight embrace, she allowed her tears to flow where her children could not see them. Their silent embrace lasted for almost a minute before Gabriella raised her head, with a smile on her face. Still clasping her husband to her, she looked into his eyes and said in a breaking voice, "Thank God! We didn't even know when to expect you."

"I didn't know myself," Béla replied as little Klari ran to him and tugged at the bottom of his jacket. He lowered his shoulder so his knapsack could drop off, knelt with one knee on the floor, and swept the child into his arms.

"I am your papa," he whispered softly in her ear as he buried his nose in her short black hair. He hardly recognized her. The last time he had seen her she was still a baby and now she was already a little girl.

"I am your papa," he repeated. "I have been away a long time and have missed you very much. Now I have come home forever." Before she could respond, Béla turned to the twins, who remained on the other side of the small drawing room. Their faces were at once eager and hesitant.

"Can you tell who is who?" Gabriella asked playfully.

Béla saw that his sons had sprouted up in his absence and now stood taller than his waist, but they remained uncannily identical to each other. As his eyes shifted from one to the other, he asked, "Miklós? Gyuri?" No one in the room betrayed a hint or clue. All Béla could do was try to hide his embarrassment at not being able to distinguish between his own sons.

The tension of the moment was broken by little Klari, who twisted out of her father's arms, ran to one of the boys, and placed her finger on the bottom of his chin. "This is Gyuri," she said, with a self-satisfied smile, "because you can feel his scar from where the horse kicked him last year. That's how you can always tell them apart. I can tell them apart anyway, but no one else can." Then she reached over and tugged gently on her other brother's coat sleeve. "And this is Miklós."

Béla suddenly felt like an intruder, a stranger to his own family. He swallowed the lump rising in his throat and, still on one knee, beckoned the boys to him. As they sheepishly approached, he took Gyuri's face in his hands, kissed his cheek and gave him a quick hug, then repeated the same greeting with Miklós. With Klari back at his side, Béla embraced all three of his children, who giggled and squealed at being playfully squeezed together by the strong and warm soldier man who had at last come home to be their father.

It was a heartwarming scene, one that all of the people in the room had hoped for in their own way. But for Gabriella it had a bittersweet tone; only she could see that Béla was not the same man who had left them four years earlier. Beneath his smiling facade she could see the deep reservoir of sorrow that lay within. Only she noticed the tightness of the skin over his high cheekbones and the hollow, inwardly turned cast of his eyes.

Later, after the children had been put to bed and Rosa and Anna had retired for the night, Béla and Gabriella were finally alone. They went to their bedroom at the end of the long hallway and shyly undressed for bed as if they were newlyweds. They lay next to each other in the dimly illuminated room and talked, although not as easily as in the days of their courtship. Even though the connection between them was still present, at this moment, Béla was imponderably troubled. He began to unburden himself.

"I know it's not rational to feel this way, but I feel so guilty for being away all these years. It hurts me to see that my children have grown up without me. And the war, the hardships . . . the defeat . . . the terrible suffering . . . I can't begin to tell you."

"You've got to," Gabriella said softly, but with firmness in her voice. "You can't keep it inside and let it damage your soul."

"How can I believe in my soul, or anyone else's? I have seen too much . . . too much slaughter . . . too many broken bodies." He spoke like a man gasping for breath, as if the images behind his own words were choking him. But

the words came out anyway, tortured descriptions of shattered bodies, fragments of limbs, bits of flesh. Now he spewed the images uncontrollably.
But part of his mind recoiled at the horror he was inflicting on his wife, as
he tried to check himself. He buried his face in his hands as if to stop his
mouth. "I am a horse doctor, that's my training, but what could I do? So
many wounded, maimed . . . young men and boys . . . dying around me,
everywhere . . . blood . . . agony . . . terror. . . . I thought I would go mad."

If there was madness in Béla's choked words, it was because it didn't feel
to him that he was the one speaking them. He felt as though he were listening to someone else tell war stories. Huddled beside Gabriella in their own
bed, Béla now forced himself to continue speaking, as if trying to reconnect
with the body and voice of the speaker, trying desperately to reassure himself
that he was not mad. "On the battlefield, in the midst of death and the roar
of the shells, I saw the future . . . ," he began, his voice filled with awe. He
held his breath a moment, then he whispered: "It's over. Everything is over.
It's the end, the end of the empire, the end of our world, the end of our way
of life."

Gabriella, who had forced herself to remain quiet so Béla could get his
words out, took his hand and squeezed it.

"What are you saying?" she finally asked. "We have survived the worst.
Whatever is coming, we'll survive that too."

Béla did not respond.

Gabriella took his head in her hands and looked into his eyes. She was trying to make contact, to draw him out, but Béla had lowered his gaze and
withdrawn into the silence of his memories.

"Tell me, keep speaking," she implored. "Don't stop speaking."

Béla remained silent for many long minutes. She listened to his breathing; every exhalation sounded like a sigh. Then, in a dry voice that sounded
far away, he said, "I can't keep talking. I only feel more distant from you and
from myself. I just want to run away from this damn war . . . forever." His
voice broke and he buried his head in Gabriella's bosom, trying desperately
to link back with normal life through the flesh and warmth of her body. When
he spoke again, his voice was muffled. "I feel like I'm driving myself crazy. You
talk. Tell me about you. Tell me about the children."

Gabriella anxiously obliged. "I've kept them fed and clothed, content and
happy," she began with a frightened smile, her voice halting and tremulous.
Then she remembered her own ordeal and the smile quickly faded. "But I'll
tell you, life was no picnic here at home. The food rationing was severe;
sometimes we didn't know what we would eat or even when we would see

our next meal. And we all worried about you. As much as food, you were our main concern."

"You've had your own war to fight," said Béla. He was grateful for the occasion to put his own experiences aside for the moment and focus on his wife.

"I'm not complaining. I prayed for your safe return and my prayers were answered. And at least I had Rosa and Anna. We were nervous hens together," Gabriella said with a hint of self-deprecating humor.

"You've managed to live and work together with your stepmother?" Béla asked with a look of surprise. Now his head was propped up on his hand as he gazed at her.

Gabriella detected a look of relief in his face. She moved her hand down to where it met his on the mattress between them. "We've never really gotten along," she said. "I still resent her self-preoccupation and emotional stinginess. And you know she's never liked me. But I have to admit that her love and kindness to the children have been a blessing."

"And how has my family been to you?" Béla hesitantly asked, as he tiptoed into the old domestic minefield.

"Your family has been helpful to us," Gabriella admitted blandly. "The children are very dear to them, too. Your mother and your sister adore them. Now that Karl has been gone for a few years, Laura has warmed up slightly."

"I wished Karl no harm. I am sorry for his death. But his stubbornness and arrogance made my sister's life miserable, not to mention other people's as well."

"Our children are fond of one another, too, although even their youngest is three years older than our boys," Gabriella continued, veering away from their shared but unmentionable satisfaction at Karl's untimely death. "Although it's not been easy during the war even to get to the other side of the river to visit them. But the boys have had no problem with that. Too many times they've run away from home, as they called it, and turned up hours later visiting your mother and sister in Pest. Once they even tried taking Klari, but she got stuck climbing out of the window and they had to turn back."

Béla burst out with a thoroughly refreshing cascade of laughter.

"Yes, you can laugh about it now, but each time it happened I was literally sick with worry," Gabriella said with a relieved smile. Béla seemed more present now. "Once, during the summer when we were at the villa, they even went to the basilica to pray. They left in the morning and got back off the tram just before dark—five-year-old boys alone in Budapest! I gave them their first good spanking." Béla was now smiling irrepressibly as Gabriella continued. "Gyuri, as usual, masterminded the plot, but Miklós was a willing accomplice. They said they went to become Christians like their father. This is what you inspired in them, even in your absence!"

Gabriella's efforts to comfort Béla came to her naturally enough, but in reality, she had long ago become emotionally depleted. It was all she could do to humor her war-weary husband.

She, too, now propped her head on an elbow, and they looked calmly into each other's eyes. Gabriella's forehead furrowed and a fleeting grimace crossed her face as she said, "But neither has your family ever fully accepted me, and I'm sure they never will. Some of them still treat me with indifference or disdain. I'm not blind to it. Anyone can see it. Sometimes I feel as if they blame me for our poverty. To them, I'm still the poor Jewish girl who captured their promising son."

"The only poor Jewish girl who could ever help me fulfill that promise!" Béla sounded indignant, but he looked more animated, and, for the first time, more normal. "They'll never realize that if the war hadn't come and you hadn't entered my life, I would still be sitting at a sidewalk café somewhere in Pest, droning on and on about turkey cholera and the mating habits of sheep. I would be Budapest's finest sidewalk veterinary consultant, dispensing my expertly half-baked opinions on any unsuspecting victim who happened by, as indiscriminately as geese exercising their bowels."

Gabriella laughed for the first time in years, and for an instant her sad eyes sparkled. As for Béla, somehow he was revived by the topic of his family's treatment of his wife and it helped him emerge from his dark mood. But as he moved into the light, Gabriella began drifting toward darkness, toward the fears she had long pushed to the back of her mind.

As they lay in each other's arms, her body stiffened and became unresponsive to his touch, even when he stroked her arms and face. She spoke slowly, as if she were not sure she wanted to share her fears with her husband. "What will happen to us?" she asked. "What will happen to the children?" As she spoke, her hesitation faded and the words poured out. "People's whispers have grown to shouts and screams. Many of them are blaming the Jews for everything!"

Béla wrapped her more tightly in his arms. "You're right," he said, sensing it was his turn to comfort her. "Things are collapsing and terrible changes are coming. I wish I could be more reassuring, but, like you said, we'll survive it."

"One thing I know for sure. We need to leave here as soon as possible. The job you were promised before the war is still there for you," Gabriella said ambiguously, not knowing whether she was making a statement or asking a question.

"I have to believe they've held it for me," Béla said. "The village desperately needs an animal doctor and it's our only hope for a livelihood now. But, to make sure, I may need to leave before you and the children."

For the moment, Gabriella seemed unperturbed by the implication that they would be separated yet again. She cupped her hand over Béla's mouth. She knew he had more to say, but a sudden impulse told her now was the moment for her to bare her soul. She took a deep breath and held it. "Béla, I'm terrified for the Jews and for our lives as Jews. Something terrible is coming. The children and I must be baptized as Catholics now, as soon as possible."

Béla scratched his forehead and looked intently at her. "Of course you and the children will be baptized. Our plan hasn't changed. But this means much more to you than just escaping from my family or from any possible danger, doesn't it? What's so important to you about becoming a Catholic? I've sensed this before, you needn't keep it a secret anymore."

"You're right. It's not just about safety or your family. I'm not interested in abandoning or hiding from anyone. We'd never fool people, so why try to hide who we are? To the outside world, we'll always be Jews."

Béla nodded. "I found out very quickly in the army that everyone knows who the Jews are, whether their name is Popper or Pogány."

"I don't blame people for wanting to protect themselves. But I think it's shameful the way many Jews think they can be more socially accepted by becoming Christian," said Gabriella. "They think they can just forget who they are and blend in with the Hungarians."

"That's not at all why you want to be a Christian, is it?"

"No, it's not about blending in or hiding. And it's not just about your getting a job in the civil service. Of course that's part of it, but not all of it."

Béla was silent for a moment. "This really has to do with your wanting a different religion, doesn't it?"

Gabriella sighed, feeling that Béla was finally ready to hear what had lain hidden inside her for so long. "You must know I've never found it easy to be Jewish. Jews are familiar to me, but it often feels like such a strain to be with them, to live among them. Don't you think it's peculiar that I feel so estranged, even from your family?" Gabriella said with forgetful naiveté.

"You're surprised to feel estranged from my family?" Béla asked, smirking. "My family epitomizes middle-class Jewry in this country, even without the religious trappings. But it's more than that, isn't it? You feel closer to Christian beliefs, don't you?"

"Yes," Gabriella continued, "it's been too difficult to find comfort in the Jewish ways and customs neither of us knows much about. I've never found warmth or meaning in the busy, marketplace atmosphere of our synagogues during those few holiday services I managed to attend. It's not alive for me and never has been."

Béla listened silently and Gabriella hoped he was agreeing with her, although he obviously hadn't thought about it as deeply as she had.

"I've read the Jewish Bible," she went on, "with more acceptance than I've ever heard expressed by our families. But God's law does not lift us out of the desert. Only His special grace and love can do that." As she began to articulate her spiritual quest, Gabriella recognized that she was leaving her husband behind. But she knew she had to continue. She had to try to make him understand.

Gabriella sat up in bed, with a pillow propped against the wooden headboard. When she spoke again, her voice was more urgent and self-assured, and a contented smile softened her lips. "Maybe I do want the cloak of Catholicism for protection and disguise. But I want it more for its warmth. It's not that I expect to find great warmth in a solemn Catholic church or a mysterious Latin Mass. But I have already found that warmth in my life, and in myself, long ago. The church names it and addresses what I already discovered when I was a child."

Béla now looked puzzled. She had never spoken about such matters before in such detail. He lay there next to his wife, his chin propped on his arm. He looked up at her as she sat against the headboard, gazing into her eyes. Their legs touched beneath the soft woolen blanket. In the faint light, he wondered if she could see the bewilderment in his face.

"I must tell you . . . ," she persisted, "How can I say this? . . . For a very long time I have heard a still small voice in my soul, like the prophet in the Bible story. . . . It calls me. He calls me."

"Who calls you?" Béla asked, raising his brow with childlike innocence.

"The Christ calls me, the spirit who became a man to teach God's love," Gabriella explained, with a tender smile.

"It must be obvious that I don't understand. But I believe more in the goodness of your soul than I do in the existence of my own."

Gabriella continued: "I think He's always called me. And I called to Him as a child, after my mother died, and when my father was away. A Christian girlfriend once told me that all anyone had to do was call to Him and He would not fail them. And I did. I called to Him and He was there, in the air, waiting for me. And He answered me. I never told anyone about it, except Elza when she was old enough to understand. She was the only one I dared to tell. She was always a comfort and never judged me. When we were kids, I protected her like a mother would protect her own baby, but I always thought of her as my little guardian angel."

"So you have felt like a Christian since you were a child?"

"Yes. From the start, I felt His love. It embraced and encompassed me. Sometimes I almost felt consumed by it. I've never known such welcome and acceptance, in this world where I've felt like such an outsider. He's been with me all this time. And He's been my home since long before this nightmare of a war was ever conceived."

"And during the war?"

"Even then, especially then. I spoke to Him and prayed to Him." Gabriella had slid down from her sitting position to lie next to her husband. "You knew that. I told you I would pray for you and for us. And I believe that's how we all survived these years. He answered my prayers. My body has always ached, I think ever since my mother died. I've been sick so much with worry and heartache. But even during these horrible years, I felt comforted. My poor mother died while waiting for my father to return from the army. The only way I've managed while waiting for you is by the grace of the spirit who is called Christ. I am as certain of this as I am of your love and devotion. I guess it's about time to let the secret out, don't you think?

"I've spoken to the children," Gabriella continued, "and they're pleased and eager to be like their friends and to be like you. But I also want them to find what I have found in the spirit of God's Son and in His Church. I can't tell you how happy it makes me that we'll all soon be baptized."

"I wish I could tell you that I've been as devoted to Christianity as you have," said Béla. "But you know it's never been anything more than a practical matter for me. I simply don't have your religious instincts. Besides, I saw such horrors in the war that I can't imagine a loving God presiding over such a world. I'm glad, though, that you've found your comfort. Our children need something more than what you and I were given. They need to know that something is true and unchanging."

For many minutes they lay beside each other. Then, with the tender awkwardness of having been away from each other for so long, Béla and Gabriella found each other again, rediscovering and reinhabiting their earthly bodies in each other's deep embrace.

❖

On a cold, bleak morning in February, a few days after Béla departed alone to Báránd to secure his position there, Gabriella set out on a singular mission. As she walked on the cobblestone path along the Danube, she held her coat tightly closed against her breast and pulled a woolen shawl covering her head down almost over her eyes. Her head was bent over her chest; such was the penetrating cold of the moist wind. There were few stragglers on the walkway and even fewer horse-drawn carriages and automobiles on the adjoining river road. It would be one of the most important days of Gabriella's life, one that would be remembered by each of her children in extraordinary detail.

Gabriella's thoughts and musings were on the city through which she now walked, this "Eastern European Paris" that had just been brought to its knees. As she looked across the frigid waters of the Danube at the imperial Parliament, it was wrapped in a dense gray mist that obscured its stately exterior. The nation for which it was the governing hub had been vanquished after four years of war. The armistice had been forced down the nation's throat in November, around the time of Béla's return, and the wartime prime minister had only days earlier been assassinated by his embittered people. The necessities of life were in short supply. For months, seemingly years, Gabriella's children had eaten their bread dipped in cooking oil or fat so their stomachs would feel full.

With the country's resources virtually depleted, the only commodity in ready and growing supply was blame. Gabriella had heard it from her neighbors and from colleagues or customers at the tailoring house, had read it in the increasingly strident newspapers. Rage and recrimination at innumerable scoundrels and villains echoed through the streets, houses, and businesses of Budapest: against the Germans and Austrians, those "foreigners" who had dominated the nation's culture and politics for so long; against the aristocratic rulers, who had exploited the Hungarian people for generations and repressed their will for reform and justice; against the newly emerging Bolsheviks, who had recently spawned the "great Red menace" in Russia; and, finally, rage against the Jews, whose religious faith had only recently been recognized by the state but who were again cursed for being Christ-killers, conniving war profiteers, or communists. After years of quiescence, even acceptance, the Jews were being publicly accused of having played a role in the ruination of the Hungarian homeland.

These and similar thoughts played on Gabriella's mind as she walked against the cold toward her destination, the synagogue near the Arpad Bridge. There, according to the accepted tradition, she would begin the process of religious conversion. As she made her way, she hesitantly wondered why she was taking her first determined steps away from the Jewish people and toward baptism in the Roman Catholic religion precisely at this tortured moment in history. She was worried about what was becoming of her beloved Hungary, but she certainly didn't blame the Jews for it. She shared their anxiety at the turn of public opinion against them. And she was troubled by the fact that the religious faith that she had secretly loved for so long had such a terrible history of cruel treatment of the Jews. The times were dangerous, and Gabriella was terrified that they could soon become demonic. Of course, she tried to rationalize, she wanted her children to be free from danger. Still, she told herself that it was not what she was walking *away* from this day, but rather what she had been determined to move *toward,* ever since she could remember.

The synagogue was a noble-looking structure facing the river. But for the Hebrew inscription below its Ionic frieze, it looked more like a Greek temple than a traditional Jewish shul. The rabbi's study was at the rear of the building. He was a middle-aged man who looked surprisingly modern to Gabriella, although his dark suit, graying beard, and the yarmulke covering his balding head conjured a sense of familiarity and security in her. While growing up, she had seen many religious Jews like him. The fact that his study was lined on all sides, from floor to ceiling, with the sacred texts of the Jews evoked in Gabriella a sense of loss—these were the riches of her people's learned tradition to which she had never been exposed. This was a treasure chest right before her eyes to which she had never been given, or been able to find, the key.

The rabbi's countenance was friendly and inviting enough, although his eyes were cheerless. He had received Gabriella without hesitation. She was respectful but straightforward. She understood that she needed to explain her wish to leave the faith by making the requisite three visits to a rabbi. It was the custom, and Gabriella had no desire to dishonor that custom.

"Kind Rabbi," she began, "I am obliged to tell you that the purpose of my visit is to begin the process of leaving the Jewish faith in order to become a Christian. My husband has received an appointment to the civil service and I'm sure you know how difficult it is for Jews."

The rabbi instantly looked dismayed. He clutched the edge of his desk with both hands and looked down as if to hide the despair in his eyes. As he raised his head, he swallowed hard. "Look," he said, "I am fully aware of the harsh realities facing Jews in Hungary. There have been waves of converts that have come through my study. You're not the first and, with the end of the war and the tide turning against us, I expect there will be floods of them after you. I must tell you, though, these visits sadden me. They are my most painful duty as a rabbi. It's one thing to bury a person as a Jew. It's another thing to mourn him when he's still alive."

In an effort to deflect the rabbi's sadness and apparent scorn, Gabriella tried to keep the conversation on a rational plane. "I don't mean to make this any more uncomfortable, but this is more than just a question of livelihood. I was born a Jew but have never received any Jewish education or training."

"What do you want me to say? Shall I patronize you and try to talk you out of your decision? I could glibly ask you, 'What makes you so sure you still cannot learn and grow in your faith?'" he said in a feigned perfunctory manner. "I've been through this useless dialogue too many times before."

Gabriella was unwavering in her need to justify herself. "It's not that I haven't tried. Earlier, before I was married and when I was a schoolgirl, I made efforts on my own—meek though they may have been—to attend Sabbath and holiday services. But despite my own efforts, I have failed to feel connected to the Jewish faith." But Gabriella secretly knew that this was not the heart of the matter. She knew she was being less than candid and was afraid that the rabbi could see her well-meaning insincerity if he cared to look. She lowered her eyes to avoid the rabbi's scrutiny and clenched her folded hands more tightly, pinching her thumbs on top of each other as if in a pose of nervous devotion.

Before she could continue, the rabbi responded, his tone seeming to have softened. "I certainly understand your plight. You may be born a Jew, but you don't feel Jewish or love Judaism unless it is taught and ingrained in you. And you clearly have had no teachers."

"Yes, that's true. Thank you for recognizing that." But instead of becoming more straightforward, Gabriella, still frightened of his disapproval, continued to hedge. "But neither has it been easy for me to feel accepted by Jewish people. I've always felt like an outsider. But, please believe me, I'm not seeking conversion because I want to separate myself from my people. I know it's becoming dangerous again to be Jewish, but I suspect that in our country, Jews will always be seen as different, even if they're Christian. So I don't fool myself into believing I will automatically be accepted and safe in Christianity."

"That's certainly true. But don't be so sure you'll not be separated from the Jews," said the rabbi. "You seem wisely aware that you'll share our fate, and though at some time in the future you may, if you seek to, be welcomed back, I assure you that when you become a Christian you'll not be treated as a Jew, at least not by the Jewish people. If you leave us, you'll be considered gone, an apostate. It's not a nice word and it has many layers of meaning—disloyalty, abandonment, betrayal of one's people and religious faith." Gabriella nodded but couldn't help feeling dejected and cast out, as if this religious leader could accept her willing departure from his beloved faith with any more graciousness than he was demonstrating.

"Don't be offended," the rabbi continued. "Our tradition is clear on this. Think about it carefully." But the rabbi's words cracked and trailed off. He seemed more regretful than critical, and then, in the same moment, nervous as well.

The rabbi now braced one hand against the armrest of his wooden desk chair. He rubbed the fingers of the other hand against his thumb, then quickly lowered his hand below his desk, into his lap so that, Gabriella thought, she would not see him fidgeting. He then asked the painfully obvious question. "So why then do you want to become a Christian?"

From the start, she had been afraid to humiliate him, and, even now, still didn't know how she could avoid embarrassing him or why she even had to bring up these matters. Yet she proceeded to answer his question, unapologetically but humbly, as her voice quivered. She knew fully what was at stake for both of them. "My dear Rabbi, I haven't been entirely forthright with you. The reasons I've given for seeking conversion are half-truths. The fault is not in the Jewish faith or the Jewish people. Since I was a child," she said, "I have believed in the Christian Savior. I have always felt like a Christian in my heart. It's a mystery to me, because I've never been taught about him, but I truly believe that God has sent His Messiah. It is His Son, Jesus." The rabbi sighed. Gabriella was certain he was about to denounce her. "I don't claim this as dogma, nor that I am right and you are wrong. I only know that He has touched my life since I was a child and kept my heart and soul alive when my husband was away at war."

The rabbi's lower lip jutted forward and his head tilted slightly as if he were quietly considering the plausibility of her statement. Wasn't it perfectly clear to him, she wondered, that the resolute woman sitting opposite him was a deep and sensitive soul, not one who was going to regain a nonexistent connection to the Jewish faith?

"You know, I like you and admire you. But I am afraid of Jews like you, because you'll be lost to us forever. At least the frightened ones might return someday. As for the social climbers who have no use for Judaism or are too embarrassed to be Jews, they could go wherever they want. You're not like either of them. You're not frightened and you're not embarrassed. You're a sincere and spiritual woman. I'm sorry we've lost you." Gabriella was touched by the rabbi's courage and recognition of her truthfulness.

"You know, though," the rabbi continued, "a chasm has opened between us, one that's been chiseled and carved out over centuries. On one side are those who hold fast to the God of Creation and Revelation. We're not fooled by the so-called Golden Age of Jews in Hungary. Our troubled history is much longer than that and, make no mistake about it, it will soon continue. Our Messiah tarries and our only redemption is God's Torah, the laws and values by which we live our lives day to day. On the other side of that chasm are those who feel reborn and redeemed in the spirit of God's only begotten

Son, the spirit who became flesh and by whose death the sins of the world were washed away—the light and the life."

Gabriella was speechless, shocked that the rabbi would utter such words. Was he blindly mocking a Gospel text or was he signaling his respect for the Christian creed and the Christian Savior—echoing a plaintive acknowledgment over the great divide he referred to? She tightened her lips and gently nodded. She knew that her own voice could not reach over that divide.

"This chasm between us," he went on, "is nothing less than a breach in the cosmos, and it's not simply bridgeable by two well-meaning people. I am obliged to be outraged with you, but my anger could not span that rift and certainly could not bring us closer together. No, I feel sadness and grief. My weeping will more readily be heard than my voice of anger." Gabriella felt a burning in her eyes and a knot forming in her throat.

The rabbi covered his eyes with his hand. He inhaled loudly, held his breath a moment, and said on the exhale, "Go then," and, unconvincingly, almost gently, pounded his fist on the arm of the chair. "Go and join the body of Christ and Magyar Christendom. I hope you find greater warmth and light in His bosom than you have found among your people. But I gravely doubt that you will."

Gabriella stood up, nodded, and faintly mumbled, "I'm sorry. I only hope you know that I never meant to attack you or the Jewish faith. Good-bye, dear Rabbi." The rabbi hesitated, remaining seated for an instant, his eyes having become moist. With one arm propped on the surface of his desk, he wiped them with the palm of his hand. She couldn't presume to know what he was thinking, but wondered nonetheless if he felt as brokenhearted as she did. Or was she just trying to console herself? The rabbi finally stood up, ushered her to the door, and obligingly opened it for her. But he could not say good-bye. As she stepped past him into the hallway, he nodded to her almost imperceptibly, more with his eyes than his head. For an instant, before she was actually by him, she saw his eyes close, as though he were shielding himself from any further display of grief. He then shut the door quietly and tightly behind her.

Gabriella left the synagogue and walked home along the promenade on Buda's bank of the Danube. It was on these very shores that Jewish descendants of Spanish Marranos had, more than four centuries earlier, built a thriving and prosperous—even if short-lived—culture under the patronage of the then-reigning Ottoman Empire. They or their families before them had fled Spain as Jews, or as expedient Christians, barely saving their lives and their faith. But they flourished once again out of their love for and eternal loyalty to the God of Israel. But some, like Gabriella, were called by a different Lord. She was leaving the Jewish faith and the Jewish people of her own accord, but she felt banished all the same. She was relieved, but not without a measure of remorse and trepidation for making such a dramatic break from her people. Just as the rabbi had seemed moved by her, Gabriella was now touched and saddened by her meeting with him, struck by his willingness to listen to her Christian convictions as well as by the realistic apprehension he awakened in her for the dramatic action she was about to take. Leaving Judaism was one thing, but being so definitively cut off from her culture and community left her feeling momentarily stranded between two worlds. She was frightened and sad, not simply relieved and liberated. She crossed the road in front of the synagogue, over to the river's promenade, and wept tears of her own. Were they tears of joy or sadness, exhilaration or fear? She did not know.

As she walked along the gray stone river wall, through the cold winter mist, a harsh and unrelenting rain began to fall, soaking her coat and shawl, chilling her to the bone and flooding the cobblestone path. The leafless birches and acacia trees on Margit's Island trembled and swayed in the downpour. The driving rain dissolved the last patches of snow on the quays of the river and leveled the few tall grasses and stiff reeds on the otherwise barren shore. The rain formed puddles and finally poured into and merged with the life-giving waters of the Danube. *Lacrimae Christi.*

✣

In earlier times, the children had been told that they would become Christians soon after their father returned from war. For weeks Gabriella had been reminding them that the time would soon arrive. Finally, after the formal preparations had been made with the local parish for Gabriella and the children to be baptized on the first day of April, she sat them down again to teach them further about the Catholic faith.

"In a few days we will all become Christians, like your father did before the war started. We will go to the church around the corner from here and be baptized, just as we have talked about before. After that, in a few weeks, we will be able to go to church and celebrate Easter, like everyone else in our neighborhood." Gabriella had been instructing the children for weeks in the precepts of Catholicism, and now, with the date approaching, she was trying to sweeten it and make it more concrete for them so that they would have a festive day to look forward to. Their eyes were fixed on her in rapt attention.

"You remember," Gabriella continued, "how we have talked about Jesus Christ, the man on the cross whose picture or statue you have seen many times, and how He died many years ago." The boys looked at each other with goggle eyes that seemed to mirror each other's puzzlement. "People killed Him because they didn't believe He was God's Son and they didn't like what He taught about God loving everyone the same."

Gabriella proceeded without a pause, not noticing the growing look of astonishment on the children's faces. "Even though His death was sad," she continued, "His suffering helped to take away all our bad thoughts and deeds. That way, if we believe in Him and pray to Him, He will make us into better people. The Friday before Easter will be a sad day because that is when we remember Jesus's death. But on Easter Sunday we will celebrate His coming back to life, to show people that He really is God's Son and to prove that He was sent by God to teach us about heaven."

Now the children were entirely confused. But they felt exhilarated that they would, from now on, be part of the fanfare they had so often seen outside their house, when virtually all the children they knew in their neighborhood went to church with their parents on occasions like Easter and Christmas. The whole country celebrated these holidays. Now it would be their holidays, too. "We'll be just like everyone else," said little Klari.

The two boys glanced knowingly at each other and smiled guardedly, more with their eyes than with their mouths, as their secret wish, nurtured throughout the years of their father's absence, was actually about to come true. They, too, greatly wanted to be like other Christian children and to enter this marvelous world of Easter eggs and Christmas presents, fragrant smoke and oil, and magical incantations in a supernatural language.

From their escapade the previous summer in St. Stephen's Basilica, Miklós suddenly remembered the refreshing coolness of that mysterious church that looked so much like a castle. He was also reminded of how strange it had felt to him, once outside the sanctuary, that the inspiring man on the cross had come to feel so distant and remote. Maybe by learning that the crucified God in the Basilica was actually dead, Miklós could begin to understand why he had felt so abandoned. But now that this dead God would be coming back to life on Easter Sunday, Miklós was filled with the hope that he would never feel forsaken by Him again.

Gyuri looked at his brother. He instinctively knew what he was thinking. Gyuri also thought of the time when he had stood, entranced, in St. Stephen's sanctuary. He remembered the eerie comfort he had experienced when he felt sorry for a human God in such terrible pain. To be told now that this man-god suffered to help make him a better person confirmed for him that God's suffering was a good thing and that his sympathy for the man on the cross was the way by which his own life would improve. Even while Gyuri remained puzzled by some questions, this sensitive and precocious boy felt relieved and encouraged that this wounded "Savior" would forgive him those times he had been mean to his sister and had mischievously run away from home with his brother. Maybe, too, this God would relieve his and his mother's sadness, her ever present illnesses, and his recurring longing for the father he had missed so terribly for the past four years and who had now gone away yet again.

The day of their baptism was an uneventful one for the children, compared to the great celebration to come on Easter Sunday, less than three weeks later. Gabriella regretted that Béla was already in Báránd and could not be with them. But she had long waited for this day and felt deeply reassured that she was finally going to enter the house of her true Lord, the One whom she had known in her heart well before she knew what to call Him. Gabriella sighed deeply and smiled. She was content and certain, and hadn't been this happy since that cold day in January, seven years earlier, when she had wed her beloved Béla.

Gabriella had dressed the children in new Sunday clothes, even though this day was a weekday. She herself had gotten a new dress, sewn for her by her mother-in-law, Regina, which Gabriella interpreted as quiet approval. Neither Béla's nor her family had given any hint of opposition to their conversion. And Elza, who lived barely three blocks away, stopped by frequently in the days before the baptism, lending comfort and support to her excited cousin. If there was any stratagem in timing the conversion so close to their departure from Budapest, it had succeeded. Even at this late moment, no one in the family, save Béla and Elza, was aware of or even suspected the real reasons behind Gabriella's conversion. Béla's relatives still regarded his family's crossing over, as it was called in Hungarian, as a purely practical matter, as a Jewish animal doctor's only hope of breaking into the Hungarian civil service.

Accompanied by their baptismal sponsor, Mrs. Ledényi, their neighbor and Gabriella's erstwhile chaperone during the early days of her and Béla's courtship, the mother and children entered the empty sanctuary of the Church of the Franciscan Fathers well after morning Mass had ended. They barely had time to look around the cavernous, brightly colored rococo interior when they were ushered back to the baptistry by the assistant pastor. The children were anxious as the priest anointed each of them with fragrant oil, poured water over their heads, and placed salt on their tongues, all the while chanting in the mysterious language the children had sometimes heard issuing from within the church. It felt to the twins and their sister a little like a doctor performing a medical procedure. Klari, especially, kept looking over at her mother, wanting reassurance that she was behaving properly and that the pastor was performing the ceremony in the right way. Afterward, the separate baptismal certificates were signed and the family members were congratulated. The children smiled but must have wondered why there wasn't more fanfare. As they left the church, they somehow did not really feel any different for having gone through such a peculiar rite, and all in such an unnerving hurry.

A few weeks later, on a balmy Easter Sunday, there was an entirely different atmosphere. The twins and their sister excitedly readied themselves to join the throngs of Christian families converging on Franciscan Fathers on their way to morning Mass. Earlier that day, Béla's brother, Louie, had even brought dozens and dozens of colorful Easter eggs for the children. Before midmorning, Gabriella and the children set out for Easter Mass.

As they walked the few steps toward the end of Tölgyfa Street and then headed up to Margit Boulevard, they joined a tide of other families, attired to meet their risen Savior, all moving toward the local parish. In barely a minute or two, the church came into view. Crossing the street in front of the entrance, Gabriella prepared the children for the crush of parishioners squeezing through the doorway to enter the sanctuary. She held the boys' hands firmly, while Klari held onto her brother Miklós's. As soon as they were inside, Gyuri looked at the sanctuary with new eyes, as if for the first time. He was single-mindedly transfixed, not by the awesome multitude of worshipers, nor by the magnificent statuary of saints, nor even by the priests, who were attired in resplendent gold Easter raiment as they stood by the exquisitely carved marble pulpit. Blind to these sights, Gyuri's gaze was focused on the diminutive crucifix over the sanctuary's altar, which he must have missed seeing entirely on the day of his baptism. The image had been on his mind for days, and he couldn't wait to see it. The sight was familiar to him, almost as if he were meeting an old friend. What had seized his imagination were the bewildering questions his mother had provoked when she explained Christianity a few weeks earlier and, especially since then, during the days leading up to Good Friday and Easter. That this human God was in terrible pain never really bothered Gyuri, because he knew from that fateful day in the basilica that he could relate his own troubles to it. But he never realized that this God was dead, as his mother had explained a few weeks earlier. That stirred Gyuri deeply and unnerved him. How could such an awe-inspiring and powerful man-god be dead? Did that mean His magically soothing inspiration worked only if He were alive? As countless people brushed by him, bumping his shoulders as they passed, Gyuri planted himself in place, resisting his mother's momentum. He pulled hard on her hand to get her to stop, and to beg her for an answer to his most profoundly serious question, one that would sound merely like the whimsical curiosity of a six-year-old child. "But, Mama," he implored, pointing at the crucifix above the altar, "how does this God come back to life?"

"I can't answer you now," his mother said as she followed the throng farther into the sanctuary. "Maybe," she added, as she turned her head back toward him, "He'll come back if we all pray hard enough now that we are Christian. And then someday He'll take us to heaven."

✤ **CHAPTER 3** ✤

Crucible

Everyone must be salted with fire.
MARK 9:49

Budapest was never an easy place to leave, even in the days following Easter Sunday 1919, when the aftermath of the war still cast a gloomy pallor over the city. The acacias and lilacs would not bloom until after the May showers, and the apricots and plums, which had been in plentiful abundance before the war around this time of year, were barely anywhere to be seen. Chrysanthemums—the symbol of the first postmonarchy government that had failed barely a few months earlier—had quickly faded and withered, mostly crushed underfoot. But early spring in Budapest once again smelled of violets from the tiny bouquets being sold along the streets by peasant women, hoping perhaps to pay for their next meal in the still starving city. The sound and smell of the rising gray-green waters of the Danube usually quickened the spirit of even this wistful and melancholy—and now defeated—people. Although the city during those postwar months could hardly be described as coming back to life, the children would later remember their own lives in Budapest, and their departure from it, as a time of innocent joy. Growing up in a war-torn city, largely in the absence of their father, they had been sustained nonetheless by their ties to one another.

Early one day following Easter, the children were awake and dressed and had gone outdoors. Though they lived in one of the poorer neighborhoods of the city's Second District, they were surrounded by many old German artisan families, who always appeared to the children as stiff, formal, and unfriendly.

From the end of their block, a few short feet away from their apartment, the twins and their little sister looked out over the river toward the once lively and robust city of Pest, where many of their relatives lived. Beyond the low-lying buildings of the prosperous Leopold District, directly across the river, waited the great flat plain of Hungary, stretching out endlessly beyond the urban life that the children had always known. They had heard about the great plain, but they didn't know that this would soon be their destination, their new home. They only knew that this was the day they would be leaving. On the surface, they were all excited, but the children were secretly heartbroken that they would no longer regularly see their Grandmother Rosa, who had taken care of them since they were babies, as well as Fräulein Anna, the governess who had taught them both the German language and good manners.

Knowing that he would be the only one going on the long train ride with his mother, Gyuri felt disconnected from his twin brother and their four-year-old baby sister. Miklós and Klari would have to wait a week or two before joining them at the family's new home in the countryside. They would be staying with their well-loved aunts—Miklós with Aunt Laura in Pest, and Klari with Aunt Bertha. These two rather liked the adventure of staying behind. None of the children relished having to travel through terrain that was being overrun by foreign soldiers as well as by ruthless Hungarian "communists," though they didn't yet know what that meant.

The source of the danger was the government that had assumed power only a few weeks earlier. In the middle of March, the Communist Party, under Béla Kun, a disaffected Jew, had promised to build a stable and equitable society based on the Russian model by which the czar had been so dramatically overthrown barely two years earlier. People had yet to feel the brunt of the evolving peace treaty, which they could only blindly hope would spare them further humiliation following their nation's defeat. But the various nationalities inhabiting greater Hungary were already clamoring for disassociation, wanting to join to their respective motherlands. Rumania especially, with its insatiable appetite for dispossessing its formerly imperial neighbor on its Transylvanian frontier, acted as the spearhead, thrusting itself into Hungary with the full support of Western nations intent on checking the spread of Bolshevism. The earlier liberal government had overlooked the pressing urgency of the nationality problem, whereas the communists now made empty and quixotic promises to thwart and manage it. In the midst of the desperate and heavy-handed idealism of the new regime, the country was in terrible turmoil.

The Rumanian Army had by now crossed the provisional demarcation lines, within which they had already been awarded large portions of Transylvania, and had advanced as far as the Tisza River running north to south near the center of the country. Hungary was now defended by the newly formed Hungarian Red Army, such as it was. The army's terrorist tactics against its own population would make travel through the countryside just as treacherous as the greedy encroachments of the Rumanian military made it. Gabriella understood the danger.

After Gabriella carefully explained the plan to Klari yet again, she hugged her tearful daughter, for whom the reality of separation was finally setting in. Although Gabriella realized that nothing in these troubled times could be taken for granted, she did not betray any overriding worry, at least not in front of fretful young Klari. Gabriella's leave-taking from Bertha was a labored one, because she did not expect to see her very often in the foreseeable future. More difficult still was Gabriella's good-bye to her cousin Elza, whom she was certain she would never see again, as Elza would soon be leaving for America. The cousins embraced with quiet tears.

Miklós was also frightened to be leaving his mother, although, like Klari, he felt reassured that he would see her soon enough. But he was surprised at how positively unnerved he felt to be leaving his brother's side. The two had never been apart, having virtually shadowed each other from the day they were born. To Miklós it felt strange, as though he were leaving a part of himself behind. When Gabriella and Gyuri were finally ready to leave, Miklós dutifully hugged his mother. But he wouldn't dare try to hug Gyuri in what he sheepishly considered an uncharacteristic, girlish way. Hugging was something that only grown-up people did. Instead, the twins looked at each other and giggled, trying to make light of their imminent separation. But inside, Miklós felt terrified. He turned his head away, trying to hide the pools of tears forming in his eyes. He really wanted to give Gyuri a big hug and not let go. He wondered if his more daring brother felt the same way.

Gabriella had been ever-so-deliberate in departing a city and a life she had grown to detest. But even she hadn't fully considered how painful it was going to be to leave. As she stood alongside Gyuri on the train platform, surrounded by their scant suitcases and a solitary trunk, she looked into the station and caught a glimpse of the street through the opposite window. She wondered if it would be the last time she would see a Budapest street. Such sentimentality surprised her, but the break she and her family were making was a dramatic one. Even through such a narrow porthole, she could see the ominous red placards still posted on the city's walls announcing the hasty resignation, weeks before, of the prime minister and the subsequent arrival of the dictatorship of the proletariat. As the train pulled into the station, the deep, hoarse voice of the announcer bellowed out its destinations: "Szolnok, Püspökladány, Debrecen." Gabriella winced and tried to swallow a knot of emotion that had formed in her throat. She pinched the corners of her eyes to squelch any further sentiment from welling up inside her. Then she gathered herself and instructed a passing porter that she and her son would be boarding the incoming train, and would he see to it that their belongings were loaded accordingly.

Once outside the sparsely settled city limits, Gyuri was in awe. The greening meadows and gardens were spotted with fewer and fewer houses as the train left Budapest. Periodically, they came upon rural villages, all exactly alike, with low, lime-washed houses and long thatched reed roofs. Gyuri felt as though he were entering another world. It was a gently undulating landscape of farmlands—ill-kept and overworked fields still partially covered with last year's husks and shafts—that grew flatter the farther from Budapest they got. Eventually, the land was breathtaking in its endless level expanse.

What happened next would so embed itself in Gyuri's mind that he would remember it always and recount it faithfully, even sixty years later. After a few hours, the train approached the city of Szolnok. As they stopped there, even Gyuri could notice the uneasiness among all the travelers as scores of armed Hungarian Red soldiers milled around the station, either on foot or on horseback, seemingly awaiting orders. Boarding the train as it was embarking, many of the foot soldiers moved about the cars with impunity, looking stiff and inscrutable.

One man seated near Gabriella and Gyuri boldly asked one of the soldiers, "What is the problem, Comrade? Is there any danger?"

The soldier responded curtly, "Rumanians, approaching the Tisza. They'll be stopped."

His words sent a shock wave through the cabin, since most people could readily imagine imminent confrontation between the two armies. Gyuri had every reason to be frightened. In the weeks leading up to his and his mother's departure, he had heard his relatives scoff at the so-called Revolutionary Hungarian People's Army. People called them a bunch of ragtag excuses for soldiers who somehow managed to survive the war, maybe even by deserting. The Tisza was just on the opposite, eastern border of Szolnok. How would the Rumanians be stopped? Compared to the Hungarians, they were fierce and formidable. Anyone paying attention could see that it was just a matter of time before they advanced toward Budapest.

To the surprise of everyone aboard, the train stopped on the other side of the railway bridge over the sandy-colored Tisza. They were past Szolnok, in the neighboring village of Szajol. Then sixty or so soldiers disembarked without a word and joined dozens of other soldiers who awaited them along the tracks.

As the last soldier left the train, he turned to the passengers and told them, "My fellow Hungarian Comrades, you are in no danger, but this will be the last train from Budapest for a while. The Rumanian Army is threatening to penetrate past the Tisza and this is where we must stop them."

"How?" yelled a number of the passengers.

"You will see shortly," he said without turning around again, waving the train on with a sweep of his hand.

The train started up again as quickly as it had stopped, barely two minutes earlier. Not yet several hundred yards beyond the bridge, a rearward explosion rocked the cabin and froze every passenger to his or her seat. Men groaned, women wailed, and the few children aboard were shaken to tears. Gyuri remained impassive but wasn't sure, probably like most of the passengers, whether they had been attacked. In their frenzy, many people turned instinctively behind them toward the receding source of the explosion. Putting their heads out the windows, they saw the billowing smoke rising from what had been the railway bridge and heard wood and metal crashing into the waters below. They sat in disbelief, most likely relieved that they were unharmed, but shocked nevertheless that their national army would resort to such a helpless and self-destructive way of fighting off their enemies. The nearly uniform look on the faces of many of the adult passengers seemed a mixture of incredulity and outrage. Even Gabriella thought to herself, "*These are the ones who are protecting us! God help us.*"

No sooner had the ringing stopped in their ears than Gabriella understood what this event would mean to her and her family. Heartbroken, she buried her face in her hands.

"What's wrong, Mama? Are you hurt?" asked Gyuri.

Gabriella quickly collected herself, and explained as gently as she could, "I'm not hurt. I'm only worried that now we may not get to see Miklós and Klari until the bridge is fixed. I don't know when that will be, but I pray, soon." But Gabriella had no way of knowing how many weeks or months it would actually be. She forced a smile to reassure Gyuri.

The train trudged along on its journey, now more than halfway to their destination of Püspökladány, the larger town just before Báránd. They were now in the heart of the great plain. Gabriella had lost sight of her surroundings and was submerged in her troubled thoughts. But she noticed that Gyuri sat entranced, looking out the window at the eerie expanse and the undulating mirages on the horizon. There were occasional herds of sheep or cattle grazing on the early spring grasses, and horses galloped across the vast flatlands. The monotonous spread was punctuated by a solitary, high well sweep—a bucket attached to a long pole on a low fulcrum, which to a child's imagination might have looked like a gallows.

The excitement of the day's events was hardly over, for they had yet to brave the constant threat, not so much of the Rumanian Army, but of the Red terrorists who were known to menace the countryside looking for so-called counterrevolutionaries. One band of such terrorists was even known to stop trains and execute people on the spot. Gyuri had heard people back at the Szolnok station say that these thugs were somewhere in the region. But he wasn't worried. He didn't even know what a communist was, much less an anticommunist. There was nothing to be afraid of, he thought. But something in that day's harrowing journey would leave its mark forever.

By the time they finally pulled into the station at Püspökladány, it was near sundown. The train had not yet come to a full stop and already Gyuri searched the platform for a sign of the short, stout man who was his father. As the boy pressed his face to the window, he saw Béla at the other end of the platform looking at him with a large smile, waving both hands.

On the station platform, husband and wife embraced first, ending this most recent six-week separation. Gabriella clutched and could barely restrain herself, but before she could speak, Béla bent down and embraced Gyuri, kissing him on both cheeks.

Gabriella stood with fists clenched, no longer able to hold back her sobs. Béla looked up.

"They blew up the bridge! The Hungarians blew up the bridge! We'll not see our children until the fighting has stopped."

Béla rose to his feet and heaved a deep sigh, trying to squelch the rage that was ready to erupt forth from his mouth. "The bridge at Szolnok, isn't it? What goddamned lunacy!" he said, stifling the words between his gritted teeth.

"What are we going to do?" asked Gabriella. She was frantic.

"Who did this?" said Béla, unable to relinquish his outrage.

Gyuri chimed in. "Those terrible soldiers blew up the bridge. And the other ones, those evil 'red' soldiers dressed in black were mean to everyone and they killed some people. We saw them. It was horrible."

Béla did not quite know what his son was getting at, but was still too angry and distracted to listen to what sounded like nothing more than his child's overactive imagination. Helpless for a solution, he shifted away from the crisis. "Let's go back to the house. We'll talk more there."

Béla sat at the reins of a horse-drawn farm wagon, while his wife and son sat alongside him as they rode over the still-softening mud of the main street of Püspökladány. Báránd was barely three miles down the road. Although the sun was setting, there was enough light for Gyuri to see the shapes and colors of this rural town—the muddy stucco surfaces of the primitive country buildings, with their thatched or red-tiled roofs and cast-iron gates and fences painted green.

The family's home was a typically modest gypsum-covered house, painted in a familiar ocher yellow, with a thatched roof of straw. It was in a row of similarly shaped and sized houses along a muddy road, only a few steps from the center of the village. The home had been handpicked for Béla by the town council, all of whose members were delighted to finally have an animal doctor in their community.

Behind the house, there was a barn and a more sizable plot of land than those of the neighbors' properties in order to accommodate the animals that Béla would treat on his premises. The barn stood next to the outhouse, and the street's artesian well was a few houses down the road. Inside the house, there was a small kitchen, including a tiled cooking area with a woodstove. There were two small bedrooms, one on either side of a central living room. When Béla had first arrived, welcoming neighbors had generously placed candles in roughly hewn copper holders and two kerosene lamps on the coarse oak table in the middle room. Candles were otherwise in preciously short supply and kerosene was even harder to come by.

For Béla, who had served more than four years on the battlefield, living in one place was luxury enough. Gabriella had modest tastes to begin with, and was undisturbed by the humble surroundings. That her family would soon be under one—albeit thatched—roof was her sole concern. She had managed to bring kitchen utensils, some linens and a few blankets for the straw-filled mattresses, and all of the clothing she owned for Gyuri and herself.

No one was inclined to speak any further about the harrowing events of the day. Béla and Gabriella must have each harbored similar fears regarding their two children left in Budapest, fears that were now left to stew privately in each of them. Gyuri was positively enthralled by his family's new home and would voluntarily wait for a more opportune moment to disclose his own tale of woe.

The next several days would be the closest Béla would come in almost five years to a normal family life. Gyuri was thrilled that he would finally be living with his father, and indeed secretly rejoiced that for the present he would not have to share him with his brother and sister. But they never had time to catch their breath, managing only a hint of stability and happiness for three or four days before the postwar tumult came literally to their front door.

Having lived alone in Báránd for several weeks, Béla had already gravitated to the local café and tavern—one in Báránd, and the other, larger one in Püspökladány—to engage in his favorite pastime of playing cards and to become acquainted with the local farmers and merchants. He had even met up with an old friend of his from the army, Imre Kovács, a decorated war veteran. Despite his urban Jewish background, Béla was an unaffected man who quickly felt at home with his new neighbors. They, in turn, quickly took a liking to him.

One afternoon, not a week after Gabriella and Gyuri's arrival in April, Béla was relaxing in the tavern in Püspökladány when a local farmer burst in and angrily blurted out that Kovács had been killed late the night before. "The Lenin boys got him! They accused him of being an unregenerate defender of the old guard." Béla's eyes widened and the veins in his neck bulged. The man continued, "He didn't deny anything. He told them that he fought proudly in the war and said he would have fought harder if he knew what was coming. He wasn't about to be pushed around by such gutless bastards. He spit in the eye of one of them!" There was a ponderous pause. Some might have hoped that the farmer was finished telling his story. But he was merely catching his breath and gathering his courage. "Then they forced him . . . ," he continued, his voice cracking, "they forced him . . . to dig his own grave in the middle of the night." He paused again, swallowing hard. "In front of his wife and children . . . and then Szamuely himself—the filthy pig—shot him and had his family bury him."

Szamuely. Tibor Szamuely. He was a nominally Jewish "officer of the revolution." He traveled through the countryside in his own armored train with an army of thirty "Lenin boys." These so-called boys were machine-gun-wielding, bomb-carrying city thugs—leather-jacketed sailors and hoodlums, some of whom had earlier escaped from prison. Like Béla Kun's ruling council, they had more than their share of Jews. With their able assistance, Szamuely interrogated and often executed alleged counterrevolutionaries, sometimes accusing them of keeping the nation's nearly nonexistent grain harvest for themselves, other times dispensing with them on mere whim or flight of fancy. A French chronicler living in Budapest at the time described Szamuely as an "insufficiently educated journalist" in his twenties, "a consumptive man . . . with the eyes of a dead fish, with a long nose . . . large mouth and thick lips . . . and heavy black hair which he brushed straight back. . . . His Adam's apple rose and fell above an impeccable collar—he was a dandy." That Szamuely was a Jew did not have to be explicitly stated by the civilized Frenchman, since the stereotypes were already amply covered. People who knew of Szamuely's reputation feared him. Even Gyuri's earlier, seemingly outrageous reference to "'red' soldiers dressed in black" killing people would turn out to be true.

While the other patrons of the tavern held their reactions in check, Béla—friend and wartime colleague to the murdered veteran—was, like the messenger, unable to contain his outrage. Pounding his fist on the wooden table and sending cups, saucers, glasses, and playing cards flying every which way, Béla shouted, "How long will this madness continue?" As the last glass and saucer teetered and then fell off the edge of the table, shattering on the earthen floor, a deeper, more cutting silence penetrated the hearts of the tavern's patrons. Not everyone, however, was moved in the way Béla was. And Szamuely's train was still at the town's station.

Béla defiantly rode home and said nothing to his wife and son on entering the house. A few hours later, there was a knock at the door. To Béla's surprise, it was the wife of a local merchant who apparently had been in the tavern. She alone knew of her husband's secret calling as an informant on counter-revolutionary activities. She had no sympathy for the murderous thugs and even less for her husband's unholy penchant for betraying his neighbors. She warned Béla that he had been informed on, and that if Szamuely were still in town in the morning, he surely would be tried by a "people's tribunal"—that is, by Szamuely and some of his henchmen. He would undoubtedly be found guilty and executed on the spot. Béla was a marked man.

Gyuri, who had been standing alongside the door, was terrified. Here, too, he would remember with uncanny precision how events proceeded from this point. He hurried into his room and took the largest white handkerchief he could find. He then ran outside to the back of the house and found a three-foot-long stick to which he attached one corner of the handkerchief. Climbing onto the empty farm wagon sitting next to the house, he stepped up the two rows of wooden barriers on the side of the wagon's platform, up onto the slanted straw thatch of the roof. Edging up its slippery surface, he climbed all the way to the brick chimney, just below the roof's crest. Risking a full standing position, Gyuri then stuck his makeshift surrender flag into a crack in the mortar at the top of the chimney. He was fully prepared to plead for the life of his father.

By now it was dark, and it felt as though Béla's fate were sealed. Gabriella looked out the window and could see three uniformed soldiers dismount horses a few yards away and approach the house. There was a loud rap at the door. Gabriella and Gyuri stiffened and stood back to the side of the doorway. Béla looked at his wife and son. He clenched his jaw, determined not to have his family see any expression of terror or fear. But his face was flushed and his hands trembled as he opened the door.

A mustached army commander, dressed in what Béla instantly recognized as a Rumanian uniform, was flanked by two of his soldiers armed with bayoneted rifles at the ready position. With unimaginable relief, Béla turned to his wife and son. "These are Rumanian soldiers. Don't worry, they are here to protect us against the communists."

He was interrupted by the lead soldier. "We have learned that you are the only horse doctor for miles. You must come with us," the commander said in Hungarian. Many Rumanian nationals spoke Hungarian and lived in greater Hungary, which was the principal reason Rumania now lusted after its due spoils of war. "We are in dire need of your services," the commander went on. "We're far from home and constantly on the move. Our horses tire and get sick easily. We need you to look after them. You'll be safe and well treated. As soon as stability returns, you'll be free to come back to your family. Your wife and son will see you in a matter of weeks," the commander said, apparently trying in a halfhearted way not to further alarm the woman and child.

Béla knew he was lying. There was no way to know when the chaos would cease. The family's terror had instantly shifted to this new crisis. If Gyuri felt relieved a minute earlier that his father would not be killed, he was now in tears. Gabriella was gasping to endure what felt like no less a lethal blow. Her husband was going away again.

"I just got back from four years of war," Béla pleaded. "I barely know my family. Find someone else to take care of your horses."

"You're the only one we could find," answered the leader. "Your horse is ready. Let's go," he said bluntly, waving Béla out the door.

But before Béla could move, Gabriella lunged at the commander, disregarding the bayonets pointing barely over her head. "You savage!" she said, managing to pound his chest once with her fist before he grabbed her wrist. The armed soldiers took a step back and pointed their rifles at the outraged woman until their leader shook his head, checking them. Even as she was physically restrained, Gabriella kept on. "You plunderer! The devil will take you! We'll not lose him again!"

Béla put his arm around her shoulder. "Are they any worse than those who would come for me in the morning?" he whispered. He knew he was trapped. He could either go with them or be killed in the morning. But he secretly wanted to be helpful to these adversaries of the madmen who had killed his friend. "We have no choice," he finally said. "I've got to go. But we've got to believe *this* war will be over soon." With that, Béla hugged and kissed his wife and son, and walked out the door to the roadway, followed by the soldiers. He mounted the readied horse and rode impassively with his new patrons toward the middle of town and then further south into the night, faintly illuminated by a waning crescent moon.

Gabriella yelled after him, above the hoofbeats of five horses, "We will find you! I will go to their leaders and to the French! We will find you!"

Four of Szamuely's men did indeed show up at her door the next day. But in her frenzy, Gabriella had no trouble convincing them that the Rumanians had abducted Béla. Fortunately for her, she was all too believable. "If my husband is in any difficulty," she foolishly barked at them, "with you lowlifes, it most likely doesn't compare to the trouble he is now in with the Rumanians." One of the men made an empty threat as to what would happen to the entire family if she was lying. Choosing not to pick a fight with such a defiant woman and her young son, he and his band of thugs left empty-handed.

The next weeks and months were terrifying. Gabriella had no idea where Béla was. But since he was not performing his civil service job in Báránd, the Hungarian government would not pay his salary to his family. Living conditions went from precarious to desperate. Sympathetic neighbors tried to be as helpful as they could, but these were impoverished times for everyone. Gabriella had to sell what few valuables she had brought with her from Budapest—a candelabra, a few pieces of crystal and china, and even an exquisite tablecloth embroidered by her mother-in-law—all to see what few crowns they could fetch for a few days' ration of bread and flour.

Physical survival and Béla's abduction were not the only trouble in Báránd. This predominantly Christian community's way of life was being assaulted. Revolutionary commissars, mostly from Budapest, had been sent throughout the country to requisition food and livestock to feed the population of the cities. Besides forcibly taking the people's precious grain, poultry, and cattle, they ordered the removal of crucifixes from schools and threatened to shut down the churches in order to turn them into movie houses. These actions convinced many local farmers and peasants that Jews were at the root of the revolution—that it was a religious war, pitting good Christians against the slayers of Christ, those eternal troublemakers disguising their self-interested hatred of the Christian way of life as quixotic egalitarian fantasies. Gabriella recognized that the haughty demeanor of these commissars, these supposedly proletarian bureaucrats—educated men or crafty businessmen dressed in city suits and ties, wearing metal-rimmed spectacles—hardly made them fitting representatives of the downtrodden masses. The ignorance of these commissars to the ways and needs of true common folk was maddening. She thought she had escaped their know-it-all attitudes when she left Budapest. Gabriella heard the various reports of their contemptible actions, naturally disregarding the fantastic ones as being steeped in ancient libels against the Jews. But she still felt outrage for the shame some of these former coreligionists brought to the innocent townspeople, as well as to themselves. Could it be that the Christian religion was now under attack by the ruling, allegedly Jewish government?

Then, in early August, the Bolshevik government collapsed under the weight of its own ineffectiveness and corruption. Although the bridge near Szolnok was still not repaired, Gabriella now saw the chance for Miklós and Klari's safe passage from Budapest. The town pharmacist and family's neighbor, Barnabas Janko, known as Barna, generously offered to travel to Budapest to retrieve the children. In early September, he journeyed by train to Szolnok, forded the Tisza by a makeshift barge, and continued to Budapest by train. His journey back to Báránd with the children proceeded similarly. Miklós and Klari felt like spies on a scary adventure, being smuggled, so they imagined, across the river under cover of darkness to their destination. The next morning, they boarded a train outside of Szolnok and arrived in Báránd within a few hours. Their mother had hurriedly fetched Gyuri, who had been playing in the rectory garden of the Calvinist church on the town's main street, and together they greeted Miklós and Klari at the train station, after nearly a five-month separation.

Within weeks of the children's return, Gabriella's fretfulness turned to Béla. She decided to set out to find her husband. She traveled first to Budapest to plead with the French patrons of the Rumanians to assist her in obtaining Béla's release. She carried with her a letter written in French by her erudite parish priest, Father Szemethy, who otherwise felt sadly helpless to be of any further assistance to her.

That initiative proving fruitless, Gabriella returned to Báránd, only to set out again, in reckless desperation, this time toward Transylvania, to try to find Béla among the ranks of the Rumanian Army. Leaving the children with a new housekeeper, whom Béla's relatives in Budapest helped pay for, she traveled with a young guide named Ernö who was familiar with Transylvania and had on numerous occasions smuggled people back and forth over the closely guarded new frontiers.

After many months of repeated forays into countless villages and towns along the Transylvanian border, Gabriella finally received word that Béla had been seen with Rumanian soldiers near the northeastern part of the region, rustling a Hungarian village's horses. With Ernö's help, Gabriella penetrated the border near the Szamos River and entered the formerly Hungarian town of Szatmár-Németi by herself. Soon after arriving in the town square, she was approached by Rumanian soldiers. She instantly felt terrified of being harmed and humiliated by them, especially by the army's familiar practice of *douâ zeci şi cinci*, Rumanian for "twenty-five," referring to the number of blows with a wooden paddle soldiers would administer to one's bare backside. Gabriella was a painfully modest woman and she knew that if the soldiers threatened to dishonor her, she would have to throw herself into the open well by which she was standing. But when she explained that her husband was the horse doctor for the army, the soldiers took her to the headquarters of the region's commander.

General Mardarescu, a robust Rumanian officer with a sharp jawline, flaring nostrils, and a wide, tapered mustache over strong, expressive lips, greeted Gabriella in a genteel manner uncharacteristic of a soldier. He was at once impressed with her fierce determination to find her husband and her reckless daring in jeopardizing her safety. "You poor woman," he said almost whimsically, in crisp German. "Your resourceful husband has been a great help to us." The general paused and smiled. "But he escaped yesterday." Then he interrupted himself with a laugh. "He deceived us, or so he thought, by confiscating dozens of sick horses. He thought he was going to slow us down. It was a ridiculous plan. His head must have become a little soft after all these months. But he still caused us some trouble. We would have been forced to court-martial him had he not gotten away." Gabriella would have been alarmed had the general's comments not seemed peculiarly tongue-in-cheek. He continued, "But we won't go after him. He's served his purpose and we have other horse doctors now. Besides, he's been a likable fellow and a good soldier. I'm sure he's ready to go home to his diminutive homeland," the general said sarcastically, greater Hungary having been carved up by the surrounding nations.

"Where did he go?" Gabriella demanded.

"I'm sure if you hurry, you'd find him in Csenger, right over the border. You probably passed him getting over here. Now hurry, dear lady, and find your good husband. You'll not be welcome here for long."

Gabriella arrived in Csenger before noon and met up with Ernö again. Watering their horses at the town's well, they met an old man who told them he had just seen Béla at the local inn, dressed in a Rumanian Army uniform.

When he learned that Gabriella was his wife and that Béla was a Hungarian, the man was delighted to take the exhausted-looking woman there. When Gabriella saw Béla, she swept forward to embrace him and openly wept tears of joy and relief.

Husband and wife set off on their long return journey home. Ernö drove the wagon and accompanied them northward until they were at a safe enough distance from the Rumanian border. The couple sat in each other's embrace on the wagon's platform. Traveling through the eastern Transylvanian countryside, they smiled hesitantly at each other and said little above the clattering of hoofbeats and clanging of harnesses.

By the end of a long day, the three arrived at the town of Mátészalka, twenty miles northwest of Csenger. At this point Ernö separated from them, expecting that he would easily find work as a border guide. He took the wagon and horses with him, knowing that Gabriella and her husband would be able to board a train for Báránd. He was never heard from again; months later, word arrived that he had been shot by Rumanian soldiers in an abortive crossing into their territory.

Béla and Gabriella retired for the night at an inn on the second floor of a tavern. For more than five years, they had barely lived under the same roof. As Gabriella sat up against the wooden bedpost of their rented room, Béla stood leaning on his hands against the wall, a few feet away. He looked older. She still felt a fateful bond to him, the sense that they were meant to be together. Somehow, though, it felt different, unfamiliar, strained, even to her, even in her avowed lifelong devotion to the man she had always loved. A certain subtle distrust had crept between them in the chilly, half-darkened room lit only by a flickering kerosene lantern at its far corner. Why hadn't he come home earlier? Why had he not escaped? Gabriella never voiced these questions, but they had grown in her heart over the months of her tireless pursuit. It must have been her weariness that made her think this way. She wouldn't dare say anything, but her doubts darted around the room, just as Béla's knowing eyes kept evading her glance. She wouldn't dare say anything. Or would she?

"I almost couldn't go on anymore," she began. "It was not like Budapest during the war. At least then we had friends and family. In Báránd we were virtual strangers. I couldn't bear it. I had to come look for you."

"I can't blame you if you thought I'd never make it home."

"I couldn't imagine you deserting us. But it's been nearly a year and the Rumanians left Hungary months ago. Why wouldn't they let you go?"

"They trusted me and paid me, and kept promising, 'Just another few weeks. We must still secure the territory.' After months, I felt duped. Long after the communists were gone, and Horthy marched into Budapest, the winter was setting in. Yes, I know about Horthy and his new government." Admiral Miklós Horthy had formed a right-wing, counterrevolutionary army and marched from the city of Szeged, in the south of the country, all the way to Budapest—that so-called Jewish/Bolshevik breeding ground he now referred to as "the guilty city"—where he formed a government and became the nation's much-revered regent. "I felt like a damned prisoner with the Rumanians."

So Béla hadn't deserted them. Gabriella rose from the bed and stepped toward him. She pulled him over to where they both now sat next to each other on the lumpy straw mattress. "I heard you had a scatterbrained plan to escape."

Béla smiled whimsically. "Well, it wasn't a very clever plan, but I was desperate."

"The general told me you tried to steal some horses."

Béla laughed and then took a deep breath and let it out. "It really was an idiotic plan. It was no plan at all. I was furious at them and tried to sabotage them by rounding up some sick horses when we raided a neighboring town. I thought their own horses would be too tired, so I could get away late that night."

Béla paused. His face had softened. A sympathetic smile cured a corner of Gabriella's mouth. He put his hand on the back of her neck and drew her head to his chest. Her voice was now muffled, "I'd almost given you up for dead."

"If the Rumanians hadn't come when they did after I opened my big mouth back in Báránd, I surely would have been dead, wouldn't I?"

"Yes, you would have," Gabriella said, lifting her head and looking him straight in the eyes. "You don't even know. The communists came for you the next day. I can't begin to tell you. Unshaven, drunken or hung over. They weren't Red, they were black and filthy."

"Terrorists!" said Béla, as he stared piercingly at the wall over his wife's head. "They destroyed what was good and decent in our country." It didn't take much for Béla to conjure his old outrage and disgust.

Gabriella's eyes had narrowed. "People in town called them 'the Budapesti commissars' or, worse, simply 'the Jews.' Not the kind of Jews we've ever known. Most of them weren't even Jewish, and the ones who were didn't care a dot about religion. But they were all painted with the same brush."

Béla shrugged his shoulders in bewilderment. "Somehow, I could never imagine the likes of Karl Schneider siding with communists. Middle-class Jews like comfort too much. What kind of fantasy is it that makes people believe it was the Jews who painted the country Red?"

"I just don't know anymore," Gabriella said. "The communists bled the local townspeople and wanted to eliminate religion from our lives." She reached for Béla's forearm and held it with both hands. "You wouldn't recognize our parish church. It was desecrated." Béla furrowed his brow in astonishment. Gabriella went on, "I was humiliated and outraged—ashamed. Is this what communism means—Jewish-looking commissars eliminating Christianity everywhere?"

Béla put his hand over his mouth and pulled at the skin of his face. "I can't believe it," he said. "Look," he continued, with his hand still grasping his chin, "I'll never forgive the communists for murdering Kovács. He was a decent man and a dear friend—a true patriot. I don't care if Szamuely and his men were Jews or not. They were the scum of the earth and deserve to go to hell. If Jews are responsible for that kind of treachery, I can understand people hating them. But this is not all so black and white."

"No, of course it's not," Gabriella added. "There are plenty of judges out there who have taken their revenge on the Jews. We don't need to join their ranks."

"Even from the Rumanians," said Béla, "I heard how Horthy had unleashed crazed militias to hunt down communists and Jews throughout the country." After the communists were overthrown the previous August, rumors spread immediately that Tibor Szamuely had shot himself with a pistol he had hidden in a handkerchief, just as he was apprehended trying to flee to Vienna. The Jews in his native city of Nagyvarod, frightened of the militias and outraged by his crimes, refused to bury him in their town's Jewish cemetery. Instead, he was buried outside its low stone walls, with an inscription on his wooden grave marker scrawled in blue: "Here lies a dog."

"I was desperate," continued Béla, "to know if you and the children were safe."

"We were. After all, there are so few Jews in Báránd that those bands didn't bother with our village." Other cities, towns, and villages where Jews lived in greater number were not as fortunate. The militias unleashed by Horthy committed atrocities throughout the country that far outstripped what Szamuely's men ever did.

Béla freed his arm from Gabriella's grasp and briefly buried his face in his hands. Then he stood up and walked over to the window. "It's just insane," he said, gazing out at the quiet road below. "Even with the communists gone, the country has gone mad."

Gabriella knew she was losing Béla. She had to find a way to bring him back. "It was curious," she said, "that the merchant who informed on you disappeared. Some people thought he fled, or that he was captured and shot. God will bless his wife for trying to help us."

"You watch," continued Béla, "the Hungarians aren't finished with the Jews." His tone turned bitter. "Do you remember? I said it years ago. I knew this was coming. Hungary doesn't need Jews anymore, so now they're punishing us for being Bolsheviks. Before this, we were profiteers, now we're communists. When I was a child, we were Christ-killers, murderers of little children so that we could drink their blood on Passover." Béla was shaking his head as he spoke. "It's just a new wave of the same old things. And this is just the beginning. I tell you, it will never end. They will never let us forget that we are not like them."

"I pray to our God and Savior," Gabriella added in a resolute voice, "we'll be able to live in peace and that our relatives in Budapest will be out of harm's way."

Béla tried to force a smile. "We'll all need a divine Savior before this mess is over. Let's hope He doesn't wait too long."

✤ CHAPTER 4 ✤

Providence

By your destined names will men call you
and in your appointed place will they place you
and give you what is intended for you.
Babylonian Talmud, Yoma 38a

After Béla returned to Báránd, some people were puzzled and thought of him as a traitor. In the town's peasant tavern, the "spitting parlor," many locals who were just getting acquainted with him as an amiable veterinarian scratched their heads. "How could he have joined the Rumanian Army?" one asked. But soon enough, others remembered him as a decorated veteran and recalled, too, his defiant denunciation of the communists. They had heard the story and knew he hadn't joined the Rumanians of his own free will.

Besides, townspeople surely hated the communists more acutely than they resented Hungary's historical rivals, the Rumanians. After all, aside from the nation's universally wounded pride for the way the surrounding countries were slicing up greater Hungary, what did larger or smaller borders matter to these farmers and landless peasants in the interior of the country? Not many Hungarians ever actually believed that the communists, or any government, could fend off the separatist thrusts of nationalities that had grown to hate the Hungarians for their age-old subjugation of them. The armistice line, the establishment of which had originally ushered the Hungarian communists into power with their empty promises of regaining the wider historical borders, was roughly thirty-five miles southeast of Báránd. Though provisional in name, to the Hungarians—at least to those in Báránd—this line might as well have become the Great Wall of China. The town was far enough from the border, and its markets were entirely local and regional. And the Hungarian government was now buying their goods again, instead of confiscating them like the communists had.

The most prominent landmark in my family's recollections of Báránd was the Central European baroque-style Catholic church in the middle of town. Such handsome, pastel-colored structures, with rococo features, spotted the Hungarian landscape and represented the efforts of sixteenth- and seventeenth-century Counter-Reformationist Jesuit emissaries of the Mother Church in Rome to attract followers back to Catholicism. The church in Báránd was the point around which the lives of these formerly urban Jewish converts would revolve.

The Pogány family became devoted members of the parish. Gabriella attended Mass regularly and confession nearly once a week. She found a great comfort in the Church. As a mother, she was devoted to her children's education and religious upbringing. All three children attended Mass with her on Sundays, and the twins served daily as altar boys. Béla rarely attended church. He preferred the company of his friends, the small cadre of white-collar professionals in the town: the new pharmacist with the noble name of Szendrei; the postmaster; the notary; even the parish priest, with whom Béla often engaged in the national pastime of playing cards. In his profession, Béla was universally respected and liked by the local farmers, peasants, and herdsmen.

Gyuri and Miklós were once again each other's constant companions. For the first time, at age seven, they would now come to know the experience of having a father, although Béla was more stiff and formal with his boys than he was with his daughter. An unflappable, even-tempered man, he proved to be an inaccessible and remote father to his sons. Yet for the first time since the boys could remember, their mother was not downcast or sickly but actually happy and energetic—despite their modest living conditions. Her pensive and occasionally ponderous spirit was now softened and sweetened with the joys of motherhood and, finally, an uninterrupted day-to-day relationship with her husband. Gabriella cooked, made birthday parties for the children, and celebrated all the Christian holidays, including marking the days of the saints after whom the children were named, with joy and fanfare.

Gyuri was not particularly enamored of his saint. George the dragon-slayer did not capture the boy's imagination or suit his temperament. Secretly, he wished he had been named after Michael, the archangel whose name fell on the twins' birthday. Miklós was thrilled that his saint's name day came right around the first Sunday of Advent, so that he would get a foretaste of what was coming at the end of the month, on Christmas.

Unlike children of the local peasants and farmers who had to help in their families' livelihoods, the three children were unessential and uninvited visitors to their father's workplace—the barn behind the house where he practiced his profession. More often than not, Béla traveled to outlying farms rather than have sick animals brought to him. He also made a daily, solitary trip to the slaughterhouse, where he served as the area's meat inspector. On one isolated occasion, Miklós went with him, riding a horse-drawn wagon along the southerly road to the county seat of Bihar. So unique was it to accompany his father anywhere, much less alone, that it remained fixed in Miklós's memory as a special event.

In school and church, the brothers had learned how Jesus had sent His disciples out in pairs to teach the Gospel and how St. Francis had modeled his brotherhood around those same preaching practices. To Gyuri and Miklós's way of thinking, now that they had renounced the opulent surroundings of the city for the humble environment of the countryside, they were a perfect, almost preordained, pair to serve God every day in church. Both boys imagined that they would someday be vagabond preachers proclaiming God's word to all who would listen.

Up to this point, their biggest religious test had occurred one early summer day when the Rumanian circus came through town and one of its donkeys took sick. The circus master would not listen to the children's plea that their father was an animal doctor and could probably cure the stricken animal. Instead he begged the boys to say five "Our Fathers" in Rumanian so that God would heal the donkey. When the animal died despite the twins' prayers, the boys could only assume that their Rumanian was not clear enough to be understood in heaven. Neither of them dared think that God had failed them.

In spite of their love for Catholicism and their devotion to the parish, there was something distinctly different about the Pogány family, different even from other white-collar families in the village. It was partly what made Jews so distinctively "other" throughout all of Hungary. This was their emphasis on learning and education. The family's social life centered around what had become a professional "intelligentsia," consisting of the schoolteacher, Gyula Mühler, who doubled as the choirmaster in the Catholic church; the clerics Szemethy and Szabo; the notary, Kolozsi; the postmaster, Torony; and, the pharmacist, Szendrei. Despite the religious differences among some of its members, this group was essentially an island of educated individuals among a sea of simple farmers and peasants. They congregated together, celebrating individual and family functions in one another's company.

Yet the Pogánys' love of books, and the parents' need to educate their children, made them stand out as particularly unique in the village. Since there was no library in Báránd, the parish priest, Father Szemethy, a learned man with his own private collection of books, fed each family member's voracious appetite for reading—providing Hungarian and German books especially. There were the Karl May adventure stories, written in German, for the children; occasional detective stories for Béla; and more literary works in translation for Gabriella, her favorite being Jack London. Gabriella, especially, stood out among the women of Báránd for being so well-read. She had developed a reputation for high-mindedly quoting famous authors whom people in town had never even heard of. At times, they'd playfully poke fun at her by paraphrasing her quotations of Hungarian classics. If the priest hadn't spoken it in his sermons, then you could be sure you had heard it from Mrs. Pogány. And she was the one who kept the village informed of national events, since she insisted that family members in Budapest keep sending her the *Pesti News,* one of the city's preeminent daily newspapers.

Ironically, in addition to the Catholic priest, the Calvinist minister of the town, Father Szabo—a former member of the Hungarian parliament—was the other major source of moral and spiritual support as well as intellectual stimulation. Szabo was no great lover of the Catholics, nor of the Catholic priest especially, so Gabriella often felt the need to sidestep the usually unspoken conflict between the two Christian communities. As the family's major objectives were worship and learning, being in the middle of these denominational rivalries made them feel even more marginal within the wider community. The boys did not understand such rivalries and paid them little mind. But the fact that the family maintained warm relations with both Christian denominations made them stand out that much more to each of the rival sides, over and above the fact that their Jewish sensibilities were obvious to all. In a way, it seemed as if the family's Christianity mattered less to their disaffected Jewish relatives in Budapest than their Jewish origins did to their Christian coreligionists in Báránd. At one and the same time, their being recent converts made them both more mobile and marginal.

❖

A few years passed. In early September 1923, Gabriella received a postcard from her beloved cousin Elza. It was written in Cherbourg, France, during her return voyage from America. Gabriella was shocked to learn from the few brief lines that Elza had met a wonderful Hungarian man in New York and married him the year before. But this husband never told her about his heart ailment, which killed him five months into the marriage. Elza was four months pregnant at the time. She was now returning to Hungary with a six-month-old daughter named Margit. Having decided she could never raise a child alone in America, Elza would return to live with her parents in Budapest. Elza implored Gabriella to contact her there after their arrival in the coming weeks.

"She's coming home! Elza's coming home!" Standing in the post office that September afternoon, Gabriella was astounded. Oblivious to who was around or whether anyone was listening, she let out a string of exclamations, each one punctuated by a laugh, a sigh, and finally a tear. Then she wiped her cheek with the back of her hand and smiled broadly, as she leaned down to repeat the news to her nine-year-old daughter, Klari.

In October, Gabriella traveled to Budapest to visit Elza and her parents, Aunt Bertha and Uncle Henrik. Although she'd presently be making her obligatory visits, as well, to those on Béla's side of the family, Gabriella did not try to hide her excitement at seeing her only family. With peace returned to the countryside, Gabriella could board the train in Báránd and be in Budapest in half a day. She would spend the night and planned to return the next afternoon, arriving home well before dark.

The trip brought Gabriella back over the great Hungarian plain that she had first traversed with Gyuri more than four years earlier. She felt an eerie sense of foreboding as her train approached the bridge over the Tisza River that the Hungarian Red Army had blown up. Her memory of the explosion and the cloud of acrid smoke barely a few hundred yards upwind now sent an ominous shiver down her arms and legs. But it was something more than the fear of reliving what had once happened there. It was something stirring in the future, something indistinct seizing her heart with an undefinable dread. No, that's ridiculous, Gabriella told herself. She was just tired, hadn't slept well the night before.

As the train trundled on through the miles of flat farmland before approaching the gentle hills around Budapest, Gabriella watched farmers hurrying to complete their autumn harvest to beat the first frost. The swiftly moving scythes leveling the tall stalks of grain, and the apparent urgency with which the harvest was being loaded onto farm carts, were harmless enough images, she thought, but they too provoked this same odd sense of trepidation. Gabriella put her head back on the cracked leather headrest of the cabin seat, closed her eyes, and told herself to rest before the real excitement of the day began.

When the train arrived at the station in Budapest, Aunt Bertha and Elza, cradling her baby daughter in her arms, were waiting for Gabriella. Seeing them from the cabin, she grabbed her overnight bag and hurried to the exit. Quickly alighting to the platform, she ran over to her relatives. She gave a warm hug first to her Aunt Bertha, savoring the embrace for several seconds, before kissing her on both cheeks. She then took Elza's face in both hands, almost as if she were making sure she was real, gently leaned forward over the baby, and kissed her long-absent cousin.

"You see," said Elza, uncovering her infant girl, "I haven't come empty-handed. "This is Margit."

"She's a most stunning little girl," said Gabriella, looking down at the baby.

Then Bertha chimed in: "People stop Elza on the street with her baby carriage and tell her how beautiful her child is. She's God's gift to all of us," said the beaming grandmother. "Only, what a terrible price my dear Elza had to pay," said Bertha, with a sigh.

Elza, apparently not very comfortable being cast in the role of a tragic figure, interrupted with a smile. "Let's go back to the house first. There's too much to talk about on this windy platform." Gabriella noticed that a gentle and self-conscious sadness had grown into her cousin's eyes since she last saw her.

Traveling by tram from the train station through the inner city of Pest to Buda, Gabriella was exhilarated to be home with her relatives. She also couldn't help notice the city, as if for the first time. It was no longer as gray and bleak as it had been during the endless years of war. Hungarians had come to refer to the halcyon days before the war as "peacetime," days of elegance and bounty that they once thought might never return. Now, peace was merely the absence of war. Nonetheless, five years after the war's end, Budapest was undeniably different. It had regained its earlier beauty and vitality. Gabriella remembered the adage that Hungarians do much better at recovering from tragedy than at taking advantage of success.

In Pest, people were about in the early afternoon: well-dressed businessmen in dark suits and writers, poets, and journalists still mulling at the cafés in the brisk autumn air. Many people had left the city, especially Jews fleeing the postwar terror. But many remained. Stunning ladies, in well-cut lamé and fashionable overcoats with fur collars, recharged the city with its former elegance and allure. In Pest, there was more movement and energy, more street-cars and many more automobiles than there had been when Gabriella left. As the tram approached the bridge crossing, she looked out beyond the silvery-green Danube toward the handsome, red-roofed buildings lining the river in Buda. Beyond the sumptuous Castle Hill and the low-lying buildings of the city's Second District rose the Buda hills, whose trees in their full autumn radiance were a richer visual feast than Gabriella could take in. But not once was her joy tinged with even a hint of remorse for having left this stunning city. Perhaps precisely because it looked so new and foreign, Gabriella could easily admire it just as a marveling tourist might. But Budapest was no longer her home. She was certain of that.

Back at the apartment on Lipthay Street, the small flat was less crowded than Gabriella remembered it. After all, as a child she spent years under its roof with seven other people. Most of them were dispersed now. Gabriella, Bertha, Elza and baby Margit, and the family's youngest daughter, Rosi, settled in the living room for coffee and pastries. Rosi, in her early twenties, was a hunchback girl who had grown too dependent on her mother to make a life for herself outside the home. She was a competent secretary at a law office but had no life beyond her family. Uncle Henrik was still at work as a foreman at Ganz Danubius, the large and respected shipbuilders.

Beneath the mood of exhilaration in the room, Gabriella sensed an uneasy quiet. As much as she wanted to know the twists and turns in her cousin's fateful life in America, she was sure that this was the source of the tension in the air. But everyone must have known that Gabriella would of course be curious.

"Well, how can we begin to tell you," began Bertha, "how difficult these months have been for Elza? She met a wonderful man in New York at the Hungarian club where she sang."

"Didn't I always tell you," Elza interrupted in nearly a whisper, trying not to wake the baby in her arms, "that the only thing that could keep me from performing in the opera was my voice?" Gabriella could tell Elza was trying to lighten the heaviness in the air with her bantering. She clearly didn't like being the center of attention, especially over such a monumental issue as going to America and then suddenly deciding to return to Hungary.

"He fell in love with her," Bertha continued, "and pursued her until they finally married, barely a year later. Elza tells us he was a romantic gentleman." Bertha smiled and glanced over at Elza before returning her gaze to Gabriella. "He worked very hard, too hard, in a factory, just to earn enough money to come back to Budapest to go to law school."

"God knows it was an unlikely dream," said Rosi. "He must have known that the new Jewish quotas would have made it next to impossible."

"But Elza tells us he was an energetic and intelligent man who would have made out," continued Bertha. She didn't respond to Rosi's cynical comment. "Even if they had returned and he couldn't go to law school, he would have taken care of his family. When he died and she came back alone, well . . ."

"My life's an open book," Elza interrupted again. She looked pained.

"Well, go ahead. You tell it, then," Bertha answered back. "I'm sorry to embarrass you."

Elza swallowed hard. She was on the spot but didn't want to give the wrong impression of her loving mother. "I came back because I couldn't imagine raising a baby in America without a husband. I felt I would have been in the way for Karcsi, so I asked Uncle Eddie for the return fare home." Károly, whose nickname was Karcsi, was the family's enterprising youngest son. In America he was called Charlie. Having been in New York since before the war, he now owned a restaurant in the Yorkville section of Manhattan, where many Hungarian immigrants lived. Eddie was Bertha's brother, a successful haberdasher in Nashville. "Eventually, my brother and uncle would have found a way for my parents and the rest of the family to emigrate to America. I guess that may not be possible now."

"I never knew you wanted to go to America!" Gabriella said to her aunt, with wide-eyed surprise.

Bertha raised her brow dismissively and glanced away, as if to shrug off its importance. But no one said anything. In that silence, Gabriella instantly understood. Of course, everyone was overjoyed that Elza had a child, but Gabriella now knew that the tension in the room covered an ocean of disappointment.

"I can only remember what it was like during the war without Béla," said Gabriella. "I had to work and Rosa took care of the children. I couldn't have done it without her." If no one else would, Gabriella would come to Elza's defense. "In another country, it would have been absolutely unimaginable. Thank goodness she had a mother to come home to."

"And, you know, fate works in mysterious ways," added Bertha. She was never an ungenerous woman, Gabriella thought. "God must have had his reasons for why Elza came back to us and why little Margit should grow up in Hungary." Elza looked comforted. It was the kind of soothing wisdom that Bertha was known to dispense to family and friends.

"You're certainly right," Gabriella answered. "It was not to be. We can't sit here brokenhearted, although I admit to being biased. This way, I get to see my cousin again and to meet her beautiful little girl. But I don't doubt for a minute, either, that there was a larger purpose to all this."

The subject was dropped, as everyone continued to look at the enchanting infant resting unperturbed in her wistful mother's embrace.

"But, tell me," Gabriella finally said to Elza, after a long pause, "you haven't said anything about your husband. Who was he and what kind of man was he?"

"His name was László. In America, they called him Lester," said Elza. "Margit and I will carry on his surname of Deutsch. He was a brilliant and ambitious man who worked too hard."

Gabriella was struck by her cousin's cool and distant description of her deceased husband. Why the remoteness, she wondered? She didn't dare ask, but looked back at Elza, hoping she would continue.

"He fell in love with me, and, I suppose, I with him. We married. But he never told me about the rheumatic fever, and the continual shortness of breath." Elza was subtly clenching her jaw, trying to choke back tears. But Gabriella could see these were not pure and simple tears of sadness.

"So he wasn't honest with you about how sick he was?" asked Gabriella delicately.

"That's right," said Elza, still in a near whisper. "At twenty-two, his heart gave out and he left me, unemployed and pregnant, living only by the grace of my brother in New York. How can anyone live that way?"

"You poor soul," said Gabriella. "You must be angry at him for not telling you about how sick he was."

"He deceived her and now look where she is," said Rosi.

With a quick frown toward Rosi, Elza looked back toward Gabriella. "I haven't wanted to put it into words. It makes me feel ashamed for feeling that way about such a dear man."

"He loved you too much and didn't know how sick he really was." Bertha tried to console her daughter. Turning to Gabriella, she added, "Elza brought his letters home with her. This man was filled with love, not deceit."

Gabriella nodded and smiled. "Does his family . . . ?" Even before she finished, Bertha gently closed both of her eyes and lifted an open hand toward her niece, signaling Gabriella to hold off. There was a tense pause. A terrible taboo had been violated. Elza bent her head over her sleeping child as if wanting to hide her eyes. Rosi winced and folded her arms. Gabriella took the not-so-subtle hint and held off. It was obviously not the best time to ask. She'd approach it another time, maybe privately with Elza.

❖

On a warm summer afternoon at the end of June 1924, Elza and Margit arrived in Báránd. Weeks after Gabriella's return from her visit in Budapest, she wrote to Elza and invited her and Margit to spend the summer months with her family in the countryside. Elza's former job as a secretary at Ganz Danubius had not materialized as she had hoped. So there was nothing that would keep her in the city. Besides, she needed to get her feet back on the ground. A summer holiday with Gabriella and her family would do her and her daughter good.

Miklós, Gyuri, Klari, and their mother excitedly went to greet them at the train station. Béla, of course, was busy tending to cattle at a local farm. The children only vaguely remembered Elza from when they lived in Budapest five years earlier. But having visitors from Budapest was a special occasion for each of them. Miklós and Klari especially liked the idea of helping to look after a beautiful and dear little girl they had heard so much about. Gyuri was more aloof, for no apparent reason. But all three children realized that their mother was not one to speak in exaggerated tones about anyone. So this little girl must really be extraordinary.

By Sunday, the third day of the visit, everyone was charmed by Margit, who, at fifteen months, was already walking and speaking several words. When the family went to Mass, Elza stayed behind since she had no interest in religion, certainly not in her cousin's adopted Catholicism. At the children's pleading, Elza consented to have Margit go along. "What harm would it do?" they said to Gabriella.

"So she is Jewish. Maybe she can be baptized," Miklós joked. The adults smiled but didn't respond.

"She'll be great fun to have around," said Klari, looking at her mother. "Papa and I can take care of her while you pray and Miklós and Gyuri serve as altar boys."

Little Margit looked in awe of the sweet-smelling, mysterious-looking sanctuary, with its crowd of people who alternately sat quietly or recited strange-sounding incantations in another language. The shiny statues of kind-looking angels and princesses and the man dressed in green and lacy white must have made the church seem a unique and gentle haven to the little girl. When everyone else went up to the altar for Communion, Margit stayed behind, holding onto Miklós's hand. For now, he was her endearing caretaker, and she was gleefully surrounded by loving family during a religious rite that her eyes, ears, and heart were not meant to behold.

After Sunday lunch, Béla uncharacteristically took the four children out for a walk, partly to give Gabriella and Elza a chance to be alone. But Béla was just as pleased to show Margit off as they strolled through the nearby paths and alleys of the village. As they walked, many people recognized the popular veterinarian and his children, waving to them from afar. There were two ragged-looking peasant women who came right up to them on a narrow dirt road. Klari recognized the women, and they must have known Béla and his family. Each woman knelt down beside Margit and gawked at the beautiful young child. When they tried to touch her face and caress her sleeveless arms with their wrinkled, dirty hands, Béla shooed them away in the manner one would drive off dogs that have become overly familiar after they have just rummaged through piles of garbage. "Don't touch the dear child," he said as he pushed their hands away. "She'll catch her death of TB." Klari had never known her father to be so harsh with anyone. He was a gentle, reserved man. She told herself that maybe he was just being very protective of his precious charge. She then looked at Miklós, maybe to see if he was as puzzled as she was. But he had a contented smile on his face, looking pleased that their father liked Margit and that he was willing to keep her from harm. Unruffled, the women walked away, still chattering about the little girl with whom they had become so taken.

"I finally think I know why you came back to Hungary," Gabriella said to Elza. Back at the house, they finally had a chance to talk. "I would have done the same thing."

"Thank you," Elza responded. She sat almost erect against the back of the chair in the kitchen. Her legs were outstretched under the rough-hewn dining table, and her nervous fingers picked at the colorful stitches in Gabriella's beautifully embroidered tablecloth, which her mother-in-law had sewn for her to replace the one Gabriella had been forced to sell five years earlier. "I couldn't bear to live by my brother Karcsi's charity anymore. He was good to me, but I knew I was a burden, especially after László died. He quietly let me know that he couldn't look after me and Margit forever."

"Understandable, maybe," said Gabriella. She was sitting across the table from Elza and leaning forward, her forearms resting on the tabletop and her hands clasped gently together. "But, you know what surprised me was how your return spoiled plans for your parents to emigrate to America. I finally remembered how they used to talk about it before I came to Báránd. I just never knew they had made definite plans."

"I suppose they talked of going out when the war ended," said Elza.

"So when you came home, it meant they'd never leave. Of course, that must be why your mother tried to hide her disappointment when I visited you last fall."

"Well, she wasn't that disappointed. Look, she and my father are no youngsters. Their life is here in Hungary." Elza had stopped picking at the tablecloth and now rested her palms against the smooth linen.

The two looked affectionately at each other. Without hesitating, Gabriella said, "You've been too proud, haven't you, to get in touch with your husband's parents, to let them know that you're here, and that you have a child?"

"Yes, too proud. With all that everyone has done for me, I don't want still more people to feel that I'm showing up at their doorstep. Yes, I was proud, but," Elza hesitated, "I was also angry."

"I think I understand that now. It's hard for you to admit, I know."

"He deceived me." There was a knot in Elza's throat. "I loved him, and I know he loved me very much. But he lied to me. Before we were married, he hid his illness from me. Once, when I saw his swollen legs, I asked him what was wrong. He made some excuse about retaining water when he ate salty foods. But after he died, the doctor told me how terribly sick he was. He wanted more than anything to make enough money as fast as he could so that he could come back and go to university. Maybe he didn't even admit to himself how sick he was. But how could he have married me? And what was he thinking when he got me pregnant? Did he think he could just ignore it and live forever? Isn't it terrible of me? The poor man died at twenty-two years old, and I'm blaming him for ruining my life."

"So you're punishing his family, aren't you, by not telling them that you're in Hungary? You *are* angry, aren't you? I wish you could hand it over to God. He would lighten your burden and help you do the right thing."

"Your God or my God?" Elza quipped, softening the tense mood.

"I'll tell you what," Gabriella answered with equal whimsy, "we'll put it out to the Father *and* the Son, and then we'll see who answers first." Then she sighed and became more serious again, but still with a sweetness to her voice. "My dear Elza. Why don't you contact your husband's family? Tell them that you've come home and that they have a granddaughter, especially such a special child as yours. Like your mother said, that little girl is truly a gift to all of us. Don't keep her from them. Margit will bring them great joy. They must have such terrible grief, losing their son and not knowing where his widow is."

"But I'm really not yet situated. I live with my parents, and this summer I'm living with you. I'm thirty-two years old and I'm not even standing on my own feet yet."

"Then I will write to them," Gabriella said boldly. "You know that I write good letters—sensitive, diplomatic ones. You yourself have even called them 'eloquent.' I'll tell them the truth, or at least part of it, that you wanted to wait until you had reestablished yourself. You didn't want to be a burden. People appreciate that. I'm positively certain they'll be overjoyed to hear about Margit—and you. You're family to them. Let me do it."

Elza was disarmed. Gabriella could tell. Elza leaned forward and surrounded Gabriella's hands with both of hers. Then, softly, she closed her eyes and nodded.

✤ CHAPTER 5 ✤

Harbingers

Drágaim, árváim, fiaim, Tik, . . . hol jártok, vagytok?
(My precious, forsaken sons, . . .
what paths are you treading and how do you fare?)
Endre Ady, "*Szegény Jó Fiaim*" ("My Poor Good Boys")

Five o'clock in the morning arrived too quickly for the residents of the orphanage. The twenty-five boys in the first-floor dormitory, and as many girls on the second floor, were given an hour to wash, dress, and make their beds before hurrying to the chapel, which was down the hall from the large common room where the girls slept. Sister Clarissa was a strict, no-nonsense headmistress who did not take kindly to any of her children being late for morning Mass. Her entire flock of nuns, dressed in the dark blue habits and winglike head coverings of the Order of St. Vincent, were uniformly known to be strict but not unkind.

The building housing the city of Gyula's orphanage was just down the street from the medieval fortress that had become the estate of Baron Venkheim, the benefactor who had charged the sisters with looking after the countless children who had been orphaned by a deadly nineteenth-century epidemic, a tragedy that had touched thousands of lives. Now, in the fall of 1924, conditions in the orphanage were less desperate. The sisters maintained the home to the rigorous standards of their Church, and life was more than tolerable for its residents. The Venkheim family had established a yearly tradition of sending a gift of hares for Christmas dinner, in spite of Sister Rosalia's ongoing complaints that there were never enough rabbits to feed everyone. In more recent years, besides caring for their orphaned charges, the sisters had begun offering room and board to students whose rural families, like the Pogánys, wanted them educated in the town's parochial school.

Gyuri and Miklós had quickly grown accustomed to the strict regimen at the orphanage and were happy to call it home. The family still lived in Báránd when the twins were sent to Gyula. At home, after passing through the four grades of elementary school, they had gone as far as they could with their weekly tutoring from Géza Varga, the train signalman's son, who would come home on weekends from school in Karcag to teach the boys Latin. Mrs. Szatmari, a local woman from Báránd, taught them math, geography, and Greek mythology. For two years, the boys had to travel by train to Kisújszállás for exams. For several days each time, they would stay with the family of the local high school professor, Dr. Hoffmann, a former Catholic monk who was now married with two children. The boys easily passed their examinations each year, and were always thrilled with the attention they got from the Hoffmann family. They took special delight in seeing the professor's collection of chibouks, or Turkish long-stemmed pipes, kept in the skull of a child, which rested stoically on Dr. Hoffmann's desk.

Eventually, though, the twins' tutor graduated high school and went off to university to become a doctor, an unusual achievement for the son of a common man in rural Hungary. Over the course of two years, Gyuri and Miklós had become even more isolated from their peers, all of whom had gone on to assume their modest places in their farming families. Now, in Gyula, the brothers were happy to be living and studying among such a large group of students, many of whom were more intelligent and ambitious than their classmates in Báránd.

If there was one sublime and carefree place to which Miklós's memory would continually return throughout his life, it was Gyula. Even while subsequent memories would be guarded by merciful forgetfulness, the precious reminiscences of the brothers' years together in that southern Hungarian town, and even the bittersweet recollections of the evolving differences in their destinies, would always be warmly welcomed guests among the stories my father would share as an old man with his children and grandchildren.

Miklós and Gyuri were always dressed and ready for Mass several minutes before any of the other children. Up until coming to Gyula, they were always dressed alike. Away from home for the first time, they now dressed as they wished, although neither one went out of his way to stand much apart from the other. Here in Gyula, just as in Báránd, they served as altar boys. The other residents of the orphanage did not give a second thought to the legitimacy of their Catholic heritage. Miklós, especially, would never feel as secure in his identity as a Catholic as he did in this cloistered environment of Gyula. While most of the residents of the orphanage stumbled into Mass, still half asleep, and mumbled their obligatory prayers and rote litanies, the twins always possessed a matchless enthusiasm for the Church that thoroughly bewildered their classmates.

During the thirty-minute chapel service, Sister Aurelia graced the assembly with her beautiful singing voice, chanting the Mass as well as reading from the breviary. She took her time to explain the meaning of the Latin prayers so that even the youngest children could follow. At one point, the children were also encouraged to pray for their parents and teachers, especially the orphans whose parents—most of them lost to the perennial scourge of tuberculosis—could spiritually benefit from the prayers of their children. Miklós typically prayed for his parents, brother, and sister. He also prayed for the sisters at the orphanage and the fiercely demanding but devoted teachers at the parochial school he attended down the street. Sometimes he added a prayer for a special favor, like improving his Latin grade, which was always a notch short of his brother's. Once, Miklós asked Gyuri what sorts of things he prayed for. These were not much different. But Gyuri also prayed for their Jewish relatives in Budapest. Miklós admired him for it, but didn't give much thought to why those people would need Gyuri's prayers. For the time being, he didn't ask.

After the chapel service, the twins quickly dispensed with their cassocks and joined the other high-school-age residents on their ten-minute walk to the high school, on the far side of the town square. The school day was a short but concentrated session of studies, from eight in the morning until one in the afternoon. It included the usual fare of religion, Latin, Greek, French, mathematics, Hungarian social and political history, and literature—a truly classical education. As Gyula was an unpretentiously ecumenical community, the few Jewish students in the school were allowed to have their own religion class.

When school let out, the students from the orphanage usually returned home promptly, since they never wanted to miss lunch. After that, there was an extended study period in the building's large living room for both boys and girls. Later, before dinner, Vespers was optional.

On Saturdays, when there was no school, chapel service was an hour later, and on Sundays everyone in the orphanage, including all the nuns, went to the Grand German Village Church for Mass. After Mass, the residents of the orphanage would retire to their own chapel, where their student choir, which Gyuri quickly joined, would sing from the Sabbath liturgy, with virtuoso solos again by Sister Aurelia.

Late one afternoon in early November, just before dark, about three months after their arrival in Gyula, Gyuri burst into the library where most of the residents were studying. Miklós was in his customary place at a far table by one of the few windows facing the front of the building. He was, as usual, wrestling with his Latin declensions.

"Come to Vespers with me," Gyuri said, in not quite a whisper, as he leaned over the table toward his brother. Three or four students looked up.

"You mean here?" Miklós whispered. "When, where?"

"At the church we pass every day," Gyuri said. "The Father is a nobleman and very dignified. It'll be good, you'll see." The parish church in the center of town was just on one side of a footbridge over a lazy stream. It was a tall and elegant, classically Roman-form Renaissance structure. The outside walls were painted in the familiar yellow of so many countryside churches of the era. There were white Corinthian pilasters set in its facade, and an imposing baroque steeple that extended well above the tops of two long rows of sycamores on either side of a tiled walkway leading all the way from the street to the sanctuary's entrance. Wooden benches were interspersed between the trees. On Sundays, before and after Mass, families strolled and sat along this charming and peaceful promenade.

Jenö Uferbach, an irreverent boy who used to smuggle Jack Carter detective mysteries into Sunday Mass, was sitting next to Miklós and playfully rolled his eyes, as if to say, "Going to *Vespers* is going to be *good*?!" But Miklós wasn't easily discouraged. He readily followed Gyuri's lead. Gyuri already had his coat on and was carrying his brother's with him. Miklós slipped it on before he was out the door. From there, the twins ran down the first-floor hall, hurtled down the five steps of the narrow central hallway, and yanked open the front door, failing to catch it before it rattled against the doorstop, nearly shattering the pastel-colored squares of peasant glass in its wooden frame. Once outside, they needed all of three minutes to run through the center of town to get to the church.

The boys were panting when they entered the sanctuary. It was larger than a typical country church, and it looked like an urban parish. Even some of the smaller country parishes were as gilded and ornate as some of the large, splendid churches in the cities. Hungarians' image of the House of the Lord included fancy statues or frescoes of cherubs and angels heralding the arrival of the divine Savior. Each community spared no expense to embody that sublime vision. Here, too, in Gyula's church, heaven and earth met as one, and a comforting feeling of peacefulness and security pervaded its interior. It instantly felt like a sanctuary to Miklós—utterly safe and embracing. With an air of self-assurance, the brothers hurried to the front pew.

Gyuri and Miklós looked around. Older students, both from the orphanage and the high school, were there. Some of them, they knew, were heading for the priesthood. There were also many older people—a number of shopkeepers who had just closed their stores for the day, some elderly women, and a few old men. Both boys felt as natural about assuming their place in this congregation as if they had been doing it forever. Of the twenty or thirty parishioners present for Vespers, the twins were, to anyone who took notice, clearly the youngest.

When the priest entered the sanctuary, Gyuri's eyes widened. Miklós, too, gaped and giggled before turning to his brother, who returned his look, as if each were saying to the other, "This *is* going to be good."

The priest, who stood barely fifteen feet in front of them, was Baron Father Vilmos Apor, a tall and dashing man with high cheekbones, a cherubic complexion, and sparkling eyes. He was from an aristocratic family and his stature was every bit that of a nobleman. He was perhaps in his thirties. Curiously, his eyes did not reflect the enlightened gaze of the landed aristocrat and devout churchman that he was. They were gentle and caring, pensive but slightly careworn eyes, as if he secretly carried a cross of his own. Even young Miklós could see it, and he wondered about it. Gyuri probably did, too. But more than anything, to the boys, Father Apor looked *important,* like the kind of larger-than-life noble and saintly soul whom the good Lord sends every once in a while for some special mission.

The service was brief, as were the Father's remarks following it.

"Salvation," he said, "does not come to those, even like myself, who spring from a good family, but those whose hearts and souls cling to the shoot of Christ's love. In the eyes of God, we are all equal. You want to be a good Christian?" he added. "Follow God's Son and live a life of love and charity. Our Lord's passion was not a way to an easy salvation. God is concerned with the way we live our lives and by how we treat our fellow man," he said, echoing the spirit of the Old Testament. "By God's grace, may you live lives of goodness and righteousness. Go in peace."

After the benediction, Father Apor did not disappear from the pulpit but came down to the pews to mingle with the small throng of evensong worshipers. By now, darkness had enveloped the day's end and the scant number of modest chandeliers and sconce-mounted candles along the walls created a soothing mezzotint reflecting off the plaster walls and shiny plaster icons. Father Apor made a beeline toward the marvelously attentive twin boys who had been steadily perched in the front pew throughout the service.

As the priest approached, tension now shot up from Miklós's belly to his throat. He tried to swallow. Were they being singled out? He wanted to look over his shoulder, but wouldn't dare, to see if he and his brother stood out in some troubling way. Maybe Miklós had forgotten that they were the only children in the sanctuary, and that for years he and Gyuri had received unwanted, fawning attention for being so uncannily identical in appearance.

But Miklós's tension instantly softened when he noticed the benevolent smile of the approaching priest.

Father Apor gently shook the boys' hands and then ever-so-lightly touched each of their cheeks, as if giving them a special blessing. "I am delighted to see you boys here this evening. If, as our Lord teaches, you must become as a child to enter the Kingdom of Heaven, then you are both off to a better start than many of the rest of us here."

Miklós was moved in a way he had never been before. As the son of Jews, he felt deeply reassured that it didn't matter that he was not born a Christian; being a Christian was in how he lived his life, not in who his ancestors were. More than at any other time in his life, Miklós felt invited into the sanctuary of Christ's House and at home in the Catholic faith. He was determined more than ever to follow in His ways. Looking at the softly penetrating gaze of the parish priest, he felt an unfamiliar calm and peacefulness. It was the kind of epiphany that heralds the appearance of a supernatural being and event. Father Apor was undoubtedly that being, and the event was Miklós's own spiritual homecoming.

✤

One brisk afternoon a few weeks later, at the end of autumn, the brothers were biding their time on a bench outside of Father Apor's parish church. Miklós turned to Gyuri and asked, "What do you think about what happened to Miki's father?"

"You mean the way he hanged himself over a gambling debt?" said Gyuri, with a matter-of-fact shrug of his shoulders. "What should I think? I suppose it's the rules of the game. You either pay your debt or you're obliged to uphold your honor. At least he did the honorable thing."

"The 'honorable thing'?" said Miklós. "Sounds a little cold. Miki's father's dead. I thought you liked Miki and respected his family."

Miki Maier was an intelligent, well-mannered, and handsome classmate to whom the twins had taken a great liking. His father had been a sophisticated man, a decorated war veteran, and a prominent attorney. His family was decidedly upper-class.

Gyuri continued, "Well, I never knew what to make of his being a Jew."

"What on earth do you mean?" In the waning daylight, with a crescent moon appearing in the sky, Miklós wasn't sure if Gyuri could see his jaw clench in response to what he had just heard.

"Miki's a very nice boy, and I feel sad for him. But Jews scare me," Gyuri confessed, "and I don't trust them."

"But you were born a Jew!" said Miklós, raising his voice. He felt peculiarly exposed. "You have Jewish relatives. What do you mean they scare you?" So that's why he prays for them, it suddenly occurred to Miklós.

Gyuri was silent for several seconds. He glanced over at his brother and then down at the ground.

"Do you remember," Gyuri said, looking up at Miklós, "right after the war, when we were going to move to Báránd, Mama and Papa decided to move us in stages because it wasn't safe for all of us to travel together?"

"So, what does that have to do with anything?"

"Papa was already settled in Báránd, so Mama and I went first."

"I haven't forgotten. A two-week delay turned into five months. So what?"

"You obviously know why you and Klari were stuck in Budapest when the army blew up the bridge. Well, that was a picnic compared to what happened afterward. You don't know the rest of it because I never told anyone and Mama never said anything either."

"About what, for God's sake?" Miklós asked, with growing irritation.

"I tried to tell Papa as soon as I saw him, but he wouldn't listen. And then, three or four days later, he was taken away by the Rumanians. After that it was just forgotten."

"Are you going to tell me or just keep leading me on this way?"

Staring off at the first stars in the evening sky, Gyuri kept returning a quick glance at his brother and now looked him straight in the eye.

"Right before we got to Báránd, just minutes before pulling into the station in Püspökladány, our train was stopped. A small and strange-looking armored train, which looked almost like a giant bullet, caught up with us and started shooting machine guns into the air to make us stop. Twenty-five or thirty dirty and mean-looking men, all dressed in black leather uniforms, got off and boarded our train. They forced everyone to get off and then their leader appeared. He was more neatly dressed than the others, in a black suit and a clean, freshly pressed white shirt and tie. He wore glasses without rims and looked kind of fancy. He actually looked more like a lawyer or businessman than he did a soldier or a bandit. But then some lady standing next to us asked him who these rough-looking men were. He asked her, in a very civilized tone, 'Have you ever heard of the Lenin boys?' But before she could answer, another passenger, an old man, said, 'These men are communist revolutionaries, and he's Szamuely.' 'Yes, that's right, sir,' this Szamuely answered. And it came to me days later that this was the same man who killed Papa's war friend and who would have killed Papa if the Rumanians hadn't taken him away.

"So then Szamuely," Gyuri continued, "started asking people a lot of questions about what they were carrying and whether they were for or against the revolution. I didn't know what a revolution was, or a communist, but I soon found out that these Lenin people thought some of the passengers were 'enemies' of the revolution. So they took three of the men, even though they looked like regular people, put them in a line, shoulder to shoulder, and shot them right before our eyes."

Miklós squirmed. Throughout the telling of his tale, Gyuri had a self-conscious smile curling a corner of his mouth, the way an adolescent does when he can't tell a deadly serious story with a completely straight face. Miklós had forgotten the point of the story, but was aghast by it nonetheless.

Gyuri went on. "Most of the women started screaming. Mama held my hand tightly and I began to cry. I think she did, too. But that was just the beginning. Some of the passengers protested that they should leave these innocent people alone. Then this devil Szamuely accused those men of being even worse enemies. He called them 'counterrevolutionaries,' ones who would dare defend betrayers of the new Hungarian government. He said that communism would soon be the government of all of Europe and that anyone who tried to slow its progress would not be tolerated." Gyuri's words moved with a suspenseful, halting cadence.

"What did he do next?" Miklós asked, helplessly captive to his brother's tale.

"Well, I didn't see this whole thing, but . . . Szamuely took the two men who spoke out to the other side of the train, the side closest to the roadway, where there were some small trees with not very strong branches. He forced the men's wives to go with them, along with four or five of his own men. Two of them were carrying ropes with nooses already tied at one end. The wives were screaming and shaking, but I think . . ." Gyuri choked on his words, halting his momentum, which by then had become that of a runaway locomotive. "I think he forced the wives to watch their husbands be hanged. I don't know if it was from the trees or from the telegraph poles along the tracks. About a quarter of an hour later, when they got back around to our side of the train, the two women were white as ghosts and couldn't speak. But everyone else was either sobbing or standing there in shock."

Gyuri kept talking, but more anticlimactically, his pace slowing, like a train pulling into a station. "Then, strangely enough, the leader told all of us to get back on the train and continue our journey. He was very soft-spoken and nice about it. But he told us that this was only what could be expected to happen to enemies of the revolution. Once we were moving again, I heard something that scared me even more than anything that had already happened that day. It gave me a new way of looking at things—at myself, and you, and our whole family. I'll never forget it, not as long as I live."

"What? What did you hear?" asked Miklós.

"As the train moved down the tracks," Gyuri went on, "at a safer distance from Szamuely and his men, I heard a disgusted man sitting near us grumble, 'This is what we get from the Bolshevik Jews!' I think 'Bolshevik' means a communist, and from that time on I realized that Jews are communists, and the communists are the ones who did all those terrible things to the poor people on the train. Don't you see? That's why Mama and Papa stopped being Jewish and became Christians. And that's why we mustn't trust the Jews."

Gyuri stopped, finally catching his breath. Miklós was stunned, frozen in place.

Gyuri then added, "That's why, ever since then, I've been so afraid of Jews. Why do you think Jewish commissars took the crucifixes off of our school walls and wouldn't let us go to church? They even came into some of the churches and put pins into the Host, into the body of Christ. Imagine that! They killed Him once and now they tried to do it again!"

"How do you know that?" protested Miklós.

"Everyone knew it. All the grown-ups told me."

"Mama didn't tell you that!" Miklós said through clenched teeth.

"Everyone in church used to tell me if it weren't for the Jews, our Savior would not have died such a terrible death. I'm glad," Gyuri concluded, "that we are Christians and not Jews. They've done terrible things and have rejected our Lord's salvation!"

Miklós was silent, dumbfounded. The moon had long moved from the horizon. It was growing late. He had never heard his brother express such harsh sentiments. It startled him, because his own feelings were so different from Gyuri's. Several minutes passed as Miklós stared up at the starry sky, not daring to look over at his brother.

"While you and Mama were in Báránd," Miklós finally said, penetrating the fear that had built up inside of him, "Klari and I were trapped in Budapest." Now he was going to tell his side of the story. His voice quivered, but he tried to speak as deliberately as he could. "I loved the idea of spending the next few weeks with Aunt Laura. I had never been to her house alone, without you and Klari or Mama and Papa." As he continued speaking, he experienced an upwelling of anger, almost revulsion, at his beloved twin brother. "But the fun stopped when I heard about the bridge exploding. I started to feel like a prisoner who would never see his family again. Well, you know that Laura and her family have never been very Jewish. We'd even celebrate

Easter with them. So it wasn't like they taught me to be a Jew or sent me to the synagogue. I just think they never really cared about religion one way or the other."

"But don't you know," Gyuri interrupted, "that's why I pray for them, because they've never accepted Christ."

"Yes," said Miklós, "I've gathered as much. It doesn't surprise me anymore. But their accepting Christ wouldn't have mattered much back then because they still would have had trouble. By the end of the summer, when the communists were kicked out—"

"Wait a minute, how do *you* know about the communists?" asked Gyuri.

"Because in Budapest, that's all people talked about. Everyone hated them, including—for your information—all of our Jewish relatives and their friends." Gyuri raised his brow in surprise. "But anyway," Miklós went on, "when the communists were almost gone, there were all these gangs in the streets who were against them. These gangs would just beat people up, especially Jews because they thought that all of them were communists. Aunt Laura didn't want me to know about it, but how could I not? One day our cousin Karl came upstairs and he had been beaten up badly. His face was all bloody and swollen. When I asked what happened, Aunt Laura told me he fell down playing football and hit his face on a rock. But that was no rock that smashed different parts of his face in. And even his arms were black and blue, and his whole body looked sore. I was only six years old, but I wasn't blind or stupid. It was those people in the streets who would curse the Jews and the communists. What could Karl have done wrong? He wasn't even twenty years old. When that happened, Aunt Laura wouldn't let me go outside anymore." Miklós stopped. His mouth was dry and he felt cold.

"But why?" asked Gyuri, with a self-possessed smile. "You could have told the gangs that you were Christian and that your whole family was Christian."

"Well, it wouldn't have mattered, because they would have found out that I was really Jewish."

"How would they have known that?"

"Because Aunt Laura knew a man who was Jewish and had become a Christian. But when these hoodlums found him playing cards in his social club, and he told them he was Christian, they asked him to recite the Lord's Prayer. When he could only say the first few lines, they laughed, took away his wallet, and beat him up."

"So, *you* would have known the Lord's Prayer. They would have left you alone."

"I would know it now, but that summer I had only been Christian for a few months. And I never got to go to church. No, I think they would have known that I was Jewish and beaten me up, too. I was sure of it. Aunt Laura didn't have to keep me inside. I was afraid to go out."

"I didn't even know you remembered being born a Jew or that you're so touchy about it," said Gyuri.

"That's not even the end of it. There's another part to this. In Báránd," Miklós continued, "I always felt a little out of place because Mama and Papa were Jews from the city and we just started being Catholic before we moved there. You probably don't remember this, but once I felt very humiliated in church, and I thought it was because people knew that we were Jewish."

"How could that be?" Gyuri said in a loud voice, with an air of haughty disbelief. Miklós saw that passersby were noticing the commotion between them.

"Remember that big fat Bible we had to carry up the stairs and across the altar to the pulpit?" Miklós said, lowering his voice to a near whisper. "Do you remember the day I tripped over my cassock and people started laughing?"

"I kind of remember that," said Gyuri. "But you don't think they were laughing at you because you were Jewish?!" he said, with a ridiculous scowl on his face. "They were laughing because it was funny that a little altar boy in an oversized cassock tripped and fell in front of everyone. Come on, Miklós, don't get carried away. Maybe it was a little embarrassing, but when you look back on it now, don't you think it's a little funny?"

"The Father didn't think it was funny. He got angry."

"Well, he probably thought they were laughing at him, maybe for something stupid he did or said."

"Maybe so," Miklós admitted. "It wasn't until he turned and saw that they were laughing at me that he started laughing, too."

"You see that, he was embarrassed and was relieved they were really laughing at you."

"Then why did I feel so singled out? And why did I feel like an outsider in town ever since that time? I think people have always laughed and said things about us. Haven't you heard Mama talk about things like that to Papa? I have."

"What are you talking about?"

"Haven't you heard Mama say that our being Christian doesn't matter to our Jewish relatives in Budapest but that our Christian neighbors in Báránd talk about us because we were once Jews and still act Jewish?"

Gyuri didn't respond. Maybe he didn't have an answer. Or maybe he just assumed that his brother had a very thin skin.

❖

As Gyuri sat in the drawing room of his Aunt Laura's flat in the summer of 1926, beads of sweat poured down his face, and it was still only midmorning. He alternately crossed and uncrossed his legs, and looked starry-eyed out the window on the other side of the room. His hands couldn't find a comfortable place to rest, so he fidgeted and picked at his fingers. A book he had brought with him from home was lying next to him. It was not one of the German adventure novels he used to read for fun as a boy. It was a more ponderous Latin classic. He had always thought of himself as an ambitious student, but Gyuri was tired out and had overestimated his willingness to plow through a book on Roman ethics on this sweltering summer day.

He sat, sinking into the large cushions of the heavy Victorian sofa. He was just plain bored, and had been that way for the past three days, since he arrived at his aunt's home for the first school holiday he would be spending without his brother and the rest of his family. The tangy aroma of the chicken *paprikas* they had for dinner the previous night, along with the doughy smell of *nokedli,* home-pressed noodles, still hung in the air of the apartment and evoked a dreamy, languid atmosphere. As much as he loved Aunt Laura's cooking, he couldn't spend all his time eating.

Gyuri had looked forward to spending time with his relatives in Budapest, whom he hadn't seen in many years. He hadn't expected that he would need to be entertained, even though he had no peers among them. But there simply wasn't much he could find to do in their company. Since the last time he had been there, Laura's household had changed dramatically. She lived in the same elegant flat in Pest, although her husband, Karl, had been dead for ten years and her four children had all grown up. Two were married, one was in the diplomatic corps in Vienna, and the youngest, Érzsi, though well into her twenties, still lived at home with her mother. Laura adored Gyuri and secretly always favored him for his adventurous spirit. Yet for the past three days he had done little more than take walks around his aunt's neighborhood in Pest, an area that was never quite familiar to him. Once, he found his way down to the river to skip stones and just watch boats go by. It was all he could do to stay occupied.

Being without Miklós was a thoroughly unfamiliar experience. Gyuri felt like half a person. Having spent virtually every day and night with him for as long as he could remember, he missed his brother terribly. Gyuri knew that Miklós had felt that it was unfair that he had to stay at home while his brother spent his summer holiday in Budapest. But Gyuri also knew that Miklós had never forgotten the dreadfully unhappy five months he had spent with Laura in 1919.

Gyuri desperately needed someone who even resembled a peer, someone with whom he could pal around and enjoy the summer—go swimming or hiking along the river's edge, or exploring the sights and sounds of Pest. Noticing her nephew's malaise, Laura had invited the Gelbs, some family friends who had a daughter named Ági only slightly younger than Gyuri. Ági's family also felt the challenge of keeping their young teenager happily occupied for the summer. So the two families decided that Ági would make a fitting guide to the rather serious and studious boy visiting from another city.

Gyuri wasn't exactly thrilled that a girl was coming over. His mild aversion, in and of itself, reassured both families about the possible impropriety of a teenage boy and girl being brought together to socialize. They didn't think that either of them was sufficiently mature to take any interest yet in the opposite sex. Gyuri's fidgetiness and boredom was ample proof that this meeting would be anything but unbecoming of modest children and their thoughtful and conservative caretakers.

As Ági entered the drawing room, sheepishly trailing behind her mother and grandmother, there was not much in her physical appearance that immediately drew Gyuri's attention. He stayed on the sofa and hardly looked up. Anyone else might have noticed that this skinny, only slightly developed teenage girl had a pretty face, a shy but warm smile, and a thinly restrained exuberance beneath a bashful exterior. Her wavy hair, shoulder-length and dark brown, grazed the shoulders of her white summer peasant dress, which had short sleeves and colorful embroidery around the neck. She wore brown leather closed-toe sandals and white socks that rose above her ankles. It was almost as if her family dressed her to look younger than she was.

In the first moments, as the adults exchanged greetings with each other and Laura introduced her nephew, Ági remained close by the side of her mother and elderly grandmother. She looked directly at Gyuri and smiled when Laura mentioned her name to him. He was by now courteously standing and had lost his initially bored gaze. He made an awkward effort to take part in the introductions by smiling and mumbling some obligatory hellos, even stiffly extending his hand to the three female visitors. He actually managed a smile when he greeted Ági, which surprised him. "Hello, nice to meet you," was, however, all he could manage to mutter.

Everyone sat down and spent the next half hour exchanging pleasantries and finalizing the plan for the day's outing, which included taking a tram over the river and up the low-lying hills overlooking Buda to a wooded park on Swab Hill, a favorite picnic area for Budapesti families. As they lingered in their seats, it took Gyuri barely a few minutes to discover that Ági smiled whenever he looked at her. It was a subtle, sweet, and always shy smile—hardly coquettish or alluring. But he couldn't help but notice that each time she did, his pulse quickened and he drew a short, shallow breath. He was conscious of how gawky he must have looked, so he crossed his legs and curled his dangling arms in front of his chest. But he was becoming more relaxed with each daring gaze in Ági's direction. Although he spoke only when the adults asked him questions, Gyuri began to smile at Ági and watched for any further signs of recognition from her.

When they got to Swab Hill, Gyuri felt more daring. He may have been a mischievous child, but at nearly fourteen, he was an introverted adolescent who was self-conscious interacting with others. Consequently, he didn't really need to make much effort to hide his pleasure in being with this likable, gentle, and pretty girl. Even while he didn't make any bold moves, Ági seemed to take notice of his interest.

"Come on, I'll show you the pond," she said, nonchalantly taking the initiative. "I often come here with my family and friends."

"All right," said Gyuri, standing up after her from where they had all been perched under an oak tree. As they began walking, he added, "I've never been here before."

"You certainly have," said Aunt Laura, calling after the two, still within earshot. "Your mother and Auntie Bertha used to bring you here with your brother and sister. It was during the war when your father was away. You were little. You probably don't remember."

"No, I don't remember," said Gyuri, smiling and shrugging his shoulders.

"So where do you live now?" Ági asked, barely hesitating, as the two of them walked on alone.

"In Gyula. It's a city in the south. I go to school there and live in an orphanage."

"Oh, I'm sorry. Are your parents dead? Was your father killed in the war?"

"Oh, no," Gyuri gasped. He suddenly realized he'd never told anyone outside of Gyula he lived in an orphanage. "My mother and father live in Báránd." It felt unnerving to be asked if his parents were dead. "My father is the village animal doctor there. They sent me and my brother to school in Gyula because there is no high school in Báránd, and having tutors was very lonely." He was talking so fast he had to catch his breath.

Ági had come to the edge of the pond where a number of children were swimming alongside their mothers or nursemaids. She sat down along the gravelly turf of the embankment next to a willow sapling, which didn't cast much shade in the sweltering noonday heat. Gyuri sat down facing her. Ági then opened a small paper bag she had been carrying, reached in, and took out two bright orange apricots and handed one of them to Gyuri. "Here, these are from the market down by the river. My grandmother says they're the best in Hungary."

"Thank you," he said, as he drew the fruit closer, putting it to his lips and then in his mouth. Gyuri's thoughts flashed to that familiar moment in church when the priest would place the Communion wafer on his tongue. But he had never experienced such surprising warmth in receiving the body of Christ. Although he sometimes felt forgiven for his sins by his Savior's sacrifice, usually Communion left Gyuri's body unmoved. Now, as he bit down on the soft and sweet apricot, he felt euphorically transported by a surge of affection for the gentle and generous girl who had given it to him. His body was alight with life and he welcomed the unfamiliar sensations with quiet gratitude.

"How do you like living in an orphanage?" asked Ági, interrupting Gyuri's secret euphoria. "It must be sad being with kids whose parents are dead."

Gyuri held his feelings in check. "Actually, the children don't seem sad at all, except the new ones who have just been sent there. Some of the kids are like me and my brother. They're boarders so they can go to the school in town. And besides, the nuns are very nice to us. Strict, but nice." Gyuri suddenly noticed Ági's mouth drop open.

"You live in an orphanage with nuns? With Christian nuns?"

"Well . . . they're Catholic." Gyuri hadn't yet caught on to the reason for Ági's surprise. "They're Sisters of St. Vincent. You know, the ones with the dark blue habits and the head coverings that look like wings," as if Ági were supposed to recognize the habits of different Catholic orders.

"Does that mean you're Catholic?"

Gyuri's hand jerked involuntarily as if he had just been suddenly awakened from sleep. "Well . . . yes . . . I am," he answered. Trying to hide his discomfort, he clasped his hands together and then quickly unclasped them, pressing his sweaty palms into the fabric of his trousers. He felt a hot breeze brushing against his face and bare arms, as if he were being pushed back and reminded of his separateness from Ági and the rest of nature. "I guess that means *you* are Jewish," Gyuri said, punctuating his moment of alienation.

"Yes, of course I am," she said with a clipped laugh. "Your family is Jewish, too. At least, your aunt Laura and her family are. I know they're not very religious, but I didn't know that your part of the family became Christian." There was more surprise than alarm in Ági's voice. She probably felt more matter-of-fact about it than Gyuri did. But what bothered him more than any religious differences was that he had been brought back to his senses after just having been so marvelously transported. A sublime moment had quickly escaped him.

"You may pray differently, but you're still part of the family," Ági continued. "You even look just like some of your uncles and kind of like your aunt Laura, too."

Gyuri wasn't reassured. It still bothered him. He and Miklós hadn't talked about this since that time outside Father Apor's church. Gyuri didn't want to make the same big deal of it now, the way he had with his brother. But his irrepressible feelings about it were gnawing at him.

"You know, they taught me in school and church that Jews killed Christ and that they're dishonest businessmen. After the war, I saw for myself that Jewish communists killed innocent people." It just wasn't the time or place to be taking this tone. In his mind, he was kicking himself for being so obtuse. He tried to backpedal. "But when I see my family again after all these years, and I meet someone like you, I realize that we get taught a lot of things that may not be totally accurate. At least, some things are open to interpretation."

"Well, all the Jews we know are not communists and wouldn't hurt a fly." Ági sounded annoyed. "And we are just as honest and good as people who are not Jewish. I just think we like business and being shopkeepers more than others do. Our family's friends who have shops work very hard and are good at business. And look at your own uncle. He has a bookbindery shop. He's not dishonest, is he?"

"No, of course not. I don't know any Jews personally of the sort I learned about in church and school. I didn't mean to get carried away. I hope I didn't offend you." But Gyuri had said too much. Ági was right to defend herself. Could it be that Jews aren't all that different from Christians? He knew that Ági herself was pure and innocent, and that there was nothing hurtful or devious about her.

Ági was not really interested in religious divisions. True enough, she attended a Jewish school, was attached to her faith, and would not tolerate any slights to her family or people. But she wasn't truly concerned about that with Gyuri. She liked him, and he was drawn to her. Religion had nothing to do with being friends. And that summer they became fast friends, spending as much time together as they could, accompanied by one or another family member—eating meals, exploring Margit's Island, swimming in the Danube. Sometimes they went to the cinema, and once to the gypsy fair.

As the summer passed, Gyuri's affections for Ági grew stronger. He had become infatuated with her, and she with him. In the occasional absence of their relatives, Gyuri and Ági took the tram together over to Buda to have lunch at Aunt Bertha's house or strolled along the river late in the afternoons. At those times, he felt a nervous fluttering in his stomach and had trouble getting his words out. Sometimes he thought he heard Ági's voice tremble a little, too. Once, the two stopped briefly in the foyer of her family's apartment house for a kiss. "There, now it is done," she said. Gyuri smiled, but his eyes were sad. He couldn't answer.

Only Sundays were disjointed, when Gyuri attended Mass. His nominally Jewish aunt and cousin would escort him to the nearby church, leave him at the entrance, and then turn to go home. It was a promise they had made to his mother, that they would help him meet his religious obligations. It was on those days, as his relatives turned and disappeared down the street and Gyuri was left alone to enter yet another gilded Catholic sanctuary, that he would feel pangs of loneliness and despair. He knew quite well that Ági could never join him there. During these moments, he felt an unbridgeable rift between his being a good Catholic and the splendid Jewish girl he was growing to love. He knew the Church would never be a place for the two of them. It was sinful even to think about being together with Ági, but he couldn't get it out of his mind. There, at the steps of the church, Gyuri asked himself if he would ever find happiness in the world. He pushed the thought out of his mind as he entered the sanctuary to pray to the God whose death had annulled human sinfulness.

At the end of the summer, as they were taking their leave in the presence of their families, Gyuri and Ági embraced with proper formality. But he had never felt such warmth, exhilaration, and passion. He tried to conceal the pounding of his heart. Promising each other they would write, the two were secretly overcome by deep affection, confusion, and longing. One might call it infatuation. But it was surely love, for it had transformed the way both of them thought and felt about life, about each other, and about themselves.

✤ CHAPTER 6 ✤

Exile

For all this I weep; my eyes overflow with tears.
For the comforter who would bring me relief has deserted me.
LAMENTATIONS 1:16

Ever since Béla was a veterinary student, he had always prepared spring-time inoculations for cattle in the same manner. Water was brought to a boil in a large vat, and then the inoculation formula was mixed in. The major difference in method between his university days and now, in Báránd, was the degree of sterilization of the equipment. Copper and iron kettles and sterile glass containers in the animal husbandry lab of Budapest's Veterinary University were always scrupulously cleaned and scoured in order to prevent disease in their animals. How Béla managed to work for nearly eight years in Báránd without incident was truly extraordinary. Cleaning and sterilizing his vats and equipment was not his strong suit. He was not slovenly or slothful, but he had a certain obliviousness to detail. Béla's mind became focused more by the task of treating animals than by the detailed preparation required for it.

During the spring inoculation in 1927, Béla had expediently used a large cast-iron soup kettle to mix his vaccine. The incident would have been comical if it hadn't had such a tragic outcome. Even if the kettle had been well scoured—which was not likely—the porous surface of the iron could easily have retained enough impurities to contaminate the vaccine. Vegetable soup with animal fat and boiled potatoes might have been a favorite of the hearty two-legged patrons who partook of it, but it was a bit too rich for the blood of unsuspecting cows.

In just a matter of days after Béla finished making his rounds to the local farms, dozens of head of cattle became deathly sick. In the end, six died. Angry grumbling was heard throughout the village and surrounding region. By his carelessness, Béla had significantly affected the livelihoods of a good number of farmers. Though he was well-liked by everyone, many felt he needed to be held to account.

László Kolozsi began the initiative. The village notary, he was an educated man whom Béla had considered a friend. Some would have said it was a sympathetic gesture Kolozsi made when he appeared in the town hall to address the local farmers. He could easily have been trying to stem the tide of criticism being hurled at Béla. But some felt that Kolozsi may have actually been the one to catalyze the hostility and bring it into sharper focus. No doubt it was part of his official duties to address possible malfeasance on the part of civil servants. But both Béla and Gabriella got wind of just how much enthusiasm Kolozsi put behind his words.

"This is certainly unprecedented in the entire region. We've never lost so many cattle," he said to the group of farmers and herdsmen gathered in the hall.

"Has he poisoned the wells too?" said an anonymous voice in the back of the room.

Kolozsi must have been aware that the faceless, not entirely intelligible voice was implying the age-old libelous accusation against Jews of killing cattle and poisoning drinking wells. This never had the notoriety of the more vicious "blood libel," by which Jews were accused of the ritual murder of Christian children and of using their blood to make matzah. A famous instance had occurred in Hungary in the town of Tisza-Eszlár in 1882, and was, no doubt, still remembered by some of the older local residents. But these kinds of vile rumors and degrading stereotypes were always under the surface of manifest calm and acceptance.

"Listen here," the notary said. "No one has poisoned any wells, or we all might have gotten sick."

"But the cows didn't die by accident," called out another accusatory, if more sane voice.

"It was not an act of God, that's for sure," spoke up another man, in an angrier tone. These voices were islands in a turbulent but otherwise navigable sea. Yet Kolozsi had to assert his control or the crowd could easily have been whipped into a tempest.

"My dear friends and neighbors, of course these cows did not perish by happenstance or divine will. The dignified Dr. Pogány has already acknowledged that it must have been his doing. He claims carelessness. Well, look here my friends, we spare no love or admiration for our esteemed animal doctor. I count him as a personal friend of mine. I bear neither him nor his devoted wife and family any ill will. But these kinds of events have not occurred in our region in recent memory, even before our village had a veterinarian, no, not until this moment. Let no one among us, however, suggest that outsiders or newcomers have deliberately brought with them such unfortunate maladies or plagues, or that Dr. Pogány is such an outsider. I am the one who must assess such events and decide what course of action to take. And I must make certain these things do not happen again in our village. Accordingly, it is my sad duty, dear friends, to request that the dignified doctor tender his resignation."

Disapproving gasps and groans went through the audience, mixed with some affirming shouts and solitary applause. The notary had done his duty, but he was not proud of it. He continued in a more resolute and defiant tone. "Now, our purpose is not to impoverish this dear family. They have lived among us for nearly a decade. They will certainly be permitted to stay on in Báránd until the doctor manages to secure another position. It doesn't gladden me to make this announcement, but I fear it is the most just decision under the circumstances."

As the crowd dispersed, there were unquestionably many who were content with the outcome. But Béla also had many friends and well-wishers in the gathering that night. Even those who had tried to keep him at arm's length had found him undeniably likable. Four or five of those who unreservedly respected and loved him walked down to the family's house after the meeting to break the news to him. As they knocked on the door and Béla opened it, no one could speak. One farmer, who was about the same age as the doctor but who towered over this small and portly Jewish convert, embraced him like a brother and wept like a child. Kolozsi, on the other hand, could not face the family until the morning. His lukewarm support that night could not have served as a more stinging denunciation, even if it may have succeeded in saving Béla from the actions of a potential mob. Béla felt disgraced. His punishment, in effect, would be exile.

Months passed. It was not easy for Béla to find another civil service position. Finally, by the end of the summer, a temporary one appeared in the village of Kondoros, in Békés county, to the south of Báránd.

Local peasants and farmers loaned the family the use of ten horse-drawn wagons—a veritable caravan. On the last day, they helped load Béla's equipment and instruments onto them, along with the family's modest possessions. As many men as there were wagons accompanied them on the journey. Gabriella rode alongside her husband on the lead wagon. The children sat in the back amidst some of the family's belongings.

An hour after they left, as they made their way toward Kondoros, Gabriella looked at Béla and put her hand on his forearm as he held the horses' reins. She was not only trying to keep her balance but also lending reassurance to the man who, she was afraid, felt that he had ruined his family's life. She gazed forgivingly at the side of his face as he kept his eyes on the horses.

"You're not surprised by this, are you, my gracious one?" Gabriella had always addressed her husband with a certain formality, sometimes borrowing appellations from a string of honorary civil service titles that went all the way up to "Count." It was truly out of reverence and affection, although it was not unlike Hungarian women to honor their men with such formal address. "I don't mean by your mistake. Anyone could have made such an error. But by the way this all unfolded?"

"Well, I'm disappointed that it's come to this." Béla quickly glanced over at his wife and then returned his gaze to the road. With people in public, he liked to banter and joke. But with his family he was quiet, standing behind the stiff formality of Hungarian men of his era. He was usually good at hiding his inner wounds and fears, except at times like this.

"It's happening now, isn't it?" asked Gabriella. "Everything we feared before, during, and after the war. You knew this would happen, didn't you? You said it years ago when things were still good."

The war, the communists, and the Rumanians had taken their toll on Béla's morale and presence of mind. He had told Gabriella of the times when he thought he would go mad, when his mind had deeply retreated, and when he imagined what it would be like to go away to an infinite distance and never return. Long ago he had told her, too, of the times during his childhood when Jews were victimized and scapegoated.

"Look," said Béla, "maybe we should just take this at face value and not get overly suspicious about it. I made a mistake and I have to pay the price. Could this possibly have happened because we have always been outsiders— high-minded urban Budapesti Jews? I suppose I could imagine it, but I don't want to."

"But things have changed for the worse in the country, haven't they?" asked Gabriella.

"Of course they have," he answered. "Things may have leveled off from the violence after the war, but after Trianon, the position of Jews changed forever. We don't tip the scales the way we once did for the Magyar minority." To be sure, Jewish financial and industrial know-how had become indispensable for the postwar Hungarian democracy to get on its feet. But it was only a means to an end for the aristocratic-conservative government that wanted to maintain and strengthen its own power. Before the war, the aristocrats had felt that the national minorities living within the borders of historical Hungary, pressing for freedom and equality, were the major threat to their privileged, feudal way of life. Now the major threat had become the Treaty of Trianon's decimation of Hungary's borders, as well as what had come to be identified as the "nefarious influence of the Jews."

"I remember," Béla went on, "how we thought that life here would be easier if we were Christians. Well, it was for a few years, after the terror brigades vanished. But now we're dealing with a more subtle and seething hatred. It all makes our conversion and move to the countryside seem pretty naive, doesn't it?"

"But you know that's not why we've become Christians," Gabriella said. She dropped her hand from Béla's forearm, and now she was the one who was looking straight ahead.

"But it is, in part, isn't it? I don't begrudge you your religious faith and the way you are raising the children. But you must admit that I would not have gotten a civil service post if we were still Jewish. We would have stood out too much."

"How do you mean?" asked Gabriella.

"Who among even our well-educated friends in Báránd," answered Béla, "have their children tutored after finishing grade school, and then pay their hard-earned money to send them away to attend high school? Who in Báránd quotes Madách or Heine in casual conversation? Who has ever read or even heard of Jack London?"

Gabriella couldn't help but smile. She'd never apologize for being cultured. And she never thought that by becoming a Catholic she'd have to give up books and stop trying to educate her children. If being cultured was part of being Jewish, then she'd always be a Jew, not unlike many Jews in Hungary who were always at least as concerned with culture and education as with religion, if not more so. But Gabriella knew in her heart that she hadn't become a Catholic to escape her Jewishness. The forces that may have impelled this departure from Báránd were unleashed after the war, and no one knew when their irresistible momentum would ease. Of course, she told herself, they were leaving because her husband had made a mistake. It was far from clear that their cultural "otherness" had led to their ouster from the community. But a painfully gnawing uncertainty remained.

"I'll miss Báránd," Gabriella said, with no hint of apology in her voice. "I'll miss our friends, even Kolozsi, and especially Father Szemethy. I'll miss the church. That's where my home is."

True enough, this felt like exile, like leaving Jerusalem for an unknown Babylon. But Gabriella's tabernacle was there in the wagon with her—her children and the husband to whom she had long ago bound her fate. And she could only hope that a new parish awaited her wherever life took them. Finally, though, Gabriella carried her tabernacle in her heart, in her enduring belief that her Lord would always be with her and would guide her to eternal life on this narrow, muddy road past the county seat of Bihar, heading toward an uncertain future.

❖

In the fall of 1927, Gyuri received another letter from Ági. Although they had not seen each other since they met two summers earlier, they had become regular correspondents. She knew that neither of them had any occasion to visit the other and recognized that with Gyuri's family's recent move from Báránd, his life must surely have been harried. Her family was well, she said, as was she, except for a bit of a cough and the nuisance of a backache she had recently developed. Her parents were worried, but Ági thought it was nothing more than the chill of winter setting in. The leaves on what few trees there were in Pest were fast disappearing. But Ági loved going down to the river, as she and Gyuri used to do, and looking out over to Buda and the glorious surrounding hills. Writing on All Souls' Day, the second of November, when many people go to the cemetery with flowers, Ági didn't need to remind Gyuri of how seriously Christians took that holiday. Hungarians, she said, are such a melancholy people; it's like the old saying that the thing they best know how to do is bury their dead. In that way, she wasn't so sure that Jews were much different. But, trying not to end on such a gloomy note, she looked forward to her friend's next letter.

Gyuri was always delighted to hear from Ági. No one but Miklós knew about his brother's infatuation with the girl he had met in Budapest. By all appearances, it was nothing more than a faithful correspondence. It would usually take Gyuri and Ági only a week or two to answer each other's letters. This one, too, Gyuri answered promptly with the usual small talk. Whatever little or much was said kept them in touch, and kept their hearts open. Then he waited.

Occasionally, Gyuri would share his imaginary excursions into the future with Miklós and would wonder if this love was meant to be more permanent someday. At those moments, he would feel tied in knots by two contradictory pulls—one his love for the church and the other his love for Ági. They were too young, and she was Jewish. Already, Gyuri's religious devotion had taken on a labored, mechanical quality. He had come to voice doubts to Miklós about what was being taught, in effect as doctrine, regarding the "hideous" Jews. Miklós felt some relief that his brother was not as rigid about this issue as he once was. Yet much of the time, Gyuri looked as if he were struggling with it. Was that why, Miklós wondered, his stride had taken on a kind of waywardness? He looked indecisive and distracted. His moods were listless and erratic. There was less light but more warmth in his life, less sorrow for Christ and more human joy and sadness.

Six weeks elapsed after Gyuri responded to Ági's letter from the beginning of November. Christmas and the New Year came and went. Still she did not write back. The boys had visited their parents and sister for the Christmas holidays in their new home in Kondoros, and no doubt, Gyuri rationalized to himself, there must have been much to preoccupy Ági's energies in Budapest over the same period. But this much time had never elapsed between letters. No one but Miklós knew the source of Gyuri's concern, but even with his brother, Gyuri tried not to let on just how worried he was. By the second week in January, he finally decided to write to Ági again.

The weeks passed and still there was no answer. Gyuri was noticeably irritable and nervous. He had less patience for the typical horsing around with his teenage friends and classmates, and was finding it more difficult to keep his mind on his studies. Every day, when he'd get back to the orphanage from school, he'd slowly pass by the front office and turn his head toward the nun seated at the desk to see if she had any mail for him. Letters from home were frequent enough, and the nuns had even become familiar with the regularly arriving letter from an unnamed "cousin" with a Budapest return address.

It was now the middle of February. Gyuri's ritual trek past the sister stationed in the front hall had become all too familiar, even while he tried to hide his tortured impatience. But his eagerness was gone and despair had set in. It slowed his steps and made him look perpetually downcast. On this particular day, as on other days in recent weeks, Gyuri walked over to the marble stairway of the central hall, sat down on one of the lower steps, and leaned his shoulder against the iron railing. He raised his head toward the vertical rise of the stairway, illuminated by a large window at the midfloor landing and extending to a corniced ceiling painted in soft, geometrical greens and golds. It was the most expansive space in the building. Gyuri looked up but wasn't really seeing anything. Then he lowered his head and supported his chin on his forearms, which rested across his bent knees. He stared blankly toward the front door.

As he sat there, one of the sisters brought an envelope over to him. Gyuri looked at it. It was a letter from home, addressed to both boys. It wasn't what he was looking for, but he dutifully opened it and read it. It was written by his mother, and contained the usual pleasantries and personal news: how good it had been to see the boys over the recent Christmas holiday; how Gabriella, Béla, and Klari had adjusted to their new home in Kondoros; and how the boys' father was trying to establish himself as a private animal doctor in the area while waiting and hoping to get a permanent position after his temporary one expired. The neighbors, Gabriella said, were friendly enough and had welcomed them into the parish. She was hopeful that they would be able to make a life for themselves there.

Then Gabriella's tone shifted as she addressed herself directly to Gyuri. She mentioned having received a letter from Aunt Laura, who had asked that she share the news with him that the girl Ági, whom Gyuri had met when he visited Budapest a few summers earlier, had died very suddenly of tuberculosis of the bone. Ági's family, said Laura, was grief-stricken by the loss and she, too, was saddened by it. Gabriella herself noted that she was sorry that the girl and her family was not known to them, otherwise they would have sent their personal condolences. "May the soul of this innocent child rest in peace," Gabriella concluded. "But may you both continue your studies with devotion and good spirits."

As he barely finished reading the letter, Gyuri couldn't move his head, and his hands were frozen in place as he continued to clutch the crumpled paper. He took a deep breath to fill his lungs with the scream that would surely collapse the walls of the building and ascend to God in heaven were he ever to let it out. But as the other residents began to stream in the front door of the orphanage, Gyuri put his forearm over his mouth to muffle his righteous denunciation of God's cruel treachery. Coughing instead, he nearly choked on his rage. Then he covered his eyes with his arm so he wouldn't see anyone looking at him. After several seconds he rose to his feet and bounded up the stairway, squashing the letter further in his fist as he went. The moment signaled the end of all happiness. And yet Gyuri had to keep it to himself. There was nothing he could do but remain silent and flee to a place where he could more freely give expression to his exploding emotions. If only there were such a place.

Barely an hour later, Miklós found Gyuri sitting hunched on his bed in the boys' dormitory. His head was in his hands, his elbows held erectly on his knees. There was a piece of crumpled paper by his side. Even from the other side of the room, it was obvious what great distress Gyuri was in. "What's the matter? What's happened?" Miklós blurted out as he quickened his steps.

Gyuri hunched over farther, keeping his face buried in his hands. Miklós picked up the crumpled letter lying next to his brother and unruffled it, glancing down at Gyuri before beginning to read it.

"Mama and Papa and Klari are all right," Miklós said, as he read the first few lines. "I thought something had happened to them. You scared the devil out of me." Miklós continued reading. "It's Ági. She died! My God!"

Gyuri did not answer. He slowly looked up with wide, terrified eyes, opening his mouth to speak. But he couldn't. He looked utterly forsaken, as if he had given up on life.

At night in the orphanage, before drifting off to sleep, the twins had gotten into the habit of staying awake in the dark, drawing their beds closer to each other, and talking about their day or sharing more distant musings. They were always careful to keep their conversations to a whisper so as not to disturb boys in neighboring beds or incur the displeasure of the nun on duty, who sat just on the other side of a wooden partition at the opposite end of the long row of beds.

Late that night, the dormitory room was still, with nearly all twenty-five boys fast asleep in their beds. Even the sister's lamp behind the partition had been extinguished more than an hour before. The full moon shone through the window between the brothers' beds, casting more than ample light for Miklós to see the silhouette of his brother's face. Gyuri, in his long flannel undershirt underneath his winter blanket, lay on his back, eyes wide open, staring at the ceiling directly above him. Miklós himself had been tossing and turning since going to bed two hours earlier.

Throughout his time in Gyula, Miklós had found a safe and secure home in Catholicism. He felt at one with the community—both with his classmates at school and with his fellow residents at the orphanage. He had been noticed by the mother superior and frequently sought her out to talk about the Gospels. He had even been asked to be the confirmation sponsor for a young orphan at the home. Miklós had recently confided to Gyuri that he was close to pursuing the priesthood. It didn't surprise Gyuri. Rather, it pleased him immensely.

"What are you thinking about, Gyuri?" said Miklós in not quite a whisper. His head was propped up on his elbow. A couple of the boys near them were awakened and tried to shush him quiet. Sister Margita pushed her head out from the partition to see what the commotion was about and simply remind the boys of her presence. Miklós quickly lowered his head onto his pillow. He waited for the nun to disappear.

Gyuri turned toward his brother and momentarily stared blankly at him. "I have lost something I will never get back," he said in an audible voice, hardly a whisper, as if he didn't care who heard him. Sister Margita again reared her head around the partition wall.

"I'm sorry," whispered Miklós. "I know how you felt about Ági."

There was no answer.

"You loved her, didn't you?" Miklós continued.

Gyuri again turned toward his brother. "You must never say anything to anyone." he said. "Even to our family, especially our family." He now spoke in a whisper, less inclined to betray all caution.

Miklós felt a large lump form in his throat. He didn't know yet about this kind of love, and he had never seen Gyuri so distraught. He didn't know what to do or say.

"We'll both pray for her salvation," Miklós finally said. "Maybe we can have a Mass said for her in church."

Gyuri continued to stare at a large crack in the plaster on the ceiling, as if he were waiting for it to cleave and the heavens to open. That way he could take his case to the supreme source of justice and mercy.

"Try to think of Christ's suffering," Miklós went on, unrelenting in his effort to say something consoling. "He thought he had been forsaken. But it was for a higher good. His suffering and death saved us. Maybe Ági's death will bring you closer to our Lord's suffering." Miklós was well versed, almost glib, but hardly insincere. Gyuri, too, had been over this ground many times. But not even Christ's passion had ever touched him as profoundly as this young girl's death.

"I can't begin to think about that now. All I care about is that I'll never see her again. Why should I care about Christ's suffering? It didn't help Ági."

"How do you know that?" asked Miklós.

"You know," said Gyuri, "the Jews didn't forsake Christ." Miklós was suddenly confused. "We did. Everyone did. We all have forsaken Him. And you know why? Because it didn't make any difference. His death didn't make anyone's life any happier. It just made us afraid that we might not be saved when we die. Once, I thought His suffering made it easier to tolerate our own unhappiness. I was wrong. It can't take away this kind of hurt. Many people discovered that, so they stopped believing. Just like I—"

"Just like you what?" Miklós wouldn't let him finish. "Just like you can and must find comfort in God's House. He hasn't failed us. God has been good to us. He protects us and He'll save us. Don't you remember how Mama told us on our first Easter that someday He'll take us to heaven? Just like He took your friend."

Gyuri turned again to look at Miklós. "My dear brother, you've outdone me. You truly are a good Catholic and I'm sure you'll make a good priest someday. Mother will be so proud to cover you in the cloth of the Church. But this hurts too much and I can't get any comfort in anyone else's suffering, not even God's." Gyuri looked back up at the crack in the ceiling and then turned his whole body away. He curled up and buried his face in his pillow. Miklós heard several muffled, wailing cries. And then there was silence.

Is all this useless? Miklós asked himself. What good is God's salvation if it's only for after we're dead but doesn't make life any happier? He felt helpless, defeated really, that he couldn't be of any greater comfort to his anguished brother. Everything he had ever learned about Christianity, everything he had ever done as a Catholic, seemed unable to soothe Gyuri's hurt and relieve his own sudden doubts. If Gyuri had stifled his cries and let go of his beliefs,

Miklós was blindly clinging to his faith and desperately trying to muffle his uncertainty. He turned over onto his side, in the opposite direction from his brother, and also buried his face in his pillow. "The Lord is my comfort and my salvation. To whom shall I turn?"

✢

Two years passed. Gyuri and Miklós completed three years of high school in Gyula. Then their father's wished-for position finally materialized. The town council of Szarvas unanimously voted Béla in as the civil service veterinarian. Szarvas was the larger town just down the road from the village of Kondoros. Many of Szarvas's inhabitants were Slovaks, predominantly Lutheran farmers and herdsmen from the north of what, before the war, had been Hungary. They were thrilled to have found in Béla someone who came from the same region and spoke their language. He and his family were welcomed and readily accepted. A year had passed since the fiasco in Báránd, and the lingering effects on Béla's reputation had run their course. He and Gabriella were confident that they could now make a fresh start. It was here, in the town's local Protestant high school, that the boys completed their studies prior to beginning their university years.

In the fall of 1930, a few weeks before their eighteenth birthday, the twins entered Franz Josef University in Szeged, Hungary's major southern city along the Tisza River just north of the three-way border with Serbia and Rumania. At the university, both boys enrolled in the Horthy Collegium, a college named after the revered Hungarian regent whose political life had originated in Szeged in 1919, when he began his march to liberate the country from the Bolshevik menace. It was here that the brothers would pursue the study of law.

In the three years that had passed since Ági's death, Miklós felt that his brother had grown increasingly bitter and disillusioned. Gyuri maintained appearances, kept his grades up and put on a brave face. He was going to make a life for himself in the world, but had grown distant from people and from his earlier religious piety. At the same time, Miklós's attachment to the Catholic Church had not been broken by Gyuri's crisis of faith. Throughout his years at the orphanage, at Catholic high school, and with the blessings of his teachers, nuns, and priests, Miklós knew with increasing certainty that his spiritual home was in the Church. But his ambition to seek his calling as a priest had never fully blossomed after leaving Gyula. Maybe it was the dislocations he and his brother had experienced that dislodged this ambition— from Gyula and Báránd to Szarvas, and now to the university in Szeged. Perhaps it was that his piety depended on an unwaveringly secure and nurturant environment, of the sort he had only experienced in Gyula. Most of all, it may have been that he knew in his heart all along that, despite his religious piety, he was not meant to lead his life at the margins of human relationships, devoted singularly to God. He felt he was called to live in the world, among women and children and a family, not apart from them.

Several weeks after their arrival in Szeged, Gyuri and Miklós were in their dormitory room. It was an ordinary-looking building of nineteenth-century German influence, across the street from more classically styled university buildings and only a few steps from the monumental Votive Church and its adjoining outdoor amphitheater.

"I've been asked to join Emericana," said Miklós. "You know, the Catholic student group." The group was a conservative religious fraternal organization under the umbrella of Actio Catholica, established at the recommendation of the pope.

"I'm not surprised," answered Gyuri. "The only thing that still surprises me is that you didn't pursue the priesthood."

"How could I?" asked Miklós, slouching comfortably at his desk chair. "I wanted to come to the university with you. And besides, I decided that the priesthood was not for me. I like being at the university too much. I don't suppose you are interested in joining Emericana with me?"

"No." said Gyuri, standing up from his bed and putting his hands in his pockets. "I'm not ready to kiss the feet of the priests," he said, with undisguised disdain.

Miklós shouldn't have been surprised by such a sentiment, but he felt stunned nonetheless by the way Gyuri said it. "So what will you do?" he asked, sidestepping Gyuri's scorn.

"I'll probably join Turul. They're just as Christian, but they put their beliefs more into action. They defend the country against the economic dangers of outsiders taking over the livelihoods of Hungarians and Christians."

"Outsiders? You mean like Jews? I heard that people in Turul used to beat Jews up when the quotas against them were imposed after the war." Disaffection from the Catholic faith was one thing, but holding Jews to account for Christian hardships was another. "Why are you still so bent on distancing yourself from your origins?"

"I'm not. That has nothing to do with it, and Emericana isn't exactly spotless. They're as little fond of the Jews as Turul is."

"I'm interested in practicing my faith, not in holding anyone responsible for my unhappiness."

"Neither am I. I don't know how you can say that."

"I've never thought of hiding my Jewishness," said Miklós. "It's not possible. But I don't have to have been born a Christian to be a good Catholic. I'm content to be who I am—a practicing Catholic who was born a Jew."

"Well, get off of it. This has nothing to do with hiding my Jewishness or holding anyone responsible for anything. I just don't need to parade my Catholicism as much as others do. It's in my heart and soul, and in my hands. I don't have to put it on a banner, or genuflect in front of others. If anything, it's important to put it into action, to protect our faith and country."

Miklós knew he wouldn't get any further with the argument. He could plainly sense that Gyuri had lost much of his earlier piety and was withdrawing from others, no matter how much he talked about so-called Christian activism. Indeed, throughout his first year at the university, Gyuri remained fixed in his solitary ways, continuing his disaffection from religious life. His character developed an edge of surliness and anger that seemed to be immutable, no matter how hard Miklós tried to reach beyond it.

✤

It was nearing dusk on a late spring day just before final examinations. Miklós hadn't seen Gyuri all day. Gyuri had walked out of the dormitory with him that morning, and hadn't said where he was going but went in the direction of the cathedral just down the street. Now, barely an hour before dinner, Miklós was back in the dorm room when Gyuri came in. His cheeks were flushed and his eyes were red. He looked as if he had been crying, although there was a gentle smile on his face.

"Where have you been? I haven't seen you all day," said Miklós.

"I spent some time in the cathedral. I like it during the week. It's very peaceful."

"You spent *all* day in the cathedral?"

Gyuri smiled at his brother but said nothing, looking slightly embarrassed by the truth.

"With exams coming, you've barely looked at your books. What's going on?"

Gyuri was silent for several seconds. "I'm . . . I'm leaving the university after this year," he finally said.

"What?" Miklós's mouth dropped open. He felt as though he had just been punched in the stomach.

"I'm not coming back," said Gyuri, sitting down on the bed.

"What do you mean?" Miklós asked, holding up his hands in bewilderment.

"I'm not meant to be at the university anymore," Gyuri said, lowering his head. Even before Miklós could ask the obvious question, Gyuri looked up and said, nearly in a whisper, "I'm going to be a priest."

Miklós said nothing. Only a blank stare.

"I don't know why," Gyuri continued, "but I've been called to the priesthood."

"Called? I don't get it."

"Maybe it was the same still, small voice that called our mother to our holy religion."

"How did this happen so suddenly? You've been out defending the rights of Christian workers, staying apart from me and from the rest of our friends. You've almost stopped going to church and now you're going to be a priest?"

"I'm not sure I understand, either. I know I haven't been myself all year, maybe for a few years. I thought at first it was just because I didn't like being here or didn't like studying law. But you're right. You've noticed what I have felt all along. I had separated myself, even from you, I'm sorry to say. Maybe I've been sad. I don't know why. But for a while I've been meaning to go to the cathedral and spend some time there by myself, just contemplating and praying. I finally did today. And do you know what I thought of?"

"No, I don't." Miklós's voice had softened. But his brow was still furrowed in puzzlement.

"I thought of the time you and I sneaked into the basilica and met Christ for the first time." Miklós felt a welling up of nostalgia and longing. "I remembered," continued Gyuri, "His bleeding hands and feet, and how much pain was on His face. From that day on, His suffering made my pain bearable, although I lost sight of it for many years. I started getting angry and thinking that He didn't have to die. I even blamed the people who killed Him. Well, today in the cathedral, His pain touched me softly and changed me forever. My heart was so filled with gratitude and comfort that now I feel and think and see things in a totally new way. I think I can finally tolerate my own trials again. But I realize I can never go very far from Him anymore. My troubles would be too much for me to bear alone. So I decided that this must be what is meant by being called and chosen to be in the Church forever. I think He wants me to be His priest in order to remind people of His loving sacrifice." Still sitting on the bed, Gyuri looked up at his twin brother and smiled contentedly.

"I am surprised," said Miklós, grasping his brother's shoulders. "But I am happy for you, too. You have found your purpose in life."

Then Miklós remembered where Gyuri's recent sadness had come from, even if he himself could not or would not say. It was clear to Miklós that when Ági died a few years earlier, his brother had never been the same. Wasn't that obvious to Gyuri? Miklós remembered how he had pleaded with Gyuri that night they learned of Ági's death to find in Christ's suffering a way to tolerate his own grief. Gyuri was finally doing exactly that. True enough, the only crying he had ever done for Ági was that night of stifled wailing and weeping. Maybe because admitting love for a teenage girl, especially a Jewish one, was so forbidden, Gyuri never succeeded in mourning her death in any other way. There was no funeral to attend or memorial Mass to say. He had to hide his feelings forever. Was it a good thing, Miklós wondered, that Gyuri forgot Ági? How strange it was that he remembered his Savior's anguish but forgot the death of his earthly love. Had Christ's redemptive suffering soothed Gyuri's grief into oblivion? Miklós would never know. But since Gyuri had not mentioned it, Miklós resolved that he would not bring it up either. Nor would their parents and sister ever suspect the human drama that Miklós felt quietly certain was the soil from which sprang his brother's lifelong devotion to his Savior.

Miklós sat down alongside his twin. He was nervous about the way their lives were going to change. But he saw in Gyuri's face a deep and steady contentment that hadn't been there in years. The corners of Gyuri's eyes were still sad. That hadn't entirely disappeared. But now it was Miklós who felt at a distance from his brother. He couldn't tell if it was his own anxiety about the future that made him feel so remote, or whether Gyuri's moment of epiphany had simply made him look more content but no less far away than he had been before. As they continued to sit in silence alongside each other, Miklós knew with growing certainty, as Gyuri probably did as well, that things would never again be the same between them.

❖ CHAPTER 7 ❖

Breach

*Our Lord Jesus taught us the elements of love; we must for-
give even our enemy. But when we are discussing an ambition to take control of the world by people of the race
that . . . can be met wherever there are revolutions, wherever the peace and quiet of entire nations is violated, wherever there is a violation of basic ethics, we do not have to
hide behind the idea of Christian love.*

— Newspaper article in *Nemzeti Figyelo* (*National
Observer*), written by a Catholic priest to his colleagues
concerning his approach to the Arrow Cross Party,
February 27, 1938

BUDAPEST, FEBRUARY 1935: As Miklós sat in Bertha's modest flat on
Lipthay Street, he remembered his childhood visits there during the war. Little had changed in the sixteen years since his family left the city. The walls of
the small and cluttered apartment were still the same discolored white and
the pictures that hung on them had never moved. The sofa in the living room
was just as threadbare as he remembered it. Could those be the same coffee
and wine stains on the crocheted tablecloth? The smell of freshly baked
mákos tészta, poppy-seed cake, made him feel as though he had been there
only yesterday.

Bertha and her husband, Henrik, were in the living room with Elza and
Margit, who had affectionately come to be called Muci (pronounced Mootzi).
Rosi, Elza's sister, was there also. She had never left. Bertha's son, Josi, was
visiting from his family's nearby flat, which he shared with his wife, Mariska,
and their two sons, Laci, short for László, and Kari, a diminutive of Károly.
The family had come together to greet Miklós, their learned cousin, recently
arrived from the distinguished university in Szeged.

"So, my dear Miklós," began Bertha, "did you have any trouble finding our
place?" she asked, with a wry smile.

"No, I'll never forget how to get here. I could have found it with my eyes
closed."

"I don't imagine," continued Bertha, "it's been easy for you to find a position yet?"

"No, it's been hard," Miklós answered, trying to hide his discouragement.

"Aunt Laura had a lead with a private attorney's office, but it didn't material-ize."

"Something will come up for you, my boy," added good-natured Henrik.

"Of course it will," said Bertha. "But for now, how do you like living at Laura's?"

"Well, it's different from her flat on Damjanich Street. It was a beautiful place, but now that Károly's been dead for so many years she couldn't afford it anymore. Her new place on Wesselényi Street is not far from the old apart-ment. It's pleasant enough, but you can tell things have changed."

"True enough," said Bertha. "The city itself probably looks the same to you, but you have entered a different world from the one you left as a boy after the war."

"Everything looks the same," said Miklós, "but I actually don't remember much except your apartment and this neighborhood where Gyuri and I used to get into constant trouble together."

"Even that has changed," said Henrik. "I doubt that either you or your priest of a brother is much of a troublemaker anymore."

"I'm sure," added Mariska, with a laugh.

"No, they don't make much allowance for mischief at that important sem-inary in Vienna," said Josi. Miklós hadn't seen him for many years, but he al-ready detected Josi's sarcasm for anything that was less than fully Hungarian. Josi had converted to Catholicism, ostensibly because his wife was Catholic. But whatever helped him feel more Hungarian was fine with him. Josi was first and foremost a patriot.

Miklós could imagine what Josi was thinking: "So, the Pázmány Univer-sity in Budapest wasn't good enough for your brother. He had to go to Vienna so he could live and study among Hungarians." Soon after Gyuri's decision to enter the priesthood, he was nominated to enter the Pázmáneum, a college for elite Hungarian seminarians within the University of Vienna named after Péter Pázmány, a seventeenth-century counterreformationist. Yes, there was a Pázmány University in Budapest, but Gyuri and his family were delighted with the honor of his nomination to Vienna. Only an ultrapatriot like Josi could take issue with the college not being on Hungarian soil.

Miklós ignored Josi. "Gyuri and I have changed, but the city looks no dif-ferent."

"The look of the city *has* changed somewhat and even improved," said Henrik. "But everything else—" He stopped in midsentence and made a thumbs-down motion.

"What do you mean?" asked Miklós, feeling some tension.

"Life has changed unimaginably since you left Budapest, truly for all of us. After the communists were defeated, the country blamed us and were brutal, just brutal."

"I remember that," said Miklós. The image of his cousin Karl's pummeled face darted across his mind.

"Well, I'm afraid that the end of the war was just the beginning of a sea change in the place we occupy in this society," said Henrik.

"Now, don't go blabbering about politics to our nephew," interrupted Bertha. "There are more pleasant things to talk about."

"Of course," added Josi, "none of this is important anyway. Why emphasize the differences between people? What's important is that we're all Hungarians."

Neither Miklós nor anybody else felt reassured. It seemed that there was no avoiding undeniable differences. Miklós turned his thoughts instead to Henrik's remarks. His granduncle had always been known as a kind and generous man. He was a strict factory foreman and yet was a soft touch when it came to signing promissory notes on behalf of his workers. Miklós had never known Henrik to be a political man, much less a religious one. But he read the *Pesti News* daily and apparently held well-developed opinions about Hungarians and Jews.

"Isn't it crazy," continued Henrik, "that before all the other nationalities were cut loose by Trianon, the Jews were indispensable to the Hungarians. Together we made up the majority. And then things turned, in an instant. This has always amazed me."

The Treaty of Trianon of June 1920, an outgrowth of Versailles, had effectively punished vanquished Hungary by cutting its historical borders by two thirds and its population by three fifths. The decimation of greater Hungary then became official. The lands that nearly a dozen national groups had inhabited for centuries were excised from the nation, ceded mostly to Rumania, Czechoslovakia, Yugoslavia, and Austria. Only two ethnic groups remained in the "rump" of the nation—the Magyars and the Jews.

The wound on the nation's soul that was Trianon had never disappeared, and one did not have to be an intellectual to understand its impact on the Hungarian mentality. It was discussed in schools and preached from Christian and Jewish pulpits. Anyone could see it in the collective outrage, the diminished stature and the self-doubt of native Magyars. The Jews, too, who were historically ultrapatriots, greatly mourned the loss of land, people, and prestige. It was the greatest collective slap in the face the Hungarian nation had had to endure in its thousand-year history, and the most dramatic turning point in the nation's relationship to the Jews.

"Look, I've never been a good Jew," Henrik continued. "Eking out a living has been hard enough without having to worry about our religion being held against us. But as far as I'm concerned, we were treated with respect before the war. You can be sure no one loved us, but the Hungarians knew which side their bread was buttered on. *Now* what are we? I'll tell you. They see us as ambitious competitors. We even get blamed for the war and the treaty. Have you ever heard anything so absurd?"

"And then look what happens," said Bertha. "All these self-righteous people come along and accuse us of killing Christ. Forgive me, Mariska," she quickly said to her Catholic daughter-in-law, lightly touching her forearm, "I don't mean to offend you." Turning to her nephew, "And you, too, Miklós. Not all Hungarians are like this. Look at dear Laci and Kari. Some people are just good Christians and take everyone at face value."

"Of course they do," said Mariska, smiling and looking reassured. "My sons are good Catholics, but they love their Jewish family. And I'm sure Miklós does, too."

Miklós felt more uneasy. "So things must be better now," he said. "In Szeged, people knew that Gyuri and I were born Jewish, and we never had any problems." It was jarring, though, to be reminded by his own relatives of what he had been taught in parochial school and church about the "perfidious" Jews. These were the very sentiments he feared his twin brother still harbored and had been exposed to all the more at the seminary. "It's fifteen years since Trianon. The country is strong again."

"Miki, Miki," said Henrik, "things are worse, my dear boy. It's obvious you've been tucked away in school for a long time."

"Henrik, don't be unkind to the boy. He's my dear sister's grandson, my flesh and blood."

"No, no, no." Henrik smiled. "Of course not; I mean him no unkindness," he said, turning for an instant toward his wife and then quickly back to Miklós. "But let me just tell you that the government held things together after the war and even abolished the Jewish quotas after five or six years. You remember the *Numerus Clausus*. It was virtually impossible for Jews to get into the universities."

"You know," said Bertha, "if dear Elza's husband had lived, he might not have been able to come back to Budapest to study law." Elza sat impassively. Political conversations never interested her, and mention of her long-dead husband no longer stirred up much disquiet. But twelve-year-old Muci's face had perked up, not because she was any more interested in the political discussion but because mention of her father provoked curiosity and longing in her.

"Well, the world finally wouldn't stand for it," continued Henrik. "The country decided it needed foreign capital more than it needed to blame the Jews. But then, when we had the depression in '29, who do you think was blamed, and is still being blamed? It's the same song sung to a different melody."

"But Christians aren't doing the blaming," said Miklós, probably not realizing how naive he sounded.

"Certainly not, dear Miklós," said Mariska, nodding at him. "It's not the Christians, not good Christians and Catholics."

"So who are these people, then?" continued Henrik, with a feigned look of bewilderment. "Who is it who's been trying to save the Christian character of Hungary? Who are in these right-wing 'cross' parties cropping up all over the place, threatening violence and vengeance—single cross, double cross, arrow cross? It's hard to keep track of them. And who's writing all these new anti-Semitic newspapers? How many new ones are there this week? And who do you think our esteemed prime minister turns to for moral and political support—the *Germans,* and his protégé from long ago, Herr Hitler."

"Look," said Mariska with a stiffer, more resolute tone. "No one denies the German influence here. But Hungary is not Germany. Maybe the Germans hate the Jews. But we're Christians. God-hating Hitler will never succeed here. No matter how much some people abuse the sacred symbol of Christ's crucifixion for their own evil ends, the Jews are like our Siamese twins." Mariska then took her father-in-law's hand in hers. "Hungary would bleed to death," she went on, "if she ever cut the Jews off. You'll see that German Jew-hatred will never take root and flourish here. We're a family of Jews and Christians. Maybe we bicker sometimes, but we don't harm one another." As Mariska finished speaking, she leaned over toward Henrik and, without the least bit of insincerity, kissed him lovingly on the cheek.

❖

SZARVAS, JULY 21, 1935: A rare surviving family photograph speaks volumes regarding what may have been the most important day in Gyuri's life as a Catholic priest. Jews and Catholics from this southern Hungarian town posed together in common celebration of their native son having come so far in the Church. My beaming grandparents were there, surrounded by family members from as far away as Budapest, as well as honored clergy and members of the local community.

On this beautiful summer day, there was a most special Sunday Mass followed by a banquet at the Pogány home for a multitude of family guests.

Miklós had come down from Budapest a few days earlier, and even Aunt Laura and Uncle Louie had made the long train trip to help celebrate this milestone in the family's life. The Christian nature of the occasion didn't really bother these secular Jewish relatives from the city. Dignitaries of the Church were sure to be on hand, including Father Fetzer, the pastor of the Catholic parish in town. Father Paul Domanek, Gyuri and Miklós's religion teacher from Gyula, who had recently taken a parish in Öcsöd just down the road from Szarvas, would be giving the homily. The entire community was astir. Young Father Pogány had come home from Vienna to conduct his *primicia,* his first Mass as an ordained priest.

An hour before Mass, the excitement of the moment had finally caught up with Gyuri. Miklós had just entered the room of the family's home, where he saw his brother pacing the floor. Dressed in a black cassock and clerical collar, Gyuri must have thought he had a rare moment alone. He stopped pacing, gazed out the window, and murmured what sounded to Miklós like a prayer for help to get through the day.

Miklós waited, not wanting Gyuri to know he had been overheard. "You look very contemplative," he finally said. "But you must be a little nervous, with all this fanfare."

Gyuri smiled. "Yes, I am a little," he said. "But there's no good reason to be. This is the happiest day of my life. To conduct Mass surrounded by my family, friends, and neighbors is more than I ever imagined."

"Do you know," said Miklós, "I remember following you around in Báránd when we played that we were in the Brotherhood of St. Francis, preaching throughout the countryside. I thought then that you would become a priest. So I'm not surprised now to see it happen. But still, you look so striking standing here in your cassock."

Gyuri smiled again, this time more broadly. "I don't feel I'm any different now than I was back then, when we both served as altar boys in Báránd." Then he became more serious. "Although I suppose much has changed. My road has been full of surprises and hardships. But whatever distractions and doubts arose along the way have vanished. That old Adam has died, and my fate is now fully bound to the Church."

"Was it really that difficult?" Miklós wasn't sure what his brother was referring to. "I never thought going to Vienna was anything but a thrill for you."

"For the most part, it was a joy and an unimaginable privilege. But at times it was hard. We Hungarians had our own enclave in Vienna. But sometimes I felt a bit isolated from everyone. I suppose that's only normal, to be an island of Hungarians in a sea of Austrians and Germans."

"I'm happy you came through it all," Miklós said, lightly grasping Gyuri's arm. "I've missed you at university. Maybe we never recognized how good it was to be together all those years."

"You're right," said Gyuri. "Life was much easier when we had each other."

It was gratifying to have Gyuri acknowledge that. But beyond that, Miklós couldn't help but wonder what kind of "isolation" Gyuri was getting at. Feeling isolated resonated deeply within Miklós. It had only been in recent yeas that he had managed to shake the recurrent feeling of being in some sort of insidiously subtle exile. But Gyuri's feelings were nothing akin to that, he told himself. Or were they? Miklós didn't dare ask.

"Our lives have gone in such different directions," said Gyuri. "Imagine, my twin brother—a doctor of law. I'm still surprised that you didn't follow me into the priesthood."

"There's only room for one man of the cloth in our family. I guess I'll have to settle for the black robes of a jurist, although I don't exactly get to wear them in my job at the bank. I'm just glad to be working."

"Well, you'll be living a normal life, Miklós, working in a respectable position in the city. Now you'll be able to follow Papa's advice to 'cherchez la femme.'"

Miklós glanced away in embarrassment. "Not all that quickly," he said. "I'm not about to go looking for women." Miklós was dressed in a light linen suit and had continued the family's longtime custom of shearing his head to offset the summer heat. While Gyuri looked becoming with his well-groomed black hair, and ecclesiastical in his priest's cassock, Miklós felt clumsy and homely, an awkward country boy meagerly impersonating a worldly banker.

"Ah, but you'll be a good catch for some lucky girl. Even our mother says so. And you underestimate yourself just because it took a few extra months to find your position."

"In our pious country," answered Miklós, "a Catholic priest would have no trouble finding work. But in these fragile times, I'm afraid it might not be so easy for a Jewish-born professional." Miklós apparently had quickly absorbed his relatives' anxieties about what was happening to the lives of Jews in modern-day Budapest. "Jews are already accused of being too visible and prominent," he went on. "These are tense—"

"Well, look," interrupted Gyuri, with what looked like a forced smile, "no one is about to check your birth certificate for your origins. Now, my being named the chaplain of a tiny rural hamlet isn't exactly an appointment to the Holy See. I am on the bottom rung of the Church hierarchy. I couldn't start any lower. But it has nothing to do with my origins. It's just how things have turned out. In one way, though, I have to admit you're right, it's easier for me.

I'll go where I am instructed and where my vows lead me." Gyuri paused and took a deep breath. "As for my origins, I leave that in God's hands. I will suffer whatever tribulations He has in store for me." It all sounded a little too smug to Miklós—a Catholic priest whose Jewish background no one need ever know.

"You've made us all very proud, my dear Gyuri," Gabriella trilled as she entered the room from the kitchen. She was carrying a platter of freshly cut choice veal that Béla had brought from the slaughterhouse. The room was cluttered with tables of covered dishes and platters of meat and fowl for the upcoming feast. "The entire parish looks up to you," their mother added, "and holds all of us now in high esteem."

Miklós wondered if she had heard the gist of their conversation about being Jewish in such unsettled times. He remembered how often he had heard her refer to their family as "baptized Jews," and how it so irritated Gyuri to hear it. He never liked being reminded.

"Now, don't be waiting around here," said Gabriella. "God forbid that you should be late for your first Mass. We'll all follow in a few minutes."

Later that morning, Father Pogány stood at the altar in front of the entire parish as the celebrant at Sunday Mass. His parents, brother, and sister sat in the front pew. Even Béla, who was not a regular churchgoer and had never truly fathomed his son's religious calling, was beaming. Father Fetzer looked unusually proud, unaccustomed though he was to ceding the pulpit to another priest, much less to someone who had risen from within his own community. Father Domanek had just completed delivering his homily, during which he praised Gyuri's religious devotion and remembered him as a promising student who may have been destined for the priesthood from an early age.

Then Gyuri stood and raised his hands over the silver chalice of wine to consecrate it: *"Hic est enim calix sanguinis mei novi et eterni testamenti mysterium fidei qui pro vobis et pro multis effundetur ad remissionem peccatorum."* Then, whispering in Hungarian, he repeated, "This is the chalice of my blood of the new and everlasting covenant, the mystery of faith, which is poured out for you and for all for the remission of sins." Gyuri's face was aglow in the performance of his sacred obligations to the Church and his home parish.

Then the high point of the service arrived, when Father Fetzer stood and invited people to receive a special blessing from Gyuri and, in turn, to kneel before him and kiss his hand, to honor and welcome him to the priesthood. Scores of people stood up and approached the altar to be blessed by the young priest whose honored family lived in their midst. But no one was as determined as Gabriella. She would later tell her family and friends that she knelt and kissed the hand, not of her son, but of a devoted new servant of the Church to which she herself was so lovingly devoted.

❖

The calm and quiet of Szarvas had never been as noticeable to Miklós as when he reentered the commotion of Budapest a few days later. Passing his banker's examination soon after his return, he finally began to feel more established and free to live a normal life. But he knew barely a soul in the city outside of the members of his extended family, and felt it would be some time before colleagues at the bank warmed up to him. Living with his aunt Laura, Miklós took to visiting his mother's relatives on the other side of the river as often as he could. He enjoyed their welcoming warmth and support, although, as a young man in his early twenties, he found no peers among them.

One Sunday in late August, Miklós was again going to visit Bertha's family. Twelve-year-old Muci had just arrived home from her yearly summer holiday with her father's family in Körmöcz, a formerly Hungarian town ceded to Slovakia after the war and now called Kremnica. Of course, the family had always been partial to the Hungarian name. Muci's grandparents and their eight surviving children had come to cherish Muci's presence. On this, the end of her first week back in Budapest, she was accompanying her mother and their family to Swab Hill, overlooking the city, on what would probably be their last summer outing. For years, Bertha had loved going with her family by trolley for picnics to a lovely wooded area with a pond and a large grassy field. This time, Miklós would be coming along, accompanying Bertha and Henrik, Rosi, Josi and Mariska and their sons, and, of course, Elza and Muci.

On the trolley ride up the hills from Buda, twelve-year-old Muci sat next to Miklós. He had only seen Muci a few times earlier that spring. As the trolley trundled up the hill, Miklós was staring past Muci out the window at the hypnotic rush of trees. But he was really looking inward, daydreaming of events that had occurred in a distant time and place. He thought of the summer more than ten years earlier, when one-year-old Muci and her mother, both newly arrived home from America, had come to stay with his family in Báránd. He remembered taking care of her and parading her proudly around the village, introducing her as his "American cousin." He noticed how skinny she was now, and that her tightly drawn, wavy black hair accentuated her thin face and jutting high cheekbones. It reminded him of how protective everyone in his family had been of her as a frail baby, when she had already been through so much turmoil in her brief life. Miklós recalled going for a walk one

Sunday afternoon in Báránd, and how his father shielded the fragile-looking child from the admiring but unwelcome advances of some local peasant women. He remembered how afraid his father was that the child would contract tuberculosis or some other terrible disease. Miklós also remembered how he himself had wanted to take her to Mass, and had suggested that she be baptized when he learned that a Catholic church wasn't a place for a little Jewish girl.

As Miklós's thoughts returned to the present moment, he looked at the already well-defined lines of young Muci's face. She smiled at him openheartedly and he felt a sudden flurry of warmth and protectiveness for the frail and tender teenager whom everyone cherished. Even after so many years, marked only by the rare visits Muci and her mother had made to Szarvas, Miklós felt that he had never really stopped knowing her, and realized that he had, in fact, known her since nearly the beginning of her life.

Fortunately for the struggling trolley, the hills had leveled off and the family disembarked at a small clearing with only a three-sided rain shelter alongside the tracks. Carrying a straw basket of food, blankets, and containers of cold drinks, the party of ten followed a handful of other picknickers down a path cutting through the woods to an idyllic pasture and hillside pond. The periodic clanking of iron wheels along the trolley tracks became more and more muted as the group retreated further into the woods and finally settled under the cool shade of an oak tree.

Miklós remained standing and looked around the area with an uncanny feeling of having been there before.

"I know what you're thinking," said Aunt Bertha. "It's written on your face. The answer is yes. You have been here before." She had a dreamy, nostalgic look on her face. "We used to come up here with your mother and grandmother during the war when your father was away. Your baby sister and your . . . brother . . ." Holding on to the last word and not being able to get the next one out, Bertha suddenly looked distressed, as if something familiar but faraway and troubling had entered her awareness.

"What's wrong, Bertha?" asked Henrik. "What were you about to say?"

Looking at Miklós, she tried to finish. "As children, you and your sister and brother loved coming here." Bertha hesitated for another instant and swallowed hard, trying, it seemed, not to betray the sadness in her eyes. "And Gyuri came here, too, during his school holiday from Gyula. We saw him a few times back then. Once he came by for lunch with—" She interrupted herself again. "And I spoke to Laura frequently after that summer, especially later, after. . . . We were both so concerned." Then Bertha's gaze dropped and turned inward. She looked sad and far away.

The moment passed. A determined smile stretched Bertha's lips, and her eyes moved deliberately, first to Henrik, then to Elza, then to her beloved Muci. No one seemed to know what Bertha's consternation had been about. Her mumbling may only have confused people more. But Miklós knew, not so much in his mind as in the sudden lump in his own throat. He looked at Bertha. She turned away. And he knew.

Then, unexpectedly, Muci jumped to her feet. "I'm going to sit over by the pond."

On impulse, Bertha said, "If neither of the boys are going to go," referring to Kari and Laci, "then please go with her, Miklós. She just got home and I worry about her so." Neither of Muci's younger cousins looked any too eager to leave his shady perch to move into the hot sun.

"Grandma, I will just be sitting by the shallow pond. It's not exactly the Danube."

"I know, I know," Bertha said. Elza nodded her approval of her mother's nervousness on behalf of Muci. By then Miklós had gotten to his feet and was following a few paces behind her. As he stepped past the circle of family members, Miklós felt a most odd thought teasing at his awareness, much like Muci's wavy hair grazing the shoulders of her summery peasant dress. Something ever-so-strange was being played out, some fateful choreography in which Miklós felt himself an unwitting participant. He played along, not knowing what the next steps were supposed to be. But as he looked back over his shoulder at his beloved grandaunt, she was staring off once again, somewhere far off. Was she viewing the present moment, Miklós wondered, in some distant mirror?

As they got near the water's edge, Muci stopped under a sturdy though not yet fully mature willow tree, which cast just enough shade to offset the summer sun. Miklós sat down facing her at a friendly but not too familiar distance.

In the years that had transpired since her summer in Báránd, Muci had become a beautiful girl just shy of womanhood. There was a sadness and innocence to her face that was easily discernible beneath her self-possessed exterior. She was uniformly indulged and spoiled by the adults around her. But there was a gentleness and fragility to her. Although Miklós was well aware that she had grown up with a devoted mother and adoring grandparents, aunts, uncles, and cousins, he also recognized that Muci had never known what it felt like to have a father, since he had died before she was born. Maybe that's what it was about her that made Miklós feel instantly paternal with her. And maybe it was also the same thing that made Muci seem so comfortable and reassured in his presence. He was older, like a father, and he, too, had had a long and painful experience of living without one. They shared similar wounds.

"You've had quite the summer with your relatives in Slovakia, haven't you?"

"I've been going there every summer since I was little."

"I remember that. Every year since the summer you spent with my family in Báránd, you went to see your father's family. You probably don't remember Báránd. Everyone in my family adored you."

"No, I don't remember. But I'm lucky to have family who are so good to me. Even though I don't have any brothers or sisters and my father is dead, everyone in the family makes me feel special. It's fun in Kremnica with my grandparents and all my aunts and uncles and cousins. The only thing I don't like about the summer is that I don't get to see much of my grandfather."

"What do you mean?"

"Grandpa David is away a lot because he's a traveling salesman. When he's home, he's either at the synagogue, where he's the *gabbay*, or he's at the tavern playing dominoes. Grandma says he gets into arguments with people over it. And then when he's home, he yells a lot."

"What's a . . . *gabbay?*" Miklós's thoughts were a step behind Muci's.

"A *gabbay* is the person in the synagogue who helps make sure that prayers and rituals are done in the right way."

"It doesn't sound like your grandpa gets much peace from his prayers."

"I don't know. I suppose he just has a bad temper. Maybe he's sad about my father being gone. Or maybe he's always been worried about how he was going to take care of so many kids, although many of them are grown up now."

Miklós was pleased Muci was so easy to talk to. She was a rather typical twelve-year-old girl; she spoke fast and impetuously once she got going.

"But if anyone in my family prays," Muci went on, "it's my grandma. She's a seamstress and works at home on her sewing machine all the time until Friday night when Shabbos comes. Then she covers her sewing machine, lights the candles, and says the blessings that she taught me. Friday night is when even Grandpa becomes a little less grumpy. And Grandma doesn't start working again until Sunday. I know my mother and grandparents here in Budapest aren't very religious, although Grandma Bertha says she will someday give me her prayer book. But somehow, at the end of every summer, when I come back from Kremnica, it always feels funny to find that some of my own family members are Christian."

Miklós smiled good-naturedly, even as he tried to escape his discomfort.

With his legs extended, he leaned back on one arm against the grass, nonchalant in response. "Well, in this country, it's not such a strange thing. Look at my whole family. We're all good Catholics and my brother's a priest. And look at Josi and Mariska and their family, too."

"That's what I meant," said Muci. "It's always strange to see Kari and Laci go to church on Sundays."

"Mariska's a believing Catholic, and so are her boys," said Miklós. "Although I think Josi would have become a Buddhist if it made him more Hungarian." Muci laughed.

"And then there are even some Christians," Miklós continued, "who become Jewish. One of your grandmother's relatives had her husband convert to Judaism, even though they eventually both became Catholic."

"Yes, I heard about that. Another one of them married the widow of the poet Ady."

"Endre Ady!" said Miklós. He was always thrilled to discuss Hungarian poets. "He's a perfect example of how strong the bond is between Christians and Jews here. He was the country's greatest modern poet but he took Hungarians to task for the way they treated the Jews. 'Your blood,' he said of the Jews, 'even if it is a hundred times foreign, yet it is mine, is mine.'" If there was one thing Miklós loved doing, it was reciting poetry. But he suddenly realized that he was going over the head of his young audience.

"Did your family convert to blend in?" Muci asked, with undaunted directness.

"No, I don't think so. My father wanted to work in the civil service and Jews didn't get many of those jobs. Maybe my mother didn't have much feeling for being Jewish. But she likes being Catholic. She goes to Mass all the time and almost as often to Confession. And she raised a son who became a priest." It must have been obvious to Muci that Miklós had not the least self-consciousness about his family's religious faith.

"Now that sounds strange, a Jewish boy who becomes a priest, in your own family."

"It's true, but it doesn't erase our Jewish blood."

✤ CHAPTER 8 ✤

Flight

Since Constantine the Great became ruler of the Roman
Empire and the persecuted Christians were able to come
out of the catacombs, the popes and church councils, year
after year, generation after generation, have engaged in leg-
islation to limit the rights of the Jews and to issue decrees
aimed at achieving this goal. . . . No one has ever canceled
these papal edicts and church laws. And so they are all
valid in our day as well.
— Newspaper article in *Magyarsag* *(Hungarianism)*
   during debate of anti-Jewish legislation
   in Hungarian parliament, January 25, 1939

Perhaps the smell of violets was still in the air during those few days in Budapest, late in May 1938. But it might as well have been the frankincense of a Catholic Mass that pervaded the air of the city. The mesdames of spring along Pest's river promenade were replaced by throngs of righteous Hungarian Christians at a most majestic Eucharistic Convention, convened by the various churches. Tens of thousands of people had taken to the streets, squares, and church sanctuaries for Masses and prayer services that heralded the rebirth of Christ's love in Hungary and throughout the world. Scores of bishops from all over the globe were present to bask in the glow of the Hungarian nation's devotion to their Christian and especially Catholic heritage.

On his way to work that morning at the Hungarian Commercial Bank of Pest, Miklós had seen the rows of stores and shops proudly displaying crucifixes from their front windows. Later, as he looked out a third-floor window of the bank, he witnessed a regal procession in Roosevelt Square directly in front of the Chain Bridge, headed by the resplendently attired, most publicly recognizable Jusztinian Cardinal Serédi, the Prince Primate of the Roman Catholic Church in Hungary. As Miklós watched the magnificent parade, he thought how ironic it was that all this show of Christian devotion was taking place just two days after the ratification of a major anti-Jewish law that would soon deprive a large segment of Hungary's Jews of their livelihoods. The bill was intended to derail the huge cultural and economic influence of the Jews and replace it with the long-overshadowed Christian culture. It was especially geared to limit Jewish influence in the press, strangely, at a time when Christian and anti-Semitic newspapers were cropping up like weeds around the city. Apologists for the bill thought that it would deflate the violent urges of the radical anti-Semites. But its supporters were naive at best and transparent at worst. The nation was on its own inexorable course to deal with its Jewish problem in the best way it saw fit.

Miklós didn't hear any of the speeches or attend any Masses that day. He only witnessed the displayed banners and crucifixes and the endless sea of fervently cheering crowds at this most Christian of national celebrations. Anyone who was Hungarian and Christian couldn't help but be swept up and carried along by its energy. Despite the anti-Jewish legislation and the growing anti-Semitic rhetoric of the past months, Miklós and other Jewish converts had nothing to fear, neither for their place in Hungarian society, nor in the Church, nor in the nation's economy. Their lives and their livelihoods were secure. They were considered full-fledged members of Hungarian society and of the body of Christ, even though some priests and ministers of parliament had had to passionately argue for the exclusion of Jewish converts from the anti-Jewish bill. But, despite his own relative security, Miklós still felt troubled that all of these Catholic and Protestant dignitaries were coming to celebrate Christ's love for all mankind at a time when the country was disenfranchising its Jewish population.

Miklós's cousin and new colleague, Pista, stood alongside him that day at the bank. Miklós was still living with his aunt Laura, and Pista had recently moved in. His family had also converted to Catholicism, and Pista himself was extremely devout. Every weekend he would travel north to his family's home in Esztergom, the seat of the nation's Catholic Church. There, his father, Sigmund Berényi, was a respected medical doctor who served as personal physician to Cardinal Serédi. Since moving in with Miklós and Laura, Pista would regale his cousin with stories he had heard from his father of the majesty of the Hungarian Holy See in Esztergom. On one occasion, Miklós and his father had even visited Pista's family there.

"Look there," said Pista, "that saintly looking man next to Serédi is none other than Eugenio Cardinal Pacelli." Miklós said nothing. Pista continued, "He is the Secretary of State in the Vatican, the personal representative of Pope Pius XI. Just think, next to the pope, he is the highest-ranking Catholic official in the world, and he is here to grace our convention."

Miklós didn't dare respond. He knew that Pista had long ago rejected Judaism. He was even afraid to look around to notice who else besides his cousin was standing next to him, much less wonder what they might be thinking. As he continued watching, arms folded tightly in front of him, Miklós tried to relax the grimace pulling at the skin under his eyes and around his mouth. His body felt tense and he struggled to keep his mind focused on the spectacle in front of him. But he couldn't keep from thinking. The pope's personal representative is here? Is he, too, oblivious to the anti-Jewish law? It just passed two days ago. How could he not know? Miklós felt a chill run up his spine. On this beautifully warm spring day, he was shivering.

Gyuri was also present at the Eucharistic Convention. Like the vast majority of Catholic priests throughout the nation, he had taken pains to attend the celebration. He had ridden his motorbike, his favorite mode of transportation, twenty miles north from his home in Hosszúpályi to Debrecen, Hungary's third-largest city. There he had boarded one of many specially designated trains that transported vast numbers of his coreligionists from all over the country, at a reduced fare, to their monumental spiritual homecoming in Budapest.

Dressed in a black cassock, Gyuri stood among an endless sea of spectators in one of the large city squares, awaiting a string of speeches from Church and government officials. His mind was at peace and readily fixed on the sights and events going on around him. He felt comfortable and at home in the nation of his fellow Catholics and Christians. The political commotion of the preceding few days and weeks surrounding the legislation against the Jews could not have been further from the mind of this rural country chaplain. He didn't read the Jewish press, having even convinced his mother, years before, to discard the liberal newspapers she was used to reading in favor of the National News, the official voice of the Catholic Church. Gyuri certainly knew vaguely of the particulars of the anti-Jewish bill, but he had dismissed the entire issue as irrelevant to himself and to anyone even remotely involved in his life. The bill's originally proposed cutoff date for acceptable conversions, August 1, 1919, didn't bother Gyuri in the least. He and his family had been baptized months before that critical day when the communists were defeated. Besides, Christian clergy had argued vehemently against the possibility of devoted converts in their own flocks being included in the anti-Jewish law. His Christian faith was, by now, too deeply rooted, and there was no compelling reason to disturb the soil out of which those roots emerged. So, this day, Gyuri stood proudly and confidently among the multitude of his spiritual brethren.

The moment was a most special one. Gyuri listened for the better part of the morning to the speeches of Christian luminaries, both clerical and government officials—the prime minister, the minister of industry, followed by Bishop Glattfelder, whom Gyuri fondly remembered from his university days in Szeged, and then the primate himself, Cardinal Serédi. They all spoke of the inseparability of religion and everyday life, that nothing was secular in Hungary, and that everything was pervaded by God's love. And that love, some like Serédi went on to say, served as a model for Christians' dual love for God and for individual and collective neighbors—throughout Hungary as well as around the world. The heart and voice of every man and woman in the crowd rose to the beat of the cardinal's syncopated hymn, "Jesus triumphs, Jesus rules, Jesus commands!" To Gyuri, and, he thought, to anyone listening, these festivities were proceeding in the absolute spirit of love, without the slightest hint of ill will or hatred.

Then came the high point of the day. Eugenio Cardinal Pacelli, the pope's personal emissary, was to address the vast audience. It was a rare and humbling privilege for Gyuri. Pacelli was a tall and gaunt, truly holy-looking man with a white complexion and hawklike nose. Gyuri smiled contentedly and waited with rapt anticipation for the cardinal's address.

Pacelli began. He established and promoted the theme of Christian love, as others before him had, especially of love in action in everyday life for the sake of "overcoming pettiness, conflict, quarreling and egotism . . . great and small." What proof, Gyuri thought, of the infinite capacity for love and compassion in the heart of this great Christian leader and at the heart of Christianity itself.

Then the cardinal's words grew more strident. "Jesus conquers! . . . He shall be triumphant in the future as well." He referred to Jesus as one who "so often suffered the persecutions of those of whom He was one" and to those "foes who cried out . . . 'Crucify him!'" Pacelli never named "those of whom [Jesus] was one," but it must have been glaringly obvious to anyone listening. To combat the cries of "those whose lips curse Him and whose hearts reject Him," the Vatican's representative offered humble hymns of loyalty and love to the Christian Savior.

Gyuri did not feel personally targeted by the cardinal's implicit accusations, but he could not have but known to whom Pacelli was referring. Gyuri had been saved, along with many other Jews. They had found their way to Christ. In Gyuri's mind, the revered cardinal must have been referring only to the communists and Jewish internationalists who had once terrified him as a boy in Báránd in 1919, and who ironically had also come close to assassinating Pacelli that same year, when he was papal nuncio in Munich. Since the time of the Bolshevik revolution, the popes had warned of the dangers of communism, and the cardinal must simply have been giving renewed voice to those warnings now. To Gyuri, it all seemed measured and thought through. His own way of thinking seemed perfectly mirrored by the holy papal emissary and man of God.

But as the cardinal was finishing his remarks, the crowd, which had given him undivided attention, grew suddenly restive. As people began moving every which way, many of those who were surrounding Gyuri inadvertently brushed up against him, most apologizing when they realized they had disturbed a man of the cloth. But then Gyuri was annoyingly prodded and pushed by the press of humanity. On instinct, he reached into the side opening of his cassock, toward the right back pocket of his trousers.

"My wallet!" he screamed. "Someone stole my wallet." He glared at the people surrounding him. "Who stole my wallet?" All his money for his trip to Budapest was gone. People around him were taken aback, probably thinking he was suspicious of each of them. Some of them defiantly peered back at him, never mind that he was a Catholic priest.

"Honorable and esteemed Father," a well-meaning bystander broke in, "you've become the victim of our famous Hungarian pickpockets."

As the man smiled and began to laugh, another man standing beside them raised a hand to eye level and made the clipping motion of scissors with two of his fingers. "It's the famous 'scissors' approach," he said. "They can clip your wallet, and even your liver, and you wouldn't feel a thing." Then many of the people around Gyuri burst out laughing. Even the priest standing on the other side of him smiled and tried to muffle his laugher. Gyuri scowled and suddenly felt his heart being pulled far away.

"Remember that big fat Bible we had to carry up the stairs and across the altar to the pulpit? Do you remember the day I tripped over my cassock and people started laughing?"

Gyuri's heart was now pounding. He took a deep breath. The taut muscles of his cheeks softened as he noticed the sympathetic, smiling faces surrounding him. Lowering his head in a surge of embarrassment, he smiled meekly as the uproar of his thoughts and feelings subsided. What had just happened, he told himself, didn't mean anything. He had merely lost his wallet and would have to rely on the goodwill of his relatives, all of whom would surely be more than gracious.

That evening, Gyuri and Miklós were together at their aunt Laura's apartment. At dinner, the brothers compared their impressions of the pageantry of the day just gone by. Miklós spoke of the visual spectacle of the parade of dignitaries proceeding silently below him from his lofty perch above Roosevelt Square. He said nothing about the troubled times in the city that had begun to poison relations between Christians and Jews, of which he suspected his brother must have been aware. Gyuri, for his part, spoke glowingly of the great spiritual luminaries he had been privileged to hear speak, and referred continually to the renewal of Christian values in Hungary. He also spoke, with what by now had become a self-effacing sense of humor, about becoming victim to the famous "scissors" technique of a skillful Hungarian pickpocket.

✤

One Sunday evening, almost a year later, in the spring of 1939, as he was nearing the end of his fourth year as town chaplain, Gyuri sat reading the *National News* in his cramped living quarters attached to the small Catholic church. There was enough space in his room for a bed, a cramped eating area with a table and woodstove, and a study space sufficient for a desk, chair, and bookshelf. Here Gyuri regularly wrote his homilies in longhand, at least those that the priest of the village, his superior, would assign him.

Gyuri had returned a few hours earlier, following dinner at the home of a family in his parish. He had become very fond of the occasional invitations he would receive from the various families in the hamlet, following Mass or special occasions like baptisms and funerals. Such hospitality helped him feel more a part of the community. If there was anything he most enjoyed doing, it was eating, especially rich Hungarian meat and poultry dishes as well as enormous quantities of cheese and eggs. It was Gyuri's solitary corporeal indulgence.

This particular evening, Gyuri had some cherished time to be alone with his own thoughts and musings. Though he still kept up with readings in Catholic theology, Church history, and canon law, he also remained well informed by the *National News*. Sitting at his desk, under the light of a kerosene lamp on a placid spring evening, Gyuri was beginning to perspire and experience a bout of indigestion. No wonder: he'd had extra helpings of stuffed cabbage at dinner, and creamed chestnut purée for dessert.

For months now, Gyuri had read about the growing alliance between Hungary and Germany. The Nazi government enabled Hungary to reacquire parts of its former homeland lost in the Treaty of Trianon following the Great War. For nearly two decades, Trianon had been Hungary's greatest historical humiliation, and now Germany was helping to redress it. Until these reacquisitions in only the past few months, Hungary had tried to steer a very cautious course in its relations with Germany, whose territorial and military ambitions were well recognized, and which could ultimately threaten Hungary's autonomy. But along with the territorial awards came a moral and political emulation of Germany's racial anti-Semitism, and this began openly infecting Hungary's religious climate.

Although aware of the new anti-Jewish legislation and its desired impact on the Jewish population, Gyuri had developed a mental reflex of telling himself, "Not me! That doesn't pertain to me." In the past, it was easy enough to believe that. For one thing, his family had decisively broken away from Judaism. He certainly had. As for his feelings about Jews, there may have been some disaffected ones left in his family. That didn't bother him. As for Jews in general, he continually wrestled with the Church's teachings. Theologically, the Jews were betrayers of Christ, and personally, they were clever and shrewd materialists whose god was money. A bounty of skewed images of Jews had been served up as common fare throughout his religious training. And then there was always the experiential bedrock from Gyuri's childhood, the harrowing journey to Báránd when he came to suspect Jews as godless Bolsheviks. But there was always one sure and ready solution in his mind to the so-called Jewish problem, and that was baptism—completion and purification of the human spirit.

Everyone was becoming concerned about solving the "Jewish problem," thanks in large part to the generous support the Third Reich gave to right-wing groups and anti-Semitic propaganda. It was becoming a hotly debated topic, not only in the national press but in local homes and taverns, even in this tiny Christian village. To more and more Hungarians, it was a problem that needed to be solved, and it had grown too large for just a religious answer. Still, it didn't involve Gyuri, personally or directly.

But now the National News was making him nervous. It was no longer voicing just the traditional, theological perceptions of Jewish mischief. German racial ideology was infecting Catholic views. Religious and political spokesmen were becoming increasingly shameless in their scathing criticism, and openly expressing the need to get the Jews under better control. While Germany's familiar rage was based on the racial otherness of Jews—on the fact that they were not Aryan—Hungary's problems with them had been based more on their not being Christian. So conversion was seen as the perfect avenue to assimilation and acceptance. But now there were more German-leaning government ministers in the cabinet of the newly appointed, outspokenly anti-Semitic prime minister, Béla Imrédy, and the voices of hot-headed politicians and clerics were becoming deafening. The tide was turning, and Gyuri could feel it.

Late the year before, a second anti-Jewish bill had been presented in parliament. On the twenty-third of December, 1938, the prime minister offered parliament a "Christmas present," a bill that would further reduce the presence of Jews from 20 percent to 6 percent in the professional workforce. Jewish converts had not suffered as a result of the first bill. Now Gyuri was reading public statements that the Jews were not only a threat to the Hungarian economy and culture, but were an alien mass that would have to be eliminated from the body of the nation. Some were openly talking about forced emigration.

Circumstances were becoming ominous. What made them even more frightening was that this latest bill had, from the start, been presented as a denial of the legitimacy of conversion. One's Jewishness would no longer be determined by religion but by race. This dimension of the bill had been defeated, but not before clerical members of parliament pleaded passionately for the spiritually transformative power of baptism. Gyuri had felt continually encouraged by these efforts, and he reassured himself that nothing would ever deny him his place in Hungarian society. But why then were these damned statements continually reappearing in the official newspaper of his Church, mentioning the need to save the Hungarian *race*? This was May, virtually the eve of the second bill's adoption, and yet the hate-mongering hadn't ceased. In the same breath that people defended the rights of converts, they voiced their bitter hatred of the Jews and their determination to be rid of them. This was getting too close for comfort. It was becoming more and more difficult to dismiss it all as "not me."

Gyuri was now sweating profusely and his indigestion had turned to intense pain. He buried his face in his hands, his elbows propped on his desk. "My dear God," he moaned in a whisper, "what kind of craziness is happening here?"

As these words came from his mouth, Gyuri's head was knocked out of his hands by what felt like a burning sledgehammer to his back, exploding down into his groin. Instinctively he tried to turn to see who his attacker was, but he couldn't. The pain of the blow was too intense. It felt as though it had broken him in two. Having lost his bearings and become delirious, he was knocked to the floor, down onto one knee, his face contorting. He tried to scream but could only let out a leaden grunt. He sank to the floor and lost consciousness.

Gyuri opened his eyes. "What happened?" he asked. He was lying in bed, with four or five concerned faces hovering over him.

"I heard a muffled scream from your room, so I came running over," said the elderly woman from across the yard. "When I came in, you were curled up on the floor, soaked with sweat and passed out."

"My groin and my back, my back hurts so terribly. It felt like someone attacked me with a red-hot metal bar."

"You *were* attacked, dear Father," said a man from the village with a benevolent smile. He had soft hands, more the hands of a doctor than a farmer or laborer. Gyuri recognized him as the area's itinerant physician. "But your attacker was not from outside, rather he came from within. And it was not a club or a rod with which you were beaten. No, honorable Father, you were attacked by stones, most likely stones lodged in your kidneys. And they may not yet have passed. If they have, others may come. We must get help for you immediately."

Gyuri was never a complainer, but he couldn't ignore this episode. He did not hesitate to heed the advice of the physician. He could have gone to the hospital in Debrecen just twenty miles up the road. But instead he decided he wanted to go home. He wasn't thinking clearly, he didn't quite know where or how he would get the best medical care. He simply reacted on the instinct of wanting to be near his mother and father.

The very next morning, Gyuri left Hosszúpályi and boarded a train for Szarvas. The pain came in waves. Knowing what it was helped him steel himself against it. But the train ride itself was excruciating. The bumping of the train along the tracks was nearly unendurable. He tried to cushion the shocks by standing on his tiptoes for most of the trip, struggling to keep from screaming out and have his legs buckle under him.

Gyuri was home in Szarvas for barely a day when the family's doctor readily confirmed the diagnosis. "It's clear you have kidney stones," the doctor said. "The rich foods of your village, and even a simple overabundance of common dairy foods and leafy vegetables, have not agreed with your constitution. You are promptly going to the hospital in Gyula," he told his patient.

In the hospital, Gyuri was given a series of medicinal baths and forced to drink abundant quantities of water. The hospital staff also attempted to readjust his diet, not knowing what stubborn delight he took in eating rich foods and how little willing he was to change for anybody's sake, including his own. He humored the nurses with his manifest obedience, even while he tried to bribe one or two of them to smuggle sinfully rich pastries in to him from a bakery. Naturally, they upbraided him for it.

During the course of his stay, Gyuri managed to pass a number of stones, much to his chagrin, though to his and the staff's ultimate relief, as well. By the end of the second week having missed one Sabbath and many more days of Confession and community ministry, he felt ready to return to Hosszúpályi. He felt relieved to be free of pain, although even touching his upper flank filled him with fear. His attending doctor, however, was not quite so sanguine. He told the young priest that stones can commonly recur, and that Gyuri might consider visiting a spa known for its treatment of kidney ailments, in Fiuggi, not far from Rome. The medicinal waters there would flush out remaining gravel in his urinary tract and reduce the likelihood of a recurrence of painful stones. Gyuri knew of medicinal waters in Budapest that had been discovered in the days of the Roman colony there. He knew they were helpful for orthopedic and arthritic conditions, and had even heard something about the medicinal waters in various parts of Italy. Yet curing kidney stones seemed a bit farfetched. And, as much as he couldn't imagine going through another episode of agony and delirium, Gyuri was not prepared to give up his ministry for an indefinite period of time.

Gyuri's medical condition was stable throughout the summer months. He took to drinking more water, lightened his intake of heavy Hungarian meats and cheeses, and became increasingly optimistic that his health had permanently returned.

By this time, Hitler's forces stood poised to extend their clutches at the borders of Poland, just as they had done the year before in Austria. They were likely to be more ruthless this time. Gyuri worried about what turmoil the winds of autumn would blow into the European plain that his own nation inhabited. But what made him truly nervous was the intensifying pitch of Nazi ideology that increasingly infected the hearts of Christians. Though he had never made any pretenses about his Jewish origins, neither did Gyuri go out of his way to mention his heritage to anyone in Hosszúpályi. He took private consolation in the fact that innumerable priests and ministers throughout the country had similar origins. It was simply the peculiar interpenetration of faith communities that had existed for generations in Hungary. Most likely, no one would have cared. Yet he said nothing. But Gyuri could feel the inexorable sea change coming in the hearts of his Christian brethren toward the Jews. Even the leader of the Hungarian Church had stated publicly that "Jews had sinned much against Christian Hungary," and saw the anti-Jewish legislation as "justifiable self-defense," entitling the state to "limit . . . even . . . the existing rights . . . of its Christian citizens," meaning, of course, converts to Christianity. Gyuri could never discuss this with anyone, but within himself he shuddered. All he could do as a Catholic priest was continue to preach Christ's love for all mankind while not betraying his coreligionists' growing hatred of the Jews. It was causing Gyuri great anguish—all the greater for it being a secret from nearly everyone he had met over the course of the previous four years. His sleep was fitful. He was having nightmares and unnerving daytime reveries of Jews being attacked and baptized Jewish priests being persecuted. He took what solace he could in his ministry, but felt increasingly like an actor on stage being stripped of his persona.

By August, Gyuri was experiencing renewed kidney attacks. His ministry was becoming precarious. At Mass, he was often distracted by pain, and what had become chronic sleeplessness made it difficult for him to concentrate in the confessional. Yet his acute medical condition helped conceal his underlying anxiety about what was happening around him.

Gyuri continued this way for the next few weeks. Then the news broke that the Germans had invaded Poland and a terrible war was about to envelop Central and Eastern Europe. While he may have hated the communists for the unmitigated evil they had already inflicted, he now feared the Nazis even more. And he was more frightened of the Christian voices in Hungary that were lending moral support to the German military cause. He didn't know what to do, but his options were limited. He felt helpless and trapped.

In early October, Gyuri paid a visit to a physician in Debrecen. The doctor's opinion was swift and unequivocal. If his medical situation was not arrested, Gyuri could suffer irreparable kidney damage. The doctor was aware of the short-term help his patient had already received, but he needed renewed treatment. Gyuri then mentioned the recommendation made by his doctors in Gyula that he take a spa cure in Italy. "What do you think of such an idea?" he asked the doctor.

"What better time could there be to consider going," the good doctor said, "than with the violence at the borders of our nation? We could all use such a rest from these troubled times. You'd be a fool not to go."

When Gyuri returned to his village, he shared the doctor's recommendation with his superior, who was concerned and supportive. He was well aware that Gyuri could not fulfill his priestly obligations in his impaired state. So the parish priest promptly contacted the administrator of the diocese to request a medical leave for his chaplain to go to Italy. Gyuri rather expected some bureaucratic haggling over the duration of his absence and the difficulty of leaving his parish for that long a time. Instead, he received a strangely swift—as few things in the church moved swiftly—and positive reply to his request. Within a matter of days, a letter arrived from Father Lindenberger, the same ecclesiastical administrator of the postwar, divided bishopric of Nagyvarod who had nearly ten years earlier nominated Gyuri to the Pázmáneum. The message was brief and to the point: his medical leave was happily granted for a period of eight months, and following that time Gyuri would be welcome to return to Hungary and his duties in Hosszúpályi.

Gyuri was pleased and relieved. But one did not have to read far into the somewhat curt contents of the note, or make outlandish assumptions about its promptness, to wonder just how happy the diocese was to permit him to leave the country. Was this lengthy leave for the sake of protecting a priest with Jewish origins from imminent danger or for the sake of finding an expedient way to relieve him of his priestly duties and expel him from the country? Gyuri did not dare raise the question with anyone. He would simply bear his cross in silence to wherever it would lead him. But there was a gnawing perplexity that would not leave him. Was he being guided to care and safety or was he being exiled?

✤ CHAPTER 9 ✤

Sanctuary

Abide with me, and fear not. . . .
With me you shall be safeguarded.
I Samuel 22:23

Not having had the time or the peace of mind to take leave of his family, Gyuri boarded the all-night Trieste Express at the end of October 1939. As it had for decades, it pulled out of Budapest's South Station at precisely 8:00 P.M. The train had for many years been a favorite of newlyweds who would board its wooden sleeping cars for a honeymoon in Venice. It traveled over the rugged Croatian mountains to Trieste and arrived in Venice eighteen hours later, sometime after two the next afternoon. Given that it was off-season and that the political situation was so precarious, more than half the seats were empty. From Venice, late the next afternoon, Gyuri boarded another train for Rome. He would have to traverse nearly as much distance within Italy as he had just covered from Budapest.

Weary from more than a full day of traveling, and feeling truly like a man banished from his homeland, Gyuri arrived at Rome's Stazione Termini during the late-night hours of the next morning. He promptly took a taxicab to the Ospizio Centopreti, the Hospice of a Hundred Priests, the place at which he had arranged to stay. When he arrived, the stucco facade of the handsome seventeenth-century building hardly gave the appearance of an austere hospice or hospital.

In the morning, after barely a few hours of sleep, Gyuri awoke to discover that there were no sick or bedridden priests confined to hospital rooms, and that this hospice was actually an elegant rooming house for clerics visiting from out of town. Bishops and even cardinals had graced the rococo halls and marble floors of the Baroque revival building, which, at perhaps three centuries of age, was considered in its mere infancy by the standards of the Eternal City.

Though Gyuri had arrived in midautumn, the air was still balmy. There were any number of guests lounging along the gallery beneath the building's Roman arches, through which they could view the Lungotevere, the scenic tree-lined roadway hugging the eastern bank of the Tiber. His initial stay at the Ospizio would be a brief one, just long enough to get his bearings before traveling to a typical Italian *terme*, or health spa, in the town of Fiuggi, about a forty-mile train ride from Rome. There, Gyuri would receive daily drafts of the naturally occurring mineral waters in order to cleanse his system of the kidney stones. A two- to three-week regimen was the usual course of treatment. The remainder of his stay in Italy would be rest and recuperation.

Gyuri was pained at the interruption of his ministry. He was afraid he would become more shepherded than shepherd. But there was nothing he could do about it. For now, he would at least be living and praying among priests. Mass was held each day in the chapel of the rooming house, although there was no shortage of churches in the Holy City. Sant' Andrea della Valle and Sante Maria in Trastevere were each a short walk away. A healthier man could have walked casually to the Vatican in less than an hour, but even that modest pilgrimage would have to wait for Gyuri to regain his vitality.

Although he had felt like a virtual prisoner in Rome, unable to view the breathtaking landmarks of the city, Gyuri found the journey to the country-side a liberating one. Fiuggi was an enchanting hill town named after the medicinal fountains that had reputedly cured the likes of Pope Boniface III and Michelangelo. Between the sixteenth and nineteenth centuries, the older, medieval section of the town was part of the Papal States, during which time its miraculous waters provided an excellent source of revenue. Fiuggi's waters were even bottled and sent to aristocrats throughout Europe as payment for their services to the Vatican. Gyuri stayed in a small rooming house on a charming lane lined with chestnut and linden trees. Wherever he went, he took with him his prayer life and his obedience to a Church that now demanded that he regain his health to conduct his ministry again. Gyuri's fellow houseguests embraced their foreign priest. They were impressed by his ready command of the language, most of which he had learned in seminary, and they loved him for his gentle piety and dry humor. As Gyuri would rise early every morning to attend Mass, some of the guests would accompany their devout "house priest" to one of the two ancient churches in the old town.

Afterward, Gyuri would walk over to the medicinal fountains located in the town's newer quarter. During warmer months, the cure could be taken from drinking fountains scattered throughout the vast wooded grounds. Now, with winter approaching, Gyuri went to the well-heated, imposing central hall of the *terme,* which was named after the pope who had benefited from its waters. In the afternoons he would walk to still a second *terme,* the Fonte Anticolana, where he would again take the cure in the company of fellow sufferers. At times he would saunter in the crisp mountain air among the dormant gardens and the spacious grounds lined with cedars and sequoias. As the three weeks of his water cure passed, so, too, did his abominable affliction.

The return to Rome proved another matter. Even though he was no longer afraid that his illness would recur, Gyuri realized that he could not endure the prospect of being a peripatetic cleric, with no flock and nothing to keep him occupied beyond his own self-indulgent health concerns. He missed his homeland and missed being a priest. After being back in Rome from Fiuggi for only two months, he couldn't imagine spending an additional five months there in such maddening idleness. He knew he had to make a change.

One cold, misty day in January 1940, Gyuri put on his overcoat and was seen crossing the street in front of the Ospizio. He stopped and stood along the waist-high stone wall overlooking the river. There, he gazed out over the silvery green waters of the Tiber, musing about his life and fate. A few minutes later, he was joined by Father Emil Kappler. Don Emilio, as he was called in Rome, was a Swiss priest who had become Gyuri's roommate at the Ospizio upon his return from Fiuggi.

"It's not like you, Don Giorgio"—thus Gyuri had come to be called—"to make such private forays into the cold. The winter wind whipping off the water can go right through you." The two conversed in German and so had an easy connection with each other.

"Oh, I don't know," said Gyuri as he turned and smiled at Emil. "I'm sure you and I are accustomed to harsher winters than this."

"But something must be bothering you for you to come down here by yourself. If I'm not intruding, may I ask what it is?" At that, Emil turned his head toward the river so as to give his friend a little breathing room.

"No, you are not intruding," said Gyuri. "I'm trying to decide how to spend the rest of my time in Italy. I've been sent here for eight months, but even after three I feel somewhat lost."

"I imagine it's not a matter of simply deciding to go home," said Emil, leaning against the river wall.

"That's right. The Germans have picked up the pace of the war, and with the Berlin-Rome Axis in place for four years, it's just a matter of time before Italy enters the war on Germany's coattails."

"So it's a matter of travel being unsafe?"

"I suppose it is. I have thought about returning to my diocese, but I must confess that I'm not anxious to go back to a small hamlet where I was unable to advance in the four years I served there as chaplain."

Gyuri's admission was honest. But it was incomplete. What he had not admitted to his Swiss friend was the hidden problem that had driven him from Hungary—the problem that Gyuri had preferred to keep conveniently submerged under the surface of his acute health concerns. No, he had not admitted to Emil, nor to anyone in Italy for that matter, that as a baptized Jew he was afraid to return to his homeland. Here in Italy, at least, Gyuri told himself, as long as his origins were not public, he was loved and respected as a man of God and a fellow Catholic.

At a time when foreign Jews and converts visiting or settling in Italy had to register their origins with the state, Gyuri passed as a plain and simple Hungarian Roman Catholic priest, sent to Italy by his diocese for medical treatment and recuperation. It was fortunate that he was not questioned about his origins. Anti-Jewish legislation had come into effect in Italy around the same time as in Hungary. And the unpredictable Mussolini was already modeling his fascist-brand anti-Semitism on the German racist model, namely, anyone born of Jewish parents was considered a Jew. The Vatican and many Italian priests, like their Hungarian counterparts, were willing to uphold the sanctity of baptism and defend the rights of converts to be exempted from such legislation. But there were those priests, too, who publicly denounced the Jews. Gyuri didn't need to be reminded of how frightening this was. He concluded that it would do him no good to confide his origins to anyone, including his otherwise trusted friend Emil. So, as he stood alongside him, Gyuri couldn't help but feel benignly subversive about who he was and why he was in Italy.

"What, then, are you considering doing?" asked Emil.

"I've got to find a suitable situation," said Gyuri, "because I can't bear another five months of being a medical patient. I've just enrolled at the Oriental Institute. I've not studied in any depth since leaving the seminary, and oriental religions is a large gap in my knowledge, even if my heart is not fully in it. But it will more than help me pass the time."

"I have an idea that might help you make a decision," said Emil. "Why don't you come with me to a place called San Giovanni Rotondo? It's in the Gargano, in the south of the country, near the Adriatic."

"Why would I want to do that?" asked Gyuri, raising his brows in perplexity. "No, wait," he said, with a look of recognition. "You've mentioned that place before, haven't you?"

"Yes, I have," said Emil.

"There's something about a saintly healer who lives there."

"That's right."

"But look here, my friend," said Gyuri. "Even though I love the Italian people, you've got to admit they're full of superstition. Why would you want me to indulge in something like that?" Gyuri smiled a gently patronizing smile.

"Do you doubt that there are saintly people alive today who are God's holy servants?"

"I've met some good and beautiful religious people, but I can't say I've met any saints." Gyuri hesitated, breathed in deeply, and then softened his tone. "But I know they exist. Our saints bring God's grace to the world."

"Yes, exactly," said Emil. "This man's name is Padre Pio. He's a Capuchin who lives in the friary a short walk from the heart of San Giovanni Rotondo. There's been talk about him in Rome in the last several years, and especially since Pius XII became pope."

Gyuri remembered having seen the tall, gaunt, ascetic-looking Eugenio Cardinal Pacelli stand in front of a pious crowd in Budapest at the Eucharistic Convention of 1938, not two years earlier. When his predecessor, Pius XI, died in February of the next year, while Gyuri was still in Hosszúpályi, Pacelli had quickly been elected pope.

Emil continued. "This man, Padre Pio, works miracles, Don Giorgio. He sees into people's souls during confession and instantly turns sinners back toward the Lord. He has healed hundreds by his prayers and has even appeared in spirit to them during illness or on their deathbed, in different places in Italy and around the world, even though the man has never left his monastery."

Gyuri pressed his eyes shut as if to resist the upwelling in his chest of spiritual certitude that, of course, God's saints walk the earth and quietly do His bidding. He didn't know whether to dismiss his friend's extravagant talk with a gentle swipe of his hand through the now rarefied air, or to give in to his own still tenuous assent to Christian mystery. Gyuri considered himself a discerning and well-educated priest of the twentieth-century church. But his heart was steeped in the redemptive possibilities available through Christ.

"Don't you know," Emil pressed on, "that this man, Padre Pio, carries Christ's stigmata? From the time he was a young man, his hands and feet and side have been impaled with the same wounds our Lord suffered on the cross."

Perhaps in that instant Gyuri turned inward and thought back to the day when, as a six-year-old boy, he stood at the altar of St. Stephen's Basilica before the larger-than-life, awe-inspiring figure suspended on the cross directly above him. Could he have remembered at that moment the uncanny comfort he felt when he sorrowfully studied the pierced hands of that suffering Lord? It was Gyuri's first childhood glimpse of the gift that God had given to the world, the Son who would comfort and redeem everyone by His Passion. Now, as then, Gyuri felt reminded of how deeply he was loved, and knew beyond certainty that God embodied that love in saintly suffering servants. Couldn't this stigmatic Capuchin friar be one of them?

Probably noticing the faraway look in his friend's eyes, Emil leaned over and gently shook Gyuri's forearm, which rested against the river wall. "Why don't you come with me to see him, Gyuri?" Giving him another shake, "Gyuri! Come with me."

Finally Gyuri's gaze returned to Emil. Standing up straight but still resting both hands on the wall, he looked at his friend.

"Maybe he can tell you what your destiny should be," Emil concluded.

Gyuri smiled and didn't hesitate anymore. "Very well," he said softly. "We'll go."

On a cold wintry day at the beginning of February 1940, Gyuri was unconcerned with the weather and the treacherous traveling conditions. His mind was clear. He had no attachment to anything that might happen during his excursion with Emil to visit the saintly monk.

Their pilgrimage would take them to the other side of the country, to what was called the "spur of the boot" of Italy. Traveling by train for nearly the entire day, they arrived in Foggia, the city nearest to San Giovanni Rotondo, in the province of Puglia. They crossed to the other side of the square in front of the train station, then boarded a bus that carried them over rocky dirt roads, twenty-five miles up the Gargano Mountains to the town. They traveled on the road of a low, flat valley, in view of rockier and steeper terrain where there were large stretches of scorched and rock-strewn earth that did not look as though it could provide, even during the height of growing season, anything more than measly stubble for the local herds of goats and sheep. There were brown, barren orchards of fruit trees and olive groves lying fallow for the winter, as well. The naked trees were captivatingly sinuous, each with an almost human personality of its own. They postured in a kind of contorted anguish, as sentinels of sorts on the road to the modern-day Calvary of one of God's reputed suffering servants. Then, as the bus crisscrossed a nearly vertical wall, rising above the pastures and farms below, Gyuri felt uncannily lifted—almost raptured—beyond the earth and its worldly concerns.

"Where we are going," said Emil, "is the region protected by the Archangel Michael."

"Michael?" asked Gyuri, with an odd stirring in his belly that rose to his heart and head. He was born on the angel's name day and had always secretly coveted the name.

"Yes, we will not be far from Mont Sant' Angelo, a community built on a grotto where the archangel is said to have visited a number of different times throughout history. His most recent visit was in the seventeenth century when he came to cure the people of an epidemic. 'Anyone,' he said, 'who uses the stones of this grotto will be cured.'"

Suddenly Gyuri was feeling much better about having made this otherwise imprudent journey. Since childhood he had loved the Archangel Michael; there was now something familiar about the region with which he could identify.

The already cool winter air the two priests had encountered in the more urban area around Foggia became clearer, with a more frigid bite to it. Emil had earlier warned his friend that atop the high plateau, and still further up the mountain on which the Capuchin friary rested, the air would be cooled by icy blasts blowing off the Adriatic, which was only beginning to come into view now that they were on the far side of the mountain road. Leaving the valley behind, they saw wayward shepherds dressed in the manner of their ancestors. Gyuri felt as though he were entering biblical times.

The bus arrived in the main piazza of their destination several minutes later and the two pilgrims disembarked. One carried a small suitcase, the other a black leather duffel bag, each with enough clothing for a few days. From alongside the bus, Gyuri had simply to look up to see the gradually sloping hillside path that led unmistakably to the airy climbs inhabited by the holy servant of God the two priests were coming to see.

Emil took his bearings, leading his companion over a snow-blown cobblestone street, past narrow ways tightly clustered with houses built with crude rocks, white stones, and chalky mortar. The two promptly walked out of the main piazza toward the winding dirt road leading more than a mile up the mountain. They were heading up a steep and rocky hill toward the Our Lady of Grace Friary.

Along the way there were patches of snow-covered evergreens, especially pines and cypresses, as well as a host of deciduous trees bearing less snow on their barren branches. Along the side of the hill, hundreds of yards below, groves of dormant fruit trees were posed, as they had been on the road from Foggia, in their motionless dance of sorrow. Gyuri was by now straining to keep his shoulders shrugged, covering his exposed neck with the collar of his coat against the bone-chilling cold. His teeth were beginning to chatter. The pair hurriedly climbed the steep hillside, hoping to arrive, if not in time for afternoon confession, then for Vespers and Benediction. By now Gyuri had surrendered his earlier skepticism and was eager to encounter the saintly healer, Padre Pio.

The two pilgrims were not alone on their mountain trek. Any number of seekers greeted them along the road. The path to the friary had not always been so well traveled, if only because of restrictions placed by Church authorities on Padre Pio's contact with the public. Ever since he had received the wounds of Christ more than twenty years earlier, while praying in the church's choir loft, authorities were afraid that throngs of hysterical and superstitious followers would detract from the sanctity of the friary. In 1931, when a transfer was being considered for Padre Pio to another friary in the region, the people of San Giovanni, fearful of losing their beloved saint, threatened to riot and tear to pieces the allegedly sinister father guardian who ordered the transfer. The transfer was canceled, but the friary had been damaged by the rioting mob. Padre Pio was confined to the friary by cautious—or, as some believed, hostile—forces within the Church. For a period of about two years, he was prohibited from hearing confessions or performing public Masses. Instead, he said Mass alone, attended by one server, in a small chapel down the hall from his living cell in a building that had once been a prison. During this time of confinement, as during earlier periods, some of Padre Pio's spiritual children would claim that he visited them in bilocation, that is, by his traveling in spirit to distant places. He would reportedly stay long enough to comfort and bless them and then disappear.

Since his release from what was described as his imprisonment, the flocks of faithful pilgrims seeking to attend the padre's Masses and, subsequently, to confess their sins to him, had increased considerably. Then, when Cardinal Pacelli, who was a great supporter of Padre Pio, became pope and encouraged people to visit the stigmatic priest, the crowds began to swell to uncontrollable proportions.

Before all the commotion had enveloped the area, mostly townspeople had come. But word spread quickly through Italy and eventually throughout Europe and America. Even now, with war having broken out on the continent, the crowds were not much tempered.

As people passed Fathers Pogány and Kappler along the mountain path, their faces were aglow and they cordially greeted the two priests, whose clerical collars showed above their overcoats. Though there may have been one man on crutches and a blind woman being led up the hill, these were not only throngs of the hopelessly enfeebled looking for miracles when all else had failed. Certainly, there must have been many of those, too, throughout the years. And they—or their relatives on their behalf—still came, and would continue to come. Padre Pio always cared greatly for people's physical well-being and would not turn them away. But these looked more like people who came to experience Padre Pio's power to touch their souls, not only to mend their bodies. "You'll see. Even Padre Pio's mere presence," Emil told Gyuri, "is, in and of itself, transformative."

By this time, Gyuri needed no additional encouragement. His youthful step, which had until recently been labored by illness, quickened even more as they continued their climb, one behind the other.

When they arrived at the white rectangular building on the rocky plateau, still well short of the mountain summit, Gyuri and Emil entered the front door of the church while it was still daylight. Down a long corridor alongside the tiny but awe-inspiring sanctuary, they found their way to the sacristy, a small, dark room at the rear of the church. They were greeted there by the sacristan, who saw that they were priests but told them nevertheless that Padre Pio was just finishing the afternoon confessions. Emil asked matter-of-factly if he and Gyuri could see the padre. The sacristan answered that, of course, the faithful and devout were always welcome in the sacristy, especially after Mass, but that perhaps Padre Pio would greet them even now. Poking their heads in the doorway, they saw the wooden cabinet of simple lines and modestly decorative curves housing the priests' vestments and sacred vessels. To the other side, immediately to the right of the door, there was an empty confessional.

"Don't worry," whispered Emil. "Women make their confessions there in the mornings. Look over there," he said, pointing through an archway ahead of them. "Padre Pio is around the corner on the other side of the arch, sitting at the kneeler. That is where he hears men's confessions." Gyuri saw a small, middle-aged man not much larger than his own low, stout stature, barely over five feet tall. The man had thinning gray and auburn hair and a beard, and was dressed in a brown Capuchin friar's habit. The habit was distinctive for its capuche, or hood, hanging down below the monk's shoulders. He belonged to a most conservative and devout order of already pious Franciscan brothers who had separated themselves from the parent order in the sixteenth century.

The padre was seated on a wooden chair, leaning forward with his arms resting on the back of a second chair. There was a penitent kneeling in front of him with hands clasped prayerfully to his chest. He spoke little while the padre smiled and made the sign of the cross on his forehead. "Go, my child," Gyuri could hear him say through the partly open door. "There is little for you to repent. Only speak more kindly to your wife. Watch your temper with her and your children. Your wife loves you dearly and is devoted to you more than you know." The man looked surprised as he stood up to leave. He collected himself, bowed his head, moved his lips meekly in thanks, tears still streaming down his face, as he walked away.

The last penitent, who had been waiting patiently at the door when the two priests arrived, approached the padre but barely had the opportunity to enter his presence and kneel before him before the friar angrily pointed to the door and roared at him to leave. "But, Father, I have traveled many hours to make my confession to you, and I have waited in line all day."

"Your confession will not be heard until you stop your evil ways. God is not interested in your empty penance. Change your ways, then come back to me and make your confession. Now, get out!"

The man looked stunned, as if he knew the padre was correct. "Yes, Father," was all he could manage to say, hanging his head in shame as he walked out the door.

Gyuri looked at Emil in amazement, his heart pounding. Was his life, too, going to be an open book to this all-seeing monk? For an instant he wanted to bolt. But he planted his feet and tried all the more to keep his knees from shaking too perceptibly. Gyuri felt that his life was about to change forever.

The two priests were ushered into the dimly lit cavernous room by the sacristan as Padre Pio stood up from the confessional. Emil took the lead and approached the padre confidently. The padre looked up with a tender smile. He then extended his wounded and bloodied hand to Emil. The Swiss priest took it and kissed it. He mustered what breath he could to say, "Father, my Italian is still very poor. But I have brought a special friend to greet you."

Gyuri took a step forward. Padre Pio looked at him with bright, penetrating eyes and a radiant and serene smile. He extended his hand humbly toward his awestruck visitor. Like his friend who preceded him, Gyuri kissed the scourged and bloodied hand of the friar. Suddenly and mysteriously, the blood from his wounds exuded a most astounding odor of roses. The moment took Gyuri deep to the center of his being.

What thoughts could have come to him at that instant, what vivid images? Christ's impaled hands, memories of which had never left Gyuri since he first beheld them as a little boy? The entombed hand of St. Stephen, Hungary's first Christian king, by which the faith in his newly found Savior was offered to the Magyar people? Perhaps the thought of his own mother kissing his hand at his *primicia*? Might Gyuri have had a strange and sudden impulse to look at his own hands to make sure they hadn't been mysteriously penetrated by bleeding wounds?

"Forgive me, Father, for being so tongue-tied," Gyuri said, with tears beginning to fill his eyes. He could barely speak, but tried anyway, in the language he had only begun to master in the preceding few months.

"And what forgiveness could you possibly require? I see only a humble priest who loves God more than himself, and one who has found his way to Christ through his own suffering."

Gyuri feared that his heart would break.

"Why shouldn't you have your own wounds?" Padre Pio continued. "Your life has been pierced by great sorrow. But, I tell you, it has all equipped you for the work of the spirit. You have exchanged your love of life in the world for the love of our Lord and the desire to serve Him."

Could Gyuri have remembered at this moment the piercing pain of the loss of one who was once so dear to him, a death that may have deprived him forever of the wish to live normally among men? Gyuri lowered his head. He thought he might die at that very moment, but he was not troubled by such a possibility. He knew he was in the presence of divine mystery and that he was eternally safe there. "My sin, dear Padre, is always one of pride," he pressed on, "as well as disappointment and anger." His words kept getting caught in his throat. "It's as if I am impatient and do not sufficiently trust the Lord."

"No, hardly," said Padre Pio, with a soothing and thoroughly loving gaze. "I know it can seem that way, but sometimes our anger arises because we love our children too much. We appear to scold them mercilessly, but only in order to turn them toward God's infinite mercy. Indeed, at times, you must watch your pride and your anger. But do not feel remorse for your disappointment and suffering. Like the path to our friary, your journey has zigged and zagged with hardship, up a rocky and barren mountain, to your own Calvary. But this is what has brought you to me today. Is it not?"

"I came to Italy from Hungary to recuperate from a kidney ailment," Gyuri said innocently. His voice still faltered. But he persisted. "I have received a leave from my diocese, but somehow I don't dare return to my homeland. The war has started and I do not know what uncertainties it will bring."

"Yes, the war. It's coming, even to Italy," Padre Pio said, with peculiar matter-of-factness. "But some things are less uncertain for some than others."

Gyuri felt puzzled by the padre's statement.

"I agree with you," continued Padre Pio. "You should not go back to your native land. But what would you do instead?"

"I'm considering living in Rome and have enrolled at a religious institute to study."

"Did you learn Italian in the seminary, and other languages?"

"Somewhat, but much of what Italian I know, I learned in the few months

I've been here. I speak English and French, and some Spanish, and German I've known since even before I spoke Hungarian."

"Look," said the padre. "I'll make no pretense about my feelings for life in our Holy City of Rome. I have always lived in the countryside and cannot bear the thought of doing otherwise. But that is beside the point. Tell me, did you come to Italy to study or to regain your health?"

"I came to regain my health."

"Then why are you going to live and study in a city that could rob you of your health?"

Gyuri shrugged.

"I will make you a proposal," said the padre before Gyuri could open his mouth. "I have need of someone who could help me respond to a mountain of correspondence—from within Italy, from Europe, some from all over the world, in many languages. I send people my prayers and whatever God shows me of matters relating to their lives or their loved ones' well-being. But I am overwhelmed by all the letters. I am not permitted to answer them by myself. Your knowledge of languages could be invaluable to me, and our clean mountain air would be very good for you. Why don't you leave Rome and become my correspondence secretary? You would be safer here, too, to make this your home. Otherwise, I am afraid, your life might be in danger."

How could he know this, thought Gyuri, and what mortal danger could he be referring to? Was the war really coming to Italy? Was persecution? Would he be in danger as a foreigner? As a Jew? Gyuri realized that Padre Pio knew more, much more, than he let on. So he accepted the padre's words and did not ask him what he meant.

"You could live in the village," continued the padre, "and serve people in the community. We also have need of priests in the friary who can hear confessions in other languages than Italian. Bear in mind, I am not asking you to take Capuchin vows. That is not your calling. But as a secular priest, you would serve as a model of probity to those worldly priests below, in the countryside."

"How do you know how much probity I have?"

"Because I know that you didn't come here by accident or as an afternoon's outing." Padre Pio smiled again at Gyuri, then paused. "But neither must your work for me take time away from your devotional life. You could serve Mass for me here at our church."

Gyuri was overcome by what seemed like such a sudden vote of confidence. Listening to the padre's gentle coaxing, he was drawn to conclude that with the uncertainties of the impending war and the ominous events in his own homeland, this might be the most prudent haven for him to continue

God's work in the best way he could. Here he was, in a remote church confessional, before a most loving seer, to whom he was willing, with such strange immediacy, to devote his life. Gyuri had been correct a few minutes earlier. This moment would change his life forever.

In remarkably good Italian, Gyuri responded naturally and confidently, almost as if he had always known this time would arrive. "Yes, Father, of course I will stay."

❖ CHAPTER 10 ❖

Betrayals

Truly I say to you, on this night, before a cock crows,
you will disown me three times.
MATTHEW 26:34

It was a cold, wintry day at the end of January 1943 in the city of Vác, upriver along the Danube between Budapest and Esztergom. The sixty or seventy labor servicemen had been stationed there since the beginning of the year, sweeping streets and digging ditches, essentially being the auxiliary sanitation crew while many of the city's men were in the Honvéd, the Hungarian Army. In spite of their being commissioned by the Hungarian armed forces, the men in the labor battalion did not wear uniforms. Since 1941, when Hungary declared war, they had been deprived of their uniform; instead they were dressed in their street clothes and whatever heavy woolen coats they had brought with them from home. The fact of the matter was that they were meant to be distinguished as much as possible from regular army units. It was felt that Jews being in uniform would have been too demoralizing to Hungarian soldiers, and scandalous to their staunch German allies, not to mention the Swabs, or Hungarians of German descent, many of whom had openly embraced the Nazi cause. Jews and other undesirables—Rumanians, Slovaks, and communists—were deemed untrustworthy to serve in the army, so they were put into work battalions to perform domestic labor throughout the country, while able-bodied, loyal Hungarians fought in the Honvéd. To tell them apart even more easily from full-blooded Hungarian soldiers and civilians, members of these battalions were forced to wear yellow armbands on top of their clothing, that is, the *Jewish* battalions.

But this particular battalion did not wear yellow. Its members wore white cloth bands around the sleeves of their coats. This was simply because they were not Jews, that is, not quite Jews, even while they were considered closer to Jews than to real Christians. The men in this battalion sweeping the streets in the city of Vác at the end of January 1943 were actually baptized Christians—mostly Catholics, some Protestants. But all of them had Jewish backgrounds; they had at least two grandparents who were born Jewish, even if everyone in their families since that time had been devoutly practicing Christians. At the start of the war, Hungary had 800,000 Jews within its recently expanded borders, most of whose able-bodied men were in the labor force, and some 200,000 converts as well, whose men were also conscripted and largely confined to labor rather than military service. Miklós Pogány, devout Catholic, *juris doctoris* and bank employee from Budapest, was among this group of "Christian labor servicemen of Jewish origin."

First thing in the morning, the men were gathered outside their makeshift barracks, an apartment building in town, in which they had been huddled for the night, eight men to a room. Now, on this freezing January morning, they were even more pressed together at the curbside, fighting off the cold, awaiting their work orders from the company commander who hadn't yet arrived.

"I still can't believe this craziness," said one man in a self-effacing undertone to whoever was listening. Miklós, standing with arms folded tightly in front of his chest to keep in his body heat, was standing next to him. Since the group had been together, Miklós had come to know most of the names of these so-called fellow soldiers. This one he knew as Bondi. He was a distinguished though tired-looking man in his late thirties who only weeks before had had a soft complexion and smooth hands. The other men did not know him as a complainer.

"We don't deserve this treatment," he went on. "We've been here more than a month and they treat us like dogs."

"Why shouldn't they? We're Jews, aren't we?" said another, faceless voice, identifiable only by the direction from which his breath was condensing into the freezing air.

"In our fine Christian country," said still another man, "where Christ's love rings forth from every city, town, and hamlet, look what's happened to us."

"It's preposterous," Bondi added. "I barely remember who the Jews were in my family. And what of it? We're respected in society. We have loved this country and we've contributed immensely to it. Look around you, do you see any freeloaders or subversives? Look here," he said as he pointed at a number of men, one after the other: "A lawyer, an artist, an actor, a musician, a banker." Then, pointing in between a number of others to a pathetic-looking, sniffling soul crouched against the apartment building, clutching at his shoulders for warmth, "This man's family," said Bondi, "is responsible for Hungary's criminal code. They're judges and statesmen, all honorable and esteemed people."

"Look," said another, "why must we go over this every single day? Can't you get it through your head? We're Jews. We *used* to be Christians but then the Germans said otherwise, and their obliging Hungarian allies clicked their heels in obedience. This country is fighting a war now and it's on the side of the Germans."

"Hey, give me my gun so I can defend our dear motherland against the Bolshevik devils," said another man, grabbing a push broom from out of the next man's hands, and nestling it in his armpit as if it were a rifle. "At least we might be working today," he went on bitterly, "unless they put us on another of those meaningless marches around the city, with forty pounds on our backs." The whole enterprise would not have been so laughable if the war were not so close to being over. The Hungarian Second Army had just been crushed barely a few weeks earlier and the government had been looking for an excuse to surrender. But then the Hungarian prime minister made the seemingly senseless concession to Hitler to step up the Hungarian Labor Battalions, so that even these remotely Jewish Christians had been inducted.

"Whatever you say, but they're going by Nuremberg now. No more half-breeds or converts, or cutoff dates for conversion—just Christians and Jews. It's as simple as that." The speaker was referring to Germany's Nuremberg Laws, which defined who was Jewish and who was not. With the passage of the third anti-Jewish law in 1941, Hungary had fallen into lockstep with Germany's more rigorous racial policy, which specified that Jews were a race, not a religion.

"So now the Hungarians have to see just how far they can bend over to kiss the feet of the Nazis," said another man in the group.

"Why outdo themselves and stoop so low, when they've already reached their backsides?"

"Don't be so smart. Look how good we have it," said another man named Andras. He was an artist—a caricaturist—who began the ordeal with a better sense of humor. But he knew the reality of their collective plight better than most of the other men and grew impatient with their complaining. "You're fortunate to be sweeping streets and being fed every day. We all know what happened in Kamenetz-Podolsk and Újvidék. Thousands of Jews have already been killed by Hungarians, or expelled from Hungary and butchered by the Germans and Ukrainians. Word spreads. And what about the Jewish labor recruits in the Ukraine? Hungarian soldiers killed them as fast as humanly possible, so they could come home at their earliest convenience. Do you think all this could be kept a secret? And maybe they'd like nothing better than to have their chance with us fine upstanding Christian citizens. But that hasn't happened, and maybe it won't. So just consider yourselves lucky and accept your fate. In comparison, it's a mild one."

"Of course you're right," said Bondi. "But that doesn't mean we have to accept this treachery with gratitude."

"Certainly not," said another, a banker from Budapest. "We're the cream of Hungarian society and we're being spit out like so much rancid *Schlag* on a Viennese pastry that had been left out to spoil. And where are our venerable Christian churches through all this?"

"The leaders of the churches have tried to protect us," Miklós finally said. Until that moment, he had been gazing pensively inward, except to glance at each speaker. He had listened with mounting apprehension to each one of them, until now he could no longer contain himself. "With each new law," he continued, "our priests tried to exempt us. I read about the speeches of Bishop Glattfelder. I knew him when I was in university in Szeged. He was a good man. Sometimes he was my father confessor. He was impassioned on behalf of converts. He once told me that baptism transforms the soul of a person. He wouldn't support the anti-Jewish laws."

"So, wonderful, he protects converts—and not very effectively at that—but hates Jews. And this is someone you look up to?"

"That can't be. He doesn't hate Jews." Miklós was feeling defensive of his former priest. "Hungarians don't hate Jews, certainly Catholic priests don't hate them—at least not the way Germans hate Jews."

"Fine! So, Germans hate Jews because they're not German, and Hungarians hate Jews because they're not Christian. The Germans want to kill us, the Hungarians only want to strip us of our dignity and make us sweep streets. Listen here: my children were baptized and confirmed in the Catholic Church. They're good, believing Catholics. But they're now considered members of the Jewish race. And what the hell do the priests care? Let me ask you something, dear friend," said the banker. "Why do you defend your good bishop? You're a better Christian than he is."

"That's not true."

"Oh, isn't it? Why, then, in the hearts of loving Christians does Christ's love not extend to His own people? We may not consider ourselves Jews anymore, but Hungarians do. And the Jews don't want us back. They detest us and treat us like dirt. Well, now we know how it feels to be despiser *and* despised. Because who among us can claim that we've never felt contempt for the Jews? Hasn't it always been easy for us to see ourselves as better than them? Well, we've been sold out by our own priests and maybe now we're being punished for hating our own flesh and blood."

Miklós stood with naive hope on this frigid cold day, alongside these other fine and good men, waiting in vain for protection and solace from the Church, or from anyone left who cared. Could he continue to deny it anymore? He tried to squelch the tightening disappointment in his chest, but there was still a storm of bewilderment whirling around his head. How could the honored Christian leaders of his beloved Church have surrendered their moral power by throwing the converts to the wolves, and then been so publicly callous toward the Jews? Miklós knew as well as most people did that the church leaders had not raised their voices to protect the Jews from the damning legislation of the past few years. Most of the Christian clerics, almost without exception, publicly supported the laws against the Jews, in spite of the lip service that a few of them paid to using the laws to deflate even more insidious anti-Semitism. These thoughts had certainly occurred to Miklós over the years. Some of his colleagues and friends had already lost their livelihoods, and his Jewish relatives were getting more and more worried by the day.

As the stern commander of the battalion came forward, holding a thermos cup of steaming coffee in his hand for all to see, he barked the orders for the day. Miklós was to remain nearby, sweeping the streets and chopping ice on the sidewalks. As he shuffled dejectedly off with his push broom, he looked around at his fellow outcasts. He thought about how much easier it was for most of them to disavow their Christian convictions and see themselves as nothing more than Jewish pariahs. But Miklós was much more painfully conflicted about it than that.

"Do you remember the bat in Aesop's tale that didn't know if it was a beast or a bird?" he asked the man walking next to him as the group disbanded.

"Yeah?"

"Well, am I a beast or a bird, Christian or Jew?" Then, for whatever reason, Miklós looked at the once soft, now callused palms of his hands, almost as if he needed to remind himself that they were human hands, and that all of this was not a dream. His thoughts shifted to the sharp turns in the road over the previous several years that had led him to this moment of penetrating uncertainty. Then he thought instinctively of Muci.

❖

Barely six months before that bitter cold day in Vác, Miklós, then nearing thirty, and nineteen-year-old Muci had sat together at a sidewalk café in Pest. It was a mild early-autumn day in 1942. Hungary had been at war since the previous summer, allied with Germany against the Soviet and Western powers. There was a tension and stiffness in the air on the streets of Pest, as well as in the gait of Hungarians as they went about their business with nervous, inwardly turned eyes. Any number of foreign tourists were also on the streets, mostly Germans enjoying the sights of the romantic capital of their new bosom allies. A group of German teenagers dressed in Nazi uniforms with swastika armbands had just gotten off a bus and were walking in semi-regimented fashion past the café at which the couple was seated. Waves of these *Wandervogel* had been coming from Germany for several years, trying to stir up interest—especially among the Hungarian Swabs—for the Nazi cause. Their mission had been more than accomplished, as they evoked more looks of friendly recognition and approval among the passersby than Hungarians evoked in one another.

As the months and years passed since Miklós had returned to Budapest in 1935, he had gradually become more and more taken with Muci. He saw her as often as he visited his relatives on Lipthay Street. In the beginning, those visits were really nothing more than to get to know his extended family again. After a while, Muci reacquainted him with the city—in much the same way, perhaps, that Ági had shown Gyuri the innocent joys of Budapest ten years earlier. They frequently went to the movies or on walks around Margit's Island in the Danube, and, on occasion, to the circus. To everyone in the family, it was curious that, just as their mothers had become such close friends from early childhood, Miklós and Muci had also discovered a strong and natural affinity for each other. He had become a familiar fixture at their dinner table and on family outings, and had come to be seen as a protective and avuncular older cousin to Muci. Muci, in turn, had quickly taken to the scholarly father figure who liked reciting romantic Hungarian poetry to her. She was flattered by it. On Sundays, Miklós would go off by himself to attend Mass, and Muci, of course, would stay behind. Their religious differences remained a subtle and unspoken divide between them and they never talked much about it. But as the years passed and Muci grew older, their relationship grew as well. Now, by 1942, despite the age difference, Muci and Miklós were in love. To members of the family it was unmistakable.

Traditional customs in Hungary would ordinarily have demanded that a young couple out in public be chaperoned. But conventions had deteriorated, and no one really bothered Miklós and Muci or even noticed. And besides, since Grandma Bertha had died a few months earlier, and Henrik a few years before that, Miklós had moved into the apartment on Lipthay Street in which Muci lived with her mother and her aunt Rosi. It was all perfectly natural and proper. The family loved him. Miklós, for his part, felt warmly welcomed in the home in which his mother had spent so many contented childhood years with her adored Aunt Bertha and favorite cousin, Elza.

"When can we tell everyone about our feelings for each other?" asked Muci as she sat facing Miklós, intently looking into his eyes.

"What feelings?" Miklós asked with wry playfulness. Muci brought Miklós to life, but he still enjoyed teasing her. It was his way of sidestepping his strong affection for her.

"That you want to be my uncle," Muci answered back. "Don't tease me. You know what I'm talking about."

"We haven't exactly gotten our families' approval," said Miklós.

"What do you mean?" asked Muci.

"Well, I know that your family likes me. After all, our mothers are cousins and we all get on pretty well. So they're not about to tell me what they really think, at least not about us. But I'm sure no one objects to us just because we're distantly related."

"It's not so uncommon."

"You're right, it's not," said Miklós, without a hint of self-consciousness. "My grandparents were both Poppers, but besides that I could tell that Bertha used to wonder if I was too old for you."

Muci gave a smile of recognition. "So, that's not news. It doesn't matter, really. Actually, it does matter, because it suits me just fine. You're more distinguished than boys my age. But what about *your* family?"

"Your mother and my mother are still good friends," said Miklós. "They write to each other. Your mother must have told my mother about us, because I got a letter from her asking me what my intentions were toward you."

"And what did you say?"

"At the time I told her it was too early to tell, and that you and I hadn't talked yet. But she's funny. You're the daughter of her cousin and good friend. They grew up together. And, from what I understand, my mother did not have an easy time convincing my father's family that she was worthy of him."

"What did they think of her?"

"Well, like all middle-class families, they only wanted the best for their son." Miklós was hedging. "He came from a fairly well-to-do family and was educated."

"So, what does that say about *her*? Your mother is a brilliant woman from a wonderful family."

"You know . . ." Miklós hesitated between words. "They . . . saw her . . . as . . . a—"

"As a what?"

"As a . . . poor Jewish girl . . . from a family that couldn't offer much to my father."

Muci clenched her jaw. "So, is that how your mother sees me?"

Miklós didn't respond. He turned aside to gaze at the passersby.

"The answer couldn't be more obvious, could it?" said Muci. "How can she think that about my family? It's her family, too. My grandmother and grandfather were saints and they loved her like their own daughter. How could she think I don't have much to offer you?"

"It's nothing more than a mother wanting the best for her son," Miklós demurred. "Look, we live in a world in which social classes stick together. My mother probably never got over being slighted by my father's family. She was a poor girl with no dowry to speak of. Since then, she has always felt like an outcast, with her only real comfort being her husband, her children, and her faith. She strangely holds you to the same impossible standard."

"So this is also about my not being Catholic, isn't it?" added Muci.

"My mother never said that. She always liked you and respected you."

"Of course. Until I wanted to marry her son."

"Well, like any Catholic mother, or Jewish mother for that matter, naturally she wants to have grandchildren of her own faith. That's understandable, isn't it? Every mother wants her children and grandchildren—"

"Where have you been living?" Muci interrupted. "Not that I would ever want Catholic children, but that's not what we're talking about. We couldn't have Catholic children if the pope baptized them, because we are not Catholic—not me, and not you."

"*You* are not Catholic," Miklós shot back.

"My dear God! You don't understand what's happened here, do you?" Muci reached across the table and grasped one of Miklós's hands with both of hers. "Don't you realize?" she said, forcing a smile. "Don't you remember? You're no longer considered a Christian. It doesn't matter who you pray to, or what kind of holy water was put on your head when you were a little boy. It's a matter of race, the 'Jewish race.' That's what the law says now."

Muci was right. Ever since the passage of the third anti-Jewish law in 1941, which defined Jews by so-called racial standards, Jews and Christians were forbidden from intermarrying and the offspring of previous intermarriages were considered Jewish.

"I don't care what the law says," Miklós said angrily.

"My dear, loving, good Miklós. You're a lot smarter than I am. The only verses of Hungarian poetry I know are the ones I learned from you. 'Though your blood be a thousand times foreign, it is mine.' Your blood is my blood, and my blood is yours."

Miklós felt his eyes welling up. "It *does* matter who you pray to. I'm not saying you're any less than me for praying as a Jew. But I am very content as a Catholic. I feel whole from it. How can I give it up?"

"Then go and be a monk like your brother," Muci snapped back, "in some other country. Because here in Hungary, you can't marry and have a Catholic family." Muci wasn't easily hurt. She sounded more antagonized. But her eyes were also filling up. "Your children would be considered Jewish. Do you see that? That suits me fine, because these crazy laws have made it easier for anyone to be Jewish than Catholic. You can pray any way you want, but your lovely Church won't baptize your children. Not that I would ever allow that. Your so-called holy water will never touch the heads of my children."

Miklós was stunned. He wiped one eye with the heel of his free palm as his elbow rested on the cast-iron table. Then he pulled his other hand back from Muci's grasp.

Muci was now crying. "We shouldn't hurt each other," she said. "This is hard for both of us. For me, if they don't allow intermarriage, and you're not considered a Catholic, then we can get married as Jews. I'm relieved that I don't have to decide to give up Judaism. But for you—"

"Yes, for me, what about me? How do I get accustomed to the fact that they are taking my faith away from me, that I can continue to 'pretend' I'm Catholic, that I can continue to pray to Jesus and go to Mass every week like I always have since I was a child, but if I want to get married and have a family, I'm really a Jew? Do I just discard my faith like a suit of clothes? Is that what they would have me do?"

❖

All this sped through Miklós's mind as he moved his arms and legs obliviously, pushing his broom along the sidewalks of Vác. The faster he moved, the warmer he felt. Not that it did much good, because a harsh, frigid wind was sweeping periodic snow squalls off the frozen river, slapping the exposed faces of the labor servicemen with icy blasts, penetrating even the elegant fur-collared woolen coats of those men who were once haute bourgeoisie. It numbed the bones of each and every man.

It was past midmorning and they had been working for at least three hours. Although the group of laborers was spread throughout the city, bands and pockets of seven to ten men worked together at different sites. The leaders of each of these smaller work units were given enough leeway to call their own breaks, between 10:30 and 11:00. The designated leader of Miklós's group bellowed out to the rest of the men to stop their work and gather together for some rest and water, which they had somehow managed to keep from freezing.

The men stood in the courtyard of a large synagogue. No one seemed to take notice of the building while they huddled for shelter from the sweeping wind. Then Miklós noticed that the back door onto the courtyard was opening. An elderly man walked out. He had a gray beard and wore a tattered hat only partially covering a skullcap, along with a threadbare wool coat and stiff leather gloves. Miklós thought he must have been the sexton, or that peculiar Jewish word he couldn't remember that Muci once used to describe her grandfather's position in his local synagogue in Slovakia. The old Jew was carrying a metal serving tray, on top of which was balanced a large porcelain coffeepot with steam rising out of its spout. The container was surrounded by a supply of china coffee cups. He ploddingly paced over to the men, whose baffled expressions must have looked as frozen to the Jew as their faces and limbs felt to themselves.

"I trust you'll all drink black coffee, gentlemen," the old man said, before any of them could say a word. "I haven't much sugar, and no milk or cream."

The bewildered men looked at each other and were uniformly speechless. One man, Stephen, who had been Miklós's work companion that morning, was the one standing closest to this humble Elijah, bearing the promise of momentary deliverance from the cold. Stephen looked at the Jew, as if to convince himself that the man was not an apparition. He then looked down at the left sleeve of his own coat and pulled at his white armband with the gloved fingers of his opposite hand, calling the old man's attention to it.

Looking up at the sexton, Stephen asked him, "Do you know what this means, old man?" He didn't wait for an answer. "It means we are no longer Jews. Some of us never were. Only our parents or grandparents may have been. We are all Christians. Jews have yellow armbands. We have white ones. You must know that."

The Jew had a gleam in his eye and a subtle smile on his lips. He looked directly at Stephen and then briefly at some of the others, catching Miklós's eye for an instant. "Gentlemen, blood does not turn to water," he said with supreme nonchalance.

The men smiled. Some laughed in disbelief. One of them began filling the cups and passing them around to the other men. Miklós took off his gloves in order to wrap his hands around the cup before putting it to his lips. He gazed at the old man with a feeling of bottomless gratitude for his modest act of kindness. *"This is the chalice of my blood, spilled in order to give remission of your sins,"* Miklós muttered to himself. But he knew this grace was nothing quite so transcendent and godlike. It was just the humble generosity of a simple Jew.

A few days later, when Miklós was back at the barracks following a full day of work, the commander came in. He was a husky, poorly shaven man in his mid-forties—a mechanic in civilian life—who had little trouble relating to the many respected, upper-middle-class men who comprised the work unit.

"Come on out and gather round. All of you boys come in here," he signaled, with a wave of his hand. In a minute there were at least sixty men huddled together around the commander.

"Consider yourselves lucky."

"Of course we do, honored commander, we always have," said one man, in hardly concealed irony. "We could be in the Ukraine shoveling bodies." The man next to him gave him a quick thrust in the ribs with his elbow.

The commander pretended not to hear the obvious reference to rumors from the Eastern Front. "The Russians have held Stalingrad," he continued. "It's a major defeat for us."

The men hardly hung their heads. They had long ago relinquished any loyalty to the government or army that had excluded them from serving their country. They knew that nothing but an Axis defeat could save them from their fate in the labor battalion. Could this be that major blow they had been waiting for? Miklós took a deep breath and held it. He tightened his fists, waiting for what the leader would say next. The commander smiled and paused, almost as if to tease the men. He knew that they would be hanging on his every word. Then, with an irrepressible charge that betrayed a basic decency, he let it out. "That's the bad news. The good news is, you're going home!"

A huge roar went up from the group. On that second day of February 1943, Miklós exhaled, raised his fists to the sky, as air once again filled his lungs, and he let out a shout of indescribable joy and relief.

Grown men, once dignified and accomplished members of Hungarian society, sang and danced arm in arm, swinging one another about. They must have carried on for the better part of an hour. After a time, the commander returned holding a piece of paper in his hand. This time he looked somber. Probably knowing that his voice would not be heard over the commotion, he didn't bother speaking. He went directly over to Miklós and handed him the written message.

Miklós took the folded paper, looked at the commander, and unfolded it. It was a telegram. There was sudden silence among the men near him. Miklós looked at the one-line message and put a hand over his eyes.

"What is it, Miki?" asked a companion.

Taking his hand away from his face, he glanced at the questioner. "My father . . . my father . . . died." As he spoke the words, the man standing next to him flapped his outstretched arms, signaling the rest of the group to be still.

"It's strange that this news comes on the day when you'll all be set free," said the commander. Then he turned to Miklós. "Get home and go to your father's funeral. Maybe this ungodly war will be over soon."

The next morning, Miklós took a train to Budapest where he met up with Muci, who had, several weeks earlier, become his fiancée. Together the two would travel to Szarvas to attend Béla's funeral.

❖

Throughout his fifteen years in Szarvas, Béla had come to be liked and loved by people in the local community. Stories of my grandfather's later years have survived intact, largely because he was so well loved by his children. He was considered a generous man, a devoted civil servant, and a respected veterinarian. He was especially appreciated by those who had migrated from the north and whose native Slovak he spoke fluently. Many of the poor farmers would pay him, if they had no money on hand, with fresh vegetables or eggs. In truth, it was not the language Béla spoke nor the honesty or competence with which he practiced his vocation that earned him his reputation. It was that he was an utterly affable man—one of those individuals to whom one takes an instant liking. He remained what he had been throughout his life, a gentle and friendly man with a ready and gracious smile, but otherwise undemonstrative, especially with his family.

Béla never became a devout Catholic like his wife. He rarely attended church. At the same time, he never tried to hide his Jewish origins. The neighboring farmers knew he was originally Jewish and would hesitate to serve him pork if he happened to be making his rounds at their farms during lunchtime. The Jewish merchants, for their part, were surprised when they learned he was a Catholic. An elderly Jew once stopped him on the street and unabashedly asked him why he had converted to Christianity. "To tell you the truth," he reportedly answered, "my wife converted for eternal peace. For me, it was for a little peace here on earth. Am I ashamed of it? Not much. I know where I come from and I know where I'm going. But for now, how many Jews do you know in the civil service?"

In the last year of his life, Béla had heard rumors of the mistreatment and deportation of Jews in his native region of Hungary, which had been ceded, following the First World War, to Slovakia. Despite his Christian faith and his disaffiliation from Judaism for nearly a quarter of a century, Béla had no illusion about these events. He knew in his bones and from his earliest childhood memories about the fate of Jews, and he never forgot how Jewish servicemen were treated during the war. Béla felt certain that even though his family was now avowedly Catholic—with a priest to show for it—they would still be in great danger if the violence ever came to their region of Hungary. He knew that day would come, and when it did, he and Gabriella— and, God forbid, his children—would be doomed.

Fortunately, Béla did not live long enough for his worst fears to be realized. He had developed diabetes in his later life, which had rounded out his stout frame and weakened his heart. On the first of February 1943, he came down with the flu, which had stricken Gabriella and Klari a few days earlier. That evening he went to bed early, telling his wife and daughter he'd be going to the slaughterhouse early the next morning to inspect the meat. Before nine o'clock that night, Klari discovered him. Béla had died peacefully in his sleep.

Miklós regretted the lost opportunity to say good-bye to his father, taking only small solace from his warm visit with him during the previous Christmas, two months earlier. He sent a telegram to Gyuri in Italy, but didn't realistically expect him to travel halfway over the war-torn continent to come home for their father's funeral. In any event, Gyuri would not have been able to make the journey in sufficient time.

Throughout his own journey home, Miklós was especially nervous about what his mother's and sister's response would be to Muci. It was far from the ideal time to introduce his new fiancée to his family, but he couldn't very well go without her.

Events that day passed in a blur for Miklós and Muci. They arrived in Szarvas on the last day of Béla's three-day wake, during which time his casket had lain in the living room of the family's home. Gabriella was still sick in bed with the flu, not bearing up well under the shock and strain of her husband's sudden death.

Ever since Béla's absence during the war and later abduction by the Rumanians, Gabriella had been plagued by nervous illnesses, especially stomach problems. In more recent years, the pains had become a constant companion to her, isolating her even further from a community in which she never felt fully at home. But even in illness, Gabriella would never abandon her true home, which was the Church. When confined to bed, she would summon Father Fetzer to her bedside to make her regular confession. But it didn't look as though she would be able to attend the funeral, at either the church or the cemetery, or be much able to get out of bed. For that matter, neither would Klari, who was even sicker, with a bad case of pleurisy in addition to the flu.

As Miklós and Muci entered the family home late in the day, the long, sharp shadows of the afternoon had softened. A vaporous light was all that remained, hovering over the living room in which Béla's body rested amidst the constant comings and goings of sympathetic farmers and peasants paying their respects. Klari was there to greet her brother, but seemed barely able to stand. Miklós saw her at the other end of the room. Nearly thirty years old, she was still pretty but had lost her youthfulness. Unmarried, overeducated, and unemployed in an increasingly hostile environment, her illness and grief had been further chiseled into her already careworn face since the last time Miklós had seen her. In comparison to Muci, who had a youthful radiance about her, Klari's eyes were darkened and bloodshot. She looked as though she had been crying a lot. Her labored breathing was punctuated by piercing fits of coughing.

When Klari saw Miklós, she made a straight line toward him and embraced him warmly. She held him for the better part of a minute. Burying her head in the shoulder of his overcoat, she sighed repeatedly as if she were weeping. Perhaps like her mother, Klari did not like any public displays of emotion. When she had collected herself, she stepped back, still holding onto both of Miklós's hands, and forced a smile as she looked into his eyes. Muci was standing beside him and tried quietly to defer to him and his sister. But as the seconds passed in which Klari would not break her gaze from Miklós to look at her, Muci nervously leaned against her fiancé's side and pressed her hand into his waist, reminding him of her presence. "Oh, yes, Klari, Muci is with me now. I'm sure you know of our engagement."

The two women were no strangers to each other. In addition to their first meeting in Báránd as children, they had seen each other in more recent years during a summer visit by Muci and her mother to Szarvas. More recently still, they had met in Budapest when Klari was looking for employment there. There was never any trouble back then. Klari and her mother, as well as everyone in the family, liked Muci and treated her well. The trouble started, just as Muci suspected, only after they learned that Miklós was going to marry her. As Klari turned toward Muci her mouth quivered in a forced smile and she nodded perfunctorily. Miklós felt a chill run down his spine, and he instantly put his arm around Muci, suspecting she must have felt Klari's coldness.

It was no mystery why Klari was responding this way, at least not to Miklós. She was obviously jealous, he realized, and resented Muci for her youth and beauty. At twenty years old, Muci was the age that Klari herself should have become betrothed. But here she was, nearly thirty with no marriage prospects whatsoever. Maybe Klari didn't realize that she was in the same predicament that Miklós was in, that under the current laws she was considered a Jew and would never be able to marry a Catholic. In effect, Muci symbolized the end of the family's Catholic heritage.

"How is mother?" Miklós finally asked.

"She's not well. She's in the bedroom, expecting you. Do go in. She will be overjoyed to see you."

If this room felt as cold as it did, thought Miklós, how much colder would it be in his mother's sickroom? He decided to go in alone first before summoning Muci, who patiently stood back from the doorway.

Gabriella was in bed when Miklós entered. Stepping toward her, he leaned over the high Victorian bed, took his mother's hand, and kissed her. He did not let his shock at seeing how sick and distraught she looked interrupt his movements.

"I'm so sorry, Mama, that I couldn't be here earlier. This has all been such a sudden shock."

"You've been through your own turmoil with the labor camp. It's a miracle it ended when it did. Otherwise you wouldn't be here even now. It must have been a very difficult journey."

"Yes, it was, for both of us," said Miklós, gently reminding his mother that he hadn't traveled alone.

Gabriella sighed and looked away for an instant. "So, where is this fiancée of yours?"

Miklós tried to ignore his mother's tone of voice. But this was not a good start. He swallowed hard. "She's here. I want you to see her."

Muci took that as a signal to enter the room. And as she did, Miklós suddenly and strangely understood everything, all within the instant it took for his future bride to greet his mother. He looked at Muci moving slowly toward him. She was a beautiful but poor Jewish girl whose eyes were perpetually sad for missing the father she never knew. Perhaps she didn't have much to offer to a middle-class family with a well-educated and promising son. That was his family's prevailing sentiment about her.

Then Miklós looked toward his mother, lying in apparent helplessness upon her stately bed. In a transfigured light, he saw before him not a sickly widowed woman but a young and beautiful Jewish girl in a black velvet dress with a tightly bound Victorian lace collar around her neck, unlike any contemporary fashion with which he was familiar. Maybe he once saw a photograph of her like this, or maybe it was an image of his mother that belonged to his family's collective memory, unwittingly shared by everyone. She had a radiant and intelligent face, but eyes that had become sad and distant since her mother had died so young and her father, whom she adored, had gone away for so long to the army. Miklós saw a lonely woman before him, spurned by her intended husband's family for having little in the way of social standing to offer their son.

Miklós now saw Muci through his mother's eyes and realized that Gabriella must have seen herself in the radiant face of her future daughter-in-law. Miklós saw it too: that self, so full of love and promise, that had evaded his mother so long ago.

Little was said—a few formalities and superficial pleasantries. There was no manifest coldness or unkindness. "It was good of you to come all this way, Muci."

"I'm so sorry for your loss, Auntie Gabriella. He was such a good man. We all loved him. I loved him always. I will never forget him."

"Thank you, dear child."

But all else was expressed through nervous, taut smiles and shallow, expressionless sighs. Miklós felt sad for it, and Muci looked especially forlorn. Sometimes, in the very choice of a mate, old wounds are redressed and even healed. But this choice and this meeting was not a healing. It could have been, but it wasn't. A pattern that had started in a previous generation had been transmitted to the next. It would forever leave a scar on Muci and Gabriella's relationship.

The next morning, it was somehow fitting that Béla's casket would be borne to the parish church in a farmer's cart. There was to be a brief service at the church, presided over by the family's minister and longtime friend, Father Fetzer. By the time the family arrived at the church, scores of townspeople and farmers had already crowded into the sanctuary. There were Catholics there that day who had barely seen the inside of the church in years, perhaps not since the time of Gyuri's first Mass as an ordained priest. A large handful of Lutherans and Calvinists were also there, Szarvas being inhabited predominantly by members of the Reformed Church. And even a few of the town's several hundred Jews came to the church out of respect for the animal doctor who seemed to have no enemies among the peacefully coexisting religious communities.

As Béla rested in undisturbed stillness in front of the altar, there was a respectful lull in the sanctuary. Miklós felt genuinely comforted by the presence of his family's supporters and well-wishers, many of whom he knew but hadn't seen in years. In the midst of the hushed crowd, Miklós could also detect murmurings at the back of the sanctuary among some men standing against the wall. Their barely subdued whispers betrayed an edge of anger that made Miklós shiver. But he couldn't make out what they were saying, much less who was saying it, and he tried to ignore them.

At the funeral Mass, Miklós wondered if his father's soul was waiting impatiently for the Latin liturgy to be done with so that he could savor, in transcendent privacy, the minister's homily. He imagined that his father would respond in as down-to-earth a way as he had always lived his life. But if Béla's spirit was impassive, then at least the myriad of those attending his funeral were visibly moved. More than a few farmers and peasants wept openly.

As the mourners and well-wishers accompanied the funeral procession on foot, a bitterly cold winter wind was sweeping off the Körös River just at the western edge of town. The cemetery was located a few hundred yards from the family's home, at the southern border of Szarvas. The ground was still quite frozen, making it easier for them to traverse the seasonally muddy, at times impassable roads. But digging the grave had been next to impossible, so rock-hard was the earth. A team of grave diggers had begun working the morning after Béla died and continued well into the night on the eve of his burial. The plot itself was as close to the front of the graveyard as earlier rows of gravestones would allow. It was a foregone conclusion that Dr. Pogány would receive the most honored burial site possible.

As the crowd huddled together in front of the windswept grave site, awaiting the priest's final benediction and recitation of the Lord's Prayer, Miklós noticed that at the entrance of the cemetery two men were standing on the road ranting and arguing. While one captively listened, shaking his head in seemingly coerced compliance, a second man pierced the frozen air with blasts of outrage. These must be the same men who had caused the commotion earlier at the church, Miklós thought. He still couldn't tell what they were saying. But there was something ominous about them.

Some weeks passed and normal life had resumed. Miklós and Muci had returned to Budapest, and Gabriella and Klari had both regained a semblance of health. Their spirits were still mournful but their grief was not as acute. The shards of frozen soil that had been packed onto Béla's grave had softened as the springtime thaw was drawing near.

It must have been the softening of the ground that compelled the loud onlooker from the day of the funeral to move into action and finally make public his private grievance. He was János Fekete, a local tradesman and Catholic in his fifties who, Miklós learned, had eagerly jumped on the nation's fascist bandwagon, becoming an official of the local chapter of the ultra-right-wing Arrow Cross, the Nyilas Party. Having lost his wife the year before, Fekete had propped up his meager stature among his neighbors by donning the party's green shirt and black tie. The armband and lapel pin carrying the party's insignia—the sign of the crucifix with the head of an arrow at each point—were, like the party itself, a sinister union of Christian passion and fascist fervor. There were certainly a handful of other similarly disposed residents of Szarvas, but it is fair to say that most people feared the Nyilas.

Gabriella and Klari soon got wind that a town meeting was being hurriedly convened on the matter of Béla's burial site. Neither of them would have dared attend, even if they hadn't been so preoccupied with their grief. They knew it was not good. And it was only afterward that a sympathetic neighbor reported back to the mother and daughter on the proceedings.

As the meeting began, their neighbor told them, a constant refrain could be heard above the exasperated sighs of just about everyone in the town's meeting hall: "What does the fanatic want now? Surely he hasn't come to dump his grief for his wife's death on us again. He's not been the same man, and we've all had to suffer for it." Fekete didn't make them wait long for an answer. As people continued streaming into the room, he quickly pounded the side of his fist on the long wooden table on the podium, as if he were a baker pounding a piece of dough before rolling it. He barked orders for people to become silent and then began speaking, even before everyone could hear him above the continuous clamor. He was clearly in a hurry to make his point.

"My friends and neighbors," he began, "it doesn't mater how well regarded the recently deceased animal doctor was." There was suddenly dead silence. "The man does not deserve to be buried in a place of honor in our Catholic cemetery."

"What do you mean? He was as loved as any man in Szarvas," an angry voice called out. "He didn't have an enemy in the world."

"Unlike some people," another voice murmured.

"Why shouldn't he be given a place of honor? He deserves it," said another. Then many more voices rose up in agreement. What did Fekete think he was going to accomplish? But there was no use in pretending. Most people could guess. Many of them knew even before they stepped foot into the hall. They knew what was coming. Their protests were rhetorical and Fekete's intentions were all too transparent. He wasn't there to protest that Dr. Pogány had not attended Sunday Mass enough times to merit a proper Christian burial, nor that the revered animal doctor was dishonest and deceitful in his dealings with the public.

"Look, my honored neighbors of Szarvas and my fellow Christians. Let me make it perfectly clear. Dr. Pogány was not a Christian. It doesn't matter how long ago he had been baptized. He was born a Jew, and, according to the laws of our nation, he was a Jew when he died. He should not be buried in a Catholic cemetery, and certainly not next to the holy grave of my dear and pious wife. Her grave is now defiled." He was now virtually screaming above an angry din. "That dear woman loved the Church," Fekete tried to press on. "We at least owe her our respect for the laws of Hungary by removing this man's body from hallowed ground."

The crowd was aghast, even while a handful of individuals in it remained silent, lowering their eyes and trying to mask their certain satisfaction at what they were hearing. Many others screamed out their protests, one more audibly than the next in the outraged commotion: "He was a good man." "He was a saint." "He lived a Christian life and deserves our respect."

Finally, one man's voice rose up above the others. "What are you proposing? We will *not* dig up the man's grave and take his body to the Jewish cemetery."

The emboldened Fekete was momentarily deflated. He couldn't have expected such defiance. He had clearly underestimated the esteem in which this Jew was held. As he stood self-protectively behind the table on the podium, above everyone else, the fascist official looked as though he were mentally revising his proposal. "No, I'm not suggesting anything like that," he said after several seconds of silence. "I'm not saying he should be moved to the Jewish cemetery. But I want his body far enough away from my wife's grave. I don't care what you do with it. Move it to the back of the cemetery if you want, but obey the laws of our country."

"What about God's laws?" someone screamed out.

"Hungary's law *is* God's law," Fekete answered. "We are a Christian nation with Christian laws. There is no room for the Jews—not on our sacred soil, and not within it. Do you honestly think there is salvation for a Catholic buried next to a Jew? I beg you, my friends and neighbors, do not let this happen. Think of my wife's eternal rest, and, eventually, of your own. Which of you would prefer to be buried on the other side of him?"

The family's neighbor paused, holding back tears. Sitting in the room where, only weeks before, Béla's body had lain in silent repose, this elderly man, with hat in hand, head hung in shame, finished his morbid story. "It was a foregone conclusion. There was no vote to be taken. Fekete pushed to have his way with the people of Szarvas. Had he not spoken up, who knows, the kind doctor's grave would be left undisturbed forever. God knows, no one wanted this. But Fekete insisted that the law is the law. Forgive me. I'm sorry to be the one to tell you this, but better me than the police." Looking directly at Klari, the man concluded, "May the soul of your dear father rest in peace."

Events unfolded as Fekete had insisted. That very same day, Béla's body was disinterred. The casket was moved only ten or fifteen yards further to the rear of the cemetery, sufficiently away from Mrs. Fekete's year-old grave. The dead woman's husband was appeased, even while many people openly grumbled that they had never known him to be such a dutiful husband while his wife was alive. The townspeople felt defeated, although some few may have taken disguised satisfaction. It turned out that the reason Fekete had proceeded with such dispatch was that Father Fetzer was away from town that day. Fekete knew that the parish priest would have vehemently protested, although he might have been unable to change the outcome; Fekete had the law on his side.

Gabriella and Klari's sorrow was bottomless. Klari promptly wrote to Miklós. He was outraged. What insidious turn, he asked, had this place taken? A nation of Christians enslaving their Jewish brethren, many of them not even knowing of their Jewish origins. And a town that digs up the grave of a well-loved civil servant, a gentle man who served his country in war and a kind animal doctor who would sooner accept a head of cabbage for nursing a sick sheepdog than demand payment from the impoverished owner. Were *these*, Miklós wondered, Christ's mystical mercies conferred on those who accepted the mantle of His cross? Dear God, has justice died on the cross with You? Where is Your mercy and Your love? Your children mock You with their cruelty. Where is Your righteous wrath?

✤

Mass had just finished in the church of Our Lady of Grace Friary. Padre Pio and Don Giorgio Pogány, who had assisted him that day, were removing their vestments in the unheated, dark sacristy. It probably felt colder within those dank stucco walls than even outside in the sweeping wind of an early March morning in the mountain air of the Gargano.

"Why are you in such a hurry today, dear Don Giorgio?" said the gentle Padre Pio to his devoted spiritual child. "You are agitated, aren't you?"

"Yes, Padre," said Gyuri with his usual reverence. "I am distressed and must leave for Hungary right away. Something terrible has happened."

Padre Pio raised a brow. "Is this how you would leave, without telling any of us? What terrible thing could possibly have happened to take you from here in such a hurry?"

"Forgive me, Father. I am beside myself, and I haven't entirely thought this through. I just received another letter from my brother regarding my father. A few weeks ago, he wrote to me that my father had died and was buried in our town's Catholic cemetery."

"Of course, I remember. Let us be thankful he received a Christian burial," said Padre Pio. "Why, then, must you return?"

"Because a Nazi scoundrel in our town resented that a former Jew was being buried in a place of honor next to his wife's grave. He had my father's body dug up." Gyuri's voice cracked and he choked back tears. "They desecrated his grave," he continued tearfully, "and moved him to the back of the cemetery."

Padre Pio's face, which was always so radiant following Mass, turned sad. "What can be done about this now?" he asked Gyuri.

"I don't know. My brother wrote to the cardinal in Budapest but has received no satisfactory response. I cannot be away while this is happening. I feel that I have abandoned my family."

"I understand," said Padre Pio. He closed his eyes for an instant. "But I am sorry to say that there is nothing you can do to correct the situation. And, besides, your father's soul is undisturbed by the circumstances of his burial. He has moved beyond that."

"I see," said Gyuri. "Your words are a great comfort. But how can I be away from my family while these terrible things are happening?"

"True enough," said Padre Pio. "This hateful war is separating families and inflicting great suffering on the world. But you must believe me, as I have told you once before: If you leave here for Hungary, it may be impossible for you to return to Italy. You remember how last year they almost sent you back. If you do not stay in San Giovanni now, your life will be in danger. It will do your father no practical good for you to imperil your life on his behalf or even your family's."

As he stood facing Padre Pio, Don Giorgio sighed deeply. His stiffened body softened as he buried his face in his hands and wept. Padre Pio embraced his spiritual child and friend, and comforted him.

❖ CHAPTER 11 ❖

Path of Sorrow

Fiam, fiam, ennek nem lesz jó vége!
(My son, my son, this will not end well!)
Hungarian Saying

When Gyuri's eight-month leave of absence from his home diocese in Hungary expired in June 1940, Italy had just declared war on the Allies. Even though his health was no longer an issue, travel out of Italy would have been difficult and dangerous. The hospitality of Padre Pio and the community in San Giovanni Rotondo had been open-ended, almost as if Padre Pio knew that it needed to be, and Gyuri had grown to love living there and serving him. From the time he arrived there, Gyuri could not have felt safer, or more accepted by the Capuchin fathers and the gracious and loving lay community in the town. He applied to his home diocese for an extended leave of absence. Again, to his surprised satisfaction, it was granted promptly and without question.

In the course of nearly his first two years in San Giovanni, among the tall cypresses and fragrant rosemary bushes of the Gargano Mountains, it was difficult to appreciate that much of the continent was being torn by war. The major hardship Gyuri and others felt was the increasing pressure from the government to become members of the Fascist Party. Eventually, people could barely get sugar or bread or other provisions without a party membership card. Padre Pio and many of the other friars and local inhabitants deeply resented it and, at least privately, held Mussolini responsible for the increasingly deplorable state of affairs.

Police presence throughout Italy, including the south, was widespread. The day after Mussolini declared war, Italian police began to arrest foreign Jews, at first all men between the ages of eighteen and sixty. They were held for weeks in Italian prisons before being transported to domestic internment camps. At the time, the Fascists were not so much interested in persecuting Jews as they were in identifying foreign, anti-Axis refugees.

Even in San Giovanni Rotondo, the carabinieri enforced the laws of the Fascist state. It was also their function there, as elsewhere, to make sure that illegal foreigners and Jews did not infiltrate the local population. Foreigners were investigated and incarcerated. Even a well-to-do American woman emigré, a pious convert to Catholicism who was devoted to Padre Pio, was sent away for "wartime service." She would have been confined to an Italian internment camp had Padre Pio not intervened on her behalf and helped arrange for her service to be fulfilled in his home village of Pietrelcina. In all likelihood, though, there was only one Jew, precisely one Hungarian converted Catholic priest, who would have come under the purview of the carabinieri in San Giovanni Rotondo. They didn't initially suspect Gyuri as a Jew, although by Italy's racial laws he was one. He simply had not registered as a Jew when he entered the country. Nevertheless, because he was a registered foreign national, it was inevitable that he would be summoned to the carabinieri office for questioning. In the summer of 1942, that day arrived.

Gyuri set out down the friary hill into town to present himself at the musty, run-down state police office on the main street. It was a typically hot day and he was sweating profusely by the time he arrived half an hour later. He was met by a mustached carabiniere who wore the black uniform with white and red epaulets of the Italian state police. The man's appearance would have raised Gyuri's anxiety but for the respectful and lackadaisical manner with which the policeman greeted him. The two were seated in a back office where a ceiling fan moved the damp, hot air around in sweltering breezes.

"Tell me, Father, what are your reasons for being in Italy?" the officer asked, in a friendly and perfunctory manner.

Having had two years to master the language, Gyuri answered in a fluent and confident voice. "I was originally sent to Italy by my diocese in Hungary to regain my health from a kidney ailment."

"You're not in any way opposed, then, to our Fascist government? You're not a communist or liberal, are you?" The man's question wasn't strident, only poorly timed and a little heavy-handed, clearly something he was required to ask.

"No," said Gyuri, as he smiled disarmingly. "My kidney stones have brought me here, not my political scruples. I am a religious man, as you can see. My political convictions are simply that I am obedient to the Catholic Church. Back home in Hungary, I was a chaplain in a tiny rural hamlet in the eastern part of the country."

"My records show that you've been here for more than two years?"

"I arrived on the second of February, 1940, almost two and a half years ago now."

"I trust you've regained your health in that time?" The officer was relaxed, not at all preemptory or trying to catch the priest in a deception. But he appeared a little pleased with himself that he had asked a more incisive question this time.

"Yes, I was treated in Fiuggi and lived in Rome for a while," said Gyuri, without skipping a beat, feeling a bit more clever than his interrogator. "Then, one day, just as I had enrolled in studies in Rome, a friend of mine convinced me to visit Padre Pio. I came, and the kind padre suggested I stay here because the mountain air would be good for my health. And I just felt that this was the right place for me to be. I wrote to my diocese back home and they granted me permission to stay as long as I needed to. I would have gone home before now, but I must say I'm very happy living here."

"You're not a monk, though, are you? You don't live at the friary."

"No, I'm a secular priest. I rent a room in town."

"How do you occupy your days, then?"

"I say Mass every day in the friary church and I try to help the Capuchin fathers in whatever ways I can. After Mass, every morning, I offer confession to foreign pilgrims who do not speak Italian and I bring Communion to sick people in their homes—every single morning." Gyuri raised a finger to emphasize his commitment to the community. "Then, in the afternoon and evening, I help with the foreign correspondence since I speak a number of languages. You must know that Padre Pio receives letters from all over the world, asking for his prayers and blessings."

"It all sounds entirely convincing," said the officer.

"It is easy to sound convincing when there is nothing to hide," said Gyuri.

"So, Don Giorgio, you're from Hungary and have been here for more than two years." Now Gyuri was getting impatient. "And before you came, you were also a priest." Gyuri tried to disguise his mounting irritation. "Then you're obviously a Christian and an Aryan, too, aren't you?"

It was almost as if the carabiniere were leading Gyuri toward confirmation of what he needed to find out and what he fully expected to hear. He seemed almost embarrassed to be asking the question.

But Gyuri was taken off guard. How much did they need to continue with this exercise in the obvious? Certainly, there was no documentation of Gyuri's Jewish origins. How could such a bumbling officer have stumbled upon such a fatefully important question?

Sitting in the stuffy police office on this hot summer morning, just before Italians typically liked to break off their serious business for an equally serious lunch and afternoon respite, Gyuri took a deep breath and composed himself. He had learned from Padre Pio that the sin of lying could be damaging to one's soul, even for the sake of saving one's life. One must always speak the truth, and leave events to the will of God.

"Me?" he said, shrugging his shoulders and innocently raising his palms toward the ceiling. "It's like I told you before. I'm Hungarian," allowing his inquisitor to draw his own conclusions about just how Aryan Hungarians were. Gyuri smiled, and actually laughed, as if to poke fun at such a self-evident question. After so many years as an avowed Catholic, and feeling so at home with his Italian hosts, Gyuri's response was nonchalant, shrewd, and . . . not dishonest.

"Very well, I thought so, Father, but I had to ask," replied the carabiniere with an apparent sigh of relief. Yet he persisted to play out his role. "But something leads me to believe that it may be difficult to extend your stay in Italy for much longer."

This was becoming serious. "What do you mean?" asked Gyuri.

"Well, it's simply that there doesn't seem to be any good reason to extend it. You've regained your health, which was the stated purpose of your visit. So now I'll need to have some good reason for you to continue living here."

"The main reason is that I have devoted myself to assisting Padre Pio. As I said, I speak many languages besides Italian, and correspondence comes from all over the world—even now during the war."

"Yes, I must say," added the carabiniere, "even your Pugliese dialect is truly eloquent. And this after only two years. You must have a flair for languages. It would certainly be difficult to find someone with your gifts who could be helpful to our local saint. I'm not much of a believer myself in Padre Pio. But I can't think of a more wholesome and holy life than in the service of the man who carries the wounds of Christ."

"Thank you," said Gyuri. "It is indeed a holy life living in his presence. I only hope that what I do begins to repay Padre Pio and the friars for the kindness and love they have shown me."

"You are certainly a man of God, I can tell that, Don Giorgio. I must admit, though, I am a little at a loss as to why you would want to cast your fate with such an irreligious and superstitious lot as us Italians."

"On the contrary," Gyuri answered. "You are a warm and down-to-earth people who don't make a great display of your piety. But, especially here in the southern countryside, I have never met such a blessed people who so love the saints and the Holy Trinity. If I have to be away from home, there is not another people with whom I would rather live. Besides, our nations have been allies for more than a year now." Gyuri was feeling considerably more deferential to even this bumbling official who, nonetheless, had enough power to dramatically affect his life.

"Let me assure you, Don Giorgio, we are not intent on being hardheaded about this, especially sending such an earnest priest through war-torn Europe. Let us see what we can do on your behalf. Believe me, between you and me, we are just stumbling through state policy here. Please try not to worry, Padre."

Gyuri had certainly impressed the police official with his religious piety, and he may have successfully evaded the more fateful issue of his ethnic, so-called racial origins. But the prospect of having to leave San Giovanni Rotondo for the certain dangers that awaited him in Hungary—never mind the journey getting there—kept him unnerved for weeks. He confided his fears to Padre Pio, who prudently advised him not to worry. Finally, Gyuri was notified that his visa would be extended and that his service in that part of southern Italy would continue to be graciously accepted.

✦

Miklós's elation at the dismemberment of his labor battalion in February 1943 was short-lived. The defeat at Stalingrad had provided only temporary respite. It may have signaled the eventual defeat of the Axis, but Germany was willing to fight to the bitter end. And Hungary, despite its own mounting chagrin over its crazed Axis ally, had to recognize this, even while the most Germanophile officials in the Hungarian government had not in the least relinquished their enthusiasm for the Nazi cause. They quickly moved to reconstitute the labor units that had earlier been dismissed. Miklós was recalled in May 1943, after barely three months of liberty, during which he lived with his relatives in Buda and worked at his former position at the Hungarian Commercial Bank of Pest. He was promptly sent from Budapest to Szentkirályszabadja, a town adjacent to the city of Veszprém, near Lake Balaton, a vast freshwater resort in the western part of Hungary—in more peaceful times a favorite summer vacation site for people from all over the country and region. Here there were hundreds, perhaps thousands of Jewish and Christian labor servicemen. The area served as a way station for assignment and transport to other work locations.

At the end of July 1943, one Jewish man in the work camp was wearing his yellow armband over an elegant fur-collared cashmere coat. In the heat of the summer, it must have appeared a bit comical. Standing within sight of Miklós's group of Christian laborers, the Jew must have just returned from a brief furlough to gather necessary belongings after undoubtedly being informed that he would be heading for a possibly "long and indefinite" trip, with hundreds of other Jews. "Where are you going, dressed so elegantly?" called out one of the Christian battalionists.

"It's not to dine with the emperor, I assure you," the antagonized man snapped back. "Where else would I be going but Bor?" Bor was a notorious copper mine in Serbia, already known among the Hungarians for its brutal treatment of its so-called requisitioned labor force.

"Isn't it a pity that you have to wear such a marvelous overcoat to Bor?" the Christian said in a sarcastic tone.

"The pity is mine, gentlemen," the Jew dejectedly responded. "How many men do you know who have returned from that hellhole? And how do you know that you will not be next? If you think that your religious persuasion will save you, you may be dead wrong." The Jew must have touched a nerve. His questioner fell silent. Miklós saw him grimace and turn away.

From the time of their arrival at the camp, work for Miklós's labor battalion began in earnest. No more idling, or sweeping, or senseless marching. Most of their days were now spent digging up and hauling rocks in wheelbarrows in order to smooth and pave a runway for an airfield. The work was backbreaking and torturous, especially in the summer heat.

Even while some of the Christian units had also been dispatched to Bor, life as a so-called Christian-of-Jewish-origin was still better than it was for Jews, if only because of the religious indulgences granted the would-be Christians. On Sundays, the Catholics were able to attend Mass at a haunting nine-hundred-year-old village church with massive foot-thick walls. Besides offering spiritual comfort and respite from the laborers' drudgery, the church was probably the coolest place to be. To Miklós, though, it only intensified the schism in his soul between being a detestable Jew who deserved only to toil in the summer heat and a man whose singular claim to dignity was the Christian god to whom he was permitted to pray. But this rock-solid country parish, which had given solace to ten centuries of Hungarian Catholics, could offer little in the way of lasting comfort to the sweltering masses of Jewish slave laborers huddled in its shadow outside its creaking and cracked oak doors. And politically, Miklós had become a Jew again. He knew, as his father had known, his fate would inextricably be bound up with that of all other Jews.

"Beast or bird?" Miklós asked himself again as he entered the church one Sunday for Mass. "Do I belong inside or outside?" he mumbled to himself, uncertain if anyone heard him or was listening.

"*Salus extra ecclesiam non est*," said one of his cohorts standing next to him, apparently in answer to Miklós's garbled question. Miklós instantly understood the Latin dictum from his school days. No, there is no salvation outside the church. The truth of the phrase should have long ago sunk into his head. It now sank, instead, into his chest and weighed upon his heart with unbear-

Taken in 1916, this photo shows György (Gyuri, left) and Miklós (right), three and a half years old, flanking Klara (Klari), one and a half years old.

Tölgyfa (Oak) Street, Budapest, where the Pogány family lived from 1913 to 1919.

The Church of the Franciscan Fathers in Budapest, where Gabriella, Miklós, Gyuri, and Klari were baptised on April 1, 1919.

A characteristic house in Báránd, where the family lived from 1919 to 1927.

Elza and Margit in 1923.

The Pogány family in 1932. Standing, left to right: Gyuri, Klari, Miklós; seated: Gabriella, Béla.

Taken on July 21, 1935, when Father György conducts his first Mass as an ordained priest in Szarvas. Gyuri (at center), Miklós (first row, far right), Klara (first row, third from left), and parents Béla and Gabriella (second row, far left).

The Catholic church in Szarvas, where Gabriella came to Mass before being deported in June 1944.

The grave sites of Béla Pogány (1883–1943) and Gabriella Pogány (1885–1944).

Miklós and Muci across the Danube from Parliament in Budapest, 1937.

The old sacristy of Our Lady of Grace Friary, where Father György first met Padre Pio in February 1940.

Padre Pio celebrates Good Friday. Father György is at right.

The Hungarian Commercial Bank of Pest, where Miklós worked from 1935 to 1944 and 1945 to 1947.

Miklós and Margit renewing their vows in 1979.

Gyuri and Miklós in
May 1980.

Miklós in front of the
Pogány family's former home
in Szarvas in 1996.

able sorrow and remorse. There may have been moments in his life when he believed the age-old maxim, but as he continued to think about it and repeat the phrase over and over to himself, Miklós's sorrow turned to desperation and outrage. He remembered the day when, as a child in the coolly refreshing basilica, he had felt that Christ's compassion quickly turned to indifference once he was outside in the sweltering church square. Following a vacuous Mass and empty Eucharist this unbearably hot day in the summer of 1943, he couldn't help being reminded of that childhood disappointment.

✤

One day in the late spring of 1943, Don Giorgio entered the Abresch family's summer quarters to teach their twelve-year-old son, Pio, his Greek lesson. The family had been vacationing in San Giovanni Rotondo for a number of years from their home in Bologna. Federico Abresch, formerly a halfhearted Protestant convert to Catholicism who was brought back to God by Padre Pio, considered San Giovanni his family's spiritual home. Over the past few years, they had made Gyuri's acquaintance and developed a warm and cordial friendship with him.

Pio was a serious student and Don Giorgio was an equally sincere teacher, even though, at times, they both rushed through their Greek lesson so that they could play a much-loved game of chess. Gyuri loved Pio and his family, and wondered if the boy, too, would someday find his calling in the priesthood.

When Gyuri came in, Pio was sitting at his desk reading the local newspaper. Actually, he was gazing admiringly at a large photograph of Benito Mussolini plastered on the front page. By this time, many Italians had become increasingly sick of the "Fascist war" and were no longer willing to have their sons die for the German Reich, if ever they had been. But some, like young Pio, naively held out hope that Italy would yet win the war. As Don Giorgio approached the boy and realized how admiringly he gazed at the image of the bombastic Duce, he grabbed the newspaper out of Pio's hand and, without a word, tore up the picture.

"Why did you do that, Don Giorgio?" asked the startled boy. "He's the leader of our country. What do you have against him?"

Gyuri hesitated. "Lets get to our lesson."

"But why? Why did you do that?"

"He's a bad and hateful man," said Gyuri. "He has ruined Italy. This is what Padre Pio himself has said."

"What did he say?" asked Pio.

"I have heard from the fathers that Mussolini sent a delegation to ask advice of Padre Pio. He told them that Mussolini has ruined the country and that nothing can save it now. I mentioned to Padre Pio that many people still think we can win the war. Do you know what he said?" Before Pio could speak, Gyuri answered, "He said that those people should be shot. And what would a victory gain? We would come under Nazi slavery, which is the worst, most diabolical evil the world has ever known." Don Giorgio held off from further haranguing the impressionable boy. The moment passed, but not without the seed of confusion being set in Pio's mind about what made his tutor so anxious and irritable.

By July, Mussolini was overthrown and internally exiled. His successor, Marshal Pietro Badoglio, arranged a secret armistice with the Allies, a move that signaled the beginning of the battle for Italy on its own soil. The Allies had landed in the south, and began their bloody push northward to displace the entrenched German troops. Travel within the country became exceedingly dangerous. The Abresches decided to remain indefinitely in San Giovanni Rotondo, and Federico opened a photography shop in the town that would become his family's new home.

One morning before the end of the summer, Gyuri moved with especial haste after Mass. He replaced his vestments in the sacristy, ran out the church door and down the hillside path to town. Ostensibly, he was off to see a sick woman who was near death and needed to have the last rites administered. She had told Don Giorgio good-naturedly a day earlier that she wouldn't make any sudden moves before he came to pray over her. Nevertheless, he hurried. But neither did he need much coaxing that day. Shortly before Mass ended, Gyuri had looked across the sanctuary and seen two uniformed German soldiers in a back pew.

Gyuri's worries were not without basis. One of the major aims of the occupying German army was to liquidate Italy's even modestly sized Jewish population. The Italians under Mussolini had taken on the mantle of Nazi anti-Semitism so as not to break ranks with their military allies. But even though many Jews throughout the country were transferred to detention camps inside Italy, not a single one of them had been deported before the German occupation in the fall of 1943. Many Italian soldiers and government officials actively stifled the designs of the Nazis to carry out the Final Solution. But now, the newspapers and radio stations became filled with anti-Semitic propaganda and the Italians realized that this was not just lip service. Although the vast majority of Italians had never considered the Jews a problem, the Germans were now in control. Gyuri was not blind or deaf to the looming realities.

The soldiers came back to the friary church a second time on Sunday. Some of the friars had learned that the mother of one of them had written and implored him to visit the famous padre in the hills, the one with the wounds of Christ. Very few German soldiers aside from these two had gone out of their way to visit the saintly miracle worker, even after German troops swarmed nearby Foggia before they were dislodged by massive Allied bombing in September 1943.

Later that afternoon, Gyuri entered the house in which he rented a room. "You look tired and nervous today, Don Giorgio," asked Maria Basilio, the gentle and holy woman who owned the house. "Your mind is elsewhere." Maria was a wealthy and generous woman from Turin who owned a parcel of land next to the friary.

"Aren't we all nervous and tired out from this dreadful war?" answered the priest.

"Of course we are, dear Father. But why do you look so especially glum today?"

Gyuri turned aside for an instant, debating with himself whether to divulge what he had long kept anxiously to himself. Perhaps it had become more habit than well-founded fear, for he had nothing but faith in and love for the good people who had filled his life for the previous three years. How could he go on not trusting them? He looked back at Maria. "There are Germans swarming over the region," he finally said. "Two of them came to Mass today. I know I have never been casual about this, but I am not ashamed to tell you that I was born a Jew in Hungary and baptized as a young boy."

"And why should you be ashamed of that? You are baptized now. You are a Catholic. Your roots and my roots are in our Father Abraham. Are we Catholics to be ashamed of that?"

"Of course not," answered Gyuri. "But with so many German fanatics in Italy, I fear there may be danger."

"Of what? How would they know anything about you?"

"Of betrayal. A few people here know my past, and my blood. I can be betrayed anonymously, and even profitably, because I have heard that the Germans are willing to pay people to denounce Jews."

"It wouldn't be the first time that a Jew has been betrayed for a few pieces of silver, would it?" said Maria, with a wry smile. "Do you think that people here care about making money by shamelessly denouncing others? What good would it do any person in this town and region to betray the safety of such an earnest and pious priest as you? Your selfless presence here has been God's gift to us. Anyone who has met you knows that. You have no enemies here. And no one I know is selfish enough to put greed ahead of your well-being."

"Thank you," said Gyuri, his eyes softening. "Of course it doesn't make rational sense. I know that some of the fathers and even perhaps some townspeople know my origins, and I know they would never dream of bringing danger to my door."

"That is absolutely true. There are probably many who could disown you. But no one, believe me, no one ever will. Maybe the Germans or people in the cities care about a person's origins. But you haven't lived here long enough to know that we don't, not here in the south, especially not in San Giovanni. Your devotion to the Lord is all that matters. You will always have a home here. Ask anyone who knows you, and I haven't a doubt in the world that they would say anything different."

"My dear Maria, I feel more accepted here than I did in Hungary. It is a blessing to live among a people who are so mindful of the blood of this one imperiled Jew."

"And aren't we all, Don Giorgio, always mindful of the blood of that other imperiled Jew?"

✢

March 19, 1944, is a day the Hungarian people will never forget. It began innocently enough, at least for the majority of the population who knew nothing of the behind-the-scenes machinations that had been going on among the higher ministerial levels of the Hungarian-German alliance for days, weeks, indeed even months. History would later note that after Italy's defection from the Axis in July 1943, the Hungarian prime minister was desperately trying to extricate Hungary from the futile war. The Germans had been equally preoccupied with preventing the country from signing a separate peace and with pressing the Hungarians to take part wholeheartedly in the elimination of its Jewish population. The aristocratic, conservative Hungarian prime minister, Miklós Kállay, while known as a "peacetime anti-Semite" who would have tabled the so-called Jewish problem for after the war, nevertheless managed for the two years of his tenure to strenuously resist Nazi efforts to deport the Jews of Hungary. But the fires of fascist hatred inside the country, fanned by the winds of a fanatically anti-Semitic press, could not be contained much longer. Ultimately, a Nazi plan to occupy Hungary, formulated in September 1943, along with Kállay's failure to respond to the Germanic elements in his own cabinet and government, led to the events of March 19. To the Nazi vultures at the gates and the calculating, Germanophile Hungarian ministers and officials, it was a day long overdue.

Late that afternoon, Muci was traveling in a tram over the Danube, going home after helping her friend Gizi, who was teaching her the dressmaking trade.

"At least," said a man in a loud, angry voice, "we'll all have more room on our tram cars now that the Germans have arrived to relieve us of our Jews." The man was a Magyar with straight brown hair and high cheekbones, and was wearing the green shirt, black tie, and ominous arrow-pointed crucifix of the Arrow Cross, the ultra-right-wing domestic brethren of the Nazis.

Muci was within earshot. "What's he talking about?" she asked the middle-aged woman sitting next to her.

"You haven't heard, child?" the woman responded. "German soldiers entered the city this morning. They say they've come to support our failing government. We even have a new prime minister."

"Yeah," said the man, overhearing the woman's comments, "someone who's a true ally of the Germans, not some weak-kneed crony of the Jews; someone who'll empty our buses and trams of Jews and load up the trains with them. Soon Hungary will once again be Hungarian."

"What are you talking about, you crazy mule?" said another angry voice. "The war's lost and the Germans have come in to take our liberty away."

"What liberty do we have when the Jews are still here?" said still another. Rage pulsated through the tram. Muci was terrified.

The woman sitting next to her turned and glanced at her, rolling her eyes as if to tell her not to take the commotion seriously.

"I don't understand any of this," Muci said to her, but this time in more of a whisper.

The woman responded in kind. "You can be sure that the Germans and Hungarians are united in one thing, and that is their hatred of the Jews." The woman couldn't have been certain that she was not speaking to a Jew, but she continued. "And you've heard of the massacres here, haven't you? Even here it's happened. It's crazy. We've lost so many boys, the war is just about lost, and all they care about is the Jews."

"What's going to happen?" asked Muci.

"I don't know, child. But if you're a Jew, be careful."

When Muci arrived home, her mother and aunt looked panic-stricken. They told her that hundreds of German troops had marched or ridden in jeeps and tanks through the streets of Budapest. Some people ignored them. But mostly, men cheered, women waved enthusiastically, and admiring girls tossed flowers. Prime Minister Kállay had been replaced by the foreign minister to Berlin, an obedient and shrewd politician sympathetic to the Germans, with no small amount of his own Jew-hatred. It must have been the work of the Germans, but it all looked so democratic. One resigned, the other stepped in. Yet the regent, Admiral Miklós Horthy, the real source of power and prestige, was nowhere to be seen. It was as if Hungary had been invaded and the government replaced, and the most powerful and respected man in the country was absent. Soon enough, he reemerged, at least as a figurehead, lulling the nation into a false sense that it was still in control of its destiny. This was a masterfully engineered plan by the Nazis, both to continue to exploit the Hungarian war machine and, especially, to carry out their designs upon the nation's Jews. Although a semblance of normalcy was maintained, the nation had, for all intents and purposes, been invaded. Muci didn't understand the politics of it, but she knew something was terribly wrong. Like many others, she feared that the reprieve of Hungarian Jewry was coming to an end.

It was only a matter of days before everyone's fears took shape. By the end of the month, Jews throughout the country were ordered to wear a four-inch-square, canary-yellow cloth badge in the form of the Star of David firmly sewn onto their outer garments, over their hearts. Any Jew found without it was subject to arrest. If a Jew's badge was not the right shade of yellow or the correct size, or had been sewn on improperly, he or she would be arrested and jailed. And the denunciations started as well. Neighbors, employers and employees, and even housekeepers denounced Jews throughout the city by the thousands, all within days of the Germans' arrival. There were unending waves of personal betrayals and isolated arrests, literally tens of thousands within the first several weeks after the Germans arrived.

And then the rumors began flying around the city—of deportations and even worse. The worst rumors, which had reached the city from Slovak or Polish refugees, were unbelievable, and so no one dared believe them. But the earlier hope of many Hungarian Jews that they would outlast the faltering Nazi war effort now turned to dread. The possibility of being deported to German labor camps was already infinitely more ominous than the domestic Hungarian labor battalions.

One of the first rumors to circulate was that only single people would be deported—that married couples and those with families would not be separated from one another. The Germans must have realized, so the reasoning went, that people separated from their families could not work efficiently. And they surely wouldn't deport entire families. People were grasping at straws, at any irrational possibility that could offer the slightest bit of hope. It was the only incentive that Muci needed. Somehow she got a letter through to Miklós and urged him to come home. It was not helpful anymore, Muci told him, to wait to get married. They should do it soon, as soon as possible, so that maybe both of them could avoid deportation.

Miklós received Muci's letter and desperately tried to get a leave of absence, which was not out of the question, although it would have been his first furlough since Christmas the winter before. Fortunately, his request coincided with the three days of Good Friday through Easter Sunday. Miklós would be allowed to leave his labor unit for these three days to go to Budapest to celebrate the holiday.

It was the seventh day of April 1944. When Miklós stepped in the doorway of the third-floor corner flat in the Lipthay Street apartment, Muci threw her arms around him, and he tightly embraced her. They held each other with bottomless, if fleeting, relief. There was none of the fanfare and exhilaration that Miklós's father had experienced when he returned from the First World War to his family's flat, only a few blocks away, to the waiting arms of his wife and young children. This war was still going on, and not on a distant battlefield but in the streets of Budapest, where Allied bombs had begun to fall as soon as the Germans stepped foot in the city.

"I had to run through the streets," said Miklós, pulling away enough from Muci to be able to look at her face. "All the way here, it felt as though the bombs were falling right beside me."

"There are sometimes blasts," said Muci, "that sound like they're coming from down the street. It's been this way for weeks, on and off. We never know when they're coming."

"And the people in the streets with stars on their chests. What kind of medieval barbarism is this?" said Miklós.

With that, Elza, who had been standing on the far side of the room, came over and gave him a perfunctory hug and kiss. She then walked over to the closet, reached in, and took out her own overcoat with the Jewish badge on it, holding it up to show Miklós. "As of just two days ago. The star of Judas they give us two days before Christ was killed. A curious coincidence, don't you think?"

Miklós was speechless. He felt rage pressing at the veins in his temples.

Elza took a deep breath and swallowed hard. "I thought at first it was only to shame us. But just today they limited our travel, and last week they tried to take away our telephones. Imagine, it's now illegal for a Jew to have a phone." Miklós shook his head as Elza went on. "Some Christian friends try to reassure us, but mostly, if they're not denouncing us, they're afraid to talk to us. And I think we've all been fooling ourselves into thinking the war will be over soon. Even if it is, the Nazis care more about the Jews than about winning."

"In the labor camp, we've also been running low on hope," said Miklós. He turned toward Muci. "I wish there were more I could do to make you feel safe. But getting married will be a blessing."

"We're all helpless," said Muci. "At least that's what they want us to think. They're taking away everything and then the threats come. Some of my friends have already been beaten up, just for having a few stitches missing from their yellow stars. And your friend Leo from the bank is gone."

"Gone? What are you saying?"

"Leo, who stupidly criticized the Germans all those years. You used to tell me he didn't care who heard him, that he thought he could say anything because he was such a loyal Hungarian who fought in the war. He thought the Germans would never take over here. Well, as soon as they arrived, the police came for him in the middle of the day. And now he's gone."

"Has the world gone mad?"

Miklós's head was spinning. "Look here, Muci. When we go to the justice of the peace tomorrow, we'll have to tell them we're both Jewish. They'll certainly believe us, because who else would be so stupid to say they're Jewish except real Jews? To the state, I'm not considered a Christian anymore. I finally understand that." Miklós paused and took a deep breath. "But, now, hear me out. If I am willing to say I am a Jew for us to get married and to help keep you safe, then I want you to consider—"

"What? Baptism, right?" Muci shot back. "Becoming a Christian! You want me to renounce being Jewish for you!"

"Of course not for me. It's for you—to save your life and keep you safe, that's all. I can't claim to have renounced my religious beliefs, but if I am willing to proclaim my Jewishness to give you more chances, then I want you to consider being baptized if it could help to save your life. Think about it."

"I have thought about it as much as I need to," Muci answered. "We're not religious Jews. But we're Jews. And it means more to me than I ever realized. I can't become Christian. I won't. This will all work out somehow, you'll see."

"Not now, Miklós," Elza said in a sympathetic tone. But she saw that Muci was weeping. "Better not now."

Holy Saturday—the day before Christ rose from the dead—was the day Miklós and Muci walked to the Office of Vital Statistics on Fö Street in Buda. Muci had just passed her twenty-first birthday and was wearing the dress she had made for the occasion with her friend Gizi's help. She also had on high-heeled shoes, higher than she'd ever worn before. She was more beautiful than ever and felt positively radiant, walking with wobbly steps over the rubble-strewn sidewalks of bomb-scarred Budapest. She carried a small bouquet of flowers and—despite the civil ceremony—her grandmother's Jewish prayer book.

At the office of the justice of the peace, the couple was greeted by two officials—one older, courteous man and a younger, haughty one in his twenties. Muci and Miklós were questioned about their religion. There, in the presence of Elza and two other witnesses, they readily admitted to the two state officials that they were Jews.

In one way, it was the happiest day of Muci's life, one she had long dreamed of. But her heart was torn. Here she was, getting married not only on the Jewish Sabbath, when it is forbidden, outside of a synagogue, but to a man whose only claim to Jewishness was his birth and his desire to shield her from harm. But it was equally apparent to everyone present that Miklós and Muci were boldly acknowledging that they were Jews at a moment of great peril, effectively binding themselves to the fate of the Jews as much as to each other. The next day, April 9, 1944, would be the twenty-sixth Easter Miklós celebrated as a Christian. But this day, this Great Saturday, marked the beginning of his return to the Jewish people.

Muci's wavy jet-black hair framed her exquisite high cheekbones. Her joyful smile finally won out over her worry and dread. Miklós looked his bride in the face and beamed, as if he were seeing the face of God—no, certainly not the deliverer of His eternal kingdom, but simply the one human being who was the major source of hope in his life.

There was no celebration following the ceremony. The streets were deserted late that afternoon, except for some Christian stragglers probably making their way to Vespers. After dark, there was not a soul left on the street. And with good reason. Inside the Lipthay Street apartment, what might have begun as Elza's heartfelt toast and blessing of the newlyweds was soon interrupted by the blast of air raid sirens. They made their way down to the basement, a dusty room with a cold concrete floor and roughly-plastered walls, which was steadily being filled by the residents of the building's fifteen or twenty apartments—mostly older men and women, along with plenty of children. Within a minute or two, there must have been forty or fifty people. As they sat on the floor amidst the coal used to fire the furnace, Muci smiled stiffly. Her body was tense, but she tried not to betray her fear and discouragement. Then the building shook and the upstairs windows rattled. The bombs could have landed anywhere in the city, but their blasts were so intense they might as well have landed across the street.

As the noise and terror receded, the residents waited several minutes before returning to their apartments. But it wasn't long before a second air raid occurred, with the same result, and then, hours later, still a third one. By then it was past midnight, and all the apartment dwellers who hadn't yet decided to stay in the basement for the night resolved to do so. On the eve of the day when Jesus rose from the dead, this is where Miklós and Muci spent their wedding night.

❖

At the friary, during the worst of times, Gyuri and those around him were mysteriously protected by a most remarkable and saintly miracle worker. Though nearby areas, including Foggia, had been heavily bombed, with thousands killed, San Giovanni Rotondo remained untouched throughout the war. However, at one time, before the defeat of the German army in and around that region, there reportedly was a Nazi munitions depot located in the town. There were numerous stories of miraculous intercession to save San Giovanni from Allied bombing efforts to eliminate the arms depot. A number of American and British airmen reported seeing the apparition of a priest or monk in the sky immediately before their fighter bombers, waving his outstretched arms in front of them as if to discourage the pilots from carrying out their bombing missions. The reports coincided with instances when the planes' bombing equipment malfunctioned, making it impossible for the planes to discharge their ordnance. There were numerous other incidents, as well, of Allied bombing missions during which bombs fell to earth but did not detonate. One such bomb, in Foggia, reportedly landed in a roomful of terrified people huddled near a photograph of Padre Pio. According to the survivors, the bomb did not explode, but burst "like a soap bubble." All of this added to the great mystery surrounding the seer of the Gargano.

❖

It was the middle of May 1944, and Gabriella was alone now in Szarvas. Klari had gone back to Budapest, if only to volunteer as a chemist in a cancer hospital, as it was impossible for her to get a paying position because of her Jewish heritage. In March, Adolf Eichmann had entered Budapest and swiftly set into motion the machinery for the "relocation" of Hungary's Jews. The Axis was in its death throes and yet Germany relentlessly persisted in its genocidal ambitions and the deportation of Jews to death camps.

Gabriella had become sickly and withdrawn since Béla's death the year before. Her heart was failing and her hands and feet had swelled. She rarely went out, except occasionally to visit a neighbor or go to church. She knew of

Miklós's and Klari's predicaments, and was fully aware of how the situation for Jews had become terribly precarious. But she hadn't much considered her own tenuous circumstances.

Early one morning, Gabriella was awakened by a loud rap at the door. There were two Hungarian gendarmes, each armed with a bayoneted rifle. Members of the domestic military police, which had a reputation for ruthlessness and brutality, they were dressed in dark uniforms and wore the characteristic cock feathers sticking up from the front of their tall black hats. These two were Magyars with angular cheekbones and dull, unsympathetic-looking faces who had opted out of induction into the Honvéd for this safer assignment to the gendarmerie, one that many men turned into lifelong careers.

"Mrs. Pogány, we wish you a good morning," one of the gendarmes said with a disarming gentleness.

"What is it, officer? What's wrong?"

"The Jews in the community have all been notified to report to the abandoned factory on the edge of town." Gabriella's heart started racing. She knew of the public call for Jews to report, but had tried simply to avoid it, clinging to her identity as a Roman Catholic.

The gendarme continued. "Apparently you are the only one in the community who has not answered that call."

"That's because I'm Catholic. I can't say that I have seen you or your companion very often in church."

"We're not from here. Believe me, I'm sure you're a good Catholic. You remind me of my mother. Your faithfulness probably puts both me and my companion here to shame. But according to our orders, we must ask that you come with us. Please pack a bag and come promptly."

"But I haven't yet been to Mass."

"I'm sorry, but that will not be possible today."

Gabriella was not fooled by the courtesy of the policeman. She knew what was coming. Ever since Béla had heard the stories of the deportation of the Slovak Jews in 1942, they both knew that this time would come. Gabriella drew a deep breath and let out a frightened, high-pitched sigh. It was the most decisive moment of her life. As she stepped away from the gendarmes and turned to enter her bedroom, she remembered the poison capsules that Béla had prepared for each of them for this very moment. Thank God, Gabriella must have thought, Béla never had to use them. But should she, now? She knew where they were and wasn't afraid to die. She recalled that day, more than two decades ago, when she was searching for

Béla at the Rumanian border. She knew back then, standing near the well, that she would have sacrificed her life if the soldiers threatened her dignity as a woman. Gabriella walked into her bedroom and rummaged frantically through her mahogany armoire for clothing to pack into a small suitcase she set open on the bed. Then she moved over to her bureau, where, she remembered, the poison capsules were kept in an old clothbound jewelry box in the top drawer. Gabriella opened the drawer and looked at the box, brushing her hand over the smooth silk cover. But as she moved her thumb over the edge of the lid, she hesitated for a fraction of a second. The she abruptly moved her hand up to her mouth and covered her lips with the tips of her fingers. No, she must have thought. I mustn't. I will meet my Lord in His time, not my own.

Gabriella was marched to a run-down, abandoned factory on the edge of town. In front of the main entrance of the two-story brick building with large, broken, mostly boarded-up windows, she was escorted by both gendarmes, one of whom courteously opened the building's heavy wooden door for her. "This is where you'll be staying for the next several days," he said, with what struck Gabriella as a puzzling expression of remorse. "You had better make the best of it. It only gets worse from here." She glared defiantly at him as she walked past him into the entryway. Immediately inside, there were two other gendarmes seated behind a table covered with stacks of papers and a large ledger with what appeared to be handwritten names and addresses inside.

"Quickly," barked one of them, as Gabriella nervously moved toward them. She had barely an instant in which to glance at her surroundings. Up four or five steps behind the gendarmes, hundreds of people—men, women, children, elderly, perhaps five hundred, maybe even a thousand—were crowded on the open floor with little space between them. For a moment, her eyes were met by the sorrowful gaze of one middle-aged woman. Gabriella recognized her. She was a Jewish woman, the wife of one of the merchants she had done business with over the years. Of course she was Jewish, what else would she be, Gabriella thought, as she stopped a few feet in front of the table.

"I couldn't guess what your name is," one of the men growled. "You're the last one here. You surely didn't think you were exempt?" He didn't give her time to answer. "We no longer have the luxury of distinguishing between old Jews and new Christians. You're all Jews now."

"Don't tell me what I am, young man. I've been praying the rosary longer than you've been alive." Gabriella felt that she didn't have to kowtow to such brash peasant boys, emboldened simply by having uniforms on their backs and cock feathers in their caps. Although she was sick and frail, she still had some fight left in her.

"Save your sass for your fellow Jews. They're going to love you for it. But don't forget, you're not dealing here with altar boys."

"Aren't I?"

The man turned his head toward his partner at the table. "Were you an altar boy?" he asked, with a feigned look of seriousness.

"Why, yes, I was," the second one answered, breaking into a churlish laugh.

"Come to think of it," answered the first, "so was I." And he, too, laughed derisively. "Those days are gone," he said with a sneer, his face taking on a steely hardness. "The only thing that's the same is that we're still doing God's work. Now take your rosary and go up there and pray for the rest of your kind. They're going to need it. Although, I assure you, they won't exactly appreciate your Hail Marys and Our Fathers."

Then, before Gabriella could step beyond the table to head up the stairs, the second gendarme poked the first one in the side. "It's an interesting twist, don't you think, to what the Romans used to do to the Christians, throwing them to the lions? Only we're throwing a Christian to the Jews. Wait'll they eat her up." Both men burst out laughing.

Gabriella was no stranger to the Jews of Szarvas. They had known her for fifteen years, and she had known and done business with them. They were well aware that she and her family were converts. But although she always appeared to them to be a pious Catholic, she was never haughty toward her Jewish neighbors. In fact, she never forgot or denied her Jewish origins and at times referred to herself as a "baptized Jew," for that is what she was. Gabriella embraced Christ as her savior, not merely to escape persecution or to elevate herself socially, but in order, as she would say, to "walk in the Light of the World."

There was not much light—at least not the spiritual light of discernment—on the factory floor among the mass of Jews. It was only the light of the springtime sun deflecting off the few cracked and broken windowpanes of the building not covered by wooden boards. The nervous adults and frightened, crying children looked less terrified of the darkness that was enveloping them than of the play of morning light that seemed almost to be taunting them.

"Go ahead, have a seat," said the woman whom Gabriella had noticed earlier. She must have looked hesitant to sit on the floor. "Don't feel it's beneath your dignity. You're lucky that there's enough room for you." Gabriella laid her suitcase flat on the floor and sat down on top of it. Before she could speak, the woman continued. "It took you an extra day to get here. You probably didn't think the orders referred to you, did you?"

"Look here," said Gabriella, trying to muffle her defiance, "I have never denied being born a Jew. But I've been baptized for twenty-five years. I have lived my life as a Catholic." Her voice cracked. "I just thought my church would protect me."

"Like they protected your poor husband when they dug up his grave?" an old man broke in. "Why should this surprise you?"

"No, it doesn't surprise me. I never used Christianity as a shield around myself and, believe me, I never thought any less of Jews. You've known me. Maybe I've been sick and involved with my family. Like all of you. I just thought that when you feel saved by your God, it helps you to . . ."

"Feel separate from others?" another woman intruded.

"So now what do you think of your salvation?" said another. "The people who brought you here were saved by your Lord, and so, too, were the sweet souls who laughed at you downstairs. Is it that they can do anything they want here on earth, as long as they know that salvation awaits them in heaven? Come, why don't you join the rest of us who are still waiting?"

"What is this place? What is it we are waiting for? Where are we going?" Gabriella asked.

"This is the ghetto, Mrs. Pogány, the Jewish ghetto," said one of her neighbors. "They tell us we're leaving here sometime in the next several days, to work for the Reich, as they call it. The Hungarians don't want us here anymore. They tell us we're not Hungarians anymore—just Jews."

Shortly after sunrise the next morning, the two gendarmes who had brought Gabriella to the ghetto came back to the factory. One of them showed a piece of paper to the guard. Then the other walked upstairs to the main floor of the factory.

Looking over the mass of sleeping Jews, the gendarme bellowed, "Mrs. Pogány, come here."

Barely had he opened his mouth than Gabriella sprang to her feet. She had heard him instantly, having barely slept her first night on the factory floor. Bending down to grip her bag of belongings, the gendarme interrupted her. "No, do not bring your bag. You'll be back shortly." Gabriella was puzzled but did as he said. By now, many more people were awake and must have wondered where in the world she was being taken so early, and so soon after her arrival.

"Where are you taking me?"

"To Mass, dear lady. We are taking you to church. Your parish priest talked to our commander. He must be an influential man. But then, it's hard for any of us to ignore the wishes of the church." Gabriella's heart melted. Yet in the next instant her spine stiffened and her skin became cold with fear. The people in the room had heard the gendarme. A Christian among them was being taken to church—by escort, no less. She was certain she would be scorned for it.

It must have taken only a day of her absence from church for Father Fetzer to realize the inevitable. Maybe he felt helpless to be of any assistance to the Jews. But he must have decided he had to do something to help Gabriella keep her Catholic faith, even while he couldn't spare her whatever was to come next.

The gendarmes walked on either side of Gabriella down the main street to the Catholic church. The place had been her spiritual home for more than fifteen years. It seemed peculiar—painfully ironic, in fact—for armed guards to be taking her there now. As they walked, Gabriella looked at one of the gendarmes, who ignored her gaze. Then she turned to look at the more vocal of the two. He briefly met her glance and then diverted his eyes, but was unable to avoid a sheepish smile. Could he possibly, Gabriella imagined, be feeling squeamish satisfaction at performing this kindness for a fellow Catholic?

When they arrived at the church, which was nestled right up to the sidewalk of the main street, the two guards permitted Gabriella to enter alone.

"Why aren't you coming in with me?" she asked them.

"It is not for us to pray, woman."

"Why, have you forgotten how?"

"No, the spirit is eager but the flesh is weak. You pray for us. We will keep vigil out here."

Gabriella entered the sanctuary and wept as she saw Father Fetzer about to begin Mass. She walked to the first pew and paused to gaze sorrowfully at her spiritual leader. He descended from the altar and embraced her.

"There was little more I could do than to get permission for you to come to Mass," Fetzer said, his voice cracking with emotion.

"Why are they doing this to us, Father?" Gabriella asked, with tears streaming down her face. "Are we guilty of killing Christ and is this now our punishment? Isn't that plainly the reason why the Jews are being treated this way?"

"Neither God nor Christians seek to punish the Jews, my dear child. The Germans do."

"Then tell me, Father," Gabriella said with anger in her voice. "Where are the Germans? Where are they? I don't see any. Have you seen them since any of this happened? I see only Hungarians—all Christians! Good Catholic Hungarian boys with rifles in their hands brought me here. One of them even blindly recited verses from Scripture. They brought me here in Christian charity. Probably more yours than theirs. And I'm grateful to you. I would not have stayed away. But they are waiting for me outside to take me back to the ghetto. And then what happens?"

Fetzer sighed deeply and looked up at the fresco ceiling. "I don't know, my dear Gabriella. I am utterly helpless, but to bring you here to church and to minister to you as long as I can. I don't know why this is happening, and why the Church permits it. I know that many priests have argued against this."

"Have they?"

"Yes, they have. Of course they have. But it has gone beyond our power to alter the minds of those in the state who make these decisions."

"Then why haven't the priests and the bishops and the princes of our church taught those boys outside, and their commanders, and the overlords of their commanders—all Christians, I'm sure, every single one of them— that Jesus Christ is a God of love. Believe me, Father, those men waiting for me outside are wearing God's crucifix around their necks. I am certain of it. And they think they are doing God's work. They told me so. But did our Lord ever call for vengeance for His crucifixion? He knew He had to give up His life. He knew it. He told us. It was prophesied. It's why God sent Him. His death and resurrection freed us from sin and showed us eternal life. But is this what you'd call being freed from sin?" Gabriella asked, as she pointed outside toward the gendarmes and the ghetto. "Did Christ ever demand that His own people be treated like dogs?"

Fetzer was silent, and that silence was echoed by the handful of worshipers in the sanctuary.

"Yes, my dear Father, that's all there has been, so much silence."

The priest dared not look at Gabriella. He lifted a hand to his face, as if to buoy his head against the weight of his own helplessness and shame.

"Forgive me, Father. You don't deserve my bitterness. You have been so kind. I am filled with gratitude to you for making it possible for me to come today."

Fetzer looked directly at his devoted parishioner. "I will see to it that you can return. May God bless you and may His mercy be upon those in the ghetto."

When the Mass ended, Gabriella turned and slowly walked out of the sanctuary. Outside, the town had not yet come to life. It was still early morning, before eight o'clock. There were only a few people out on the main street going about their business. As Gabriella looked around, to her surprise, she did not immediately see her two police escorts. She walked a few paces to her right, to the side of the church, and looked around the corner, where there was a small, shaded garden with blooming bushes and a ten- or fifteen-foot-high beech sapling. At the far end of the garden, by the corner of the main crossing of the building, Gabriella saw the two gendarmes leaning against the side wall, with eyes closed, rifles held to their sides. Next to them, nestled in the corner, stood a small stone statue of the crucified Christ.

Gabriella went over to them and shook one of the men by his upper arm. "At such a time as this you are sleeping and taking your rest?" she said.

"Save your self-righteous insolence, woman. I'm tired of your pontificating."

Gabriella held her tongue. There was something farcical about these men falling asleep on their watch. But she realized it was unwise to belittle them, especially because she wanted to return the next day. Maybe she'd even get to stay for Confession.

As they arrived back at the ghetto, Gabriella paused in front of the factory and nodded to both of the men. "Thank you," she said softly, feeling almost ashamed for having to acknowledge her gratitude. She then walked back into the building.

From the instant of her return, just as she had feared, Gabriella was shunned by everyone. They would not look at her or make any room for her to sit down. Women kept their children away from her and told them not to stare. Being personally accompanied out of this hellhole by brutal gendarmes must have been unfathomable to them. Just having the chance to leave for a little while was an unheard-of privilege. The torturously crowded place had quickly become intolerably hot and squalid, with one bathroom for so many hundreds of people.

"And where did these devils take you, as if it's not obvious?" one woman asked.

"They took me to Mass," Gabriella answered, biting her lower lip and not looking up.

"Does your Lord Jesus give comfort, too, to the generous men who took you to church?"

Gabriella could not respond. How much more obvious could it be, she thought, that the state was in league with the Church, if a Jewish convert was allowed to leave the ghetto by police escort in order to attend Mass? What could she possibly say to defend herself? The law of the state insisted that Gabriella was a Jew. But in the otherwise hardened hearts of the state's police, she was counted as one of them—a worshipful member of the Church, and therefore she was permitted religious liberties. What could she do but try to find a place to sit and remain silent?

Two weeks later, shortly after sunrise, on a warm spring morning in early June 1944, nothing in Szarvas was as usual. The tension in the air had blanketed the town, and especially the ghetto, in an uncanny stillness and silence—not because there was no movement or sound but, rather, that people's fear and uncertainty had muffled quotidian sights and sounds. The multitude of finches, blue jays, and sparrows had surely begun their morning opera, but they might as well have hesitated. No one noticed. The cocks from surrounding farms had most likely sounded their wake-up calls. But they might as well have postponed them. No one was paying any attention. And even if the angel of death had been hovering over the town in bated anticipation, there was not a ruffling of leaves to be detected on the acacias or the drooping willows along the banks of the Körös.

Then the rumble of automobiles penetrated the collective oblivion. Stopping in front of the Jewish ghetto, a handful of gendarmes carrying rifles or semiautomatic weapons got out of the cars and rushed into the building while people still slept on loose pieces of clothing, against the wall or each others' bodies. A shot rang out, hitting the plaster ceiling, awakening the trembling inhabitants. Children squealed and screamed in terror.

"Everyone up, immediately," said one of the gendarmes. "Pack your bags. You are all leaving this morning. You're going north, where you'll be relocated for labor outside the country. Don't worry, your families will stay together. No harm will come to you. You'll be fed shortly."

Gabriella was dazed by the gunfire and looked up from the floor. On hearing the announcement, she had no illusions left. She was a Jew now, and would share the fate of the Jews. They had all heard about such "relocations," mostly of Slovak Jews, and the less frequent but more unbelievable tales of Polish Jews. Some of them had even heard the outrageous stories of their own Hungarian Jewish men in the labor battalions being shipped to the Ukraine and murdered by the thousands. At first these preposterous stories had sounded as if they were the tales of deranged people who had lost touch with reality. They were not to be believed. Yet some of their own men had not returned from labor service. Now, ever since the remaining Jews of Szarvas had been stuffed into this hole, anything, any horror or nightmare, was plausible. There were no secrets or surprises left. The children didn't suspect it, as long as their parents could put on a good face. And some of the adults may have still deluded themselves otherwise. But just as the sun was now rising, so too was there a dawning awareness in the minds of the many hundreds of

Jews of Szarvas that there was little cause for hope remaining, and that this could end only in the worst possible way.

As Gabriella stood up, she stuffed her belongings into the small brown leather suitcase she had brought with her and snapped the bag shut, her hands by now swollen, as were her feet and ankles. She grabbed the handle of the suitcase. In her other hand, she clutched a wooden object closely to her breast and her racing, terrified heart. Amid the chaotic pushing and shoving, she made her way down the stairs, moving through the throng of bodies, leaning against the railing, having no free hand and receiving no assistance from anyone. As she neared the front door she could see that one by one, at riflepoint, the Jews, young and old alike, were being forced onto any number of wooden farm wagons obviously obtained from the local inhabitants—how freely given no one dared speculate—and probably amassed in the middle of the night.

As she stepped toward the farm cart, Gabriella saw the two gendarmes who had escorted her to church throughout the previous two weeks. The men looked at her, almost—she would have liked to imagine—with solicitude and remorse. Her gaze quickly turned into a scowl. This was the final treachery, she thought, that those who had taken her to Mass were now loading her onto a farm wagon. But by now Gabriella was too sick, exhausted, and frightened to cling to her rage.

"Vengeance is the Lord's. I turn it over to You, dear Jesus," she said, looking up at the cloudless sky. Yet she could not find it in her heart to ask that these devil's accomplices be forgiven for what they were doing. She dejectedly lowered the hand in which she had been clutching the unseen object to her breast. As she rested it upon the wooden barrier of the cart, the gendarmes looked and saw that it was a carved crucifix. "Look," she finally said with her last ounce of defiance, staring at the leader of the pair, "my betrayer has drawn near."

"You ungrateful Jewish bitch," said the second man, hearing Gabriella's words. "This is the thanks we get for taking you to church." He raised the butt of his rifle and was about to strike her.

The other man pulled his arm down to restrain him. "No need," he said with a self-satisfied smile. "Our work is done here. Let the Germans finish her off with the rest of them." But by then Gabriella had turned away and moved toward the front of the wagon. She would not dare face them again. She lowered her head and placed her hand, holding the symbol of her faith, to her breast.

In another moment there were almost a dozen more people on the wagon with her. Gabriella's breathing was shallow. She was gasping for air and her heart was pounding furiously. Now, as the creaking caravan of the condemned inhabitants began its procession through the town in mute certainty of its fate, it must have seemed as though the cries of birds and the crowing of the cock were the only sounds to be heard. Could Gabriella's thoughts at that moment have possibly turned to the Gospels, where it had been revealed that the cock's call signaled the final betrayal of her Lord Jesus Christ?

The Jews had a parallel tradition regarding the significance of the cock's call. It was told that Reb Izak, the Tzaddik of Nagykálló, once, while taking a walk through a meadow, overheard a shepherd boy singing a beautiful and haunting tune about the crowing of a cock. The words of the song spoke to the rebbe of a time of deliverance, always in the indefinite future. Reb Izak instantly learned the song and, over the ensuing years, it was embraced by Hungary's Jews. It came to symbolize the heralding of the Messiah, God's Anointed One, who would deliver the Jews from their centuries of oppression. But on that day in 1944, there were no saviors present.

Accompanied by many people on foot, the carts creaked through the town toward the train station, lurching over the cobblestones of the main street and with painstaking stops and starts through the viscous, redolent mud of the side roads. A warm sun shone, the blossoms were on the crab apple trees, and spring was in the air. As Gabriella's wagon passed the houses in the main part of town, she gazed at the onlookers, many of them her neighbors. Some stood boldly within view of the wagons. "Get out! We don't want you anymore," some of them yelled out. Others were frozen and inert, looking on with sympathetic helplessness, or perhaps disguised but malicious joy. Others of them dared only peer sheepishly and secretively from behind the drawn curtains of their windows. Gabriella saw some of her fellow parishioners, with whom she had knelt in church to receive the body of their common Savior. Some of them had even been blessed by her son at his first Mass. How could they now stand so idly by? A few civil policemen from Szarvas, but mostly armed gendarmes, lined the street. Shame on them all. The One who had been sent to make them more human had failed. Their first Hungarian king, Stephen, canonized for bringing them the gift of a divine savior, had been utterly misguided. And, just as she had suspected, Gabriella did not see a German soldier anywhere.

The rest of the morning passed in a daze—the smell of the horses, the commands of the guards, the boarding of the train, and finally the slow trundling of wheels over iron as they headed north toward their destination. The first stop was Szolnok, where the Jews were collected, with several thousand others from the same region, in an old sugar factory that served as the city's ghetto. When she learned where they were, Gabriella must have remembered how, twenty-five years earlier, she and six-year-old Gyuri had crossed the nearby bridge over the Tisza only moments before it was blown up by the Hungarian Red Army; she must have counted up the years her family had made its life in the great Hungarian heartland.

One or two people died each day in the overcrowded conditions. On the twenty-fifth of June, the first trainload of Jews was dispatched. Gabriella was not among this first transport. No one was told where the trains were going. Two days later a second transport departed with all the others. Like her fellow prisoners, Gabriella didn't know about the separate transports or the different destinations, much less the separate fates that awaited them. Those who remained were told they were being relocated to the east to work for the Reich and, once again, that they would not be separated from their families. But by now, those assurances were absurdly transparent. All that she could be certain of was that they were being cast out from the vast interior of their nation. They would be carried north and eastward, where it was perhaps best that they didn't know what precise fate awaited them. Sick and nearly exhausted, abandoned by Christians and scorned by Jews, Gabriella knew she would not survive. The thought did not frighten her. What filled her heart with terror at this moment was a piercing question: If her Savior had been betrayed by His own flock, would He still be there to receive her in death?

✤ CHAPTER 12 ✤

Samaritans

A csillagok szégyenkezve hunyták be szemüket.
(The stars closed their eyes in shame.)
Miklós Radnóti,
Hungarian-Jewish poet shot in October 1944

One day, barely six weeks after she was married, Muci returned home from the job she had recently managed to get in a government factory after she had lost her work as a dressmaker for her friend Gizi. It was a nominal job for meager pay—cleaning factory floors and machinery. But being employed by the government was rumored to be an effective strategy to stave off deportation, so it could prove to be a lifesaver. Jews in Budapest were still making important life decisions based on rumors. It didn't matter how improbable they were. Avoiding deportation was the only truly important concern that required any decisive action. If marriage to a labor serviceman would not help, then maybe this job would. She knew it would be temporary at best, but at least to Muci's way of thinking it bought her some time and gave her and her mother a little peace of mind.

The deportation scare arose from the fact that Jews in the countryside had been confined to ghettos in April and May. The deportations started within a few weeks after that. Gabriella and every Jew and converted Jew in Hungary, except for those in Budapest and the labor battalions, were gone in a matter of weeks. Only a small handful of Jews in Budapest clearly foresaw where their brethren from the countryside were being taken. They could barely imagine that nearly 150 trains from all over the country were carrying human cargo—nearly 450,000 people. Much less were they prepared to believe that the vast majority of those deported were being sent directly to death camps. But however little the survivors in Budapest knew for certain, perpetual fear, dwindling hope, and complete desperation were taking over their lives.

No sooner had Muci entered the apartment than her frantic mother began to tell her that a Hungarian immigration detective had come to the apartment looking for her. Elza said he was a big, husky man with a respectful and mild manner. But his message terrified her. He had informed Elza that her daughter was to report immediately to the immigration office near Roosevelt Square, that there were some irregularities that needed to be cleared up. Elza knew that, despite his sympathetic look, there was something ominous in his tone. She had pleaded with him that Muci was her only child. She had two days to appear.

In the meantime, Muci got back in touch with her friend Gizi, knowing that her husband was a lawyer and possibly could be helpful. But since Mr. Somogyi was a Jew who had lost the right to practice his profession, he recommended a Gentile colleague, a Dr. Szappanos. Elza desperately made the contact with the obliging-sounding attorney to assist Muci with her "immigration" problems. The lawyer agreed to meet them in front of the immigration office and accompany Muci to her appointment.

When Muci and her mother arrived at the building at the agreed time, one hour prior to the appointment, they waited anxiously for Dr. Szappanos to arrive. Ten minutes passed, then twenty and thirty, and still no lawyer. After three quarters of an hour, in a frenzy, Elza found a telephone and called him.

"Kind doctor, sir," she said, pulling herself together, "my daughter and I have been waiting at the immigration office for nearly the entire hour since you had promised you would meet us. Is there a problem?"

"I believe I miscalculated," said the voice at the other end.

"What do you mean, sir? If there is a problem of time, perhaps we could get an extension."

"I should have known who you were if you were friends of Somogyi."

"Why is that a problem?" asked Elza, with a gnawing fear in the pit of her stomach.

"Because," blurted out Szappanos, without further hesitation, "I don't take care of Jewish cases." He had slammed the phone down before Elza could respond.

Before she could hang up, the fifty-three-year-old widow broke into sobs with her daughter standing next to her. By now there was a sinister-looking black sedan parked directly in front of the immigration office. Two young, dark-haired, Jewish-looking women and an elderly man had already been escorted into the backseat of the car. Muci was afraid that this would also be her fate and was certain that her mother was thinking the same. Elza wanted her to run away. But Muci thought otherwise. She was intent on keeping her appointment and had even come prepared. Having worn her wedding dress and high-heeled shoes, she loosened her long, wavy black hair and let it fall to her shoulders. No, she didn't fancy herself a seductress, and had always been shy and self-conscious in public about her dark Semitic beauty. But Muci had learned only recently of her power to influence Hungarian men. She prayed that the officer, whoever he was, would not take her allure as more than innocent flirtation. With Elza still pleading with her not to go into the building, Muci pried her mother's clinging hands from her arm, kissed her on the cheek, and stepped past her toward the front door. Elza was frozen in place and continued to weep.

Upstairs, Muci waited several minutes, during which time others were summarily gathered in an adjoining office after meeting with the detective for no more than a couple of minutes each. Some of them were being led downstairs. A few of the women tried to muffle their tears as they walked past Muci toward the stairway. Another woman was inconsolable and wailed piercingly, her cries ricocheting off the walls and doors of the narrow hallway, penetrating Muci's heart like a bayonet.

When it was Muci's turn, the immigration officer proved as kind and decent to her as Elza said he was when she met him. He was a big man, perhaps in his early forties, with blue eyes, auburn hair, and boyish good looks. "You know, your dear mother was worried sick when I went to find you at your home," he immediately said to his young detainee.

"I'm sure she explained, as she always does," said Muci, "that I'm her only child, that she's a widow of many years, and that both her parents died just a few years ago."

"Yes, she did, as a matter of fact," he said, in a quivering voice. "I was touched by it." The detective appeared nervous in Muci's presence, rather than she in his. She could tell he was taken by her. She thought it was curious that only moments earlier he had been able to send helpless, terror-stricken people to an uncertain fate. He looked at her and then down toward his desk, stealing a glance at her breasts. His eyes came to rest on a document on top of a small stack of papers in front of him. He then hesitantly lifted it off the stack and slowly handed it to Muci, seated across the desk from him. "I must tell you, young lady," he said, before she could even glance at it, "that we simply are not able to establish your citizenship."

"But I've lived in Hungary since I was a baby. My mother is Hungarian. I was born in America and my father was from what is now Czechoslovakia. It was Hungary back then."

"But you are not native-born. You admit that. You have no passport, and we are at war. Your citizenship here is unclear and you have no diplomatic protection from any country." The immigration officer stopped, looked up at the ceiling, and bit his lip. "What you are looking at is an order," he said, pausing and clearing his throat, "for your . . . arrest."

Muci gasped. She could not answer. She looked at the paper and then helplessly looked the detective in the eye.

"I am compelled," he pressed on, stumbling over his words, "to have you join the other individuals in the next office, and then someone will escort you downstairs. You may have noticed the car outside the building. I'm afraid you will be taken with the others to the city jail, and from there to one of a number of internment camps around Budapest. It's not for me to say what's to become of you there." The detective sounded as though he was trying to evade the terrible gravity of the order.

Muci looked down, then shut her eyes for an instant. Her heart was pounding, but she didn't want the detective to see how frightened she was.

"Why are you telling me all this? To terrify me, I'm sure."

"No, I'm so sorry if I have. I thought it might be better for you to know than to be kept in the dark. Forgive me if I've used bad judgment."

The detective sounded genuine in his concern. Muci thought that he certainly had some hint of decency to him. But she had trouble believing that it was her sadness or desperation with which he sympathized. It was her face—the charming and beautiful face of a Jewess that betrayed just enough Magyar features to make a Hungarian man feel that she could be his wife or his lover, at least his daughter or sister. She looked up and into the man's eyes again. Muci was too constrained by nature to play the coquette, but the deliberate way she had dressed, and, now, the way her eyes connected with his, accomplished the same purpose, only, to her great relief, not with unintended consequences—not yet, at least. Taking a deep breath, her body subtly tightened with renewed resolve.

The man turned away from Muci's imprecating gaze. He fumbled with the papers on his desk and then covered his mouth with his cupped hand, as if trying to think of alternative ways to proceed.

"Look here," he finally said, "it's not that we're all monsters. Officially, this is an immigration problem. But these sorts of things have been going on for years in every country our German allies have occupied. It's 1944 and we haven't yet allowed it to happen here. Believe me, I do not hate anyone. But it's as if Hungary doesn't belong to the Hungarians anymore." Maybe he was a sensitive man, Muci thought, but the more he revealed of himself, the more she squirmed in her chair. It wasn't so much lustfulness that frightened her anymore. "And now," he went on, "we are being pressed to solve this problem."

"So this isn't really just about my not being born in Hungary." But Muci was not about to talk politics with the detective. "How am I a threat, sir? My father died long ago and my mother has worked in a factory for years. We have no designs on the country. We've simply lived here and have been good citizens. It's been our home. I consider myself a Hungarian. I actually loved this country before all this happened."

"I'm afraid there are too many people who believe that your Jewish ways have flown in the face of Christian Hungary."

"*My* Jewish ways?" Muci said, coldly glaring at the man. "My husband's entire family are devout Catholics, even though they were born as Jews." Muci knew this was a calculating and disingenuous gambit. Her throat began to tighten and her chest became heavy. But she continued, "My husband serves in a Christian labor battalion and is worked like a dog. But he still has the heart to attend Mass on Sundays. What does that fly in the face of?"

The detective overlooked his charge's impudence. "Your husband's in a Christian labor battalion?" he asked. "He's a pious Catholic, you say?" Then he sat back in his chair, extended his legs out in front of him, folding his hands in his lap. He seemed to breathe a sigh of relief. "What if," he said, "I were to sign off on your case? 'This has been a mistaken arrest,' I will say. This woman's husband is a fine Hungarian Christian. He serves in the Honvéd, on the front, as a . . . lieutenant, yes, a . . . *first* lieutenant.'" He sat up in his chair and then leaned across his desk, smiled, and looked Muci straight in the eye. "He's a first lieutenant, isn't he?" he said, plying Muci with her husband's newly invented identity.

Muci's brow furrowed. Then for the first time she smiled. "Yes," she said, nearly swallowing the word. "He's a first lieutenant in the Honvéd," she went on, her widened eyes gleaming. She couldn't believe what she was saying, nor what she had just heard.

In an even more dramatic turn, the man continued, "You know, it may not be such a bad idea for you to get baptized yourself, or at least apply for papers. In this country, it's safer to be a Catholic than a Jew."

"You sound like my husband. Why should I renounce my Judaism? What possible salvation could it bring?"

"Heavenly salvation should not be your concern. But being baptized might save your life. We in the Church welcome converts into the body of Christ. Look, this may be a racial divide for the maniacs here and in Germany, but most of us just wish the Jews could blend in and be like us."

"We *are* like you. Why should we dishonor our religion and yours by acting as though we were taking off one suit of clothes and putting on another?"

"Look, by its own canons, the Church allows for emergency baptism to save a person's life. No truly decent priest should care about the insincerity of a conversion under these circumstances. We all know what's happening to the Jews, or what will happen soon enough. After the war, you can pray to whomever you want. For now, baptismal papers might just save your life."

"I can't think about that now. As I've told my husband, I may not be a good Jew, but my parents and grandparents were Jews, and I would feel like a traitor."

"If anything should ever happen," he went on, apparently looking for another way by which to express his interest, "if things get worse—as you know they might—let me know. I will help you in any way possible." Then the officer handed Muci a slip of paper. "Here is where I live. Before your train pulls out of the station, think about it. You would be safe with me."

Muci appreciated the detective's generosity, but knew what he was unspokenly getting at. "After the war," he must have been thinking, "you can love whomever you want, but for now, coming to me might just save your life." The detective signed the necessary papers and discharged Muci. As she got up to leave, she lightly extended her hand. "Thank you, sir. Thank you for your decency."

"Go home to your mother. She's worried sick about you."

As Muci walked down the hallway of the stuffy office building, she heard the heels of her shoes knocking against the wooden floor, the sound reverberating through the long corridor of drab stucco walls and wood-framed glass doors. She felt, as if in a dream, temporarily spared, at least a few more days.

✤

By late June, Muci, Elza, and Rosi had been forced to move to Király Street in Pest, alongside the Jewish quarter. All Jewish residents of the city had been forced to crowd into designated "Jewish buildings" called "yellow star houses." It was a major step in the process of disenfranchising and segregating Budapest's Jews. Many of them feared that it was simply preparing them for easy transport. During the last few days of relocation, the city looked like a medieval town expelling its Jewish inhabitants. There were untold thousands of people carrying whatever belongings they could load onto horse-drawn wagons, handcarts, and wheelbarrows. Many carried bags or furniture in their arms or on their backs as they desperately tried to meet the midnight deadline of June 25.

From that day on, there was a curfew imposed that prohibited the Jews from going outside their living quarters except between the hours of two and five in the afternoon, and then only for essential shopping. Muci had lost her factory job and was confined to a small apartment along with her mother, Aunt Rosi, and twelve or fifteen other adults. They could receive no visitors, nor could they visit Christian homes or public parks and esplanades. Food was in short supply, and with money coming in only erratically from Miklós's labor service, living had become even more precarious. At times, Muci would boldly rip the yellow star off her clothing and venture out during curfew among the Christian population, being exquisitely careful to sew the star back on properly when she came back in. At other times, she was accosted by policemen or Arrow Cross who would have arrested her if they had been able to fit a pencil between the stitches holding her star onto her jacket.

Muci and her relatives' circumstances grew graver by the day. News of what had happened during May and June in the provinces was now out in the open, although the remaining Jews in Budapest still refused to believe that the deportations meant anything more than being transported to provide "labor for the Reich."

The residents of the Király Street apartment where Muci and her relatives lived were cooped up in a cluttered, stuffy room on a hot day during the second week of July. Muci, her mother, and her aunt sat on wooden chairs as close to the window as they could, where at least there was an occasional movement of warm air. Oblivious to the others, they talked about the food Elza had just bought during the two-hour hiatus in the curfew, and how long their provisions might last.

Just then, an older man burst in, a resident from one of the other apartments in the building. "I want to make you all aware," he said, "there is a rumor that the Prince Primate of the Catholic Church has made an agreement with the prime minister to suspend deportations of Jews in Budapest, and that if they resume, converts would be excluded."

"So what good does that do us?" said a middle-aged woman. "Why should we care about that? What are you suggesting, that we convert to Christianity? Don't you have any loyalty to your people, or do you just plain lack the intelligence to understand that this doesn't amount to anything? It's just another ploy."

"I'm afraid, dear lady," the man said, "it's less of a question of loyalty and more one of saving your life."

"Then let us perish as Jews," said still another woman. "Why be so anxious to stay alive in this hell?"

"It is a hell, for sure," the man answered, "a rat hole, and we are the rats— not holy Jews. We've been abandoned by everyone—by our country, by the world, and by the churches," he said, shaking his finger as he mentioned each one. Punching the air with his fist, he continued: "The government only cares about Christians, for God's sake! They are the only protected ones. Have you ever heard one churchman, even a lowly priest, never mind the church leaders, come out publicly in support of the Jews? I'm damn certain you haven't."

"So why do you want to become one of them?"

"Because I don't want to die like a rat," the man answered. "And what is there to be loyal to? Even our own people are bickering amongst themselves—the Neologists and the Orthodox, the religious and the secular. The Germans must be laughing at us for the spectacle we are making of ourselves."

"Don't be so self-loathing," said the first woman. "The Germans planned on this happening."

But the man was persistent. "And then our own Jewish leaders tell us to listen to the commands of the Germans and Hungarians, and to follow every order so that we might save ourselves. Tell me, my Jewish sister, to whom and what must we pledge our loyalty? Who will save us? Where is our Messiah? Have you seen Him?"

"You don't really think the churches would welcome us now with open arms?" asked another. It was becoming a chorus of voices.

"You're absolutely right," said the first woman. "Go to a church and try to get yourself baptized and see how openhearted and loving they are to a desperate Jew who only wants to save his skin, not his soul. Go see how welcome you'll be."

"Of course it's a farce," said still another, "just to avoid danger or death.

But isn't that exactly what the Marranos did during the Inquisition? Do we hold it against them for trying to stay alive?"

"Exactly. I don't deny my Jewishness by wanting to stay alive, if getting baptized will help me do that. So it's a ruse, I don't care. I don't believe that God demands that we be martyrs. By the Church's own canons, a person in danger of death does not have to receive instruction in the faith but can be converted without delay. Why should we willingly oblige our persecutors?"

Muci had kept silent. She hated hearing it all. Was this what her life as a Jew had come to—the choice between being trapped like an animal in a tighter and tighter net or trying to escape by betraying her people and their history? She felt paralyzed with fear and indecision. Miklós had not stopped urging her to consider conversion. Now she looked over at her mother, sitting barely an arm's length away. Muci knew what she was thinking. Elza wasn't afraid of being deported. She was only terrified by the prospect of being sep-arated from her daughter or of anything happening to her. Muci was Elza's life, the only thing—human or divine—that sustained her heart and soul. If Christian conversion would allow her to live another day, Elza would beg her to go ahead with it. And this was precisely what showed in her eyes at that moment. Maybe this was the only way that Muci could rationalize what she decided to do at that instant. She realized that her life was vitally important to someone else's. That's the way it had always been for this child so cher-ished by everyone in her family. Their happiness had always hinged on hers. And, although Muci had never thought about it until that moment, this obligation to others' well-being was more important to her than remaining a Jew. She knew how self-serving it was, and would later say it was the most painful decision she would ever have to make, however her life might turn out.

The next afternoon, during the two-hour hiatus in the curfew, Muci walked the few blocks to the rabbinical offices on Wesselényi Street to fulfill her obligation to announce her desire to leave the faith. Long lines of people were already there for the same purpose. She had only a few hours and she knew she couldn't wait. She hurriedly walked several blocks in the other di-rection, making her way over to the parish office on the corner of Nagymezö and Proféta Streets. The two lines there were immense. Hundred of Jews waited to declare their intention to convert. No wedding dress or special ex-emptions would help Muci here. She would have to wait with the others. She queued up at the back of one of the lines. It wasn't long before sinister-looking Arrow Cross militiamen, in their familiar green shirts and black ties, along with plainclothes civilians, were beginning to taunt the lines of Jews, first from across the street.

"You are violating our sacred church and desecrating its sacraments," said one bystander. No one responded. But Muci could tell that people were nervous. They all looked stiffly ahead of them, perhaps not wanting, either, to be noticed by their fellow Jews.

"You're turning our churches into stinking synagogues," burst out another. "Have you no shame, being baptized for crude, sacrilegious reasons? Our priests must not allow this."

Finally, like a knife thrust into the collective heart of the helpless Jews, another man from across the street pontificated, "Our Lord will drive you bloodsucking peddlers out with a whip. And we will help him."

Muci was sure that violence would break out. It did. Some Arrow Cross men walked over to between the church and parish office and picked a fight with some in the waiting crowd. A few of them entered the church and must have beaten up some of the Jews waiting inside, because they looked bloodied when they were shoved out of the sanctuary doorway. "Go to your dark and dismal business elsewhere," one defender of the faith yelled after the Jews just dislodged from the threshold of the church.

Most of the rest of the crowd dispersed, while others steadfastly stayed on, evading the looks of the angry Christians and hoping still to enter the church. Muci had had enough. She had never expected to be warmly welcomed. But neither did she expect the visceral hatred that greeted the Jews this day. She walked back to the apartment on Király Street, feeling not only her earlier guilt for betraying Judaism, but terrible shame that she had considered entering a religion with such hate-mongers as its defenders.

But the next day, Muci mustered the brashness to go again, this time to a different church, this time during the curfew. First thing in the morning, she carefully cut the thread that connected her Star of David to a light cotton jacket. She put the jacket on over her summer clothing and slipped out of the apartment, ignoring the frightened stares of the others. They were certain that she was risking arrest and imprisonment in an internment camp, and possible deportation. She looked into her mother's eyes as she turned the doorknob, and knew that it must have been obvious to Elza where she was going. Her mother gently closed her eyes and smiled contentedly. "Be careful," she told her daughter. Muci smiled back at her as she opened the door and left the apartment.

She walked into the inner city of Pest, losing herself among the crowd, and continued westward toward the Danube. She got to the Chain Bridge and proceeded to cross it by foot, being frightened that she would be arrested were she to board a tram car. On the other side of the river, Muci had walked nearly

two miles, and would walk as far again before arriving at her old neighborhood. From the quays of the Danube she could begin to see the area around
the foot of Margit Bridge where she had lived her entire life until only a few
weeks earlier. Muci then proceeded up the cross street and passed Lipthay
Street, not daring to show her face near her home for fear someone might recognize her. A bit farther she passed Tölgyfa Street, where Miklós had lived as
a child. She walked another block, up to Margit Circle Road, where she immediately saw her destination—the Church of the Franciscan Fathers.

Muci had come here because she seemed to remember that this was
where Miklós had been baptized. It gave her no comfort that she was following her husband's path to apostasy. It was painful to think that her Jewish
faith had arrived at the steps of this Catholic church.

Muci waited across the street until the last few stragglers had exited the
church after morning Mass and confession. Then she walked in the open doorway of the sanctuary and approached the altar, where the priest stood in wistful solitude.

As she walked down the aisle, Muci felt a peculiar glimmer of familiarity,
as if she had been in such a place before, accompanied by family members
who talked of having her baptized. She couldn't remember where or when. It
just felt like a long time ago. Maybe it was just in a dream. She somehow remembered shiny statues of kindly regal-looking people and magnificent frescoes on the ceiling. It seemed that she had once seen such a majestically
dressed priest standing in front of her. And there was a ghostly echo filling
her ears with strange-sounding incantations. All of it made Muci feel that she
was in an unearthly province, surrounded by gossamer memories of people
who loved her and wanted to protect her.

"What is it, my child? Is anything wrong?" the priest asked her in a comforting tone, just as she got close enough to hear. He could probably tell that
with each step Muci's gait became more nervous and stiff, and her face grew
more contorted with agitation.

At hearing the cleric's words, Muci felt an icy chill run down her spine.
She was freezing. Her teeth were chattering as she attempted to answer. "Sir,
may I speak to you in private?" She was unable to say the word *Father*.

"We are alone here and unlikely to be disturbed, at least for several minutes. Speak in comfort and I will listen faithfully. First tell me, who are you?
You've not been here before."

"My name is Margit Pogány. I have come here from Pest because this is
my husband's former church. He came here as a child and I believe he was
baptized here." The priest looked pleased. "It was many years ago," Muci
added, "after the First World War."

"You are very brave to walk so far through the streets of Budapest. There's no telling when we'll be bombed next. But it's been practically every day, hasn't it? It must surely be something very important that has brought you here at such risk."

"I have come, sir, to try to save my life. That's really why I am here." Muci could feel her heart pounding.

"What do you mean?" the priest asked.

"I am afraid I would be deported if—"

"If what?" he said instantly, in a harsh tone. "If you remain a Jew? Is that it? Of course it is."

How quickly the cleric caught on, Muci thought. He suddenly looked stern and scornful. "I have no difficulty," he continued, "admitting you into the body of Christ, but I wouldn't dream of baptizing a Jew with insincere or selfish motives. Have you prepared yourself for this spiritually? The Catholic Church insists that one who aspires to be baptized pursue sixty hours of instruction spread out over six months."

Muci was beginning to feel defiant. "How insincere and selfish is it, kind Father"—there, she had said it—"to want to escape persecution and deportation? You surely must know that this has happened everywhere in Hungary. And it's bound to happen here in Budapest very soon."

"Our sacred Church has fought valiantly against these things. I know that the cardinal is sorely troubled over them and is strenuously using his offices to halt, or at least slow, the persecution. It's truly a sin against God."

"That's very peculiar, Father, because we in the Jewish community have not heard or read a word coming from your leader about his trying to save the Jews. All we've heard are rumors that converts might be helped." Muci had to remind herself of the purpose of her visit, but was not easily able to squelch her rising hostility.

"I assure you that everything that can be done is being done—privately, diplomatically, quietly."

"Quietly, Father, yes, very quietly. I'm afraid, though, that we Jews have no illusions left except maybe this last one, that conversion might yet save us."

"But baptizing insincere converts is not a legitimate weapon in this fight."

"I ask you again, Father, how insincere is it to want to save my life? And doesn't your church make emergency provisions for baptizing souls who are in danger of losing their lives?"

"Who says so? How do you know that?" The cleric sounded indignant, as if he had to be reminded by a Jew of what his own church's canons stated.

"Isn't it true?"

The priest winced and looked away.

Muci sensed he felt trapped between his church's enmity toward Jews and its laws governing conversion. "And is it not the depth of indignity," she said, more humbly driving home her final plea, "for a persecuted woman to stand before a priest of your church and beg for sanctuary?"

The priest cringed a second time, forcing his eyes shut for an instant, for it is in one's eyes, Muci well knew, that one displays shame. Then his face softened, if ever so slightly. He had no place to go but toward compassion. "As a priest, I have no sympathy for those who have crucified our Lord. As a man of flesh and blood, I see a frightened child in front of me who is willing, however meekly, to renounce the error of her people's ways and accept the yoke of our Lord's suffering. May he grant all the faithful eternal life, and, if there be sin in what I am about to do, may God forgive me. Step over to the baptistery, child, and kneel before me."

Was Muci being saved or executed, she wondered? She had succeeded in finding that the priest had a heart, yet her own was pounding even more furiously than when she entered. She had never been extremely well grounded in her Jewish faith, she knew that. Yet Muci never held so fast to it as she did at this moment, and never felt as much anguish as now, at the moment of leaving it. "Dear God, forgive me. Dear God, forgive me," she repeated over and over to herself. "Dear God, please forgive my desperation. I vow to you that whatever happens, I will bring Jewish children into this world and they will pray to the God of Israel." Muci began weeping. To her they were obviously bitter tears, but to the priest they may have looked like tears of gratitude and contrition. So may it be.

"What do you ask of God's Church?"

"To be baptized."

"Do you clearly understand what you are undertaking?"

"Yes."

"Margit, the Christian community welcomes you with great joy. . . . Let us ask our Lord Jesus to look lovingly on this woman who is about to be baptized. . . . Bathe her in light and welcome her into Your holy Church. . . . All holy men and women pray for us . . . ."

"All holy men and women pray for us, indeed," repeated Muci under her breath.

"We pray for this woman. . . . Set her free from . . . sin . . . and send Your Holy Spirit to dwell with her . . . who lives and reigns for ever and ever. Amen."

"Amen."

"Do you believe in God, the Father Almighty, Creator of heaven and earth?"

"Yes, I do."

"Do you believe in Jesus Christ, his only Son, our Lord, who was born of the Virgin Mary, was crucified, died, and was buried, rose from the dead, and is now seated at the right hand of the Father?"

Muci's heart nearly broke.

"I . . . believe," Muci mumbled, "with perfect faith . . . in the coming of the Messiah . . . and though . . ."

"Do you believe in Jesus Christ, . . . our Lord?"

"And though . . . he tarries, I will wait for him." The priest must not have recognized the creed of Maimonides that Muci had learned so long ago in Jewish religious classes.

"This is our faith. This is the faith of the Church. We are proud to profess it, in Christ Jesus our Lord. Amen. . . . Is it you will, Margit, to be baptized in the faith of the Church?"

"God have mercy on me." Again, was the priest ignorant of what she was implying, or was he being merciful?

"I baptize you in the name of the Father . . ."

"*Sh'ma Israel,*" Muci silently mouthed the Hebrew words of the Jews' proclamation of the oneness of God.

"and of the Son . . ."

"*Adonai eloheinu . . .*"

"and of the Holy Spirit."

"*Adonai echad.*"

The fragrant oil of chrism with which the priest then anointed Muci's forehead, and the holy water that he poured over her head, streamed down into the flood of tears covering her cheeks, all flowing into a common stream over her lips and touching the tip of her tongue with a strangely pungent tang that permeated her mouth and the whole of her face and head.

"Margit, you have become a new creation . . . and have been reborn in baptism. . . . May Almighty God, the Father, and the Son, and the Holy Spirit bless you. Amen."

The priest paused. "Wait here," he said, anticlimatically. He disappeared behind the altar and reappeared a few moments later with a document in his hand. "This is your baptismal certificate. You see, our perfect Church moves slowly and cautiously. But the body of Christ has a sacred heart when individuals are in need. Go in peace, my child."

"Thank you for your kindness, Father," said Muci, as she stood up from the altar and nodded her head in gratitude, if not in reverence.

She left the church and began the long walk home along the Danube. God help me, she said to herself, I know that I will forever remain a Jew. But will I ever dare tell my children what I have done today? She felt deep sadness, and not a hint of relief or liberation. But Muci also felt undeniable gratitude to the priest who baptized her. She let herself believe that simple human compassion had actually broken through his church's rigid scorn.

As she walked along the gray stone river wall, through the momentarily placid and balmy war-torn city, Muci still felt a chill that penetrated to her bones. She pulled the collar of her jacket up over her neck, but it did nothing to warm the cold that suffused her body. The leaves on the birches and acacia trees on Margit's Island, slightly back over her shoulder, barely moved in the tepid, motionless air overhanging the city. Only the rumble of distant exploding bombs periodically set them into fluttering motion. The world was crumbling in what felt like its final days. Yet the river's edge was rife with summer's tall grasses and red and yellow wildflowers that had not all been trampled by frenzied citizens or desperate fugitives, or squashed by the debris of buildings or motor vehicles thrown over the river walls and now cluttering the shoreline. With the sham baptismal certificate inside her jacket pocket, Muci didn't really think it possessed much power to change the course of events in her life. And with the crumpled yellow Star of David clenched tightly in her hand inside her other pocket, she knew, with greater certainty than ever before, who she was. Her fate would be that of her fellow Jews, and her destiny was the Jewish children she hoped and prayed she would one day bring into the world. Knowing that, Muci felt at peace with whatever was to befall her.

❖

The radio reports in the early afternoon of October 15, 1944, had left the Jews of Budapest in a mood of wild jubilation, for they thought that a unilateral armistice declared by Regent Horthy signaled the end of the war. Many of them threw off their yellow stars and were ready to dance in the streets. Yet later that same afternoon, the Germans moved in and ousted Horthy and his government. Military leaders instructed Hungarian troops, over the same airwaves, to remain in their fighting positions on the outskirts of Budapest in order to defend the city against the Russians, who were quickly approaching. Celebration turned to utter despair in a matter of hours.

A new government, headed by the Arrow Cross, was now in control. Jewish expectations of the worst materialized immediately. Within hours of the German-installed Nyilas government taking power, bands of their armed, uniformed thugs, many no older than teenagers, took to the streets in murderous rampages. Jews, or those suspected of being Jews or of helping Jews, were shot on the streets or marched in groups to the Chain and Margit Bridges and there were shot and thrown into the Danube.

There is a Jewish legend of how, at times of great distress, when the Messiah had tarried for too long, some Jews angrily threatened that, if only they knew where He lived, they would break all the windows of His house. During the last months of 1944, the streets of Budapest were strewn with broken glass. Allied bombers were unrelenting, and even when buildings had not been directly hit, the concussive blasts of the bombs blew out windows for seemingly miles around. After the war, one of the few things Elza would mention about wartime Budapest would be the glass—the mounds and piles and rivers of glass.

About a month after the Arrow Cross took power, Miklós's labor battalion was reassigned to Budapest, where they would clean the streets. For the past several months, the unit had been in the city of Hatvan—as denoted by its name, sixty kilometers from Budapest, to its east. There the men had worked on an electrical power station where they had been interrupted continually by Allied air raids. During the raids they had been forced to evacuate the building and bide their time playing cards in the overgrown meadows below. The men were worn-out and disheartened. But for infrequent one- or two-day furloughs, they had barely seen their families in almost a year and a half. They didn't know many of the actual details of the war, but they couldn't believe that the Axis was continuing to fight.

Miklós himself had managed to survive. Many of his peers had not. He watched as they had perished from the cold during the winter before, or from the previous summer's scorching heat while they insulated the suffocatingly hot power station in Hatvan. Some had died from starvation or were shot to death. Some had escaped or simply disappeared. Others had gone mad. Though they continually reminded themselves of their good fortune in not having been sent to the Ukraine or Serbia, their human dignity and any earlier optimism had virtually disappeared.

In more buoyant times, Miklós's friends in the labor unit had nicknamed him Hoot Owl for his constant, anxious refrain, "We're never going home. We're never going home." But now there was a mixture of rage and despair in his voice. Perhaps, like his father before him, he was leaning over a precipice from which, if he were not mindful, there would be no return.

The best part of being transferred to Budapest for Miklós was being able to live with Muci. The commander told the men who had families in the city that if they failed to return each morning to their barracks for their daily work assignments, the entire remaining company would be marched to the Austrian border and then out of the country. "That day might soon come, anyway," he told them, "when you will be needed to help fortify Austria's eastern wall against the Russians. But why hurry the day and push fate's hand? It's better here than there, believe me."

But another of Miklós's companions from the labor unit, György K., did not feel duly warned by his commander's statement. In November he tried to escape from the two-story barracks on Columbus Street where they had been stationed since their arrival. György tried to seek shelter with any Hungarian Gentiles who, he hoped, would be charitable and courageous enough to take him in. After three days, however, György returned to his unit, having come to believe that he was endangering the Christian friends with whom he had gone into hiding, not to mention his colleagues in the labor unit for having fled. "Boys," he told his companions, "we can't do this kind of thing. We run and hide with friends decent enough to take us in. But they only risk getting killed or ingeniously tortured for it. You're fortunate enough to knock on someone's door and have it slammed in your face. If you're less fortunate, you're denounced on the spot. There's no escaping this."

With fifteen people or more living in a one-bedroom apartment, even the consideration of other residents could not accommodate Miklós and Muci with the privacy they had never gotten during their married life. But they slept on the same mattress and managed to keep each other warm in the ill-heated apartment during the cold, snowy November nights. Their sleep was punctuated by the rumbling of bombs and the screeching of distant or nearby sirens.

"How did you manage to get those potatoes for our supper?" Miklós asked one night, in a faint whisper. The money from his salary was running out and it was getting hard to get food, especially since Jews were being robbed, beaten, and even shot on the streets.

"It seems amazing now when someone behaves decently to us," Muci said. "Mr. Schindler's daughter went shopping for me during curfew." Schindler was the manager of the apartment building. "She said she hated to think what could happen if I went out myself, with all this ugliness."

Just then, Miklós grimaced, reminded of something he had quietly carried around from the day before. "Do you remember my friend Otto from the labor unit? He came to visit us the day after our wedding."

"What about him?"

"He was wounded by low-flying Allied planes that strafed our unit with machine guns when we were marching in the street last week. They thought we were soldiers. I told you about that."

"I remember." She had been terrified by Miklós's story.

"Otto was one of the men who was wounded. They took him to the hospital. But yesterday, when I sneaked away to visit him, he was gone." Miklós paused and swallowed. "An old man who was a patient there told me that the hospital had been raided by the Nyilas, looking for Jews. They were almost finished with their search when he saw a nurse slip one of the militiamen a note. She must have denounced Otto as a Jew because he was dragged from his hospital bed, taken out to the street, and shot. They threw his body into the river with the others."

Muci let out a deep, sorrowful sigh, covering her eyes with the palm of her hand.

"I just don't get it," Miklós tried to finish. "The nurse had nothing to gain. She didn't want his money, or his house, or his job. She just wanted to be rid of another Jew." Miklós's voice was trembling.

"Dear God," said Muci, "we're living in a jungle with no laws. I'm sure there's no other place like this in the universe, where cruelty is right out in the open. People are either letting us be butchered or gladly handing us over to the Nazis. Why do the Christians hate us so much?"

"I don't know." But Miklós *did* know, yet he still couldn't admit what was all too obvious by now. He knew why Christians hated Jews. He had always known. But he always tried to deny it and push it out of his mind with every ounce of strength in him. And still he persisted in his denial, even while the drama was being played out on the streets of Budapest. The indifference and passivity, the rage and the hatred of the people who had lived as neighbors for nearly a thousand years was finally and fully out in the open. Miklós knew why but could not say it.

❖

The morning of the third of December proceeded in what had become the usual manner. Miklós left the apartment early to get to Columbus Street in time to receive his day's work assignment. When he got to his barracks, there was great commotion. In the large building next door, there were a lot of police and gendarmes milling around. Miklós didn't suspect any personal danger and went ahead with his assignment to shovel snow on Rottenbiller Street, a main thoroughfare barely five or six blocks from their apartment on Király Street.

When work finished that evening, no one responded to Miklós's repeated knocks at the apartment. Finally, the kindly house manager, Mr. Schindler, appeared in the foyer. As his sad voice cracked with emotion, he told Miklós that after he had left that morning two armed Nyilas militiamen had come to the apartment house and blared out with a megaphone that all Jews had to report to a certain address on Columbus Street.

"They were all told to take a few days' belongings with them," said Mr. Schindler, with a look of grief on his face. "I'm so sorry." He barely could finish speaking, and he buried his face in his hands.

Miklós gasped. His head was spinning.

Mr. Schindler lowered his hands. "They all knew," he said, "that this day might come. We did, too. My family and I trembled as much as your dear wife and her mother."

Miklós took a deep breath. He grasped Mr. Schindler's arm. "Thank you, dear man," he told him. "You and your family have helped us survive until now. God will bless your goodness." Schindler squeezed Miklós's forearm and nodded, forcing a meager smile.

Then, as he walked to the front door of the building and opened it, stepping out into the dark, snowy night, Miklós turned around once more before shutting the door behind him. Mr. Schindler was weeping as he looked straight at Miklós.

"God will judge our nation," Schindler finally said, "for what we are doing to the Jews."

Miklós ran furiously through the streets, gasping for air. He had just put in a full day of work shoveling the early winter snowfall. He was exhausted. But still he ran. Though his legs felt quickened by panic and terror, he could taste the vaporous blood from his lungs in the back of his throat from the sudden and unaccustomed exertion. Panting and heaving, he must have run two miles without stopping, over icy and snowy sidewalks, hoping to find out where on Columbus Street his wife might still be.

When he arrived at his barracks, breathless and nearly delirious, he guessed by the continued commotion in front of the adjoining building that this was where Muci's group was being held. The building had been some sort of large civilian institute before the temporary barracks had been built in its courtyard and garden. Still wearing the white armband of a baptized Jew around his coat sleeve, Miklós knew that the several Arrow Cross militiamen hovering around the front of the building had no regard for acquired religious differences. He dared approach only close enough to catch a glimpse inside, where guards and city police were seated and apparently still processing a crush of new arrivals. He realized he would have to wait until the morning to find out if Muci was still there.

After a sleepless night at the barracks, Miklós arose, considerably earlier than the others. As the sun began to cast its first light behind the row of buildings, he went outside carrying a small duffel bag with a few scant changes of clothing, and watched the internment building from a distance.

Barely fifteen minutes after the sun had risen, Miklós noticed three or four city police vehicles and a small number of army trucks pull up to the building. Within a matter of minutes, there were armed police and gendarmes, soldiers and Arrow Cross militiamen swarming around the front entrance. Through their megaphones they gave blunt calls, first outside, then inside the building for people to awaken, come outside, and begin moving over to a nearby field. Within a matter of minutes, hundreds of weary and frightened-looking people streamed out of the building. Miklós spotted Muci leading her terrified-looking mother and aunt out the door and across the street, heading toward the snow-covered field. He had to act quickly or else he would lose them in the swiftly moving flow of people.

Miklós walked over to the side of the building where he could not be seen by the militiamen guarding it. There was a wrought-iron fence, about four feet high, separating the building from his barracks. Without hesitating, he pulled off his white armband and let it drop to his side, grinding it with the heel of his boot into the snow. Then Miklós quickly scaled the fence so as not to be detected by any of the guards. He ran over to where he had seen Muci less than a minute earlier and moved in double time with the flow of the crowd until he caught up with her. He called out her name and grabbed her forearm from behind before she could turn around.

"What are you doing here?" Muci gasped as she turned and saw him. "How did you get here? Get out or they'll take you, too."

"Your blood is my blood. Where you go, I will go. Your people will be my people."

Muci tried to mask her smile. "This is a time to recite poetry? Don't be stupid." Then she became more serious. "You know, they'll take you, too. And maybe you don't have to go."

"No, I'm sure they will take all of us sooner or later. What good might a few more days do me, especially without you?" Miklós's voice cracked as he continued walking with her.

At the open field, just down the street, people had only a few minutes with their loved ones before guards barked out orders for them to separate—first, women on one side, men on the other, and then people younger or older than forty. "I will find you," Miklós called out to Muci, shouting over the blaring megaphones and the press of people. "We will be together again. I will always be with you." But as the crush of the crowd carried them away from each other, Miklós struggled against the awareness that he might never see his wife again.

Soon Miklós heard that the older people would be discharged to their homes. He dared not imagine how utterly panic-stricken Elza would be to have to leave her daughter behind. Then he and the other men were ordered back toward the internment building, where transport trucks waited.

Arrow Cross stood at the rear of each truck. Before they started boarding the men, they relieved each one of them of whatever he had in his pockets. They collected wallets, loose money, valuables, and whatever else. Feeling his back pockets, Miklós suddenly realized that, ever since his return to Budapest, he had been carrying a printed document in his back pocket, signed by the papal nuncio in Budapest, Angelo Rotta. All of the men in the labor unit had been given such a paper, in an effort to extend to them at least the belated protection of the Vatican. Miklós, like many of the men in his unit, felt it was a useless courtesy, coming when it did, so late in the process—a mere token of assistance given to those whom it had little real chance of helping. The nuncio had been in Budapest for fifteen years, considerably longer than the Germans had. Many of the more cynical men in the unit suspected that he surely must have known long before this—either through his own offices or directly from the Vatican—what would soon happen to the Jews of Hungary, and eventually, to those remaining in Budapest and the labor battalions. The nuncio's handing out of protective papal passes in November, after most Jews had already been deported or massacred, was meagerly anticlimactic, simply too little too late.

But it wasn't the usefulness of the papal document that concerned Miklós now. He was more worried that it would betray him as a deserter of his labor unit. He dreaded he might be shot on the spot. Since it bore his name and the nuncio's signature, he couldn't very well just toss it out as he had his white armband. Feeling panicked, Miklós took the document out of his pocket, crumpled it up into a small ball, and stuffed it in his mouth. The taste of the paper on Miklós's tongue felt like a bitter Communion, the final sacrament of his failed church, like no other he had ever received before. Having long ago lost its power to redeem from sin and evil, it sat on his palate like a stone before he gagged on it and, finally, spit it out.

After the Arrow Cross men had emptied his pockets, Miklós boarded the back of a truck with dozens of others and was promptly taken to the Joseph Municipal Train Station. That same snowy winter afternoon of December 4, 1944, he was crowded with approximately eighty other Jews into a cattle car, which sat alongside scores of other similarly packed boxcars, and taken on* what would prove to be a horrific journey.

Muci was detained for another day in the internment building on Columbus Street, after her delirious mother and aunt were discharged back to Király Street. Early the next morning, Muci, too, was boarded onto a truck and taken to a transitional apartment not far from the train station. There she was placed in a one-room flat on the building's second floor with about thirty other women, where they would stay briefly but wait endlessly for the next move to be made. They were guarded by one armed and uniformed Arrow Cross militiaman, a boyish-looking teenager who couldn't have been older than eighteen.

Late that afternoon, the guard stuck his head into the room where the women were standing or sitting, helter-skelter, nearly on top of one another. "You, come here," he said, pointing his finger at Muci. "You're going downstairs to buy some food."

Muci felt self-conscious for being singled out. She walked out with the guard as the heavy wooden door shut behind them. They were not going far, only downstairs and out the front door to the next building, where there was a small grocery store.

Within view of the guard, who remained standing outside the apartment building, Muci walked over to the store and bought barely enough bread and apples for the thirty women. It would hardly take the edge off their growing hunger, but it was something. When she returned, the guard, still outside the front door of the building, gazed a Muci, this beautiful young woman barely three years his senior.

"You shouldn't come back in the building," he said to her.

"What do you mean?" asked Muci, holding tightly to the bag of groceries.

"You're just going to be deported. You know that, don't you?"

"I suppose I do. But why are you telling me this?"

"I didn't want any of this to happen. I need for you to know that. I didn't know what terrible things would be done to these poor people." The boy sounded sorrowful and pleading. "Look here, I live in a farming village. My family is not like this. The Nyilas came to our home and made all these promises of a fancy uniform and a rifle, and the chance to win Hungary back from our enemies. I didn't realize they meant the Jews. All I've seen is cruelty, terrible, terrible cruelty toward innocent people—old people and children. Please believe me, I didn't want any of this."

"I've also seen those horrible things," answered Muci, "done by men who enjoyed what they were doing. You seem more innocent. Maybe I do believe you."

"Then please run away. Take off your yellow star and find a place to hide. Because if you don't, they will take you away tomorrow to Germany or to Poland. It's not for labor, like they say. You would die there. I know it. They would kill you."

Muci paused, looked back toward the street, and then inward toward her own thoughts.

"If anything should ever happen, if things get worse—as you know they might—let me know. . . . Before your train pulls out of the station, think about it. You would be safe with me."

Muci thought about the detective's offer, but not for very long. She told herself that she was the wife of the man she had always loved, and she was a Jew, and would decidedly always be both. She would not try to hide who she was, not with the help of the officer or anyone else. Nor could she just bolt into the street. She would surely be arrested and shot if she were found. Though she had always been the pampered and cherished child of a widowed mother and adoring grandparents, uncles, aunts, and cousins, there was no one left to watch over Muci, and nowhere to find safety. In the biting cold of that December afternoon, with the Star of David sewn firmly to her coat, she was weary and resigned to her fate. "I have no place left to go," she told the young guard as she stepped past him, back into the building.

✤ **CHAPTER 13** ✤

Death and Resurrection

Örök bolygók, örök riasztgatók, Idők kovászai,
megyek én is veletek, bélyegesen, csillagoson.
(Eternal wanderers, eternal alarmers, leavens of time,
I too go with you, branded, bestarred.)
Endre Ady, *"A Bélyeges Sereg"* ("The Branded Host")

As the doors to the boxcars swung open, the sign over the train station read CELLE. It had been cold enough when the men left Budapest at the beginning of December. Then for days frigid winds had swept into the train cars and lanced the men's faces. But it was now weeks later into the winter; they seemed to have traveled considerably northward and could well be in Germany. After all of them got off the train, they stood shivering outside the boxcars, waiting for the next order.

"You have some walking left to do, gentlemen," barked one of the guards. "It's more than a couple of kilometers from here. It will get your blood circulating again."

As the deportees walked along the frozen ground from the train station to a yet unknown destination, they saw townspeople lining the road, most of them standing several yards removed from it, but still within a short distance.

As hundreds of exhausted Budapesti Jews trudged on, any number of the local inhabitants along the road began yelling angrily and hurling stones at them. At first, Miklós couldn't really hear what they were saying. But then, as a second and then a third onlooker from the roadside began repeating the same refrain, he was able to make it out all too plainly. The words pierced him painfully: "Christ-killers! Christ-killers! You dirty Christ-killers!" Three, four, five times, then a dozen more. Then it became countless, the rhythmic ranting of the angry scattered mob, come out on such a stinging cold day to honor the coming birth of their Lord with their accusatory howls at the ones who were finally—after nearly two millennia—about to pay for their damnable crime.

It felt like the death blow to Miklós's life as a Christian. Walking down the road, the cold winter air closing in on him, Miklós heard the echoes of all the accusations in all the passion plays, on all the Good Fridays throughout his entire life as a Catholic. He knew that this was the answer to Muci's question, which he had resisted answering days earlier in Budapest, "Why do the Christians hate us?" It was now fully out in the open. The Jews were cursed by God for killing His only begotten Son, and they would be eternally damned for it. He had been taught this, had recited it and sung it in church. In riveting clarity, he now remembered his cousin being attacked and beaten during his childhood. He remembered the laughter of the people in church in Báránd. And then, for a fleeting instant, Miklós remembered his former joy as a Catholic—the Masses he had served with his brother as an altar boy and the festive weeks of Advent they had always celebrated together throughout the years of their childhood. He remembered how they had walked through the narrow roads of Báránd pretending to be in the brotherhood of St. Francis, spreading the Gospel of Christ's love and heralding the Kingdom of Heaven. And Miklós remembered the day at Sunday Mass in Szarvas when he had knelt and kissed the hand of the new priest who was his identical twin brother.

As stones continued to whirl past him, and the shouts had grown so loud he couldn't even hear himself think, Miklós wondered if, somewhere near the Adriatic, in a tranquil friary, his mirror image knew that Christ had died without benefit to those who now viciously held the Jews to account for His suffering. Did Gyuri realize that those who expressed love for his Savior's life and hope in His death had utterly forsaken His compassionate heart? How would Miklós ever explain this to Gyuri? And would his devout brother ever believe that the world that Miklós inhabited was not likely one to which God's only begotten Son might ever dare return? Would Gyuri hate Miklós, as those along the road did, if not for killing Christ, then for defining His death as bereft of meaning and vacant of the power to annul the sins of those along the roadside who now dared invoke His name? For if Christ's death could purify *these* sins, then Miklós would all the more willingly share the fate of those whom they now condemned.

He walked on. The sky was gray and night was falling. The damp, cold air penetrated to his bones. He was shivering, but he didn't know if it was from cold, fear, or despair. Another stone whirled past him and missed. Miklós closed his eyes a moment. He could still hear the people yelling. It was the longest walk of his life. A few miles later, he passed under the gates of the place called Bergen-Belsen, with little hope that he would ever walk out under them again.

Miklós and a group of about forty men were placed in what was called a *Sonderlager*, or special barracks, of the camp. All of the men wondered what made the barracks so special, aside from the fact that they were allowed to wear their civilian clothes rather than the chafing blue-and-gray-striped camp uniforms worn by others. He had heard mention of some prisoners having been sent earlier to Switzerland in exchange for trucks, supplies, and money. He wondered if his group might be exchanged, as well. It gave a few of the men some hope. Others of them, separated from their families and having witnessed their way of life disappear, had nothing left to hope for. It no longer mattered to them. For Miklós, it mattered only insofar as it meant possibly being reunited with Muci. It was as if each of them had a responsibility to the other to stay alive.

A few days after his arrival, Miklós stood outside his barracks with a group of five or six other men in his *lager*. They watched as a newly arriving trainload of prisoners was trekking down the same road they themselves had traveled a few days earlier. On the other side of the barbed-wire fence, perhaps a few hundred women moved toward the gate, thirty or forty yards away from where the man stood. Then he saw her. It was Muci in her familiar gray woolen coat. Her curly black hair was matted down under a dark-colored scarf, which she clutched with both hands in front of her throat. He looked for several seconds to be sure it was her.

"My God, that is Muci," he screamed in a fit of rage. "The world has gone mad. It's gone totally mad." Some of the men next to him grabbed his arms and pulled him back. One of them put his hand over Miklós's mouth, trying to stifle his scream, hoping to spare him any jeopardy. This usually soft-spoken and stoical man had quietly endured untold suffering and humiliation. But to see Muci at this moment moving toward the gates of hell unleashed an explosion of rage and panic in him that burst the walls of his impassive character. "Those goddamned Nazi pigs. They are destroying everything. The world has gone mad."

He had avoided thinking about it before, but Miklós now felt certain Muci would never survive. She was too fragile and could never endure the hunger and cold. This was a girl who had been sickly throughout her childhood, who needed virtually an army of loving caretakers to help her feel that life was bearable and worthwhile. In Budapest, she may have acquired a wily instinct to use her beauty and charm to fend for herself. But here, thought Miklós, under the physical hardships of this depraved place, Muci was a weak and frightened child who didn't stand a chance.

Miklós tried to tell himself that at least he knew where Muci was, that she would not be killed outright, and that perhaps—for all he knew—she, too, might be handed over to the Swiss. Maybe he was just rationalizing, giving in to the tricks of his mind, but he convinced himself that her nearness now offered him some hope. Somehow he felt it would magically give him the strength to survive for both of them. If neither God nor Jesus Christ could save them, then Miklós himself would hold on to the hope of survival for both himself and the beloved wife whose presence gave him the will to go on.

✤

Muci and her group of new arrivals were promptly given blue-and-gray-striped coarse camp dresses, which itched and chafed terribly. They were given flimsy coats that hardly protected them from the frigid cold of the northern German winter. In the *lager*, the women slept on boards stretched across makeshift bedposts, with mattresses of frozen and rancid straw stuffed into sacks. Muci was grouped not only with Hungarian women with whom she had traveled on the train, but also with women from Slovakia and Poland. Some of them had been interned in one concentration camp after another for nearly the entire duration of the war. Most looked sallow and embittered, some as if they were the walking dead, with no discernible expression of emotion left on their drawn and emaciated faces.

It wasn't long before Muci was barely able to endure the starvation. They received one meal a day of brown, watery soup with slivers of horse meat, along with a small ration of bread. She thought of almost nothing else but food, and had to guard her meals, for they would frequently be stolen or simply grabbed away by desperately starving women.

One night Muci dreamt that her loving grandmother Bertha, her *Nagy-mama,* had come to her with a tray of her favorite pastries to soothe her terrible hunger. As Muci began to eat them in her dream, she was awakened suddenly by the woman who squeezed next to her on the wooden plank on which they all slept in the cold, dark barracks. Roused and startled, Muci looked up and began to cry. She complained out loud to herself, or to whoever else was listening and understood Hungarian, "If they don't give me food here, why can't I at least eat my dear grandmother's pastries while I'm dreaming?"

"Don't be stupid, you whimpering sissy," said a Polish woman who was awakened by the commotion. She spoke in Yiddish, the only barely understandable language between them. "No one cries about anything anymore in here. Where did you get those tears, anyway? I haven't seen anyone cry in years." Then she let out an inhuman laugh. Muci was sure the woman had gone mad.

A Hungarian woman who had been in the camp already when Muci arrived rose up from her bed, two bunks away from Muci's, and came and knelt down beside her. She began to stroke Muci's face, wiping her tears gently off her cheeks. "Look at these, my little sister," she said in their native language, lifting an open hand that was wet with Muci's tears. "These will keep you alive and keep you from losing your mind. Don't be bothered by the laughter. If your grandmother visits you in your dreams, remember that she is not coming to feed you, but to remind you of your tears. Your tears will keep your soul alive. I have only been here a number of months, but I have seen the souls of many die who have lost their ability to cry."

Muci smiled and felt comforted for the first time in a long while. To be reminded that she still had a soul was comfort enough. She took the woman's moist hand in her own and kissed it. The lump in her throat had softened and, though tears still flowed down her face, her heart felt lighter. In the midst of all the sorrow and self-pity her heart contained, there was now a little space for gratitude. She felt she had been comforted by an angel.

In the morning, Muci approached the woman again. "Thank you again for your kindness," she said to her. "I am Margit, but I've always been called Muci."

"And I am Éva. You must be from Budapest," the woman replied. "You just got here several days ago."

"Then you know that we were the last to be taken."

"Yes, I do. I'm from Budapest, too, but I was visiting my parents in their village in the south just before the Germans arrived in the country. As soon as we had to begin wearing the yellow stars, it was impossible for me to get back to Budapest. So when the Germans came for my parents in the spring-time, naturally I was taken, too. I pray that my husband is still alive in Budapest, that maybe they didn't take him. We had just been married and we were so sure that God had meant us to be together. I don't know if either of us could survive without the other."

"I was just married, too, and feel the same way. It's good to find someone so kind as you whom I can speak to in my own language."

"You'll find enough Hungarians here, don't worry."

"There are others here from Hungary?"

"Oh, plenty. They saved the camps up for us, at least those of us they didn't dispense with right away."

"Dispense with? What do you mean?"

"Did the Germans and Hungarians really manage to keep all of this such a secret for so long? Most of us were taken right away to Auschwitz, a camp somewhere in Poland. Many of us, like my dear parents, never returned. They were killed." Now it was Éva who was weeping. "You see, my parents are gone, but they are still with me. My tears for them keep them alive, and they revive my soul, reminding me to stay among the living."

"I don't mean to make your burden greater," said Muci, "but I don't understand. What do you mean they were killed? You mean they died? Of hunger?"

"Dear child! It is unspeakable. You don't need to know, not yet. It's just not good to know. Soon there will be no more secrets. You'll find out soon enough. But why should I make your life even worse than it already is? Please don't force me to be the one to tell you these things. For now, regardless of how they died, I am certain that all of them died for *kiddush ha'shem*, the holiness of God's name." Muci hadn't been aware that she was speaking to an Orthodox girl.

"I am not so religious as you, and not as hopeful. I don't know how I could go on if my family were killed in this place, or if my own hunger gets any worse."

"You can go on," said Éva, in a gentle voice, "by making a promise to God and making sure you keep it when you leave here. We Jews have always made bargains with God. Even our teachers Abraham and Moses did it in order to save lives. Even if you are not a religious girl, you can still make a promise to become a better Jew, just in some small way, and maybe God will save you for it."

"What kind of promise?" asked Muci.

"Something as small as keeping a kosher home or lighting the Shabbos candles."

"My grandparents kept kosher. I remember in the summers when I visited them in Slovakia, the *shochet* would come to their house to slaughter the animals in the right way, to make them kosher. I used to love the way my grandmother would cover her sewing machine on Friday night and light the Shabbos candles."

"So keeping a kosher home wouldn't be so hard for you. Believe me, God may spare you for it. He doesn't want us to disappear. We have survived these things before, and we will again. There must always be a vestige of us to fulfill the commandments."

"But I don't know if I can promise something I'm not sure I can keep," said Muci. "The only thing I am sure I can promise God is that I will have Jewish children. I would tell them about what happened here to the Jews. And I'll tell them about you, too, about how you tried to make me a better Jew." Muci paused as tears ran down her face. She touched the tears with the tips of her fingers and held them up to show Éva. "I'll tell them how your goodness kept my soul alive. I know I can do that. Yes, all right, I would also cover my sewing machine on Friday night and light the Shabbos candles. But I can't make other promises that I may not be able to keep."

"Then that will have to be enough." Éva smiled. "I myself have made promises, but I'm not sure it is intended for me to return. I suppose I don't mind, because even here I can keep the commandments, like not eating the miserable *trayf* soup they give us. It's certainly not kosher."

Muci was stunned. "How do you stay alive?"

"My soul is still alive and I want to live a long and happy life with my beloved husband. But seeing my parents and sister die tore up my heart and I may need to be with them. I know I am commanded to eat to preserve life. But I just can't. I won't. One thing they can't take away from me is my observance of the commandments. Listen, if I should die while we are together, please find my husband, Moshe. Tell him I loved him as much as life, and that I died from a weakened body and a broken heart. But tell him that my soul was whole and that I sanctified God's holy name in the way that I lived and died. Can you promise me that?"

"I promise you and hope that I never have to keep it," said Muci.

It was only a matter of a few more days before Muci discovered other Hungarian women in the same barracks. One day, Éva pointed to a group of four or five of them in a far corner of the barracks. "You see those women over there?" she asked. "I was with them in Auschwitz. Their families are gone, too. They're the only ones left. They're from the southern regions of the country."

Muci's eyes darted up in curiosity. "My husband's relatives are from Szarvas."

"You see that one over there, squatting down against the wall with her head down? I think she's from Szarvas."

Muci swallowed hard and clenched her hands in order to steel herself for what she was about to do. She walked in small, hesitant steps over to the woman Éva had pointed out. With Muci standing above her, the woman didn't look up. Squatting, her shoulders and back hunched over her knees, the woman's head was bent onto her chest. Twirls of brown, greasy hair were matted against the woman's scalp. She had a wild look, as though she were broken by sorrow.

"Are you the one from Szarvas?" asked Muci, touching her on the shoulder.

The woman looked up and stared blankly at her questioner. "Yes, I am," she said in a flat voice. Then she lowered her head back down onto her chest.

"My husband's relatives lived there. Did you know them? The Pogánys. The father was the animal doctor and—"

"I knew them," said the woman, without raising her head a second time. "They were converts. The doctor was a good man." Then the woman looked up, almost with a glimmer of life. "Everyone liked him. We all knew them. But they kept to themselves. The doctor died before they took his wife." The woman paused.

"What happened to her?" Muci's voice was tremulous. Her knees felt weak.

The woman winced. It was almost a scowl, a crazy scowl. She pressed her thumb and forefinger onto her eyelids and rubbed them back and forth, as if considering whether to answer at all. "What do you want me to tell you?" the woman said with the same disconcerting monotone. "Do you want to know she was the only Christian in the Jewish ghetto in Szarvas? That she was taken to church by the same people that put the rest of us on trains to come here? Do you want to know that the Jews scorned her for it? Shall I tell you she carried her crucifix with her on the train? I saw her. I saw her before she died. I was there, in the camp, by the entrance to the gas chamber."

With those words, Muci's head began to spin. "Gas chamber?" she asked with childlike incomprehension. "Where is she now?"

The woman pointed her finger up to the sky.

"I don't understand," said Muci. But she was catching on, her fears rising like smoke and twirling heavenward.

"There are things that are not to be spoken," the woman continued with no hint of feeling, as if her emotions had either died long ago or there were none that could have matched the reality of what she was saying. She didn't seem to notice Muci gasping and looking upward. "Many of the people getting off the trains were already in great pain. The guards took the last of their jewelry before they went in, in whatever way they could—the rings off their swollen fingers. Then I watched as the people went into the room, to be showered. That's what they were told. They all knew they would die. They cried and they prayed. In the midst of all those *Sh'ma Israels*, I heard the doctor's wife cry out and pray to her Savior. Then I heard her say the names of her children as she walked on and disappeared with the rest of them."

❖

Weeks passed. Muci grew weaker and weaker. It was a miracle she survived at all. Éva was still there, too, which was even more of a miracle. Muci got strength from her, as well as from her grandmother, who, she was sure, kept calling to her in her dreams from God's kingdom, reminding her, in whatever way she could, of life's goodness and sweetness.

Before much longer, though, Éva's strength had all but vanished. She was frail, almost a skeleton, and seemed to have surrendered any final hope of surviving. But there was still warmth to her smile and a glow to her eyes that never disappeared. One winter morning late in January 1945, Muci was still asleep on her freezing bunk when she heard a voice, more inside her head than in her ears: "Good-bye, dear sister, remember your promise." Then, a jolt roused Muci awake—something very strange and powerful. She leaned up onto her elbows and saw that the barracks was still. It must have been just before daybreak. She looked over at Éva, lying only a few feet away, on her side, with her back to Muci. On an impulse, Muci reached out to touch Éva's back. The flesh under the coarse striped camp dress was stiff and taut. Her body was impassive. Muci swallowed and was afraid of what to do next. Taking her friend's shoulder, she pulled Éva's body and rolled her over, fully onto her back. The arms moved stiffly, in unison, like a mannequin's. Éva's hands, with fingers prayerfully intertwined, were wedged against her chin. Then Muci saw that Éva's eyes were open and were staring blankly up toward the bed planks above her. Muci touched her face and closed her eyes. They were icy cold—colder still from what appeared to be streams of frozen tears that had hardened onto her cheeks before they could dry. Éva had died in the night and must have wept final tears of sorrow and longing. Her body was dead, but her frozen tears told Muci that her soul was alive.

Muci tried to believe that Éva was with God now, and with her parents. But she truly didn't know. She had always been afraid of death, truly terrified of it—the child who grew up without a father, never understanding the explanations of why he was not there. As far as Muci knew, death meant bewilderment, absence, even abandonment. And just at that moment of doubt and terror, she saw, hovering over Éva's stilled body, a black and smoky apparition of a woman's scornful face, an amorphous body and a shrill, evil laugh. Was this the angel of death, Muci wondered, seeing in her fear an opportunity to taunt her? Or was she simply losing her mind? In the early morning light, she dismissed the specter with a swipe of her hand through the heavy and foul air, now thick with fear and death. She would not be intimidated by a trick of her mind or of the devil. She thought instead of her promises to Éva and felt reassured by her determination to fulfill them. She couldn't promise God anything, but she would fulfill her vows to her gentle friend. She reached out and once again touched Éva's cheeks. "Farewell, dear friend. You are the only sister I ever had. I will remember my promises."

✤

The next day, an SS guard came into the barracks and singled out Muci, along with a handful of other recently arrived women, and ordered them to assemble and ready themselves for transport.

"You have been chosen," the guard said as he paced up the aisle where the women were lined up against the row of bunks, "to provide labor for the war effort in another location. Since all of you are young and have only been here a matter of weeks, you have some strength left to work on other important projects for the Reich. And besides, you haven't had your heads shaven, at least not yet," the guard sneered. "So you've retained your healthy appearance and good looks," he said, interrupting his remarks with a sinister laugh. "Since you'll be going to a more civilized place, we wouldn't want anyone wondering why we are employing such wretched-looking corpses. So, for the time being, dear ladies, you'll keep your hair."

The women were given their daily food rations and then marched back to the train station at Celle the same way they had been marched to the camp weeks before. On that freezing cold morning, as they once again boarded the cattle cars, Muci stood on the wooden platform of the car and reached up to grab hold of an icicle hanging from the roof outside. She had no bread or soup left, but this way she could ease her thirst by eating the long, dirty stick of ice.

Nearly a full day later, when the women arrived at their destination and the boxcars were pulled open, they were told they were in a place called

Raguhn. It meant nothing to any of them. But as they left the train, some of them overheard mention of the city of Dresden. The women were promptly marched a short way to a makeshift barracks in an industrial area, alongside a large factory. At the building's ground level there were large windows through which they could see airplanes being manufactured.

By the next day, Muci and her company of recent arrivals were put to work in the factory, assembling airplane parts and munitions. Their ration of food had not improved substantially since Bergen-Belsen, which to Muci seemed stupid on the part of the Germans if they expected important military hardware to be assembled properly. She was put to work fitting and riveting wings of airplanes. After several days of relentlessly exhausting work, Muci wasn't sure if she was deliberately sabotaging the plane parts she was working on or if she was simply too weary to hold her arms in position to do the job right.

"You should find yourself a scarf to wear around your neck," said the SS lieutenant. "You'll catch a cold in this damp factory."

"Where am I going to get a scarf?" answered Muci, who had been working on the floor of the factory for an hour in the early morning chill. She didn't dare express a fraction of her disdain for the officer's obtuse solicitude.

"I guess you're right," said the lieutenant. Did he have any idea, Muci wondered, how maddeningly ridiculous he sounded?

Then, looking around the production floor, he caught the attention of the *Aufseherin,* the female supervisor, and barked an order at her. "Find this worker a scarf, or at least a pin for her collar. We don't need them getting sick, do we?"

Later that same day, as the women were returning to the barracks, the lieutenant once again appeared on the factory floor. Noticing that he was watching from a distance at the other end of the floor, Muci was afraid that he would see how slowly she was walking. For weeks she had had open blisters on her feet from the oversized army boots she was forced to wear. As she had feared, she saw him approach out of the corner of her eye. She bit her lip and tried to keep her eyes straight ahead. But continuing his approach nonetheless, he walked up directly behind her and gave her a hard, swift kick in the calf. "You're holding up the line, you bitch. Keep up with the others."

Muci cried out and sank to one knee, holding her leg. When she looked up pleadingly at the young guard, he quickly changed his tone, apparently recognizing the young woman with the pretty face and the pin fastening her collar together. "You know the whites of your eyes have turned yellow. You should be on a diet. Be careful what you eat."

"Maybe I'm taking too much butter with my toast in the morning. Or is my Wiener schnitzel too greasy at dinnertime?" she thought to herself. "You are either a moron or a sadist, or both, you crazy son of a bitch." She knew exactly what she would say, but dared not open her mouth.

A few days later, in mid-February, during the Allied bombing of Dresden, with sirens squealing, the women workers were being marched down to the factory basement for shelter. Anxious guards prodded the women with their bayonets, trying to get them to move more quickly. Once again, Muci was singled out. Moving no faster than before in her ill-fitting boots, she had been repeatedly poked on her back and arms by one of the guards, with so much force that the blade penetrated the coarse material of her camp uniform. She was certain her skin had been punctured and she was bleeding. She shuffled on. Then the frantic guard, who must have been terrified for his own safety, even more forcefully thrust his bayonet toward her, this time lancing Muci's backward-turned palm. Blood spattered the floor and the front of her camp dress. She held the hand under her opposite armpit to try to check the flow of blood. "Forsaken, we are forsaken," she said, under her breath, not even knowing where the words were coming from. "Why have you forsaken us, dear God?"

❖

Miklós never set eyes on Muci again during the weeks they were both in Bergen-Belsen. He, too, was kept in lice-infested squalor, on a near-starvation diet consisting of the same thin soup, small pieces of bread, and black water that passed as coffee. Along with the Hungarian men with whom he had been deported, he had been moved from one barracks of the *Sonderlager* to another. Deliverance to Switzerland never materialized. Eventually, though, the men began receiving packages of food from the Swedish Red Cross, about every two to four days. They suspected that most of the provisions were stolen by guards and camp personnel. But it was obvious to them that what little food did get through saved their lives. At times, the men would spread margarine onto Swedish crispbread and sprinkle sugar on top. Though the food was not very nourishing, it was infinitely better than camp fare and at least gave them the energy to fantasize about the Hungarian delicacies they might someday eat again. Miklós and two of his fellow prisoners, Béla and Taki, whom he had been with ever since the Columbus Street transport in Budapest, even traded recipes for those dishes. They meticulously described the preparations, down to the kind and quantity of spices to be used and the cooking time. Entire conversations centered around food.

"Of course, you start with soup, like chicken with noodles."

"Unless you make goulash soup the whole meal. Isn't it amazing all the things you can make with paprika and onions, green peppers and tomatoes?"

"Goulash or *lecso,* whatever meat you put in the *paprikas* gravy becomes food of the gods. I personally like *virstli* [frankfurters] in the *lecso.*"

"*Töltött kaposzta* [stuffed cabbage] is my personal favorite, stuffed with tender meat and real sauerkraut, not that imitation sweet stuff."

"And for me, even the thought of *solet*—its beans and smoked goose—takes me back to my family's dinner table. Just talking about it, I can smell it."

Wednesday evening, March 28, 1945. Miklós was still in Bergen-Belsen. It was the first night of Passover. As the sun set, he watched a group of starving men observe the seder. Obviously, there was no available Haggadah (the prayer book for the seder ritual). But some of these men were sufficiently learned that they knew the prayers and blessings by heart. And if they happened not to know the precise wording of the story, they certainly knew the story itself and could tell it with conviction and compelling detail, in both Hebrew and Hungarian. The words of the songs, of course, must have been etched in their minds since they understood language—the tunes even earlier. Instead of matzah, a number of the men had traded their bread rations with other inmates for *dürgeh müzeh,* scant Swedish wafers that were part of the Red Cross packages. Miklós stood watching the group of twelve or so men along the narrow middle of the floor between the rows of wooden bunks. He was deeply touched by their willingness to sacrifice their more tolerable rations for such flimsy wafers.

In a near whisper, a religiously observant man recited the Hebrew blessing for the traditional cup of wine. This was a rusty container of black coffee that a number of men had saved up from their morning rations. Then, he held up a stack of three wafers of the makeshift matzah in a piece of soiled cloth that had been covering it. There, in the dark and sordid barracks, cold and damp with early spring, he recited the blessing in Hebrew, again in a faint whisper, and then repeated it in Hungarian:

"This is the bread of affliction that our forefathers ate in the land of Egypt. Let those who are hungry come and eat with us. Let all those who are in need come and share our meal. This year we are here. Next year may we all be in the land of Israel. This year we are still slaves. Next year may we all be free."

A few moments later, an older and equally knowledgeable man sitting next to the leader raised the cup of "wine" and recited God's promise to the children of Israel. "Though you will be strangers and slaves in a land not your own, your enslavers will be judged, and you will at last go free." Then he gave the Jews' response, in a tear-choked voice:

"This is the promise that has sustained our forefathers and ourselves. For it was not one man alone who rose against us to destroy us. In every generation they rise up to destroy us. And God, blessed be He, saves us from their hands."

Miklós was speechless. He was moved to tears. As the speaker finished, another man looked up at him as he stood across the aisle against the row of bunks. The man waved for Miklós to come sit next to him. Miklós walked over and sat down. Other onlookers sat down as well. Without hesitation, another man handed Miklós a piece of the wafer that had been passed around. He took it and awkwardly held it, looking around to find out what to do with it next. He saw that the others all waited until a blessing was said over it, and then they ate it. Miklós followed suit. How strange and, yet, how dear it felt to him.

"This was your Lord's Last Supper, wasn't it, Miki?" said Miklós's friend Béla, sitting next to him.

"It feels more like ours, doesn't it?" replied Miklós. "I always learned and believed that His death erased sin and brought us closer to God's kingdom. But there is no kingdom of heaven here, or even close at hand."

Béla was a short, stout lawyer from Sopron. "No," he said, "here it's just the kingdom of the damned. And we Jews have always lived in it. It's not a very savory place, but we don't trouble ourselves much for eternity."

"Aren't you afraid of death? Don't you pray for redemption, for the salvation of your soul?" asked Miklós.

"We've always prayed for it. It's part of the Jewish liturgy. But our loudest prayers are the ones you're hearing tonight. It's when we remember being liberated from slavery in Egypt. We pray for liberty as a living people more than for the salvation of our individual souls after we leave here. This is the bread of affliction," Béla continued, holding up the wafer. "Tonight we pray for liberation from this modern-day Egypt."

"How curious," Miklós said. "With one wafer, consecrated as the body of Christ, I enter eternity, freed from sin. With this one, I accept the fate of the people into whose midst I was born."

"Miki, my friend, we Jews don't ask for Christ's salvation—not yesterday, not tonight, and not tomorrow. We just want freedom to live as a people in peace and dignity. The only redemption we seek is from Christian hatred and Nazi evil. What more desirable salvation can there be than that?"

"Salvation," said Miklós, "we have no control over. But dignity: I can't think of anything more dignified than what we are doing here tonight."

"Then you, too, are bearing witness, my friend," said Béla, placing a warm, reassuring hand on Miklós's forearm. "You have reclaimed your Jewish soul."

"So I have," said Miklós, returning Béla's gaze. Miklós felt he had just crossed a great divide and had returned from a long journey. He had never felt so free.

✤

The bread of affliction in Bergen-Belsen was still the body of Christ in San Giovanni Rotondo. There, in the friary church, Gyuri was serving Padre Pio at Easter Mass. Over the years, he had learned that the holy padre had long experienced horrible episodes of spiritual torment during many nighttime prayer vigils, as if he were literally being attacked by the devil. As Gyuri now stood alongside this modern-day suffering servant during the consecration of the Host, he knew that Padre Pio agonized over the scourges suffered by Christ, which he himself carried as open wounds on his own hands, feet, and chest. This was easy to notice, even for people who were unfamiliar with the padre's stigmata. He shouted and then bit off the Latin words, which transformed the Communion wafer into the body of his Savior. Then he jerked his hand violently back from the chalice of wine, which was to become Christ's blood, as if he were in too much pain to grasp it. His facial muscles twitched and he shed tears of agony. His head lurched from one side to the other as if the devil were striking him invisible blows. Many years later, Gyuri would say that there was nothing as miraculous and moving as the moment that Padre Pio transmuted the wafer and wine into the body and blood of Christ. Upon the completion of the consecration, the padre looked greatly relieved, as if the devil had lost yet another battle.

The war years only added to the trials of the saintly padre. He prayed, he wept, he suffered over the ferocious evil that was sweeping the world. He feared that an Axis victory would enslave the world and threaten the existence of the Catholic Church.

"Do you know," Padre Pio asked Gyuri one day toward the end of the war, "what I would do with Hitler if I could get my hands on him? I would have him put in a cage and taken everywhere in the world so that he could hear what people are saying about him." Men's hearts had turned away from God,

Padre Pio complained, and were not ready to turn back to Him. He was said to be aware of the tremendous suffering that the war had caused so many innocent people, and of the hundreds of thousands of victims of human cruelty. But was he being circumspect in not mentioning any specifically targeted group? Or did he just not know?

What might Padre Pio have thought of the religious justifications of those who participated in, or passively stood by for, the cruelties against Gyuri's brother and his fellow Jewish victims? Could he have discerned the darkness in Christian hearts by which men, women, and children stood along the roadside to Bergen-Belsen and hurled stones at the murderers of Christ? Was he aware that the body of Christ had somewhere on earth reverted back to the bread of affliction? And could all his years of dark nights of spiritual torture, inflicted on him by the devil himself, be compared to the anguish Padre Pio might have felt from such knowledge?

✤

It was the seventh of April, 1945. At least a part of Bergen-Belsen looked as though it were being evacuated that day. Miklós and the surviving prisoners dragged their worn-out and rag-covered bodies out of the gates of the barbed-wire enclosure and began the nearly twelve-mile trek back to the train station in Celle. No one knew where they were going, but they were elated to be actually leaving the camp.

At Celle, the prisoners all boarded a waiting train. Small children and the very ill were placed in passenger cars. They wondered if this signaled an imminent end to the war, even though armed SS were still visible. The rest—men, women, and teenagers—boarded boxcars. Only about forty people filled each car, half as many as had been crowded in on the journey to the camp.

Over the course of hours and days of traveling, the doors of the boxcars were occasionally swung open by the guards. It was April and the snow had long since melted. There were thousands of birds that could be heard even above the rumble of the train. Spring was in full flower and foliage on trees was budding. Miklós would never forget the sight of white poplars brushing against the open door of the moving train. Equally unforgettable were the stunned faces of the children and field-workers who gazed at the trainload of these tattered "enemies of the Reich" as they passed by. And there were also the awful inscriptions on the train station walls, inciting German citizens to persist in a fruitless war.

The train journeyed for five days through the German countryside. On the night of April 12, Miklós and the others heard furious gunfire. In the morning, the guards were gone. But the prisoners, too long accustomed to their captivity, did not dare budge from their prison on wheels. Miklós could hear others mumble about how unwise it would be to try to disperse into a countryside where people had been taught to hate them. They were stunned and afraid. Yet when guards still failed to appear by noon, Miklós and some of the others made their way to a nearby brook to drink and wash. Some had gone foraging in the woods and farmlands for anything edible.

By the time they all got back to the train, it was already late afternoon. The sky was painted red. To Miklós, it seemed as if all the blood that had been shed in the war was strewn across the heavens. The wind had blown all day but had now stopped, leaving an eerie stillness and silence. A war-torn world had finally become quiet. It was a natural pause, nothing as other-worldly as the silence of the heavens, nor as transcendent as the echo of God's—or His Son's—stilled voice. God's world and man's were now irreparably riven apart, and even echoes of one could no longer be heard in the other. But it was a majestic silence nonetheless, replete with promise of a final end to war if not the beginning of a heavenly peace.

A few minutes later, while there was still light at dusk, as the mass of prisoners sat quietly along the side of the train, there was a rustling in the nearby bushes. Then armed soldiers appeared from out of the brush. But these were not Germans. They addressed the crowd in English, and told them that they were Americans of the Ninth Army. They told them that the war was over and everyone would be safe. Those who understood translated the few essential words for the others, into German, and Hungarian, and Polish. Miklós and many of the others stood up, shouted, and wept for joy. They hugged and kissed the American boys and thanked them in whatever language they could for giving them back their freedom and dignity. It was the thirteenth of April 1945, somewhere near Farsleben, Germany.

Seeing the wretched state of their new charges, the Americans began distributing food rations. It was meager army food, to be sure, but it was overly rich fare to camp inmates who had not digested a good meal in months. Some of the people who had earlier gone to the brook had found potatoes and wild fruit, which they had already devoured. A good number of them bolted the army rations, filling their stomachs as rapidly as they could. They could not stop putting food in their mouths. Some of them instantly became violently sick. A few died within hours.

By the next afternoon, the entire group was put back on the train, to be taken, they were told, to Neu-Hillersleben, where they would be cared for by the British. The sick would be hospitalized. By this time, disabling weakness and burning fever accompanied Miklós's bottomless hunger. He suspected that he, too, had symptoms of typhus, the scourge that had already taken countless thousands of lives among the prisoners in Bergen-Belsen.

✦

"What is it, Don Giorgio?" asked one of the friars in the convent garden. "You look like you bear grim news for us today."

"I'm afraid I do, dear Father. Even now, toward the end of the war, the news is not good. I have learned from the radio report that the world has lost a great leader. Yesterday, the twelfth of April, 1945, President Roosevelt of America died of illness." A few friars standing nearby frowned and kept silent.

"He was a great man," said Padre Pio, who had been listening. "If it wasn't for him, we would not be coming out of this war."

For some months now, Gyuri had been listening to Radio London from his room in San Giovanni Rotondo for news of the progress of the war. The war bulletins on Italian radio were utterly discouraging for their brevity and unreliability. In the evenings he would bring word of the London reports to the Capuchin fathers in the friary garden, where they would congregate every day in between their religious obligations.

Even Padre Pio would join the friars in the garden—albeit usually for briefer, perhaps twenty-minute periods—before quickly returning to his rigorous regimen of prayer or hearing confessions. Sometimes he would take walks with Gyuri or any of a number of friars through narrow, cypress-covered archways of the garden, or would watch as some played bocce. At times, he would sit with the friars and listen to Gyuri's war report. Though it seemed that the war was nearly over, the news within Italy was usually terrible, and in other parts of Europe it was not uniformly good. To be sure, it was an exceedingly narrow window onto the world, but it was a tremendous relief to the fathers to receive reliable information.

Gyuri had once written to his parents and family in Hungary that in San Giovanni Rotondo he often had difficulty imagining that there was a world war going on. Since that time, it had become increasingly impossible to avoid the kind of news bursting over the airwaves this day. Yet even the reports of Radio London would never be able to bridge the gap between Gyuri's twin brother's experience in the heart of war-torn Europe and his own life in this loving monastic community nestled along a mountainous plateau overlooking the Adriatic.

✦

One morning in the early spring of 1945, while walking into the airplane factory in Raguhn, Muci caught a glimpse of herself in the ground-floor window.

She did not recognize the emaciated, skeletal figure in the striped, blood-stained camp dress that returned her gaze. She saw unfamiliar eyes, sunken and hidden in the darkened folds of her eyelids. They had become the desolate eyes of a child who had long ago forgotten how to cry. Muci held her hands up in front of her face and touched her cheeks with the tips of her fingers, as if to convince herself that it was indeed her own sorrowful gaze in the window. As her eyes scanned the dusty, darkened glass, Muci saw the body of a withered old woman who could never again be loved or desired by even her adoring husband. She was terrified that, having lost the ability to cry within the last few weeks, her soul had left her body, and that it was only a matter of time before that body would shrivel and die. She thought once again of the dark, ugly specter that had harassed her the terrifying day in Bergen-Belsen when the body of her young Hungarian friend lay next to her, staring blankly up at the wooden bed plank above her. It felt to Muci as if even death would provide no respite from her misery. For what was there to look forward to but blackness and emptiness? She wished at that moment that she could pray. She still felt ashamed for being baptized, for even pretending to abandon her Jewish faith. But if God were alive and were really God, He wouldn't be letting all this happen. She wouldn't let herself pray to someone whose existence was so dubious and whose loving-kindness was so lacking. Instead, Muci thought of her grandmother Bertha. "Please help me *Nagymama*, you've got to help me," she repeated to herself. For an instant, Muci almost felt a tear coming into the dried-up wells of her eyes. And then she thought, too, of her prayer—no, it was her promise, to Éva, maybe even to God—to give birth to Jewish children, to teach them and always remind them what happened here, to her and to the Jews.

Finally, in April, Muci was taken from Raguhn to Theresienstadt, a camp in Czechoslovakia that had, at least at one point, been paraded as a "model" camp by the Nazis. There, earlier in the war, Jewish families had been displayed living together in supposedly tolerable circumstances. Now tens of thousands of people occupied a space meant for five or six thousand. In early May, wardens and guards hurriedly abandoned the camp following a dramatic uprising in nearby Prague. A few days later, Soviet troops arrived. In June, Muci was put on a train transport back to Budapest, this time by open boxcar.

At one station on the return journey, a number of the women with whom Muci had been together for many months were huddled together in the rear of a boxcar, afraid of being approached by Russian soldiers. They had stationed Muci at the car's door, her frame and face having become so wasted and shriveled that they were certain that she would act as a human scarecrow, discouraging any soldier's interest in having his way with any of them. A hacking, consumptive cough only intensified her repulsive appearance. Holding onto the sides of the door's opening, her arms outstretched, Muci was exploited now only for her misery. "Look at our sorry substitute for a divine savior," she overheard one of the girls say in the back of the train car. "There's no salvation or even comfort with this one," said another. "Just a little protection."

When Muci finally arrived at Budapest's Keleti Station, there was pandemonium on the platform. The Russians had provided a Jewish relief agency a list of returning survivors. Even those whose relatives were not on the list came to look for loved ones. Muci saw her frantic mother almost instantly, although she had to look twice, because Elza's hair was now as white as snow.

Elza, dear Elza, had remained in the Jewish ghetto for the duration of the war. She had nearly given up hope of ever finding her daughter alive. At that moment, standing on the train platform, she couldn't have imagined that someday three little children would call her *Nagymama,* Grandma.

She saw a sickly woman with hideously protruding bones and only a stubble of hair walking toward her with wide eyes and a broad smile, in apparent recognition and anticipation. Elza looked through her, either because she simply didn't recognize her or because her mind froze at the possibility that this human skeleton could be her daughter.

"*Anyukam,* my sweet mother," said Muci when she was finally close enough to speak. "It's me, Muci." Elza then fixed on her daughter's face for a brief instant, gasped, and promptly fainted.

"Éva . . . Éva . . . Éva," a man desperately repeated in the middle of all the chaos and excitement. Elza had barely revived to have a moment together with her daughter when Muci turned her head in the direction of the persistent and desperate voice. She saw a young Orthodox man, no older than his late twenties, with a scraggly beard and very thin white arms dangling from the short sleeves of his white shirt. Muci felt an instant lump appear in her throat, and she began to cry. Tremendous, unendurable sorrow flowed from her eyes. She thought her heart would burst. She kept looking at the man until he saw her.

"Do you know Éva? Do you know my wife, Éva?" the man asked in profound anticipation.

"I don't know," said Muci, her words punctuated by heavy sobs. "From

Budapest?" she wanted to ask, but couldn't. "Gone to visit her parents in the south?" But she just stood in place and said nothing.

"Do you know her?" the man asked.

"I knew someone by that name in Bergen-Belsen," said Muci evasively. "We were together." She couldn't come right out and tell him. "She saved my life and my soul and tried to make me a better Jew," she managed to say in a faint whisper, almost mouthing the words in total silence.

"Where is she now?" the man persisted. "Do you know where she is?"

"She taught me the meaning of my tears," Muci wanted so much to say, "and told me not to forget to cry. She helped me stay alive." The man surely must have thought Muci was deranged as he looked upon her uncontrollable weeping. But still she couldn't speak.

"I beg you, if you know where she is, please tell me. I beg you."

Muci took a deep breath and stiffened her body. "You are Moshe?"

"Yes," he said.

Muci must have wished at that moment that her tears were words and that the man would understand. She must have wanted to say, "Your dear wife has left me with all her tears. I guess she doesn't need them anymore. I promised her I would never forget." But Muci just stood, her lips trembling, and continued to weep.

❖

In Neu-Hillersleben, American troops replaced the British, and were soon replaced by the Soviets. Miklós spent two weeks in a hospital ward with other typhus victims, where, ironically, German physicians conducted rounds with junior doctors-in-training and lectured them on the medical conditions of the former concentration camp victims who were their patients. "Not exactly a classical case of typhus we have here," said one of the pedantic senior physicians as he stood next to Miklós's bed, when he had just spiked a fever of 40° centigrade.

The hospital staff was carefully instructed not to feed the emaciated patients overly rich solid rations. But Miklós's hunger was unabating and he grew impatient. He summoned his friend Taki and asked him to smuggle heavy cheeses and even whole salamis into his hospital ward at any opportunity. Taki threw them in to Miklós through the first-floor window, none of the hospital staff being any the wiser for it.

The Russians were an inscrutable presence. No sooner had they taken over command of the post than they emptied out the camp and loaded up the train with the recovering survivors. Without being told where they were going, many people suspected they were being taken to a Russian internment camp. When they arrived at their destination, even from the train station, they saw that it looked ominously like an abandoned German concentration camp. Most people were too paralyzed with fear and indecision to make any sudden moves. But Béla, Taki, and eight other daring souls, including Miklós, stayed behind and hid inside an empty boxcar on another track. By the time the others had entered the camp, the group of nine men and one woman didn't have to think about what they would do next. The train started moving and traveled nonstop for hours, until late into the night.

When the stowaways got off the train in the morning, they saw that they were on what appeared to be the outskirts of a most peculiar, otherworldly place where there was hardly a building fully intact. Miklós looked around and couldn't believe his eyes. It was a place of nearly total devastation. As far as the eye could see, there was almost a solidly leveled plain of charred rubble. "Look for the sign over the station," said one of them. "Find out where we are." They found the station building, which was nearly destroyed, its ceiling collapsed and large sections of its outside walls lying in huge chunks of brick and mortar. The sign identifying the city was dangling from one end of the metal canopy facing the railroad tracks. It read DRESDEN. But the place might as well have been a planet in a distant galaxy. Or maybe this *was* the planet Earth, Miklós thought, that unique corner of the universe he remembered Muci once talking about, where cruelty had fully burst forth and become the custom and all pretensions to civility had disappeared. The scorched plain in front of them was the inevitable outcome. It looked like the end of days.

It was the middle of August. The war was over. The group of ten stayed in Dresden only as long as it took to get their bearings. They found food and shelter through a relief agency they heard about on the streets from shell-shocked local residents who had no place left to live. Desperate to find a way to get back to Budapest, they managed to get passage on a train going south to Prague. It covered only the first leg of their journey home, but it would have to do.

Prague had returned to a far greater semblance of normalcy than Dresden. Relief agencies were hard at work and there seemed to be at least a thin layer of civil authority operating in the city. When they arrived at the train station late on the afternoon of August 18, Miklós and his companions looked at the arrival and departure board above the ticket window. They discovered that a train was scheduled to depart for Budapest the next day. With his companions hanging over his shoulder, Taki stepped up to the uniformed official at the ticket window and asked him matter-of-factly, in German, "How do ten Hungarian refugees from Germany get back to Budapest?" The man answered, with equal nonchalance, that they would have to get transit passes at the transportation ministry in another part of the city. He told Taki there would be enough time to get them before their train departed. Hearing this, Miklós turned to the others and reassured them with a smile, "We need passes, but we're going to make it. We'll be home soon." No one dared say anything, but a mood of muffled elation showed on all of their faces.

In the morning, having spent the night in a school building converted for refugees, seven of the group went back to the station while Béla, Taki, and Miklós headed for the transportation ministry, located along one of the side streets of the downtown thoroughfare. Inside, seated at a desk in the middle of the marble floor, a glum-looking ministry official greeted them.

"We're here for ten passes to go to Budapest," said Taki, in a peremptory German. For all that they had been through, Taki, for one, was not about to tolerate any authoritarian haggling.

"I would keep my voice down, if I were you," the man answered far more hesitantly in the same language. "People have been beaten up on the streets, you know, for speaking this damned language."

"Excuse me, sir," Taki said, nodding and lowering his voice. "The last thing I need is for someone to think of us as German."

"It's obvious you're not. I already know that you're Hungarian. And I can guess from looking at your emaciated faces where you're coming from. I probably know more about you than you think."

A puzzled look crept over Taki's face and creased his brow. But he didn't ask what the man meant. This official, thought Miklós, was not as bureaucratic as he had expected.

Taki pressed on. "We were just now in Dresden. There is nothing left of it. Before that, we were taken care of by the Americans and British after we left the camp called Bergen-Belsen. It's somewhere in the north of Germany. If we hadn't escaped when we did and wound up in Dresden, I'm sure the Russians would have taken good care of us," Taki said with a wry smile.

"Yes, I'm certain," said the man, nodding, looking as if he were trying to squelch a smile of his own, "I know quite what you mean. Now, what was it you needed? Ten passes to Budapest I recall, for ten Hungarians longing to get back to their well-loved homeland. I imagine it's been some time for all of you since you were there."

"We return with mixed feelings," added Béla. "But it's our home."

As Béla spoke, the official had already begun to fill out a single piece of paper that would serve as transit pass for all of them. There was something unusually kind about him.

In a matter of minutes, the work was finished. The man handed the pass to Miklós, who stood alongside Béla. He smiled at all three as they said, almost in unison, "Thank you."

"You're welcome," he said. "You should know," he added, "there is no charge for these special transports."

"Lucky us," answered Béla. "All of our transportation these past several months has been free of charge." The ministry official smiled again.

Then, just as the men turned to leave, the man finally said, "One more thing, gentlemen. In the past, I'm sure you have been exemplary Hungarians. Maybe it's time now to be better Jews."

The men looked at the official and then at each other. A chill stiffened Miklós's spine and spread into his limbs, for at first he wasn't sure how to take the man's comment. But then Miklós's eyes softened. He realized he had been openly recognized for the first time in a very long while, as if by a relative who hadn't seen him in decades. Yes, he thought to himself, maybe it's time to be a better Jew. What a strangely reassuring thought that was.

The train traveled through the entire night, over the Moravian hills and the Slovakian frontier, through Brno and Bratislava, and arrived early the next morning in Budapest. It was the twentieth of August, 1945. The group of ten fellow survivors had now been together for four months since leaving the camp, and a number of them since entering it four months before that. They would not forget one another. But each of them had vital family interests to look into. Were their family members alive? Were they taken away? Did they come back? Or did they manage to survive in the city? These were questions that must have been swirling around the minds of all ten of them. As soon as the train screeched to a stop, they all took off like bullets in different directions, having already said their good-byes, knowing that they would surely reconnect with one another again.

On that hot summer day, as Miklós stepped onto the platform at the Keleti station and walked out to the street of the city, he felt in a daze. "I am home now," he said out loud, as if trying to convince himself it was true. "This is my city, my home." But his heart and his body were numb, as if he were a man pinching his paralyzed arm to see if he could feel anything. He couldn't.

Then, by some cruel irony, church bells rang out in tandem in different parts of the city. Miklós didn't understand why they would on a Monday morning. Feeling hollowed out by the sound, he stopped walking and stood in place just outside the station, searching his mind. It's Monday morning, the twentieth of August, 1945, Miklós said to himself. What's so special about today? Across the street, he saw a throng of people exiting a Catholic church. He crossed over and singled out a man about the same age as him.

"Forgive my ignorance," he said to the buoyant worshiper. "But what's the occasion for the Mass?"

"It's St. Stephen's Day," the man said. "Our holy king's name day. Where have you been, brother?" he asked as he hurried on to keep up with the crowd.

"Of course, where have I been?" Miklós muttered, not knowing if the man heard him. "Where have I been?" he repeated, with his hands clenched in fists.

As the church bells continued to toll, Miklós thought back to the summer day in 1918 when he and his brother first entered the church named after the sainted Hungarian king who was presently being memorialized. It was then that Miklós first beheld the passion of his future savior.

Now, nearly three decades later, in the shadow of the tattered and bombed-out city, Miklós's redeemer's passion had lost its power to help him tolerate his own suffering. The day's celebrations seemed hypocritical and offensive, as if Catholics cared more about the founder of their faith—whose entombed hand they were parading around the city—than the suffering they themselves had had a hand in inflicting on the nation's Jews. Miklós's Savior was remote, vanished, absconded. He now felt ultimately forsaken and betrayed—by God and by Christian charity. Only the love and support of his fellow Jewish survivors, and the slim possibility that Muci was still alive, now sustained him. He had to try to find his wife.

Miklós got his bearings and promptly found the Joint Distribution Committee, the major relief agency for Jews. He approached the front desk, where an official had a list of names of survivors. He swallowed hard and took a deep breath. "Pogány, Margit Pogány is my wife. Did she return?" The man looked down at his list. "She was taken to Bergen-Belsen in December and then I—"

"Yes," said the man, interrupting Miklós. "Mrs. Pogány, née Deutsch. Margit arrived back from Theresienstadt some weeks ago."

"She's alive? My wife is alive?" Miklós covered his face with both hands.

"Yes, she's alive," said the man, smiling. "She's in the hospital at the Elizabeth Pulmonary Sanitarium in the Buda Hills. She has tuberculosis. She was originally in grave condition but, God willing, she'll survive. Go see her. But be prepared, dear man. She's probably very wasted, like many others."

Within hours, exhausted from his travels, Miklós journeyed to the Buda Hills and found the sanitarium where Muci was a patient. He ran up to her room and found Elza standing outside a closed door, stationed there like a watchdog. Miklós hadn't seen her in eight months. It might as well have been ten years.

"Elza? It *is* you, isn't it?" Miklós said, looking intently at her. He had known her since he was a small child. But she was so drawn and wizened.

"Yes, of course, Miklós," she answered, with smiling eyes. They hugged warmly and stood for several seconds in each other's embrace. "We all look a little different, don't we?" she continued. "My hair started turning gray when they took Muci away, and then it became completely white in the next few weeks, when the bombs fell closer and closer to the ghetto."

Miklós had also changed. His shirt and pants hung from his emaciated frame and his heavy-rimmed eyeglasses now appeared too big and severe for his gaunt and bony face.

"The ghetto?" But Miklós had already turned his eyes toward the closed door in front of him.

Elza picked up on it right away. "Of course you want to go in. But please let her rest. She's finally getting a little sleep."

Miklós looked back at Elza. He suspected she was afraid of having him see his wife in such terrible condition. For the moment he tried to oblige her. "The ghetto? What ghetto?"

"About a week after you and Muci left, Rosi and I and the other Jews on Király Street were taken around the block to a fenced-off and guarded area they called the Jewish ghetto. There were thousands of people and barely any food. We ate raw onions and the carcasses of horses that died in the streets. Many people died of hunger or typhus or were shot by crazed mobs of 'Death Brigades.' We had to cart the bodies through the streets and pile them up in the synagogue courtyard on Dohány Street."

Elza's report was shocking, but Miklós was already numb from his own misery and impelled by his urgent need to push past Elza and open the door. "You had your own variety of hell to live through, didn't you?" he managed to say, his words dribbling out with no conviction behind them.

"If it were not for wanting to stay alive for Muci," Elza answered, "I would have wished that the bombs had fallen right on top of us. The streets, I can't begin to tell you, were filled with glass from the bombs. There was never a day, not even a moment, when we felt safe, not from one side or the other.

The Russians finally came in January. But then we heard rumors that the Germans were going to blow up the whole area before they ran. I'll never understand it, Miklós. I'll never understand the hatred."

Miklós winced, feeling that he couldn't listen to any more. He was sinking into his own emptiness.

But Elza still pressed her luck, trying to buy a few more moments. "You just came today, didn't you? You look exhausted. But I also have some good news." Miklós couldn't even raise his eyes to look at her. "I have seen your sister, Klari." Now Miklós looked up with a start. "I was visiting others in the hospital when I saw her."

"How is she?" Miklós finally asked. Elza now had his attention.

"She's recovering. The poor woman. She just got back a few weeks ago from her own ordeal. She was also in a camp and was beaten terribly when she tried to escape." Miklós gasped as Elza drew a more measured breath before continuing. "The doctors don't think she'll ever be able to have children. But Klari's got a strong spirit and I have already introduced her to a gentleman, a patient in the hospital whom I knew years ago." Elza had an almost whimsical look on her face. "He's also a convert and a survivor. Maybe they'll find some things in common. He's a very sick man. But God knows they both have to go on with their lives somehow."

"You always were the matchmaker, weren't you, Elza? Even at a time like this." Miklós couldn't resist smiling.

Elza glanced toward the door behind which Muci lay. "I want you to see her, but I know you'll be shocked. You won't recognize her. She barely has any hair, and her head is still bandaged from lice and infections she had on her scalp. When she returned home, she was barely sixty pounds. She's not much more than that now. I'm so afraid the shock of suddenly seeing you will harm her, and that you will find her hideous. Please be patient with her."

"What are you saying?" asked Miklós, glaring at Elza. "I've waited too many months. Do you think that matters? I'm going in."

Elza nodded, with an anxious look on her face. She pulled open the door and Miklós looked in. The figure in bed, draped in white sheets and bandages, turned her head toward the squeaking door. Their eyes met. Muci moved her mouth but no sound came forth. Miklós remained quiet and walked into the room.

Elza was right. Her daughter was unrecognizable. Muci looked as though she had returned from the dead. Miklós went over to her and leaned down to embrace her. She could do no more than lift her shriveled arms. He gently lifted her fragile body and held it close to his, keeping to himself his shock at seeing her wasted frame. He touched his face to hers and gently kissed her cheek. Then he carefully lowered her back down onto the bed and sat down beside her. Neither spoke. They wept together in silence. It was the happiest moment of Miklós's life.

"Looking forward to this moment," he finally said, "was all that kept me going."

"And me," whispered Muci.

"You are the only savior left in my life."

"Don't be silly," said Muci, her sunken chest heaving in labored breathing. "I'm a simple Jewish girl." Her words were punctuated by short bursts of coughing.

"And I'm a simple Jewish man."

"What do you mean?"

"Your blood is my blood. It always has been. When I was a child, they taught me that baptism transforms the soul. But in the end, they didn't want me as a Christian. They treated me as a Jew, and lo and behold, I will be one.

"I heard stories," Miklós went on, "from my friends in the labor unit that Jews were not kind to converts. But they have never been anything but kind to me. When I got to the camp, these people prayed and sang on Passover. They had barely any food, and they gave away their bread for measly little crackers. And they asked me to join them. I'm telling you, I've never experienced anything like it."

"I'm glad something good may have come of this. I have memories, too," said Muci, "and promises that I've made. I haven't been a good Jew, but I will always remember."

"The only thing I know about being Jewish is knowing how to hope. That's what I learned from the Jews. If I still believed in God, I would thank Him for making me a Jew."

Muci was breathing heavily again, but she pressed on. "In the camp, I had so much trouble thinking of God. . . . I couldn't pray. All I could think of . . . was you, . . . and my mother, . . . and my grandmother, . . . and the children I'm determined to have someday. But for that, we'll need to find a way to believe . . . in a kind God who cares about us."

✦ CHAPTER 14 ✦

Ascension

Hol a tiszta szavak nem dadognak,
El innen, végre, a magasba, föl! (Where sacred words do not falter,
Away from here, finally, heavenward, on high!)
Attila József, *"El Innen"* ("Away from Here")

September 1945: "Giorgetto," said Padre Pio in his unforgettably sweet voice, which immediately implanted itself in any listener's soul. "You haven't been yourself for several days now." The padre and Gyuri were taking their daily walk around the friary garden of Our Lady of Grace. Padre Pio was gentle and natural and did not put on airs. He was fond of telling jokes. But on this day his faithful secretary did not seem in the mood to hear any.

"You've noticed," answered Gyuri.

"Of course, it's not difficult for any of us to tell. People at Mass could see it. And when I sit with you over the correspondence I know that your mind is elsewhere."

"I didn't want to burden you or any of the other fathers," said Gyuri. Padre Pio dismissed his statement with a mildly piercing look. Gyuri proceeded. "I've received a letter from my brother."

"Your twin. In more ways than one."

Gyuri wasn't sure what the padre was referring to. "He told me my mother has died a terrible death in a place in Poland where Germans put many people in gas chambers." The padre looked horrified. Gyuri paused. "He and our sister also were taken to concentration camps, but, thank God, they returned. So did my brother's new wife, a Jewish woman who is a distant relative of ours. She and our sister heard about the fate of our mother from different sources, but my brother didn't want to believe it. I don't either."

"Why not?" asked Padre Pio, his horror having turned to a look of more composed concern. If he knew something, he was not saying. "If it is reported from two sources, perhaps it should be believed."

"Do you remember," answered Gyuri, "the Hungarian monsignor who visited here last week from Rome? He left just the other day."

"Of course. He joined us for Mass and I heard his confession."

"I shared the news with him and he tried to reassure me. He told me that many people are still returning from those camps and that some of them are in displaced persons' camps or hospitals until they are well enough to return home."

At that, Padre Pio grew silent. He turned and lowered his head slightly and closed his eyes. For an instant he looked pensive, almost as if he were seeing or listening to something inside or beyond himself. "Giorgetto," he said softly, "your dear mother is dead. I am certain of it. She died a martyr, bearing her cross. You can be sure of that."

Gyuri's hands shook as he raised them to cover his mouth. He looked at Padre Pio through the pool of tears that had suddenly filled his eyes.

"We should pray for her," Padre Pio continued. "She needs our prayers, not because she was without faith—she had great faith, you know that—but because there was terrible turmoil surrounding her death. I can see it even now. Her soul is released, but it is still troubled. We will say a funeral Mass for her here, and then we must pray for her."

❖

On an early spring morning at the end of March 1946, Josi, Elza's brother, that most patriotic Hungarian, took time off from his work as a customs inspector and walked through the streets of Budapest to resolve a dream that had turned into a nightmare. He was determined to attend the public execution of two men who were among the most notorious officials in Hungary's campaign of liquidation against the Jews. Many Hungarian collaborators had proceeded with enthusiasm in that campaign, but none with as much relish as these two, and few with as much power to implement the plan.

As Josi continued walking, he hardly noticed the soft, gentle breezes that had lost their chill in the previous few weeks. Nor did he notice that the usually gray sky of Budapest's late winter was a crystalline blue, with only occasional wisps of clouds crossing the path of the morning sun. Josi was not a pensive or complex man. But on this particular day he was turned inward. His thoughts were vague, as usual—insufficiently formed, not entirely coherent impressions. His emotions were heavy and painful. Josi was feeling defeated by the terrible outcome of the war. All his life he had loved Hungary with a passion that countenanced no criticism, neither before nor after its terrible defeat and decimation in both world wars. Although Hungary had fought alongside Germany each time, Josi had never been an admirer of the Germans. He had always feared that they would deprive Hungary of its independence, almost as much as he feared that the Bolsheviks would do the same. He took little solace in the fact that the Hungarian government had managed to retain its autonomy until 1944. After that, it had all but collapsed and Germany had showed its true colors.

By the third anti-Jewish law of 1941, Josi's sons should have been considered Jewish, despite their mother's being Catholic, and should not have been entitled to serve in the Honvéd. But they served nevertheless and fought valiantly, even while they regretted their Jewish heritage, which barred them from becoming officers. The law had caught up with Josi, too. Both his parents were Jewish. For the longest time, his patriotic facade quelled any suspicion of his origins. He kept his job as a customs inspector throughout the better part of the war. Then, when the Arrow Cross took over the government in October 1944, Josi, too, would have been rooted out and persecuted had he not taken refuge in his wife's native village outside Budapest. In spite of his Jewish origins, he had all but embraced his nation's abiding belief that Jews were not good for Hungary. Was he an anti-Semite, or a Nazi? God knows he wasn't. But his irrational love for his homeland might have quietly justified in Josi's own mind some kind of solution to what most Hungarians considered "the Jewish problem."

As defeat became more and more inevitable and the Russians were fast closing in on Budapest, he begged his sons to supply him with a bomb or a grenade so that he could end his misery and not face his nation's imminent dishonor. But his sons had not gone mad. Instead, they just felt sorry for their father.

So why was Josi so decidedly going to the execution of such notorious war criminals? It was, he told himself, to remove all illusions from his mind. He could not go on believing in Hungary's greatness and innocence when the world was rightly prosecuting such horrific monsters. At least this way, Hungary could begin anew, with a clean slate and a fresh reputation, provided, of course, that the Russians would not seize control of the government. But that had not happened, at least not yet, and the Hungarian nation was desperate for cleansing and renewal.

When Josi arrived, a crowd was already forming in the courtyard of the Marko Street Prison, where the sentences were to be carried out—soldiers, government officials, photographers, foreign journalists, and even a handful of civilians like himself. Many stood peering out the second-story windows overlooking the courtyard of the prison, in order to get a bird's-eye view of the proceedings. The makeshift gallows were nothing more than wooden posts driven into the ground to stand at a height of perhaps nine or ten feet. The noosed ropes around the men's necks would simply be straddled over the top of the posts. Their bodies would then be hoisted and suspended only a few feet above the ground until the men expired.

Twenty minutes after Josi's arrival, the two condemned officials, László Baky and László Endre, were led out the prison door, their hands tied in front of them. What was most impressive to Josi about seeing these ruthless murderers was their cowering weeping and whimpering, especially in one of them. He was weak-kneed and had to be almost carried to the hanging post by a man at each arm—this, thought Josi, from the man who wanted not only to kill Jews but to cook them and eat them in goulash. Then, as each man was led to his hanging post and before their legs were tied together, a Roman Catholic priest appeared from along the wall of the prison where he had been standing.

"Father, I don't want to die," said one of the terrified prisoners. "Please commend me to heaven. Don't let me die," he cried, "without giving me my last rites."

"Do you wish to confess your sins?" responded the priest.

"Yes, Father, I have sinned against our people and against God. Will God forgive me? Please tell me, will God forgive me? Don't let me go to hell."

"Then, you confess your sins and seek the comfort of Jesus Christ our Lord and Savior?"

"Yes, Father, I do. Don't let me go to hell. Please forgive me." The man was speaking in loud, uncontrollable sobs.

The priest laid his hands on the man's head and then anointed his forehead and his palms with oil. "Through this holy anointing may the Lord in His love and mercy help you, with the grace of the Holy Spirit. Amen."

"Amen, Father, amen. Thank you, Father, thank you. I am saved now, aren't I?"

Josi was an artless, uneducated man who was never very religious. He could hardly have been called a spiritual man. He had never given much thought to heaven or hell. If being Catholic helped fortify his identity as a patriotic Hungarian, then that's what he would be. That is how he had lived his life. But as simple as he was, even Josi felt diminished by the ease with which a servant of his own church—his wife's beloved religion and the one in which his sons had been raised—could provide dignity to the death of such a devil. Of course, even Josi realized that it was never for the priest or the Church to judge a man before his death. All that was needed was sincere contrition in order for one to merit the supreme unction of the Catholic Church. It was the unquestioned obligation of all priests, he knew that. But something was terribly amiss in this scene. If everything the newspapers were saying about this man were true, Josi finally concluded, then the Church itself should usher him to the gates of hell rather than accept his terror of dying as true contrition. Is that all a man has to do, mouth remorseful words before being executed for unspeakable crimes against humanity, for a priest to provide the obligatory blessing of the Church? Josi was not interested in high religion or theology, but even he felt a knot in his stomach and the kind of shame that makes a man want to be invisible. Though these government officials had proudly carried the banner of Christian love in their efforts to eradicate the Jews of Hungary, they were now receiving the final blessing of their church.

✤

In 1947, with the establishment of the Soviet-supported Hungarian Republic, the thousand-year-old Kingdom of St. Stephen had come to an inglorious end. During the previous two years, war criminals had been brought to justice and survivors had returned from the camps. Miklós grudgingly lived in Budapest, reemployed in his earlier position at the Hungarian Commercial Bank, while Muci continued her recuperation in a tuberculosis sanitarium in the Tatra Mountains in Slovakia, which one of her uncles had helped arrange. Muci and Miklós saw each other a few times a month.

At the sanitarium, it wasn't long before Muci learned the details of her father's family's fate. Her father's mother had died before the war. The youngest son in the family, Arpad, had fled to Sweden soon after Czechoslovakia was invaded. Muci's uncle Alexander, who had arranged her stay, told her that, as a dentist, he had been pressed into serving the invading German soldiers in his town of Liptovský Mikuláš, not far from the sanitarium. He took small comfort in quietly subverting his patients' dental care, sometimes deliberately pulling healthy teeth. When the Nazis came for Alexander's elderly father—Muci's grandfather—the eighty-year-old man hid in a closet until his pursuers threatened to take the dentist's wife, Munci, instead. At that point, David, the erstwhile scoundrel of a father and husband, decisively stepped forth from the closet and willingly bartered his life in exchange for the safety of his daughter-in-law. He was promptly deported to Auschwitz. When their own lives became endangered, Alexander and his family fled to a neighboring village and successfully blended in among the peasantry for the duration of the war. The grim task presently fell to Alexander of informing Muci that her other aunts, uncles, and cousins, thirteen in all, had perished in concentration camps and before firing squads.

Throughout this time, Miklós had remained in contact with some of his camp comrades. His friend Béla had been imprisoned by the Soviets for Zionist activity. The one woman in their group of ten, Vera, had already left Hungary for Palestine, despite the odds against her getting in. Taki could barely wait to regain his strength before leaving for Canada. He would make a life for himself anywhere, but never again, he vowed, in Hungary.

One day, on the street outside the bank, Miklós ran into a former fellow labor battalion and camp inmate. Miklós recognized him right away, even though he looked dramatically different. He was formerly a tall and strapping man, with red wavy hair and a wide, muscular chest. But now he looked hunched over and morose. The gleam in his green eyes had disappeared. "I just can't get my life moving," he told Miklós. "There's nothing left for me."

"What do you mean? Is your family gone?"

"No, I have my wife and children. Thank God, they survived. But all my friends, everyone who was in my life before, are all gone. They're dead or disappeared. Life has no direction. I just don't know what to do with myself." Miklós looked at his former companion. He understood his emptiness. He himself had had days and weeks of such feelings and in idle moments still had to fight them off.

"And you, how about you?" the man asked automatically, as if it were a struggle to muster enough concern to ask.

"My wife survived," answered Miklós. "That's how I can go on. But . . . my mother," he hesitated. "They killed . . . " A knot formed in his throat. It had been the first time he had ever spoken the words and had no idea how hard it would be.

The man put a hand on Miklós's shoulder. "Don't, it's all right. I know. Forgive me for saying this, but in a strange way, I envy your sadness. I should be grateful and relieved that things turned out as they did for me. But all I feel is emptiness."

"I'm relieved, yes," said Miklós. "But grateful? No, I don't think so. What should I be grateful for?"

"I seem to remember that you were such a devout Catholic in the labor unit. You wouldn't hear any criticism of the Church."

"You have a good memory. Yes, I used to feel that the Church would do everything in its power to prevent those things from happening."

"How about now?"

"How about now? My mother is dead, my faith is dead, and the Church is morally bankrupt. It's not just that Christians didn't help. They jeered at us on our way into the camp. I'm sure you remember that."

"Of course I remember," the man said without much emotion to his voice. "But I don't feel any of it. I'm numb. I just don't care," he said as he started walking away. Looking back at Miklós, he added, with almost a trace of interest in his voice, "Don't I also remember that you were the one who was so fond of the Bishop of Győr?"

"The Bishop of Győr?" Miklós was puzzled. "I don't know who you mean."

"Your priest from when you were in school, Father Apor?" He had halted several steps away.

"Yes, of course, Father Apor," Miklós smiled. "When I went to school in Gyula. I remember now, he became a bishop." He suddenly felt a wave of nostalgia stream over him. "Apor helped me become a believing Christian. I almost became a priest because of him. Not that it matters anymore, but what about the dear man?"

"I had relatives in Győr. Some were converts. Some stayed Jews. They praised him and heard more than just rumors that he tried to do all he could for them. He always spoke up during the war, some say even to the cardinal, who apparently didn't do much. Not many people in the Church helped. But the few like Apor should be blessed. He kept speaking up for the Jews, protesting their mistreatment and deportation. I heard they almost put him in prison to shut him up."

"That would have been a first, wouldn't it—a Catholic priest being put in prison for trying to protect the Jews? And where is he now? Is he still bishop? People like him should be the leaders of the Church."

"Maybe he would be, but the Russians got to him first."

"What do you mean?" Miklós asked, swallowing hard.

"Apor disappeared," the man said, with no awareness of the impact of his statement on Miklós. "The rumor was that some Russian soldiers shot him when he tried to protect some nuns from being raped. He meekly raised his arms to keep them away and they shot him."

The image of Christ flashed through Miklós's mind, the humble Savior with arms outstretched, trying to protect the world from its blind lust for life. Then Miklós thought of poor Father Apor, the noble and gentle priest who had once blessed him and his brother and inspired their faith by simply touching their faces. Miklós could still remember his homily that day, when he suggested that salvation was not some lofty gift utterly disconnected from the way one lives one's life. "Our Lord's passion was not a way to an easy salvation," Miklós remembered him saying. "God is concerned with the way we live our lives and by how we treat our fellow man. By God's grace, may you live lives of goodness and righteousness." The best in the Church had been killed.

"What will you do?" Miklós asked his fellow survivor. "What will become of you?"

"I don't know," his friend replied. "I have a family. I should behave like a responsible man, shouldn't I? But something's missing and I'm afraid it might never return." Then, with a glimmer of emotion, he looked Miklós in the eye. A faint smile creased a corner of his lips. Without another word, he turned and shuffled off up the street.

"Good-bye and take care," Miklós called after him. But the man just walked on. Miklós couldn't be sure whether his friend had extended his hand to wave good-bye or was simply adjusting the sleeve of his overcoat.

✤ CHAPTER 15 ✤

Reunion

And Esau ran to meet [Jacob] and embraced him,
fell upon his neck and kissed him; and they wept.
GENESIS 33:4

In October 1949, Miklós wrote to Gyuri in Italy from his home in Gothenburg, Sweden, where he had lived with Muci and Elza for the previous two years. In the letter, Miklós shared with his brother his great joy and satisfaction that Muci had just given birth to a fine baby boy (my older brother, Peter). Both mother and son, said Miklós, were fine and would spend a few more days in the hospital. He then told his brother that he had chosen the occasion of the birth of his son to inform Gyuri that he had decided to return to the Jewish religion and raise his son as a Jew. It seemed, he told his brother, that after what both he and his wife had been through, it was the only sane thing to do. Miklós was careful not to explain too much about his reasons for leaving Christianity, to avoid impugning Gyuri's beloved faith. He had always admired his brother's piety and praised him for his religious calling. Neither did he wish to imply that his move was entirely the fault of Christianity, although he noted that the war had changed his feelings about the faith in which the two of them had been raised. He simply wanted to explain that, because of what he had personally experienced, he had lost faith in God and found faith in the Jewish people, and, of course, in his Jewish wife, who had given his life renewed meaning. Miklós expressed the hope that the news he was sharing would not keep him and his brother apart.

✤

"It is perhaps time for me to make my confession to you again," said Padre Pio to Don Giorgio.

"Why do you say that?" asked Gyuri. "It is always difficult for me as your confessor. I don't believe you've ever sinned."

Padre Pio smiled tenderly. "It is as St. John said, that the man who thinks he is without sin is a fool."

Gyuri was Padre Pio's occasional confessor. It was a supreme privilege for him to serve him in this way, although he never stopped believing that Padre Pio was truly one who had never committed a sin, not even a venial one. Yet the padre was not as certain of his own spiritual purity as others were. At times he felt thoroughly rejected by God for his sinfulness and smallness, and incapable of gaining His favor. Forever an obedient Catholic, he felt that everyone needed to submit to confession for the purification of his soul. It was not an idle exercise for someone who considered himself above it all. It was altogether the contrary.

"Yes, but . . . all right. But why does your confessing to me seem so urgent to you now?"

"Because I haven't given sufficient comfort to the holy friars and priests who rely on my counsel."

"To whom are you referring, Padre?"

"I am referring to you, Giorgetto."

"How could that possibly be?" said Gyuri, raising his opened palms in puzzlement. "You have been a spiritual comfort to me since the day I arrived."

"I have allowed bitterness to enter your soul."

Now Gyuri was dumbfounded.

"I have not discouraged you strongly enough from believing that only Catholics are saved."

"Do you say this because you know about my brother?"

"I do. It's not easy to keep secrets, either from me or from the other friars. We live in a loving community and are of one heart. There are no walls between us. I know that your brother has lost faith. But I also know his suffering was great."

"Christ's suffering was great. Shouldn't He be our model? And my brother's? It is not right that he renounced our faith to become a Jew again. He has imperiled his soul."

"Don't be self-righteous," said the holy padre. "Of course, Catholicism is the only true faith. Even other Christian faiths are founded by men. Only Catholicism has its direct source in Jesus Christ. But that does not mean salvation is not possible through other paths. The Jewish faith is an ancient one and was given directly through the great prophet Moses to the Hebrew people. I have great respect for God's chosen people. You should know that by now."

"Faith, yes, but my brother has not taken on the faith of the Jews, only their ways. He considers himself one with the Jewish people because, he says, of what he went through with them. And he has a Jewish wife, which seems like a more convenient reason to turn away from Catholicism."

"And who are you to judge him? I know that you, too, once had dreams, which never came to pass, of living a normal life among men."

Perhaps Gyuri chose not to grasp what the padre was referring to.

"It has become your cross, hasn't it," Padre Pio continued, "that has led you to Christ? Well, your brother's suffering has led him away from Christ. It pains me, too. But he can still live a life of goodness and find salvation. Suffering is our holy purpose here. It helps save souls. But it is not everyone's. You must consider the possibility that your brother and others have suffered more than any mortal man could endure—not only the death of dreams or even physical torture and hunger, but the pain of being rejected by the world. Our dear Jesus knew that kind of suffering. But not all men are meant to follow Him."

"I don't understand."

"I know that your mother suffered greatly and kept her faith in Christ. She has received her heavenly reward. But we now know, don't we, that others suffered just as much and either lost their faith or remained faithful to the Holy Father, the God of the Jews. Is it for us to impugn that? He will save the righteous among His ancient people, just as He will save the righteous among the Christians. Christ is our life, but turning away from Him does not mean turning toward evil. Look at our bodies, dear Giorgetto. Are they not frail, very frail containers of God's light and love? Not everyone can tolerate the great suffering that our Lord did."

"I still don't see what sin you have committed that you would need to confess to me."

"It is the sin of not teaching you sooner that it is God who judges our brothers and saves their souls—not us. I have been granted the grace to be helpful at times, but it is not ultimately my power. It is God's. All any of us really has is the power of prayer."

There was a long pause.

"Will my brother ever turn back to Jesus Christ?" Don Giorgio finally asked.

Padre Pio was silent.

✤

In October 1956, Gyuri wrote a letter to Miklós. It had taken him seven years to come to terms with his grief over his brother's abandonment of Christianity. In his letter, Gyuri responded to Miklós's invitation of a few months earlier to visit his family in America. It was not the first time Miklós had invited him, but it was the first time Gyuri could respond positively. He planned to make his visit in December.

Miklós's invitation had been a timely one. In May, the community in San Giovanni Rotondo had dedicated the hospital that had been so many years in the planning and construction. Everyone was overjoyed about it and Padre Pio had been devoted to it since its conception. Yet there had been much hustle and bustle in the community for many months. Life had become less peaceful than it once was. And with the apparent failure of the Hungarian Revolution, it no longer looked as though there would ever be an opportunity for Gyuri to return home and find a parish. Now, with many Hungarians bound for America, perhaps there would be a place for a Hungarian priest among them. Gyuri planned to take his portfolio of credentials in the hope of finding a parish in the United States. In a gesture of conciliation, he extended his warmest regards to Muci and Elza and told his brother that he looked forward to being called Uncle George by Miklós's three children. Finally, he promised to adhere to his brother's request not to bring up matters of religion with the children. Seeing someone who looked just like their father wearing a priest's collar, Gyuri said, would be confusing enough for them.

Gyuri had finally decided to leave the place that had become his beloved home. He had even become an Italian citizen—no easy feat for a foreigner. His work in the community was rewarding, and being in the daily presence of Padre Pio was ample reward in itself. He was well liked and greatly appreciated by the friars and townspeople. But Gyuri had come to recognize that there was something missing in his life. He felt cut off from the only family he had left in the world. In addition, he terribly missed having a parish of his own. In all his years of serving Mass for Padre Pio, Gyuri had been asked to preach only occasionally. Since September 1943, when American troops had dislodged the Germans from Foggia, he had preached to the Americans stationed there. These times had reminded him of what most drew him to the priesthood.

Gyuri had thought of leaving before, but he hadn't been able to imagine giving up the privilege of living in the daily presence of the saintly Padre Pio. He surely would never forget the many miracles he had witnessed or heard about from the friars or townspeople: the padre's instant conversion of non-believers; the many healings. A blind child who was brought to Padre Pio's Mass at the friary had begun looking around the sanctuary even before the service was completed, his sight restored. Gyuri remembered the man whose eye was destroyed by an explosion yet whose vision also returned—indeed, his missing eyeball was regenerated. Unbelievers would scoff at such ridiculous tales, but reputable physicians had no way of explaining the events. He was intimately familiar with the story of how a short, stout fellow from Yugoslavia, a good Catholic, had driven his car into a remote part of the Adriatic Sea, only to be saved and pulled through the window of the sinking car by the figure of Padre Pio, who had appeared in a great white light above him. Gyuri knew the man, for he had moved to San Giovanni Rotondo following the incident and devoted his life to the padre, as well as to the construction of the hospital next to the friary. Padre Pio's reputed odor of sanctity, whereby a room would mysteriously fill with the fragrance of flowers, had visited Gyuri on a number of occasions. He never doubted, from his very first meeting with the padre, that the man was a saint. But he was touched more by Padre Pio's gentleness, practical kindness, and infinite humility than by his miraculous accomplishments. When Father Emil Kappler, Gyuri's Swiss friend, visited in 1947 and boasted, following the canonization of a fellow countryman, that the Swiss now had two saints, Padre Pio said to him, *"In Paradiso, lo stesso"* (In heaven, it's all the same).

Padre Pio himself had mixed feelings about Gyuri's leaving. He surely must have known that, despite Gyuri's contentment over the previous years, he had missed having a parish of his own. Earlier on, when Gyuri had considered taking Capuchin vows, Padre Pio knew that Gyuri's destiny was not as a monk but rather as a secular priest—and perhaps not always in San Giovanni Rotondo. But Padre Pio loved Gyuri, always referred endearingly to him as "Giorgetto." He didn't want to see him leave, but he knew that this was an opportunity Gyuri might have to seize. The padre quietly supported him, telling him to have an open mind about what the future held in America, even while he pleaded with Gyuri not to go. "Once someone has been held in these hands," Padre Pio finally told him, holding up the encrusted, bloodstained wounds of Christ penetrating his palms, "he will never get far away from them."

Regarding the fact that Gyuri was going to visit his Jewish brother, Padre Pio maintained a respectful silence, except for whatever may have transpired in the confessional between him and his penitent and occasional confessor. In that silence, could there have been an implicit plea for the reconciliation of Catholic and Jewish brothers in the aftermath of cataclysm?

✛

At the end of that year, as planned, Gyuri left San Giovanni Rotondo and came to the United States to meet his twin brother, who had been living in East Orange, New Jersey, since 1950. Miklós and Muci, along with Elza, had left what they considered the permissive atmosphere of Sweden for the U.S. in order to raise their family. On their arrival, they were quickly advised by relatives who had been in the country for years: "Listen, don't talk about what happened to you during the war. Americans would not be interested, and they would never understand." Thus, the couple began their lives in America carrying dark and ugly memories that they felt compelled to keep to themselves.

Gyuri arrived in the port of New York on the sixth of December, 1956, his brother's name day in the Catholic Church. As Gyuri disembarked the ship, the brothers saw each other for the first time in nearly twenty years. Gyuri had a bushy black beard and wore an overcoat over a black suit and clerical collar. Miklós had no trouble recognizing him. They embraced warmly for several seconds and kissed on both cheeks.

"The first thing we need to do," said Miklós, "is to visit a barber. If you're going to stay for all these months, you'll want to look more modern, even as a priest."

Looking taken aback, as if he were about to be stripped of his familiar identity, Gyuri smiled nonetheless and nodded.

"That way, too," Miklós added, "it will be more fun for the children to try to decide who is who between us."

The car ride from New York in the family's new wine-colored DeSoto had been too distracting for the brothers to talk about anything but the bare details of Gyuri's trip. As they drove on the highway along the New Jersey wetlands, the sight of New York City's skyscrapers was awe-inspiring to this rural priest who had lived in the mountains of Italy for so long.

Before they went home to the family's third-floor apartment in East Orange, the brothers paid a visit to Miklós's Italian barber. As Gyuri's bushy whiskers fell in clumps onto the floor of the barber shop, the other patrons looked on in wonderment at the sight of the priest and a layman who became virtual mirror images of each other in front of their eyes. Even to Miklós it felt that, despite Gyuri's slightly more robust frame, he was looking at his own reflection.

Later that afternoon they arrived home. My mother and grandmother were there to greet them. Five years old at the time, I was downstairs with my brother and sister, playing in the narrow, asphalt-covered backyard of our three-story brick apartment house. We had grown impatient waiting for our uncle's arrival. I suppose that my mother approached Uncle George with a smile, probably hiding whatever discomfort she had acquired over the years. We understood even then that George had suspected her of being the cause of our father's defection to Judaism, although the excitement of the day overshadowed the vaguely understood tension between the adults. The two of them graciously reached for each other's hands and then more cautiously embraced and kissed each other's cheeks.

My grandmother Elza, whom we called Nagymama, had accompanied my parents from Sweden and was living with us. She must have followed suit, also probably harboring worries about the religious rifts that could erupt in the family. Standing now in front of my father's Catholic counterpart, she was continually reminded of the love she once felt toward his mother, her dear cousin and friend, Gabriella. But Nagymama would never mention that love, because of the hurt she felt when her daughter was snubbed as a suitable marriage partner for my father. And she would never bring up that bitterness, because of the way that Gabriella had died. But these forbidden sentiments were likely being conjured up at that moment, as she greeted the pious twin brother who had by some ridiculous twist of fate escaped the whole nasty ordeal.

My mother told us later that as Uncle George was coming out of the bedroom, my father saw my brother and sister and me come in the apartment door. He quickly reversed course and ducked into the bedroom, pulling his brother by the shirtsleeve so that they could walk out together to greet us. Catching on quickly to what my father was trying to do, my mother and grandmother ushered the three of us into the living room to await their entrance.

As the two men came out and stood side by side, we looked at one and then the other and for a few bewildering moments we could not tell the two apart. At least, I couldn't. Neither man spoke. All four adults watched us in bemused amazement. Not wanting yet to give away the twins' identities, my mother and then my grandmother asked the three of us if we could tell which one was our father and which was our uncle.

Our father and uncle turned and glanced at each other, looking as though each knew what the other was thinking. Despite the different worlds they had inhabited for half their lifetime, the two of them were still indistinguishable in their looks, and maybe even their thoughts. The buildup of almost intolerable tension for the three of us was finally broken when my father spoke softly, "I am your father," and my uncle, smiling, said, "And I am your Uncle George." He extended his hands and gently touched our faces, first my brother on one side of the row of three and my sister on the other, and then mine, in the middle.

✤

As the initial excitement of my uncle's arrival subsided, the twin brothers retreated to a back room, where Gyuri would continue to unpack his sizable black trunk. My mother and grandmother were in the kitchen, cleaning up after dinner, and my brother and sister and I were in the adjoining living room, still bouncing around from the excitement of our uncle's arrival. Alone now in a more settled moment, my father and uncle would have the encounter that would color their relationship with each other for the next four decades. Although I was not in the room with them, I got a sense of the spirit of their conversation by looking at each of their faces later on that evening. Many years would pass until I learned the seminal content of that fateful talk, and still more years until I could truly imagine what they may have been thinking and what they might have said to each other to have created the ensuing decades of silent disappointments and implied recriminations.

"I'm grateful for your hospitality," began Gyuri, as he started moving clothing from the open trunk to the top drawer of the dresser, which had been cleared out for his arrival. "I'm sure I won't need to stay here for more than several days before they make room for me at the Benedictine Fathers."

"That's fine," answered my father.

There was a hesitation. Gyuri's eyes darted toward him. "Your children are lovely." He looked away again. "I'm glad to finally meet them . . . and to see you after all these years. It's surprising, isn't it, that we still look so much alike?"

"Yes, I suppose we do, especially after the beard is gone," said Miklós.

"And especially surprising because life has taken us in such different directions for the last twenty-five years. You would expect our faces to reflect those differences. Now, our frames are a slightly different story."

Miklós smiled but did not respond.

"You can probably tell that I still enjoy my solitary vice of eating a good home-cooked meal," Gyuri continued. "And I haven't had such a wonderful Hungarian meal as Muci and Elza cooked since I left Hungary. It brought tears to my eyes."

"But the children didn't notice. I think we actually fooled them. You always did carry a few more pounds than I did. I suppose in that way you took after our father. The dear man. He, too, enjoyed the hospitality of friends and neighbors, and his portly frame reflected it."

"Ah, yes," Gyuri sighed. "He was a dear man. You know, I often thought while I lived in Italy that Papa was the best father in the world, when we had him. But he was away for such a long time. I sometimes wonder if that's what made both of us so intensely inward and independent when we were young. When you think of it, he was not around to guide us and discipline us for almost five years of our childhood. We weren't bad children, but poor Mama couldn't handle us alone. Do you remember," Gyuri continued with a laugh, "how we would run off in different directions on the street and she would have to yell at passersby to stop us?"

"Well," said Miklós, with a facetious smile. "Haven't *you* become the Freudian psychologist!"

"Of course," Gyuri answered, "that's from studying at his university in Vienna." He seemed just as willing as Miklós to sidestep weightier matters for the time being. The ways they had broken loose in their youth, their mutual feelings of abandonment—these were probably the last things either of them wanted to bring up.

"I don't mean to ignore your remark about our father's absence," Miklós pressed on, "but it was much harder for Mama than it was for us. I think she felt that she had no one there for her, just three little kids and a disagreeable stepmother."

"That may be true," said Gyuri. "But that's what helped her find her way to Christianity. That's why it became so important to her."

A grim look came over Miklós's face. He knew the conversation was proceeding innocently enough, but he could sense the sudden turn it had just taken. Where else could it go? he thought. It didn't really sound as though Gyuri had been strident in his remark, just natural, inadvertent. After all, he was a priest who had lived among monks for so many years. How could Christianity not come up?

Sitting on the armrest of the overstuffed chair in the corner of the bedroom, Miklós looked up at Gyuri standing a few feet away. He swallowed hard and looked aside, his eyes darting toward the corner of the ceiling and then downward while he remained in self-conscious silence. Gyuri hesitated, too. For an instant, maybe he didn't know either how to break this sudden tension. After several seconds he finally said, "God has favored you with such beautiful children. I'm afraid we have waited too long to finally come together. But I must take the blame for that. Our parents would be filled with joy to be grandparents," he went on. "They would be very proud." Miklós appreciated Gyuri's changing the subject.

"Just as I know they were so proud of you for becoming a priest," said Miklós. "Especially Mama." He was instinctively kind in return and realized the subject of religion could not be avoided.

Gyuri was nonchalant. "Mama was proud, I know that. Papa never had much use for religion."

"I have to admit," said Miklós, "I have not thought much about our mother. I try not to. I can't. I guess it's too painful."

"It hurts me, too," Gyuri said right away. "But my prayers have helped, and I hope they've helped in the salvation of her soul."

"I'm glad that you still believe," said Miklós. "I've sometimes wished I could pray, at least for the benefit of our parents. But I can't. Not anymore."

Gyuri did not respond. He turned his head and looked out the window at the December early evening darkness.

Miklós knew he must have hit a nerve. How is a Catholic priest, he wondered, supposed to respond to his brother telling him that he has lost his faith? Miklós felt he needed to spare Gyuri the weight of his religious doubts, at least for now.

"You'll tell us, won't you, about your life in Italy?" Miklós said, trying to salvage the moment.

Gyuri pulled his gaze back from just beyond the green canvas awning at the entryway of the apartment building. He looked as though he had been mesmerized by the flickering of the streetlamp over the hard urban landscape outside the window. Cities had become so foreign to him. Appearing pensive, almost sad, he looked back at Miklós.

"Yes, of course," Gyuri answered, as if from a distance. "And you'll tell me about what life is like in America."

"That's a deal," said Miklós.

"I once learned," Gyuri continued, "from an American woman who wrote to Padre Pio that in America, God is powerful but money is omnipotent. I will never forget that," said Gyuri, with a halting laugh.

"There's some truth to that," Miklós answered. "The profit motive is a powerful force here. If you have money, they treat you like a king, even if you're an ignoramus. In Europe, they judge you by your education and manners. I'll tell you, this is a great country. I was ready to kiss the ground when we got here. But it doesn't quite suit our temperament."

"How has it been for you and Muci and the children? I don't imagine it's been easy. You've had to learn the language quickly and then find a good enough job to support your family."

"We wouldn't be here if it weren't for Charlie, Elza's brother. He's been here many years and was very helpful to us. He and his wife, Helen, visited you, I think, a few years ago in Italy."

"Yes, I remember that. I had to be in Rome, and I showed them around the city."

"Charlie's had a successful business," continued Miklós, "and I worked for him for several years, until just the last few weeks."

"His plant went on strike and I had to find temporary work. Luckily, I guess, Muci and I both got jobs as interpreters for people leaving Hungary after the revolution." Thousands of Hungarian refugees had come to the United States after the failed October revolution. Many of them came through the former army station that had become the immigration processing center at Camp Kilmer, New Jersey, near Brunswick.

"I mentioned this in one of my letters to you," continued Miklós. "I thought it would be a good time for you to see if a Hungarian priest might be needed."

"It must be very interesting for the two of you," said Gyuri.

"Interesting is putting it nicely."

"What do you mean?" asked Gyuri.

"I think under the best of circumstances I would have had a hard time working with Hungarians again. I wanted to leave Hungary as quickly as I could." Miklós had left as soon as Muci was well enough and they had the opportunity to travel to Sweden. At the bank in Budapest, they had wanted him to join the communists. He was sure he would have gotten a promotion if he had. But Miklós wanted nothing to do with it. He wasn't interested in politics. "I have to admit," he added, "that I only wanted to see Hungary punished."

"You sound so bitter," said Giörgi.

Miklós paused and bit his lip. He was startled at Gyuri's ignorance, or naiveté, or both. He couldn't hold back. "Of *course* I'm bitter. They dishonored our father, killed our mother, and they treated us like nonhumans. They were a crazed mob, glad to be finally rid of us."

"But that wasn't the Hungarians. That was the Nazis," Gyuri said, with seemingly forced composure. He sounded more like he was asking a question than making a statement, as if he were looking to have his own fears dispelled.

"And who do you think the best Nazis were? You know, Muci was in Budapest the day the Germans marched in. But after that almost no one saw them. It was all the Hungarians. The Germans conceived the plan and pushed for it, but the Hungarians engineered it and executed it with diligence: the anti-Jewish laws, you remember those; the labor camps, I must have written to you about the happy months I spent there; the persecution and murder in the streets—yes, Hungarians all; and, finally, the deportations. There was little left for the Germans to do. And where do you think some of these helplessly coerced Hungarian collaborators are now? They are escaping the Soviets' iron fist as fast as they can. They're showing up here, in America, in New Jersey, at Camp Kilmer."

"That's wrong. I don't believe it," Gyuri finally said. He looked antagonized. He was looking straight into his brother's eyes as if to defy Miklós's arguments by his piercing gaze. But he said nothing further. He gritted his teeth, bracing himself for what was likely still to come.

"Don't get me wrong, Gyuri. Not everyone flocking to America from Hungary is a fascist or a Nazi. Far from it. And no one should have to live under the domination of the Soviets. I don't wish that on anybody. But America hates communism so much that they are welcoming these former Nazis with open arms. I know that war criminals are getting in without thorough background checks simply because they profess anticommunist sympathies. Muci and I are just interpreters. We are powerless. But one of these monsters was let in and he settled only a few miles from here. At Camp Kilmer, I overheard him talking about his having been a commander of a labor battalion in the Ukraine. 'The faster the Jews were killed,' he said, 'the faster we got to go home.' I tell you, they hated us with a passion that they didn't inherit from the Nazis. It came from a much deeper place than even that, one that is not unfamiliar to either of us, I'm afraid." Gyuri was holding his fist over his mouth, as if to restrain himself from speaking. "And someone like this," Miklós still went on, "should be welcomed into the United States of America?"

Miklós stopped to catch his breath. He hadn't been so worked up in a long time. But he could see his brother's face turning red and his brow being pressed into a scowl.

In that instant, Gyuri seized the floor. "He's no worse," he said, "than an apostate!"

Miklós felt as if a bullet had burst forth from a revolver. He slouched over for a fraction of a second as if he were wounded physically by his brother's verbal assault. Then he stiffened himself bolt upright in the chair. The mortal blow of Gyuri's words resounded in Miklós's heart and shattered any coherent thoughts that were still in his mind. He was shaken to the core and sat speechless, looking blankly at the wall in front of him.

Gyuri now had the floor. "I know what you are implying," he said, moving quickly to fill the heavy air in the room still reverberating with his outburst. "And I can't listen to it anymore. You can call them Hungarians or Germans, Fascists or Nazis, but what you really mean is Christians, don't you? Well, listen here. None of this catastrophe had anything to do with Christians. If it did, then the guilty will surely be judged by their deeds in the world to come. These were the actions of people who hated God, both the Father and the Son. The Nazis hated Jews *and* Catholics. But whatever happened to anyone, it did not prevent good, decent, devout Catholics like our dear mother from praying to our Savior the moment of her death. At least He used to be our Savior, until you forsook Him and betrayed the faith in which she raised us."

Now Miklós was the one gritting his teeth. As he glared at his twin brother, his head was still spinning and he could not respond.

"Don't you remember," Gyuri persisted, "those years together in Gyula when you talked to me late at night in the orphanage about Christ's love, about how you wanted to become a priest?" His tone had softened but he sounded patronizing. "You would have been a better priest than me, and maybe I wouldn't have become one at all if you hadn't brought me back to Catholicism when my own faith was failing. If you had been baptized in your adulthood, even if only to save yourself during the war, who could blame you for returning to the religion of your birth and upbringing? But you had been a good Catholic for most of your life. How could you turn away and become a Jew?"

Gyuri was irrepressible. He hardly gave his reeling brother a chance to collect his thoughts. "As the Lord is my witness," he continued, "I would not have wished this catastrophe on the Jews—"

"Well, it's easy for you to defend the Church," Miklós interrupted. He was regaining his footing. "But that's just not how it was. In effect, the Church supported the Nazis—if not with its complicity, then with its utter indifference."

"That's preposterous."

"Is it? It came out later that the cardinal knew full well what was happening and he didn't lift a finger. The papal nuncio in Budapest also knew. They would argue over each other's inactivity. The nuncio warned that if the Hungarian government persisted in its complicity with the Nazis and the cardinal persisted in remaining silent, the Pontiff would have to raise his voice in protest. And do you know what the cardinal answered? He said that the nuncio was the one who was not doing enough, that his presence in Budapest had never been any use, especially when the Vatican had direct relations with the Germans."

"Fine, so all this took place behind the scenes. But I'm sure they did all they could have," said Gyuri.

"Yes, the nuncio sent a strong letter of protest to the Hungarian government, which was in no mood to heed his demands. But he, too, was more concerned with the converts—with the whole issue of Jews not being seen as a race, so that baptized Jews could be granted religious liberties. But it was curious that he made his appeal specifically on behalf of converts and not, as he said, from any 'false sense of compassion' for Jews. Wasn't that shrewd of him?" Not waiting for an answer to his rhetorical dig, Miklós continued: "I'll give the nuncio credit, though, that he did speak out and that he gave out documents of protection to converts *and* Jews, stating that they were under the protection of the Church. It was a noble effort. But I will never understand why it took him so long.

"As for the cardinal," Miklós continued, "a statement was read on the radio to the parishes at the end of the summer that he was proceeding quietly and diplomatically to do everything he could to be helpful. Until then, people didn't hear a word from him."

"He wasn't a well man, either. I know that."

"He wasn't well? He might as well have been dead or in prison. That's what people thought. All these people running around, denouncing, brutalizing, and deporting Jews, and the head of the Church was sick and silent. Deafeningly silent, for five months—from the day the Germans arrived. Almost half a million people deported from the countryside and he didn't say a word. The Germans were thrilled by his silence and the Hungarian collaborators were egged on by it!"

"But he didn't stay silent. I am certain he wrestled terribly with how to respond."

"Yes, but even from the start, it was always in defense of the converts: the converts should have their own labor battalions and be able to practice their faith; the converts should be exempted from wearing the yellow stars; the converts should not be put in ghettos and deported with Jews."

"He must have done everything he could," answered Gyuri. "He was obviously powerless to defend the Jews."

"Of course, and no one can blame him for that. The whole thing wasn't his idea. But once the thing started, it was painfully obvious that he didn't give a damn about the Jews. I even heard that in June he prepared a Shepherd's Epistle that he was going to have read to all the parishes in the country. He barely mentioned the Jews by name."

"There were government censors. He couldn't speak freely."

"Well, he all but said, 'Take the Jews but leave the converts alone.' But he even reneged on that when he struck a deal with the prime minister to protect the converts. The epistle never got read. So much for his moral voice."

"So you see, the cardinal didn't even have the power to help the converts. Look what happened to our mother."

"Our mother was already gone, along with every other Jew and convert from the countryside, by the time the cardinal even got around to writing his epistle. And when word spread that all these efforts were being made to help converts, many desperate Jews still in Budapest thought it would be a way to find sanctuary. For a while, the churches were helpful in providing baptisms or baptismal papers for them to help save their lives. I even hoped and prayed that it would help Muci. But they stopped when too many Jews began flooding the churches for so-called insincere baptisms."

"What would you expect them to do, rubber-stamp insincere conversions?" asked Gyuri.

"Tell me," Miklós continued, "which is worse, the hypocrisy of Jews wanting insincere conversions, or the hateful self-righteousness of the churches for refusing to help them? You should have heard what they called the Jews standing outside the churches. They were looking for safety and were turned away. They might as well have been handed over to the Nazis and Nyilas on a silver platter."

"I don't believe it." Gyuri's nostrils flared as his words sputtered through his clenched teeth. "I just don't believe it. What would you have had him do instead? He simply didn't have any real power to influence the government."

"If he had told Hungarian Catholics on the radio that they would be punished or excommunicated for their violence, do you suppose that things might have turned out differently?"

"Then he surely would have been arrested, probably killed—martyred—and the Church would have been seized and destroyed."

"Maybe so. I couldn't insist that anyone be a martyr—not Jews, not Christians. But after so much silence and indifference and hatred, what's worth saving in the Church?"

"You must realize that Hitler hated the Christians as much as he hated Jews. Probably half of those who died were Christians or converts."

"If that's what you've heard," said Miklós, "it's absolutely false. The number was far, far fewer. And if Nazis hated Christians so much, then why were those of us in the Christian labor battalions in Hungary taken to Mass on Sundays but forced to work like slaves at other times? And do you know that in the concentration camp, I heard that Jews who insisted on fasting on Yom Kippur had to work in the kitchen, and then were offered pork at the end of the night? And I was there to see the virtual feast prisoners were given on Christmas while they literally starved us to death the rest of the time on thin soup with slivers of turnip and horse meat in it. Would you call that Nazi fervor or Christian charity?"

"As I said," answered Gyuri, in a somber voice, "evil done by individuals will not go unpunished. But regardless of how much the Jews suffered—and I don't deny their suffering—you have to understand that the life of the body is not as important as the life of the soul. But it is not so much the souls of the poor Jews that I am concerned about. I probably should be, but I can't pretend to be so pious that I would pray for them. It is your soul's destiny that troubles me." Standing over his brother, Gyuri put his hand on Miklós's shoulder. But Miklós brushed it off and turned his head aside.

"I don't know why you gave up Christ's love and His promise," Gyuri went on almost tearfully, "but I fear you have endangered your salvation. Although you might consider it self-righteous, I see it as simple solicitude that I continue to pray for your salvation."

"That's it?" asked Miklós. "Your fraternal prayers for my soul? Are you still so much in the dark about what it was like, what we went through, what might have driven a good Catholic to renounce the religious faith he once loved in order to become a Jew again? You can patronize me with your prayers. But you refuse to comprehend what I witnessed?"

"I can't imagine such terrible things, because that's not how it was in Italy," Gyuri said. "The people in San Giovanni Rotondo knew I was born a Jew and that I would have been in danger if the Germans or Italian Fascists found out. But everyone kept quiet. Throughout Italy, we heard later, priests and nuns and laymen hid Jews—in their homes, in monasteries. They even hid men in convents. They fed them and sheltered them."

"Things may have been different there," answered Miklós, "but in Germany good Christians threw stones at us as we walked to the concentration camp from the trains, and they accused us of killing the Savior. The Savior who sustained my heart and soul for so many years. Do you think I could bear that blame? I don't deserve it and the Jews don't either. It's what we've been accused of for two thousand years. I would rather renounce Christianity than have to share Jesus Christ with such viciously self-righteous people. They accused me of killing Christ when they were the ones who annihilated His spirit. Maybe God's Son can endure that kind of scorn. I can't!"

"So you still do believe in God's Son?"

"I believed in Him and I loved Him since we were children. But my love was crucified by those accusers and haters, and my faith in His salvation will never be resurrected. I prefer to remember the victims and share my life with fellow survivors."

"But so many people found faith in the camps. Look at our mother. She died a martyr."

"You were not there!" said Miklós, nearly shouting, pointing his finger at Gyuri. "Do not judge me. I survived hell with people who conducted themselves with dignity and honor, even while they were starving to death and dying of typhus. Maybe I haven't found faith in the God of the Jews. Maybe I will never pray again to any god. I know I'm not alone in that," he said, lowering his hand back into his lap. "But I refuse to be judged by you or anyone who wasn't there. After the war, my religion became my wife and children, and my connection to the people I survived with. If you want blasphemy," said Miklós, craning his neck toward his brother, "my wife—who nearly died, and was treated with unspeakable cruelty—is my savior, and my family and people are my salvation, at least here on earth. I wouldn't trade any of it for God's glorious kingdom. If you want to pray for anything, maybe pray that you and I can live in some degree of harmony, despite our differences. That is something that even I might be able to pray for."

When Miklós was finished, Gyuri stayed quiet. "It is time for my evening prayers," he finally said as he turned around to leave the room.

Miklós couldn't help but feel that Gyuri was going off, undeterred, to plead for Miklós's salvation. He watched him go. He knew he would never again discuss the suffering of Jews or the behavior of Christians. And Gyuri would not likely bring up his brother's apostasy, nor the eternal rewards of Christian faith. As Gyuri closed the door behind him and went to pray, Miklós put his head in his hands and wept.

❖ CHAPTER 16 ❖

Disarmed

El se mondom majd a csillagoknak, Hogy a teremtő ember öldököl.
(I'll not even tell the stars of the murderous spirit here.)
Attila József, *"El Innen"* ("Away from Here")

On a distant and strange planet, a man dressed in a white ceremonial robe is standing in an enormous amphitheater and holding a giant silver sword. A few feet away, another man dressed the same way, also holding a sword, is standing across from him. Surrounding them are lots of other pairs of people with swords. They are all taking part in some kind of war ceremony or dance. Their movements are slow and graceful, except that some of them end up killing their partners. The first man kills two others and then puts his sword down on the ground. He walks over to an old man with white hair and a long gray beard, dressed in a colorful robe with glittery stars and lightning-bolt designs on it. The old man wears a pointy hat and looks like a magician or a wizard.

The warrior comes up to this wizard and tells him that he doesn't want to play in the deadly game anymore. It's not the violence that upsets him, he tells the wizard, as much as the pretense on the surface of people's behavior. He would rather be in a place where civility has broken down, where violence is out in the open, and where gentleness and restraint have to grow back from the inside out in order for people to live together in peace. "Is there a place like that anywhere in the universe?" the warrior asks the master. "And can you send me there?"

I awoke in the morning of a summer day in 1960, having fallen asleep the night before with my New York Yankees baseball cap still on my head. I had been listening to a late-night ball game, keeping my portable radio under the covers next to my ear with the volume turned low enough so that my eleven-year-old brother wouldn't start screaming at me for waking him up. Since he lay in the twin bed barely the distance of the cast-iron radiator from mine, it didn't take much volume for him to start yelling for my mother or father. I emerged from the dream, opened my eyes, and looked around. My brother was already out of the room. Although the sun was shining in from the corner of the window over the bed, it didn't feel too late in the morning. I heard music and voices coming from under my covers and realized that the radio was still on. I turned it off and then looked down over the edge of the bed and saw that my thirty-three-inch baseball bat, with my fielder's glove draped around it, was on the floor, sticking out from just under the bed.

1960, the year I turned nine, was the year I became a full-blown Yankee fan. The Yankees were not a great team that year—not, at least, for the first half of the season. They were scrappy underdogs, which was exactly why I had an easy time identifying with them. It was also because they embodied such raw talent and great heart. As hope sprang eternal inside every nine-year-old Yankee fan's heart, I was sure they were headed for the pennant and, no doubt, the World Series. But I took nothing for granted. I was wrapped up in every game, every inning, and every pitch. I wouldn't dream of not watching or listening to a game if there was any way to avoid it. At night, after saying the *Sh'ma Israel* and before going to sleep, I always added my own prayers, not only to be able to pitch well in Little League the next day but also for the Yankees to keep winning.

My parents were from a foreign country and never grasped, much less participated in, my love for baseball and the Yankees. My father repeatedly confessed—with disarming pleasure—that his only connection to baseball was what he was forced to learn about it by the U.S. immigration official in order to become an American citizen. He rarely came to watch my prodigious talent as a pitcher in Little League. We lived in Newark, which was less than an hour's ride from New York, but we never went to a Yankee game together, either, like other fathers and sons. I sometimes wondered if the roaring crowds would have evoked unwelcomed memories in him. For my love of the Yankees and as the child of an immigrant and convert, I might as well have lived in the House that Ruth Built. There was nothing that made me feel more American than being a die-hard Yankee fan.

Before I crawled out of bed, I thought about the dream I'd had. It was all so clear and colorful and detailed, about things I couldn't have imagined before, much less known about. I didn't realize it right away, but this must have been one of those dreams that told me who I was and what I was supposed to do with my life. It was something about having to trade in a killer instinct and weapons of ritualized combat to learn how to become kind and gentle. Surely I had heard and seen plenty about graceful and solemn rituals, especially coming from a family where there was a lot of religion. But I didn't know what to make of savagery being masked by people pretending to be nice. And, at the tender age of nine, I wasn't about to trade in my killer instinct for anything. It helped me be a good ballplayer and feel like a powerful and invulnerable American kid. But I never forgot the dream.

✤

I am standing in synagogue as a small boy, alongside my father and mother. I have been attending Jewish school for a few years, so the rich melodies of the Hebrew prayers come readily to my lips and flow forth in a natural and confident way. I am a Jew, I say to myself. This is my home. These are the people to whom I belong.

My mother and father have been determined to make a Jewish home for their children. My mother hasn't become a highly observant Jew in America. She has never gone to a *mikvah,* or ritual bath, nor does she keep a strictly kosher home. But she does light Shabbos candles, has taught us the *Sh'ma Israel,* and makes certain we go to Hebrew school and Sabbath services in synagogue. She tells us all the time about the promise she made to God when she was in the concentration camp to teach her children to be Jewish and tell them about what happened to the Jews in the war. She is keeping that promise.

On the outside, I feel bothered about having to come to synagogue and learning to chant the Hebrew prayers. It doesn't seem as if any of my friends are forced to do as much of this as I am. But secretly I know that there is something very special about being Jewish, although I don't know what it is. I can't admit it to anyone, even to myself. But I keep looking for it, as if it were a buried treasure and all I have is a frayed and crumpled map to find it. I look for it in every Jewish turn of phrase that I hear—and in every ethnic slur against the Jews by the Gentiles and against the Gentiles by the Jews. I look for it in every pained expression in the faces of my parents or their European friends when memories of the war come up.

As I look up at my father standing next to me in synagogue, he is silent— stern-looking, remote, and maybe a little sad. Or is it my sadness? I wonder whether he is not singing the prayers because he doesn't believe in God, or whether he just doesn't know the Hebrew words. Even Jewish fathers who aren't religious surely must know the Jewish prayers enough to sing them with their children in synagogue, I think.

My father and I don't have a very easy relationship. He is a smart and educated man, so he tries to teach me chess and talk to me about European literature and Austro-Hungarian history—never his own—and Greek myth-ology. He even has me learn the Gettysburg Address because he thinks it is important for American kids to know it. Needless to say, I feel disconnected from this stoical and stodgy European immigrant.

One day, when I am about ten years old, I am sitting next to my father in the front seat of our Biscayne Chevy as he drives us home. There is an un-comfortable albeit familiar silence between us. It isn't that there is nothing to say to each other. It is probably that there is too much. The silence between us is dense. He can't relate to my interests and I have to struggle to connect with his.

The past weighs heavily on my father. There is too much he cannot tell me about himself—everything, I fear, that diminishes him in my eyes and, perhaps, in his own. I don't know quite what it is, but I know. I absorb it the way kids usually learn secrets in their families, through the pores of my skin rather than the synapses of my brain. I know it is a combination of sorrow over how some people in our family had died and nostalgia for a way of life that had ended abruptly. Of course, I don't know the details. I only know that the sadness in both my parents' eyes and the knotted silences in conversa-tions fill me with more dread and outrage than any vivid facts could. I also know that a vitality enters my father's voice when he speaks about the history of his former homeland and about his former religious faith.

As he continues to drive, I innocently ask him, "How can Christians be-lieve in Jesus coming back from the dead?"

"Well, people have to believe in certain things," he says matter-of-factly, "so that their lives have meaning, even if no one can prove their beliefs. But I don't know how they can believe in something like that, either." He does not give me the impression that he is secretly harboring any lingering faith in Christ's resurrection. I want to ask him, "Then if you don't pray in temple and you don't believe in Jesus, what do you believe in?" But I don't. I am too afraid of his answer. I wish he would believe in something rather than noth-ing at all. I think he believes in being a Jew, but I don't know what that means to him.

A few minutes later, after a long silence, we start talking about something else. My father says that so-and-so is a cheap Jew even though the man has a lot of money. He sounds angry. I ask him what he means. He tells me that not every Jew is so honest. I feel I am supposed to agree with him because he is my father, and that it is all right to agree with him because he is Jewish—that it's not as bad for Jews to criticize other Jews. But I also feel hurt and confused, because I don't know if he is speaking as someone who was once a Christian. I sink down in the seat and don't say anything.

Another time, not long after that ride home, my father and I are home alone together. On the rare occasions when he talks about himself, he never directly mentions much of anything about his own past, but rather takes delight in his knowledge of Hungarian history, and even church history. "There is no history," he says, pedagogically, "without dates." So he regales me with dates of battles and the reigns of various Hungarian kings before he'll fill in the stories. He also knows stories of popes from centuries ago, and revels in recounting them. Today he smiles as he recites the consecration over the wine from the Latin Mass: *"Hic est enim calix sanguinis mei novi et eterni testamenti mysterium fidei qui pro vobis et pro multis effundetur ad remissionem peccatorum."* It has been many decades since he last heard it in church, and many more since he learned it as a child. Easily piecing the phrases together from memory, he looks delighted with himself. There is a look of dreamy nostalgia on his face that I have rarely seen throughout my childhood. He never talks about his years as a Catholic, except for occasional comments about various holidays or how his family might have celebrated them. In the day-to-day, I have heard my father refer many times to himself as a Jew. He has always seemed comfortable saying it, and it has always pleased me. Yet he surely has never learned Jewish liturgy quite as thoroughly as he is able to recite from the Catholic Mass. At times like this, I worry that he feels more attached to the Catholicism of his youth and early adulthood than to the Judaism into which he was born and which he chose later on in life.

❖

It was a typical Sunday afternoon at our house. I was still about ten years old. Uncle George was over for a midafternoon dinner. He often came over to our house for dinner on weekends, especially on Sundays after his religious obligations at church were over. On this occasion, nothing too important was said at first. It was easy for my father and uncle just to sit around the table and enjoy my mother and grandmother's home-cooked Hungarian meal. George got plenty of dinner invitations from his parishioners. But there was something special for him about his own family's cooking. My grandmother Elza had probably traded recipes with my grandmother Gabriella, whose name was never mentioned in our house.

During dinner, my mother and grandmother didn't sit down until all the food was on the table. Sometimes when Uncle George was there, it was almost as if they waited a little longer to take their places at the table.

"Well," said Uncle George, "my parish had a very successful church dinner. We rented the hall at a good price and made a very nice profit for the church."

"So," answered my father, "good business sense hasn't left you just because you put on a priest's collar. As for me, I dare anyone to show me a business that I couldn't run into the ground in a matter of weeks," he said with a self-deprecating laugh. I suppose my father was trying to be light, but his comment was a bit leaden.

Uncle George smiled anyway. "I've always been the businessman in the family, haven't I?"

"All right," my father continued, still upbeat. "I'll grant you the business skill in the family."

"That goes without saying," my mother bluntly added. "But you've been successful in a different way." She was always quick to jump to my father's defense, especially when she heard him being so self-effacing. "Look at our family. That's where your success is." My brother and sister and I were still at the table. We forced self-satisfied smiles; we were being shown off as our parents' trophies. "You're the one," she said, looking at George, "who would have been a good Jewish businessman if you hadn't become a priest."

"I don't know about that," answered Uncle George. He stopped smiling, and even I could tell that he was bothered by my mother's implication. "I think it's the other way around," he said, looking directly at her. "I think if Miklós hadn't been a successful Jewish husband and father, he would have been a good priest." Without a word, my mother bolted out of her seat and started clearing the dishes, even before some of us were done. My grandmother sighed and followed her into the kitchen.

My uncle turned toward the kids and bantered with us for a few minutes, trying to act as though nothing had happened. But that wasn't easy to do. Before long, my brother and sister and I got up and retreated to different parts of the house, leaving my father and uncle alone at the table. I went into the living room, hoping to stay inconspicuously within earshot of them. I couldn't make out much of what they were saying. I always felt protective of their relationship and often secretly tried to guard against there being too much tension between them. But I knew that in this instance there already was.

The rest of their conversation died down. Their voices were calm and they laughed and joked together. There was an undeniable affinity between them to which even my mother sometimes had to take a backseat.

A few minutes later, my mother and grandmother served the obligatory dessert, which gathered everyone back around the table. Regardless of what was going on between them, no one was willing to forego my grandmother's *mákos tészta* (poppy-seed cake) and my mother's *gesztenye piré* (strained chestnut purée).

It wasn't long after these delicacies were eaten that Uncle George said his good-byes and beat a hasty retreat. After his departure, my mother and father were not very talkative. They glanced at each other, one waiting for the other to start the conversation. But neither of them did. My mother looked irritated and my father seemed edgy. I read in the silence that something had been stripped away, down to the core, and I figured it had something to do with our being Jewish and my uncle being a Catholic priest. My uncle didn't really have to say it out loud, although he had come close. His unspoken message was that my father was not really a Jew, that he was a Catholic impersonating a Jew.

It all struck me as curious and confusing, because whenever I thought of my father being Catholic for all those years in Hungary, I thought he was really a Jew impersonating a Catholic.

"I know what you're worried about," my father finally said to my mother.

"Tell me, Einstein, what?" she asked.

"You're worried that my brother doesn't respect our being Jewish."

"Well, it's obvious, isn't it? It's always been that way."

"Look here," said my father, "he's more Jewish than I am Catholic, not because he believes in it but because of who he is. I think it's harder for him to leave behind his Jewish past than it is for me to let go of Catholicism. You can see he's a good businessman and he respects the business sense of Jews. And I respect him for being a priest. I think he's a good one. The biggest difference between him and me is where we spent the war."

"Then why does he care so little about what happened to us?" my mother snapped. "Why has he never asked what we went through? Does he think we were at a picnic or off on vacation?"

"Of course not. The truth is that if he had been in Hungary at the same time we were, he probably would have been taken away, too, no matter how pious a Catholic priest he was. He was lucky and smart that he got out when he did. Although I can tell you, from the way we were both educated by the Church, that his being a priest can easily get in the way of being sensitive to his Jewish brother. But you have to admit he's been basically respectful, and he's been good to the kids."

"I don't deny that, but why are you defending him? It was easy for him to be a good priest in the mountains of Italy under the protection of some Christian saint. He was living with monks out of harm's way. I'm sure there were good religious people in Italy, but where we were we had monks carrying guns against the Jews and priests standing with crucifixes in front of the trains, yelling at the Jews, 'Now go to your punishment in the name of Jesus Christ.' How can you defend your brother?"

"Because he's my brother!" my father said, pounding his palm onto the table and rattling the remaining dishes. "And I can't defend what Christians did. I have to keep the two things separate. That's the only way we can live as brothers."

In the kitchen, my grandmother stopped rattling dishes. Suddenly there was a thick and heavy silence in the air that you could cut with a knife. My father winced and looked down at the floor. He looked as if he were trying to restrain sadness or embarrassment.

"There's nothing to be ashamed of," my mother added. "Your parents are at peace for it, believe me."

"Don't be so sure."

"Well, I am. Your mother and father would be proud of you for what you have accomplished. I only wish you could be more at peace with it yourself."

I didn't think my sister had been listening, but she promptly stood up from where she had been sitting in the corner of the living room and walked off into her bedroom. My brother had been listening intently also, alternately turning his head between my mother and my father. It had always been Peter's way to tune in to what needed fixing with our parents. But strong emotions were less his province than practical, real-life considerations. Sometimes all he could do was act as a dutiful son. This was way over his head. He seemed to be getting more and more nervous as he sat transfixed on the living room sofa.

I, too, felt frozen in place. I sat there thinking, *We are Jews but we have some heavy-duty Catholics in our family and Dad actually used to be one. He could have been a priest! That's unbelievable.* I had never seen things become so tense in our family.

"Do you think we could stop talking about this in front of the children?" my father said finally.

My mother threw him a dirty look, which I thought said, "It's too late for that."

My mother was right. It was too late. It had all been said and it couldn't be taken back. In a way, I actually felt some relief to see and hear these things out in the open. I had always known that there were feelings hidden under the surface of my family. I just never knew what they were. Now at least I knew.

✦

From early on in my life, I knew, even in my child's heart, that the God to whom I prayed for the Yankees to win the World Series was thoroughly out of

His league when it came to fixing my father's and our family's unhappiness. This God could not disentangle the knotted silences and muted recriminations that bound us to each other. As hard as I tried to find my place as a Jew in my family, I feared that the personal God of the Jews would not show His face, and neither would His commandments be compelling, until my father's history and interior life became more comprehensible to me, and until the chasm that divided him from his brother and from himself began to heal.

Despite my prayers, the Yankees lost the World Series in 1960. They outplayed and outscored the Pirates, but in the ninth inning of the seventh game, Bill Mazeroski hit the series-winning home run. When I saw the ball sail over the left-field wall of Pittsburgh's Forbes Field, my heart sank to my belly like a lead weight. I darted out of the house, ran five blocks up to Unterman Field, climbed over the chain-link fence, and sat down in the upper corner of the cement bleachers where no one could see me. There I leaned forward onto my knees, buried my head in my arms, and cried.

After that, the driven childhood warrior that I was began to soften. I still played ball with great tenacity and still loved the Yankees. They would be great again, even better the next year, when they would win it all. But somehow I knew deep in my heart that that moment, sitting alone in the bleachers, signaled the time to put down the weapons of this choreographed warfare of my American childhood. Until then, I felt I had been cast down against my will from some other, more dynamic and powerful world into this quiet and somber family, where my only connection to myself and others was in playing baseball and identifying with a veritable dynasty of warrior-athletes. But from then on I knew that the time would soon arrive for me to take my place among these exiles from a distant and gruesome world they had once called home, a place where they had been disarmed, dispossessed of all power and pretensions to it, and were left with barely restrained undercurrents of rage and recrimination among themselves. It was precisely in this family that I would be forced to embrace the message of the disenchanted warrior from my dream— to put down my sword, to leave my world and my identity behind, and then to learn gentleness and compassion from the inside out.

✦ **CHAPTER 17** ✦

"Jew Priest"

Come, tread the winepress!
The blood of the ages squeezed from our flesh
shall be our loving cup: Red river of life, drawn from martyrs and sages,
shall bear you on its tide till your Lord shall raise you up.
Olga Levertoff, "The Ballad of My Father"

"Father Pogany is a Jew!" said a female parishioner standing outside St. Mary's one Sunday, just before going in to Mass. It was during George's first year there as pastor. "Why should we have him as our priest?" she continued. "Why don't we leave and find another church to pray in?" Her listeners remained silent. But someone was sympathetic enough to get word back to George that same evening.

Uncle George had planned on a five-month visit to the United States. There had seemed to be only a slim possibility that he would fulfill his hope of being assigned a parish. As it happened, he never left. Following the 1956 Hungarian Revolution, the ranks of an already existing refugee community in New Jersey dramatically swelled. That predominantly Catholic community was spread out in and around the New Brunswick area, but extended throughout New Jersey. One of their parishes, in Newark, rented the sanctuary of St. Mary's Abbey from the Benedictines. After Easter of 1957, when their Hungarian pastor, Father Olajos, relocated to California, along with a number of Hungarian Benedictine monks, George had come to the end of his five-month stay in America. He had been attending St. Mary's and many parishioners realized how well suited he would be for the vacancy. George presented his portfolio to Archbishop Thomas Boland, on the enthusiastic recommendation of Monsignor Glover, who treated George with exceeding kindness, paving the way for his appointment. Being precisely in the right place at the right time, George promptly became pastor of the Hungarian National Parish of the Archdiocese of Newark, New Jersey. He had gotten his wish of a parish ministry and would make his home near the community in which my father and our family were living.

The morning after the parishioner's insult toward her new parish priest, George called the woman and asked her to come into the church as promptly as she could. She obliged him and came in that afternoon. He greeted her at the front door of the church. Looking at her with a frown that bordered on a scowl, he twisted his head slightly to the side, more to signal her to follow him than to acknowledge her presence. Without saying a word, George escorted the disgruntled parishioner back to the rectory and into an office he had been offered there. As she entered and helped herself to a chair alongside an old oak desk, George grasped the tarnished bronze knob of the heavy wooden door and shut it with a slow and deliberate motion. He then walked around the woman's back to face her. Still standing, he held onto the back of his chair and looked her straight in the eye.

"Look here," he said, dispensing with formalities, "what you say about me personally, I don't care in the least." Each word was delivered with scornful precision. "But when you discourage others from coming to my church, that is my business, and I will not stand for it." In the brief instant it took for George to deliver the message, the woman was in tears and seemed unable to answer. "Do I make myself clear?" he added.

The woman nodded sheepishly, at which George concluded, "Now leave."

There was no lilt in George's voice or demeanor when he defended himself in this way. He was a soulful and deep-thinking man, to be sure, but he did not believe in being gentle and warm with everyone. "Sometimes nothing works as well," he was known to say, "as a well-timed slap in the face."

The incident had less to do with George's being an oppressed Jew than with his being a determined and devout Catholic priest. "I am simply defending my right to be a Roman Catholic priest," he told Katharina Lamping, a member of the parish who would one day become his housekeeper. "I am defending my parishioners' prerogatives not to be discouraged from going to church. Do you think I feel ashamed of being Jewish? Not in the least. I merely feel entitled to be a good Catholic." George had been a priest for a quarter of a century, and nothing could force him to relinquish his hold on his life's calling. He had never given much thought to feeling singled out and threatened for his Jewish origins before he'd found sanctuary in southern Italy. And in that safe haven, George had been insulated from the tragedy that befell Jews in Europe. Perhaps he never fully appreciated the sanctuary he received.

✤

Several years passed. In 1967, after the race riots in Newark, members of the Hungarian parish housed at St. Mary's Abbey dispersed into the surrounding suburbs. Soon the remaining members could not afford the rent they were paying the Benedictines for use of the church. So in 1969 George bought a house in Irvington, near the Newark border, and moved his parish into the first floor. His residence and rectory would be upstairs. For seven or eight years, he lived and served alone in what became the Church of the Assumption of the Blessed Virgin Mary. Then, when he was in his mid-sixties, George took Katharina in as his housekeeper.

Katharina was a devoutly Catholic Hungarian immigrant, an energetic blond-haired, blue-eyed Swab whose family of German descent had lived in Hungary for three hundred years. Despite her deep roots in the nation, the Hungarian Communist government had forced fifteen-year-old Kati, her widowed father, and her grandmother, along with many other Swabs, to emigrate to East Germany. She and her family eventually managed to get to West Germany, where they lived for several years. Katharina finally came to America in the midst of a troubled marriage to a fellow Swab. She began attending St. Mary's, where she met my uncle before he became pastor.

Over the years, having been a seamstress, Katharina helped George with mending and altering his vestments, stitching his cassocks or attaching buttons and labels to them. She sewed curtains for his new church in Irvington and designed an elaborate and colorful tabernacle cover. When Katharina's husband finally died, she moved into the rectory as George's housekeeper and parish assistant. She agreed to work for Father George and the church with the one stipulation that he untiringly continue to teach her the articles of the faith, the ways and rituals of the church, and guide her into the perpetual light of the Holy Spirit. He gladly agreed.

One Sunday afternoon, George and Katharina sat relaxing for a few minutes in the living room of the rectory following the customary morning Masses in Hungarian and English. A blood-red Turkish rug covered the floor, an oil painting of a typically Hungarian pastoral scene hung over the mantel, and a number of religious statues, including the Virgin Mary, flanked the doily-covered sofa. The room, and the entire rectory apartment, had a definite European flavor to it.

"You look like something's wrong," said Kati. "What is it?"

"It's the same thing all over again from years ago," George said. "It never stops." He shook his head. "I'm almost beginning to understand what my brother went through."

There was a pause. Kati raised her brow.

"I was at St. Mary's only a few months before it started," George continued. "And now, a few years later, it's happening again."

"What's happening again? You haven't told me."

"The same brand of anti-Jewish lunacy." George lowered his head slowly and touched his forehead with his fingertips. Then he quickly raised his head. "Look," he said, "I have never denied being born a Jew. But why should that matter now? I was baptized as a little boy. My faith is Catholic. My soul is Catholic. Don't they know baptism transforms a person's soul?"

"Why are you going on like this? What are you getting at?"

"Well, be quiet and listen. I'm telling you," said George. Kati lowered her eyes, looking sternly reprimanded.

"Do you think that an ounce of this hatred ever happened in Italy?" George went on. "They revere their priests there. I was treated with dignity and honor. During the war, of course, there were fanatics in the government, and my neighbors could have turned me in in the blink of an eye. Do you know what they said instead? 'So, he is Jewish. He is a good and earnest priest. Why should we let any harm come to him?' What do you think people here would do if they had the chance to turn me in? They would shout it from the rooftops, or report me in secret."

"So, please tell me: What happened?" Kati said in a quieter, more cautious tone.

Still, George grimaced like a schoolboy being asked to recite his lesson. "I was invited to someone's home for dinner," he began again, this time more measured, "and a remark was made." He was still being evasive.

"Who was it?" Kati asked.

"It doesn't matter. Let's just say you used to see them in church, but you probably will not anymore."

"What did they say?" Kati persisted, looking for some question that George might be willing to answer.

"As I said before, I've never made any secret of my Jewish birth. But they were new to the church, so maybe they didn't know. Somehow the conversation turned to the subject of Jews. And then the ignoramus woman said something like, 'Baptism doesn't work. There's no changing the Jews. You should have seen them in Budapest during the war, rushing toward the churches to be baptized as if it were the safest insurance policy in the world. But of course it didn't work. And why should it? They're a race, not a religion. There was only one way to deal with them.'"

Kati looked stunned. "Something tells me, Father, that she's not just an ignoramus. It's as you said: Baptism changes the soul. If it didn't, many people would still be barbarians. But we all must struggle against the devil. Isn't that what you have taught me?"

"Yes," said George, "baptism is no insurance policy against malice and evil."

"How did you answer her?"

"I couldn't and I didn't," said George. "I stood up and walked out of the house. I'd prefer never to see those people again."

Kati furrowed her brow in surprise.

"I know, I know," responded George. "I'm sure they're aware that if they came back to the church, I would have to minister to them. That is my obligation as a priest. But as people, I couldn't even look at them."

"If they did return, maybe it would be a sign of their shame and remorse. But, dear Father, I pray you do not feel that you yourself have anything to feel ashamed of."

"No shame," said George, "only despair and desperation."

"What do you mean?" asked Kati. She bit her lip as if to squelch her growing impatience with her revered mentor for being so dour.

"Look, I'm not just parading my scorn in front of you. These things are coming up because it's happening again. Don't you know about my efforts to be appointed to the empty pastor's seat in the archdiocese? It's a larger parish that would suit me well, and I'd be well qualified for it."

"Of course, I do know about it," Kati said, softening her tone. "I'm sorry, I mustn't forget the atmosphere of high tension around here for the past few weeks. What's happening with it?"

"There's no official word but it's as good as dead," said George, both hands clenched in tight fists on his lap. "I've heard that some people in the parish council don't want a 'Jewish priest.' I'm as good as disqualified from consideration."

Shaking her head from side to side, Kati was speechless. George himself didn't know what else to say. As both of them looked down at the geometric pattern in the rug, there was a long pause.

"You know," George finally said, "if I didn't have my faith and I didn't have you to speak to about this, I would not be able to go on. It would drive me to despair."

"Yes, you do have your faith," Kati hurriedly said, "as I have mine." She was moving quickly to check her spiritual leader's gloom. "But yours is mightier than mine, for your teachings have lifted me toward God's light. You have pointed me toward the eternal rewards of our suffering, and I would not be here without your help. I am a better Catholic because of you, and so are many other people. It is my privilege to sit with your heartache now. God knows," Kati said, with a laugh, trying to soften the mood, "you have sat with plenty of mine."

George smiled, almost in spite of himself. He lifted his eyes and noticed Kati's gaze turn inward and become more pensive. Then she bit her lip.

"You look as though there's something else you want to say," said George.

"Well . . . yes," Kati said. "I was just thinking. Am I the only one whom you could talk to about this?"

"What do you mean? Who do you have in mind?"

Kati swallowed hard. "Well, have you ever considered mentioning any of this to your brother? He has certainly—"

"No!" George barked, cutting her off.

Kati jumped with a start at the outburst. Then she collected herself. "I can only imagine the two of you have never spoken about these matters."

"We have and we never will again," George shot back.

But Kati persisted. "He surely would understand what it feels like to be a Catholic humbled for being a Jew."

George looked at Kati piercingly. She was on very shaky ground. She was always so careful not to be impertinent with him. "It's not enough," said George with a sigh, "to have suffered the humiliation. Padre Pio suffered humiliation—obediently, willingly, in order to take on the suffering of others. Like Jesus, he did it to redeem souls from suffering and sin—not to give up his faith. My brother lost his Catholic faith in the process."

"Forgive me, Father, but who are you, and who am I for that matter, to judge him—a Christian minister protected in Italy and a little German girl living in Hungary during those terrible times for the Jews? How willingly would you or I take on that same humiliation? Please take no offense, but you chose not to. You left Hungary."

"I was lucky. I had to leave for health reasons."

"Was that the case, Father? You yourself told me that Padre Pio said that your life would have been in danger if you went back to Hungary."

"That was later. That was in 1943 when I wanted to return to look into the shameful way my father's grave was treated."

"Oh, I see. Are you saying that from the very beginning Padre Pio knew nothing of the dangers that awaited you outside?"

"I don't know how much he knew from the start. Maybe he did say something. But it wasn't some mystical vision of what danger I was in. He was a practical man. He had common sense. He put it in the terms that my health would be better in San Giovanni than in Rome."

"So there would have been no danger, then, had you stayed in Rome, or anywhere else? But didn't the Nazis deport Jews from Rome and other parts of Italy, too? Maybe Padre Pio knew more than he let on."

"Look, maybe he did. I'm not going to argue with you about this," said George, shaking his finger at Kati. "It's not a matter of what Padre Pio knew or of how fortunate I was to escape. It's about how much faith a believing Catholic has in the face of mortal danger."

"Thank God you never had the chance to be tested in that way. I'm not sure how faithful I might have remained if I had been deported by the Nazis or assaulted by the Nyilas."

"And I'm sure I would not have been a hero or a saint," admitted George. "I would have been afraid and meek."

That kind of admission was one that Kati had not often heard from her hardheaded priest. "But there is no sin in meekness," George continued. "Our mother remained faithful, even though she went meekly to her death. Padre Pio said she died a martyr's death."

"Your mother, but not you. You don't know how you would have behaved in her circumstances or in your brother's. They each had their trials. Maybe this is yours."

"I'm not giving up my faith in God or in the holiness of the Catholic religion. I'm just losing my faith in people."

"Your brother had to make decisions about how to live his life. Maybe he'll still convert. Maybe all the Jews will. But for now, neither you nor I can judge him. You've told me yourself that Padre Pio had his dark nights when he felt that God had abandoned him. Even our Savior had doubts on the cross. 'Eli, Eli, lama sabachthani? Lord . . . Why have you forsaken me?' That was the human part of Him, the part that felt pain, and knew He would die, and didn't know what came next, or for what purpose. He always knew, before and after that moment. But in that moment, maybe just for that one solitary instant, our Lord forgot. Shall we judge Him for His cowardice or His loss of faith? Or could it have been that even the Son of God was trying to teach us how fragile our faith can be in the face of unimaginable suffering and death? Why can you not be more forgiving of your brother?"

George had been listening with his head lowered. Maybe he couldn't stand to hear his spiritual child upbraid him for his harsh judgment of his own brother. But then he raised his head and looked Kati firmly in the eyes. "I won't!" He paused, looked down for an instant, and then in a softer voice finally said, "I can't. I do not have God's infinite love and mercy. I just can't."

✦

Eventually I learned from my father that, a few years after this episode, on another Sunday afternoon, George drove over to see my parents. He had not been a stranger throughout the years, despite occasional flare-ups, which the brothers did their best to minimize. After a typical midafternoon lunch, the twins continued to sit around the dining room table, talking about events and people in their lives that, at least initially, were not likely to stir up any tension. Then the conversation took an unexpected turn.

"I never told you," George said, "that you were right about the prejudices of some of the people who came over here from Europe."

"What do you mean?" asked my father.

"You remember that work battalion commander you told me about who was so cruel to Jews in the Ukraine?"

My father sat up in his chair. Of course he remembered. How could he ever forget? "What about him?" was all he could say, his eyes darting away.

"Well, of all the peculiar coincidences in life, the man wound up joining my parish." My father sighed and shook his head in disbelief.

"He's still not very fond of Jews," said George, "nor of good Catholics who happened once to be Jewish." He raised a brow and glanced over at my father to see if he was looking at him. My father's mouth was slightly agape and he looked frozen in place. George continued. "Over the years, I learned about his history, and have had to make quite an effort to be a good pastor to him. But it wasn't long before he found out about my being Jewish. And then word started spreading, and all of a sudden I was being called a 'Jew priest.'"

After all those years of carrying his hurt, my father could have said something bitter and retaliatory. But he didn't. He pursed his lips and nodded in silent acknowledgment.

"But you know," George continued, "God works in strange ways."

"How do you mean?" asked my father.

"I was contacted by the Immigration and Naturalization Service and asked if I could support the man's application for citizenship. There wasn't much I could tell them that was useful. Certainly I could never divulge anything I had ever learned in confession."

"Believe me," answered my father, "they had a big file on him at Immigration in the late fifties. I'm sure you didn't tell them anything they didn't know. What they probably need are eyewitnesses to come forward, and that's not very likely to happen."

Nothing more was said. But even after the brothers went on to another subject, my father sat and dwelled on why my uncle would have brought up such a thorny topic. Was this George's way, Miklós wondered, of finally admitting that maybe he caught a glimpse of his brother's suffering?

For a fleeting instant, it must have felt to my father as if some of the dust had been rubbed off a tarnished mirror, revealing an imperfect reflection. Maybe he almost recognized himself in it, face to face, for the first time since he and his brother were children.

✢ CHAPTER 18 ✢

Revisiting

And still it is not yet enough to have memories.
One must be able to forget them when they are many
and one must have the great patience to wait until they come again.
Rainer Maria Rilke, *The Notebooks of Malte Laurids Brigge*

One typical morning, probably in the early 1980s, George had just come upstairs from the sanctuary after morning Mass and hearing confessions. Arriving at the top of the stairs, he saw Katharina in the kitchen. With a deep but good-natured sigh, George said to her, "You know, after hearing the same absurdities hour after hour, if someone else dares to suggest that confession was invented by priests, I would punch them in the nose."

"Now, Father George," Kati said good-naturedly, "I know that no one more than you believes as firmly in this blessed Sacrament. How many times have you yourself told me that it is one of the greatest gifts our Lord gave to the Church?" As she spoke, Kati was already making her way into the living room, carrying a tray with a pot of tea and some toast for a light breakfast.

"That's exactly the point," said George. He was following close behind her as they both took their customary seats in the living room—she on the sofa and he in the armchair. "What man in his right mind," George continued, "would think up such a difficult and dreary institution if the Church hadn't vested him as a priest to serve people in this way? Who else but a priest can offer only that which the Church can give—absolution from sin and the grace to help fulfill one's Christian calling? If I had to just listen, without having the power to absolve and reconcile, I'm sure I would go crazy."

"Now Father George is beginning to come back to life. Of course, for a man, this work is too hard. As God's gift, it is a joy. So have some toast and tea. Replenish yourself a little."

But George's mind was astir. He wasn't finished. "Do you know," he asked, with a whimsical look on his face, "when I was in high school in Hungary, one of our religion teachers—who were always priests," George said, raising an instructive finger, "told us that once when he worked in a large city, the rabbi there came to him and asked, 'Father, please would you hear my confession?' The priest was surprised and explained to the rabbi that he would be happy to listen to the man's sins, but that genuine absolution could only be given to one who is baptized."

Kati took a sip of hot tea. She replaced the cup onto the saucer resting on her lap. She looked off at the corner of the room and then glanced delicately at the spiritual mentor whom she revered. "May I venture to guess that you are thinking of Hungary now, and maybe your brother as well?"

George was startled at Kati's pointed intuition. "Am I being that transparent, or are you dreaming up my thoughts for me?"

Kati smiled and nodded deferentially. "Do I need to be a psychologist, Father, to guess that when you mention a Hungarian Jew who requests absolution from a priest, maybe you are thinking about your brother? It doesn't take much to realize that your morose mood these past several days has to do with your brother's trip to Hungary. Clearly you are not happy with his going."

"It's not that I'm unhappy. It's that he's going for what sounds like frivolous reasons—a simple pleasure trip along with his wife, who is called there on business."

"So, what's wrong with that, Father?"

"What pleasure or purpose is there in going back there if not to honor our dead, especially our mother?"

"I hope you don't mind my saying that it's been well over thirty years since you left, and you have never wished to go back. Why do you hold your brother to a higher standard?"

George craned his head toward Kati and looked her right in the eye. "I have prayed for my parents every day since I learned of their deaths," he snapped. "But as a priest, I can't go back, and I wouldn't—not to a nation, even my homeland, that is oppressed by communist Satans. I wouldn't choose such a thing. But he has, and for what? At least his wife visits the graves of her relatives. But tell me, if they are already in Hungary—which is not a big country—why couldn't he take a train or a car to Szarvas to visit our parents' graves? They have been to Hungary a number of times now, but not once has he returned to Szarvas."

"Is there a grave for your mother in Szarvas? But she didn't die there. Isn't that true?"

"Of course that's true," George said, raising his voice in pained irritation. "My sister went back after the war and had a grave covering put in next to our father's, and a beautiful headstone. Our mother's name was added to it. It gives dignity to—"

"—that which had no dignity," Katharina interrupted. "Forgive me, Father, but do you think even with all the prayers that you've said for your parents, you could bear going to a place of such terrible memories? How do you imagine your brother can ever go back there?"

George looked away, avoiding Kati's penetrating gaze. Another man might have felt sad and seen the point she was making, might even have shown it in his eyes and instinctively moved his hand up to check a sudden upwelling of tears. But George was not a sentimental man. Indeed, he was a spiritual and dutifully religious one, whose prayers were genuine and heartfelt. He believed that those prayers could help ensure his parents' eternal rest—even his parents, whose graves were either desecrated or empty. But could George bear going back to a place of such haunting memories? He could not answer Kati's question. Nor could he begin to understand the power of his brother's untapped grief.

❖

Klari was visiting from Sydney, Australia. It was early in the autumn of 1984. She had never been to America and had not seen my father since the end of the war, almost forty years earlier. She had married Max, the man to whom Elza had introduced her in the hospital in Budapest after the war. They had made a life for themselves in Sydney as two Jewish converts to Catholicism. Max had died ten years earlier and, for some reason—bewildering at least to Klari and George—had requested, as his last wish, to be buried in a Jewish cemetery. Perhaps finally feeling safe from the clutches of the Nazis, Max preferred that his body be buried in the midst of his Jewish ancestors rather than that his soul be redeemed in the kingdom of those among whom he had never felt entirely at home. "Repent one day before you die," Jewish sages have counseled. If he was following this precept, Max had accomplished his turning in barely enough time to recognize who he was and where he rightly belonged. Surviving him, Klari had led a solitary existence as an entomologist and then as a museum curator.

After our first dinner, we sat together at the dining room table and the siblings reminisced about their lives together in Hungary and about the members of their extended family. I listened to their stories, at times grilling them with questions about people and events. Things started innocently enough. The twins and their sister seemed to gravitate toward familiar but safe stories that would not evoke disquieting or painful memories.

My father, uncle, and aunt's interactions sometimes revealed more than the content of their stories. It was difficult for Klari to seize the floor to tell her own version of things.

"How was that?" my father would ask, with a skeptical look on his face.

"No," George would interrupt, rolling his eyes. "That's not how it was."

"Quiet," Klari would say, firmly standing her ground, "I'm telling the story."

The friction between Klari and her brothers was continual. In one way or another, her credibility was often called into question by either or both of the twins. Her memory was just as good as theirs, and she appeared to fend well enough for herself. But I could see George catch my father's eye and signal a little smirk with the corner of his mouth. I wondered if that was how they used to collude with each other as children against their hapless sister. Probably little had changed in the sixty-five or so years since the twins had to cancel their plans to run away from home because their inept little sister couldn't make it out the first-floor window.

The conversation unavoidably gravitated toward treacherous ground. Sweet and inconsequential anecdotes about family members turned instantly sour when one or another sibling would ask, "Whatever happened to him?" And there was always an underlying clash of perceptions and beliefs among the siblings over how and why things happened the way they did.

Why, for example, had their father's cousin and childhood playmate György Szanto, who had become an artist and writer, escaped deportation? Klari was preoccupied with telling innocent stories of their father's relationship to the mischievous boy Szanto, as well as of how, for years later on, she would visit the blind writer during the summers at his home in Arad. The fact was that Szanto and a tiny number of talented Jewish artists and intellectuals were granted exemptions by a Hungarian government mindful of their enormous contribution to the nation's culture. George saw it as the admittedly meager benevolence of a government that was otherwise tricked into participating in the persecution of its Jews, in a country that had for years served as Europe's last haven for them. My father saw it as an insignificant concession by Hungarian rulers who otherwise cared little or not at all for the destruction of the vast remainder of its talented as well as "dispensable" Jewish population.

And then how was one to understand the de facto exile in 1938 of Sigmund Popper, a wealthy Viennese uncle, when the Nazi *Anschluss* took over Austria? Did he hand over his bank to the Germans as ransom so that he and his wife could escape to Switzerland, or was his estate "Aryanized" by the Nazis before he managed to flee, dying a broken man in Switzerland before the war's end?

And why was a converted uncle, Sigmund Berényi, the well-loved physician of the Hungarian cardinal, not given sanctuary before he and his family were captured and shot by the Nazis? Were those who loved him so entirely powerless to offer him protection, or did they simply fear that they would jeopardize their own safety by extending him asylum?

These were explosively complex and unbridgeable differences of opinion that never fully emerged but were always right under the surface among the three siblings—a priest whose understanding of events was indirect at best, and a Jewish brother and Catholic sister who directly experienced and survived the events from vastly different vantage points.

Finally, that evening, George must have thought he was on firmer and higher ground when he brought up an event in which he himself had participated while he still lived in Hungary. "Now, one of our Aunt Laura's sons, Miklós, Miki we called him, and his wife were baptized by me in 1938, before I went to Italy. It must have been after the anti-Jewish laws, which made it hard for many people to earn a living. I also thought at the time that they sought baptism out of conviction. I wasn't sure it would help them in their livelihood, but I was happy to try."

"It didn't make any difference," said my father. "Miki wound up in the copper mines at Bor."

"Yes," said George, with little expression on his face. "I think I knew that."

"You know," my father went on, "both Miki and his wife became Jews again after the war."

"That I didn't know," said George, with barely disguised shock in his voice. "But, then, it's understandable. They were adults when they converted, so maybe their religious convictions were not as strong as I let myself believe. But I didn't know they were such good Jews to begin with."

"Maybe they didn't have to be," insisted my father. "Maybe all you need is a Nazi telling you you're a Jew, deporting you to a camp, or killing your Jewish friends. Or maybe it helps to see Jews who bore their crosses with dignity for it to take on renewed meaning."

At that, the conversation trailed off into a shamed and tense silence that must have been the echo of so many similar moments—a lifetime of them, fraught with unspoken rancor and unredeemed anguish.

✤

The next day, undeterred, I intended to meet again with my father, uncle, and aunt, this time at George's rectory apartment, where Aunt Klari was staying for the duration of her visit. There was lingering tension from the day before, but I didn't think I would ever again get the three siblings together in one room.

Before leaving, I turned to my father. "I trust you're coming with me."

"Why don't you go ahead without me today? I think you'll learn more about your uncle and aunt that way, which is what you want, isn't it? You and I will talk at another time." I probably couldn't have expected a different outcome.

It was a delicate position to be in. I was the Jewish son of the brother who had renounced my uncle and aunt's beloved Catholic faith and who saw events entirely differently than they did. I didn't want my father feeling that I was after either the rewards of Christian faith or an understanding of the events of the war as seen through Christian eyes. But neither did I want my uncle and aunt to see me as indifferent toward their experience or discrediting their point of view. I simply felt compelled to discover more about what remained undisclosed in our collective past.

When I arrived, Kati greeted me. George and Klari were already seated in the living room.

"I'm sorry my father couldn't come," I said before sitting down. "But he wanted me to be here."

"Well, okay, then," said Klari, putting on a cheerful face. "It's too bad, but we'll still have plenty to talk about."

George and Klari promptly took up the gambit. They proceeded to speak freely about their lives for almost two hours, their reminiscences punctuated at quarter-hour intervals by the chiming of the grandfather clock. George, especially, spoke with dramatic flair and historical precision about some of the childhood events that had forever colored his and his siblings' sensibilities. His stories of their years in Budapest were sentimental and almost lyrical. Naturally, he spoke of the twins' escapade in the basilica in Budapest and recalled their baptismal day in 1919 with an ease and sense of uncontested authority. He gleefully spoke of his perplexity over how the statue of the crucified Christ was supposed to come back to life. "Even back then, as a six-year-old-boy, I was taken by such questions," George said with an endearing laugh.

He also enjoyed talking about the communist debacle of that year, especially his run-in with the Bolshevik terrorist Tibor Szamuely. But his comments were not without ironic and caustic subthemes woven throughout the blithe exterior.

"This Szamuely was a big communist revolutionary," said George, "and a murderer, just like the rest of them. He and his band of hooligans traveled in their own train and absolutely terrorized people. They were worse than the Nazis. They—"

"No," Klari snapped, "they couldn't be worse than the Nazis."

"They killed people whom they suspected of being against the revolution. In front of their families, they hanged them on trees or shot them in front of graves they were forced to dig themselves. It was a scandal. Thousands of Hungarian people throughout the country suffered for it."

"All right, but they couldn't have been worse than the Nazis," insisted Klari.

I assumed that the communists George mentioned by name were also Jews, and I was afraid of where the conversation was heading. I couldn't go directly to the heart of the matter but felt I had to change the direction of the conversation.

"When you were in Italy," I said to George, "did people there know that you were born Jewish?"

"Yes, of course," he said. "You have to remember, Italy did not have many Jews, and even Mussolini didn't readily follow Hitler's plans to deport and kill them. In my village, in San Giovanni Rotondo, they knew that I was Jewish, but they said 'So he's a former Jew. He's a good priest and he's not doing anything wrong.'"

"So the Italians were good to the Jews?" I asked.

"Even the pope!" George answered emphatically. "He gave the Nazis fifty kilograms of gold to save the Jews of Rome. Kilograms! That's more than two pounds each. Do you know how much money that is? After the war, we heard that he hid hundreds of Jews in the Vatican, just as the Nazis came into Rome in 1943. Naturally, he couldn't save all of them. But some of those who were not taken were baptized. Even the chief rabbi of Italy accepted baptism. Maybe he thought it could serve as an example to his people. Naturally he lost his position in the synagogue, but then was given a teaching post in a Catholic university. If baptism didn't preserve the Jews in life, at least it saved their souls."

I felt as though I had just run into a stone wall. How could I respond to such a sectarian impasse? I was dumbfounded by the way that members of the same family could have such thoroughly different versions of events. Had I been living in some other reality than my uncle's? I had heard of the fifty kilograms of gold, but I understood it was a loan that Pius XII offered to the Jews of Rome to avert the Nazi plan to deport them. The Jews gathered the gold themselves and never had to accept the pope's offer. Needless to say, it was all a greedy ruse by the Nazis to plunder Jewish wealth before getting rid of them. They never intended to halt the deportations. As for the chief rabbi of Italy, his conversion was a most bizarre event, hardly intended as an example to his flock to avoid Nazi wrath. At a critical time, the rabbi had been absent from Rome for nearly nine months. No one knew where he was. When he emerged from hiding, Italian Jews were stunned and disheartened. Less than a year after that, months before the end of the war, he and his wife and daughter were baptized. Some suggested that he converted out of spite for being scorned by his community after his return to Rome. That is how the story had come to me. And, as for Jews being hidden in the Vatican, I had read reports of a Jewish family of eleven receiving shelter there after the Catholic fiancé of one of them secured the assistance of a sympathetic Vatican official. Hundreds? Perhaps many people wanted to believe that, including my uncle. As a matter of fact, I dearly wanted to believe it, too.

Maybe George saw how stunned I looked. He seemed to soften his stiff self-assurance. "I don't know what it was like in Hungary, but as for the Italians, I appreciate what they did for me."

"You don't know what it was like in Hungary?" Klari angrily interjected. "For one thing, they dug up our father's grave from its place of honor in the Catholic cemetery because he was born a Jew. Everybody loved your grandfather in Szarvas," Klari continued, looking over to me. She looked more sad than angry. "Hundreds of people wept at his funeral. He didn't have an enemy in the world, until the Nazis came, of course. Then one loudmouth bully had his way with the whole town. Talk about a scandal. It was terrible, shameful. Your father and I were upset about it for months, although we tried not to say too much about it to our dear mother."

"Yes, of course I knew about that," said George. There was no combativeness in his voice. He looked as sad as his sister. "Miklós wrote to me. I wanted to come back right away to protest what happened, but Padre Pio told me I would be jeopardizing my life. He said going back would do no practical good. But he was very humble. He knew many things supernaturally. Of course, I respected his opinion, so I stayed away. But it was hard, very hard."

"Your father wrote to the cardinal," Klari added, still looking at me. "But nothing was ever done. After the war, I learned that the people of Szarvas drove the bully out of town when the war ended. I will never forget what he did to our father's grave. But I can tell you that, as a Christian, I can forgive."

Now I was even more stunned than before. Did I hear Klari correctly? Did she say she could forgive the man who desecrated her father's grave? Trying to have him held responsible would have been more consistent with my own sense of justice. But a Christian's forgiveness of such malevolence was beyond me. I didn't know whether to pity my aunt or revere her. But I had to understand what she was getting at. "You mean you would forgive someone for doing such a terrible thing? Maybe with that particular man because you knew him personally? But you're not saying, are you, that you could forgive all of the atrocities such people committed during the war—in particular what was done to your mother?" I couldn't be delicate about it. I had to ask.

"Look, no one gets away with murder," interrupted George, "certainly not those savages. They will all be judged for their deeds in the next world."

"I can't think about the people who did that to our mother," said Klari. "That is God's work. No, I can't forgive everything and everyone. Like George says, God will judge them by their deeds. But as far as our mother—your grandmother—goes, I know, because I was told by someone who saw her at Auschwitz, that she died holding her crucifix. As she entered the gas chamber, she prayed to our Lord, 'God bless my Gyuri, Miklós, and Klari,' I'm certain she was saved."

"Padre Pio knew," George added, with palpable sorrow in his voice, "when someone was no longer in life, and he felt it when they had left purgatory to go to heaven. When I wasn't willing to believe that our mother had died, he told me that she had, and that she would be saved. He told me she had died a martyr. That gave me great consolation, I can't begin to tell you."

I sat quietly and stared off into the adjoining room, at the middle of the dial of the grandfather clock as it began to strike five. My body was motionless, but my mind was racing with everything I still needed to say, and everything I wanted to ask my uncle.

"A Christian martyr or a Jewish martyr?" I wondered but wouldn't dare ask. I knew that my grandmother had died with a crucifix in her hand and a prayer to Jesus Christ on her lips. How much more obvious did I need it to be? Still, I thought, she wouldn't have been killed if she were not Jewish.

I could almost anticipate how my uncle would respond. She never denied her Jewish origins, so why I was feeling so insistent on claiming her as a Jew? Why would I want to define her as something against her will, the way the Nazis did? Undeniably, in the moment of her death, she affirmed her love for Christ. Shouldn't that be the way by which she is defined spiritually, by what she lived for and what she was willing to die for? In my imaginary dialogue, I was boxing myself into a corner.

But I quietly pressed on. All right, my grandmother was a Christian martyr in Auschwitz. Was she the only one Padre Pio singled out from among all the millions of Jews who also died? Did he ever mention them? How I wanted to ask this question! According to what I had already heard from my uncle, Padre Pio never specifically said anything about Hitler's murderous actions toward the Jews and no one in that part of Italy could have dreamt what terrible things were happening. I suppose Padre Pio mentioned my grandmother because the subject came up, but that was only after the war was over. Did he really not know? Was he indifferent? Was he so preoccupied with the wider war—perhaps especially after the Italian armistice in 1943, when the Germans turned on them—and with the survival of the Church that he paid no attention to genocide? He was fully prepared to have Hitler punished and was certain that Germany would lose the war because it was cursed by God, but it had nothing to do with their diabolical designs on the Jews? My uncle was a Jewish-born refugee whom Padre Pio considered one of his dearest assistants and friends, yet never did the holy padre mention a word to him or to anyone else about the evil that was being perpetrated on the Jews. Even though Padre Pio believed in the primacy of the Roman Catholic faith and had baptized a number of Jews himself, he had frequently expressed his reverence for God's chosen people. So, when he warned George, presumably a number of times, that his life would be in danger if he returned to Hungary, was George simply afraid to ask him what he meant, and was Padre Pio only trying to spare him the pain of telling him?

I recognized that even if Padre Pio was as much of a mystic and visionary as he was said to be, he certainly could not have known the anguish of everyone on earth or the reasons for it, much less do anything about it. I had learned and could accept that he had changed people one soul at a time, working for their salvation—in Mass, in solitary prayer, and in the confessional. Even though it was jarring and confusing to my Jewish sensibilities, I had also heard of the physical torment and spiritual agony he took on himself in order to save souls from damnation, in the same manner as his Savior had. I knew that there were saintly souls and great luminaries in all religious traditions. If Padre Pio could have supernaturally taken on the suffering of the world, I am willing to believe that he would have.

But why is the value of suffering measured against salvation? It is one thing for a man of God to voluntarily take on the suffering of others, and another for an entire people to have great suffering inflicted on them regardless of whether their faith in the face of death would merit God's kingdom. The Jews who went to their deaths uttering the Sh'ma Israel did so not to ensure their salvation but because they were proclaiming the oneness of God—for the sanctification of His name, not for their heavenly reward.

A story came to mind. A devout German woman went to see Padre Pio after the war and told him that she had helped save a large number of Jews by lying to the Nazis. Padre Pio told her that she shouldn't have lied, that she should have left things to the will of God.

"It is one of the laws of Moses," I could imagine my uncle saying. "A soul is tainted by lying."

But surely that didn't necessarily imply that Padre Pio would oppose lying in order to save people's lives? How could I possibly understand that? Jews believe that if you save one life, it's as if you save the world. Would Padre Pio have us believe that if you save many lives but have to lie in order to do so, you damage your soul in the process? On the face of it, this was preposterous. Did he value the purity and salvation of the soul more than life itself?

Maybe Padre Pio would have found an ingenious or clever way to "reserve the truth," as he was known to say, when confronted with peril to innocent life. Or maybe he would have sacrificed his own life and safety, keeping silent in order to protect innocent people from persecution. Even that would be easier to believe than that he could view the suffering of countless innocent victims, as other pious Christians have, as a sacrifice to help redeem the world. But I couldn't avoid the conclusion that he would have been incapable of flat-out lying to the Nazis, not because he didn't care about Jews or because he saw their suffering as redemptive, but because he couldn't accept those kinds of challenges to his spiritual purity. Having lived so many years in the daily presence of the holy padre, my uncle would often state very matter-of-factly that Padre Pio was a saint and that someday the world would recognize it. I would not dispute his saintliness. But is saintly purity the same as righteousness—that is, being able to act virtuously for the highest good, even in the face of perilous danger, not only to oneself but to others? In the real world of good and evil, righteous people sometimes diminish themselves even when they are acting for a higher good. Was Padre Pio simply not capable of diminishing the truth? Perhaps he could have not deliberately sinned if he wanted to.

"Look," said that still, small voice inside my head, "the most important thing to Padre Pio was that no soul is lost to God, not any individual soul, nor even the souls of many innocent people who died terrible deaths."

"Then let others die as martyrs," I screamed silently, "if they believe they will gain salvation for themselves or others through their suffering. But those Jews whom that dear lady saved did not choose their suffering, and their deaths would not have been the will of God, only the will of the Nazis—regardless of whether their souls would have been saved or lost. It's righteousness versus purity of the soul." I wondered how my uncle would have reacted to the same dilemma. I tried to convince myself that he was, despite his soulfulness, a fallible man of flesh and blood who, like that German woman, would have willingly compromised his candor, as any other feeling person might have, in order to help save others.

Maybe, I thought, that is why George ultimately left San Giovanni Rotondo after so many years. Perhaps he needed to live among men and be subject to the moral flaws and challenges of the world. And maybe that, too, is why Padre Pio always knew that his dear Giorgetto would leave him one day.

There was so much I could have said, so much I wanted and needed to say, and so much more that I needed to hear from my uncle. But I was afraid of irreparably opening up old wounds between him and my father and only deepening the rift between George and our family. I also respected my uncle's reverence for his spiritual mentor and would not dare impugn Padre Pio's saintliness and goodwill, certainly not in my Uncle George's presence, not to his face. So instead I said nothing. I continued staring at the grandfather clock as it finished striking five o'clock , and I remained silent, frozen and inert.

✦ CHAPTER 19 ✦

Memoria Passionis

And I will betroth Thee to me in faithfulness;
And you shall know the Lord.
HOSEA 2:20

In the spring of 1979, on the occasion of my parents' thirty-fifth anniversary, my mother and father renewed their marriage vows in a Jewish ceremony at their home. For my father, it was his crowning moment as a Jew, the time when he returned to the core of his being.

As my parents stood under the *chupah,* the wedding canopy, their children and grandchildren surrounded them. After reciting the *Shevah B'rachot,* the Seven Wedding Blessings, the cantor instructed my father to repeat in Hebrew the bridegroom's vow: "I betroth you according to the laws of Moses and the people Israel." It was the first time I had ever heard my father recite Hebrew words—not Latin incantations, not Hungarian poetry, but the Hebrew words of his wedding vow.

Those ancient words resounded through my mind, speaking to me of my father's life as a Jew, perhaps even giving me a moment's access into our family's collective memory. My thoughts reached back seventy years to that pivotal moment when my Jewish grandfather was baptized. What ironic counterpoints that moment and the present one were in the life of our family. My father and his father had fallen in love with poor Jewish girls who were suspected of having little to offer them in marriage. My grandfather had taken temporary refuge in Catholicism. And now, by way of his own Jewish wedding ceremony, my father had fully found his way home as a Jew.

" . . . according to the laws of Moses and . . . the people Israel," repeated my father, this time in English, his voice cracking in the process. It was as close as I had ever come to seeing my father weep.

Though it had taken him many years, I felt that this particular day marked my father's full and complete return to the Jewish people. He was no longer someone who had been accidentally born a Jew, nor someone who happened to have been persecuted along with other Jews. Much less was he someone who had simply married a Jewish woman and accepted her faith in order to raise their children in one religion. My father's life was sustained, more than anything else, by the love he and my mother had for each other, and by everything his life had become, since the end of the war, because of that love.

As I stood next to him and held one of the four corners of the tallis that served as the *chupah,* I couldn't help but wonder what had occurred to my father at that moment that would have caused his voice to falter. Was he reminded of the day in August 1945, at the Elizabeth Pulmonary Sanitarium in the Buda Hills, when he was tearfully reunited with his living wife? Or was there something else in addition to that, something unspoken and unspeakable but present nonetheless? At such a crowning moment, I wondered, could my father have reopened his heart to his wife, to the Jewish people, and to the laws of Moses but not to God, as well? And might he have remembered not only God the eternal Father but also the Savior whose love had filled my father's life as a child and young man, at a time when Jesus was still Christ and when my father felt safe in the world—reassured of his home in it and his eventual welcome in the Kingdom of Heaven? Or would he have banished such intrusive thoughts as quickly as they had come—that taste of redemption on his tongue that had turned so bitter over the previous four decades?

Somehow, as our family stood under the *chupah,* I decided that this moment must have touched the wound in my father's heart that dated from the time when his God had fallen silent and, even more sorrowfully, when his beloved Savior had failed to save him and his fellow Jews from suffering, failed to save the Christian world from bodying forth evil, genocide, and indifference. Maybe, at that very instant that his voice cracked, my father remembered the sweet promise of redemption and recognized the bitter truth: that the world was still unredeemed. And through that remembering and that recognition, more than in any other way, my father truly became a Jew again.

❖

A few years later, on a spring day in May 1988, the Cathedral of the Sacred Heart in Newark was crowded with worshipers and well-wishers. Father George Pogany's devotion to the Church was about to be celebrated at a Mass officiated by Archbishop Theodore McCarrick. A declaration by His Holiness, Pope John Paul II, would be read, recognizing George as a Chaplain of Honor. It would constitute his elevation to papal prelate, after which time he would be referred to as Monsignor Pogany.

Parishioners, colleagues, friends, and family filled the front pews of the magnificent Gothic cathedral replete with stained-glass windows and vaulted ceilings. There was great joy and exhilaration in the air. George's parishioners, many of whom sat together in the front pews, were astir with pride that their shepherd of more than thirty years would now be taking a step up the Church's honored ecclesiastical ladder. Even George's twin brother was present, with his wife and members of their family. My father knew how important this event was in his brother's life and would not deny him that recognition. It surely marked the culmination of George's spiritual betrothal to the Church.

As George rose to his feet in the front pew and listened to the reading of the papal proclamation, his mind must have swept across the terrain of the previous seven-and-a-half decades. It was as if he were once again at the baptismal altar, about to die to the life of the body and be born again in the life and spirit of his Lord and Savior.

Sitting in the midst of my family, I was puzzled by the serenely humble countenance of my uncle as he stood before a prince of his church. I had always felt regret and perplexity: what kind of man, really, was my father's twin brother? His spirituality always seemed austere to me, and his religious calling mysterious and arcane. Certainly his enforced silence kept it that way. But what could have been going on inside his mind and heart when he witnessed his brother's seemingly happy family life? Was he jealous or envious? Did George ever think about how his life had turned out so differently from his brother's? Had he ever longed for a more normal life with a wife and family? I simply didn't know.

By that point, in 1988, my uncle had spoken to me more about his past life than my father had about his own. But our conversations always seemed to revert back to his Catholicism and his calling as a priest. There was great soulfulness to his person but little observable flesh and blood. I simply could never fathom what human emotions shaped and directed George's piety. Even at this marvelous moment in the Cathedral of the Sacred Heart, I discerned more of the sacred heart of Christianity than the human heart of my father's twin brother, standing so proudly near the altar. I wondered what secret wounds had pierced his own heart and hands in the course of his life. What buried disappointments in love, what forgotten longings for a normal life among men and women lay at the concealed stations of George's path of tears, leading to his personal Golgotha? In this glorious house of God, a place of priests and bishops, scepters and miters, and the sweetly transporting smell of frankincense wafting heavenward from swinging silver censers, I thought of more quotidian scenes around our family's home, where the familiar aromas of chicken *paprikas* and *nokedli* evoked secret memories, all-but-forgotten longings, and fantastic speculations in the deeper, inaccessible silences of each of our own hearts and minds. Despite all those years of receiving avuncular kindness, manifest cordiality, and occasional rumblings from George, too much had gone unsaid.

✤

By the early 1990s, the time had come and gone when Father George celebrated daily Mass at his own parish, the Church of the Assumption of the Blessed Virgin Mary. Members of his flock, mostly Hungarian immigrants and refugees, had long ago stopped coming during the week to George's church near Central Avenue in Irvington, in an urban neighborhood that had become increasingly crime-ridden. Although his parishioners still journeyed from the suburbs into the city to attend Sunday Mass, on weekdays George had, in recent years, conducted two morning Masses each day at St. Lucy's, not far from the cathedral in Newark, in the midst of the much-loved Italian parish of his good friend and colleague Monsignor Joseph Granato. But more recently still, he had been forced to say Mass privately in the rectory of his own church.

George had been confined there ever since an automobile accident had nearly taken his life. He knew he shouldn't have gone out that night. He had prayed for many years to various angels, one of whom finally communicated directly with him that night, telling him in a small but distinctly audible voice that he should not venture out. In his self-avowed bullheadedness, George refused to heed the angelic warning and drove to visit a friend in New Brunswick, where he must have fallen asleep at the wheel, because he didn't even see the stop sign, much less the car that broadsided him and put him through the windshield. The police found him lying twenty feet from his car. Miraculously, George survived with only a fractured facial bone and severely bruised ribs, which impaired his breathing for weeks and required that he be kept on oxygen. With his wounded chest and labored breathing, he would surely have died if pneumonia had set in. George was certain that his angelic guardian had saved his life, for he knew he easily might have been killed in the accident. There was no other explanation for why and how he had been spared. After that, George never got behind a steering wheel again, but his life and health were never quite the same.

Many years earlier, a pious and prescient lady in San Giovanni Rotondo had predicted that George would have many fortunate turns in his life and that he would die at a ripe old age. Years later, in America, an Italian woman at St. Lucy's who had the gift of seeing into the future confided to him that he would go to his heavenly reward at the age of eighty. By the spring of 1993, precisely at that age, George was grievously ill and too weak to receive visitors. By the summer, he was resigned to his imminent death. He stubbornly refused hospitalization and accepted palliative care in his rectory apartment only from his housekeeper and his personal physician. He was unwilling to receive even family members.

By the end of July, on a hot summer afternoon, Kati thought better of George's isolation and finally summoned my father to his bedside. George had earlier received the last anointing and was going in and out of consciousness. He became aware of my father's presence as soon as he entered the room. He partially opened his eyes and tried to speak.

"Miklós," he said, speaking in the language of their childhood and youth, "Do you remember the basilica, when we were children?"

"Of course I do," answered my father.

"Do you remember how we prayed there for the first time in our lives?"

"Yes," said my father with an undisguised smile. "We were good Catholics, weren't we?"

"I've been so sorry you left the Church," George said, in a breaking voice.

"And I'm so sorry for our separation," my father responded, straining to keep his composure.

There was a long pause. "I'm not angry anymore," said George. "And I'm glad we have been reunited. . . . I will continue my prayers for you when I'm gone . . . but please pray for me until then."

"I wish I could pray, but I don't know if I can. I can only hope that you rest peacefully, here and now," said my father. "What happens in the hereafter, we must leave that to God. As for me," he continued, "whatever prayers you or anyone has ever said on my behalf, please believe that they have been answered. I can't ask for any more than I have already received. And as for what awaits me after I'm gone, I suppose I, too, will find that out in the not-too-distant-future."

George seemed not to hear my father's last words. His eyes opened wide, and his gaze was directed toward a distant inner horizon. Then, suddenly, he turned to my father and said, "Do you remember how shocked I was when I found out that the poor crucified Jesus on the cross was dead?" George was stumbling over his words, as if he needed to get them out quickly.

"Yes, I remember," said my father.

"It's not true. He has risen. He died as a man only to redeem our sinfulness. I tell you He's alive. I can see Him. There you are, my dear Lord. I see You now. You've always been . . . alive."

At his funeral reception a few days later, I sat quietly before George's crimson-clad body and studied the peaceful countenance that could have been my father's. Behind him was a statue of his crucified Savior, and clasped gently in my uncle's hands was a rosary with a small cameo photo of Padre Pio. Inside the large hall of the funeral home, mourners approached his body one by one, touched his cassock, and bowed their heads in prayer. As I sat with my family among the congregation of those who had come to pay their respects, I softly spoke the words of the Kaddish for this child of Israel become the son of the Mother Church. *"Exalted and magnified be the Name of God in the world of His creation . . . "* I wanted to find a way not only to lift George's soul heavenward but also to surrender my grief for the missed opportunities between the twin brothers, and their respective houses of faith, to more fully heal the unresolved estrangement between them. If only posthumous efforts such as saying the Kaddish could diminish the inner barriers between this devout Christian minister and the quietly courageous Jewish husband, father, and grandfather who was his twin brother.

Shortly afterward, at the same Cathedral of the Sacred Heart in which George had been elevated years earlier to monsignor, he was honored and eulogized at his solemn Christian funeral. Priests, monsignors, and bishops crowded the altar surrounding the coffin of this tireless servant of the Church. In his eulogy, Archbishop McCarrick made respectful but unobtrusive reference to George's Jewish origins, suggesting that his "knowledge of the Hebrew Scriptures" had informed his ministry. George was also praised in personal words of tribute by his friend Monsignor Granato, in whose Italian parish he had often conducted Mass. "Father George," he said, with an affectionate smile, "was a selfless, 'old-fashioned' priest who was utterly devoted to his prayer life, his ministry, and his Church."

I suppose that it would have been neither timely nor appropriate on this occasion for anyone to disclose the complex web of grief and disappointment between George and his Jewish twin, much less the deeper historical wounds between the brothers' houses of faith. But the searing irony of George's identical twin brother's entire Jewish family being seated in the front pew of the magnificent Christian sanctuary could not have escaped the awareness of everyone who knew of George's circumstances.

I never suspected that George ever considered my father's being Jewish an impediment to his standing in his own religious community. His own Jewish origins may have presented a greater obstacle to his advancement within the archdiocese than his brother's rejection of Christianity. To George, my father's readoption of the faith into which they were born represented a private spiritual rupture between the two of them. He was not in the least concerned about what people thought of him for the way his brother lived his life. But now, with George's passing, any possibility of mutual discernment and embrace between him and my father would have to depend on the belief that they would one day meet again, face to face. Or was there something that the surviving brother could still do to help heal that troubled relationship? What that was, I didn't know, but as I passed through the day, listening to the many heartfelt eulogies and being greeted warmly by so many of my uncle's friends, colleagues, and parishioners, I continually pondered the possibility.

Though the spiritual schism between the brothers was never fully or outwardly resolved, it seemed odd to me that the twins came to fulfill such kindred life tasks within the same area of urban New Jersey. George tended to the spiritual lives of his parishioners at his small church in Irvington. My father eventually worked for the better part of his career as a social worker, assisting residents of Newark's west side ghetto to stay one step ahead of poverty and shame, even while his unending devotion to his wife and family had always been the most central part of his life's calling. While George offered his flock salvation in the world to come, my father provided his family and community with dignity and pride in this world. The brothers were both loved and appreciated for the lives they lived and the work they did, by the people they served and by those who served alongside them. Their natural, undeniable affinity for each other, their similar vocations and, perhaps, the unseen hand of their loving parents finally braided together the very separate strands of their lives, just as perhaps God Himself—we are told in the Midrash—braided Eve's hair.

✤   CHAPTER 20   ✤

Mourning

Ugy faj nekem hógy te vagy halott és nem én.
(I hurt so badly that it was you and not me.)
Peter L. Fischl, "To the Little Polish Boy Standing with His Arms Up"

It was eight years after Klari's visit that I finally sat down with my father to ask him all the unasked and unanswered questions that were either too frightening or implicitly forbidden to me as a child. It was September 1992. It had taken years to get to this point. I was over forty years old, married, and now the father of two young sons, and I still didn't know my father's story as well as I knew my uncle's and aunt's. Even now, I was afraid that this exchange would be dangerously heart-wrenching.

On the surface, my father was willing. But he seemed nervous—legs crossed, hands folded, leaning against the back of the sofa in a strained show of nonchalance. He looked as though he were about to be interrogated about sworn secrets. Although, at nearly eighty years old, he was still passionately involved in literature, poetry, and astronomy, he wore the usual poker face of a man whose deep emotions lay under an impenetrably stoical exterior.

Up until then, no one in the family had ever asked our father about his past, aside from that solitary occasion during Klari's visit. Before and after that, we didn't dare. He never directly said much about it—very little about his brother and sister, and virtually nothing about his father or mother, nothing of the manner in which they lived and died. Usually he would hide behind pithy phrases like "survivor guilt" and "tacit consent" (meaning the cooperation of onlookers, by which so many Jews were killed). He used to love to quote Martin Niemöller's famous statement about a man who witnessed the deportation of different groups of people but never took a stand because he himself didn't belong to any of the groups. Then, when the man himself was deported, there was no one left to speak up for him. I found out only later that Niemöller was an impassioned opponent of the Nazis but confessed his own anti-Semitism following the war. My father never knew that. But I always wondered why he chose to quote a Christian clergyman who felt so unconnected to the plight of the Jews until he himself became a victim. No mystery, I suppose.

I was as clumsy in my questioning as he was evasive in his answers. "Can you tell me anything about yourself from before I was born that captures something about your life?"

"No, I don't think so."

I was a professional listener to people's life stories. But my father was not a patient, and I was not a dispassionate listener. As I sat across from him in a stiff-backed chair behind my own stiff persona, I was frightened of his sadness and, in truth, of my own.

I backpedaled, asking the more chronological and factual questions that would suit a man more comfortable with providing name, rank, and serial number. Gradually I was able to ask more substantive and poignant questions.

After about an hour, as my father continued speaking, I sensed that we were silently conspiring to stay away from subjects that were too highly charged. I decided I had to steel myself and move into more dangerous territory. "Can you say anything about your time in the concentration camp?"

"Well, first I was in the Hungarian labor battalions."

"What was that?"

"It was an alternative to the army for so-called undesirables like Jews and communists. I was in a group with other converts for almost two years."

"Why only converts?"

"Because they separated the Jews and the converts. A lot of times it was easier for us, because the Jews were usually treated miserably. We even got a chance to go to church. It was absurd. But by the time we got to Bergen-Belsen, it didn't matter. I had lost my faith in Christianity and I didn't know what Judaism was about. There was no religion in the camp, only fate and luck. That is how any of us survived. No, I take that back. I remember some religious Jews celebrated Passover. That impressed . . . me . . . very much." There my father's voice cracked.

"When did you find out about your mother?"

"After the war, I found a card from her written one day before she was deported in 1944. She knew what was coming. So I feared the worst."

"Can you tell me more about her, about what her life was like at the end?"

My father winced, swiftly shifting his head to the side as if seized by a tic. "What do you need to know? I really don't know much."

Throughout my life, whenever I mentioned my grandmother's death in Auschwitz to anyone, my voice cracked and I choked back tears. Actually, without knowing it, I avoided mentioning it whenever I could. Even the name Auschwitz was too powerful for any of us in the family to mention casually without clutching or choking up. So we children, too, all kept an unspoken vow of silence about it. But as the years passed, my grandmother's memory lay darkly hidden in our consciousness, undispelled, as powerful as if she had just died within our own lifetime and our own memory.

"She was in the Jewish ghetto in Szarvas," my father went on. "That was the town we lived in after we left Báránd. My brother and I finished high school there. Our mother was deported with the other Jews of the town."

"But she wasn't a Jew. Why did they take her, too?"

"The Nazis didn't care. The Hungarians didn't, either. My sister told me that our mother was taken to Mass every morning by Hungarian gendarmes. Our parish priest helped arrange it. The Hungarians cared about being good Christians, I'll tell you that. But in about six weeks' time, from the time Eichmann entered Budapest, the Hungarians helped deport almost every single Jew from the countryside, including your grandmother and other converts."

I always tried to pretend that my grandmother's Catholicism did not matter, even to her, that she was persecuted simply for the fact that she was a Jew, and that I as a Jew had only Jewish relatives who were killed in the Holocaust. But it did matter, much more than I'd ever wanted to believe.

"If the priest could help your mother that way, why couldn't he help her escape, or hide her?"

"I don't know. I don't know," was all my father could say.

"When did all this happen?"

"In May and June of 1944. Like I said, when I got back to Budapest from the concentration camp in '45, I found a card my mother had written to me. She expected to be deported the very next day. She had no illusions. She knew."

I had never seen my father so choked up. His eyes were sad, yet his voice was angry. I instinctively fled from the emotion and changed the subject to a lighter one. But several minutes later I gathered my strength and returned to it, needing to probe further. "Why have you never talked about your mother before?"

My father glanced at me and then turned away, staring off in limitless silence at the corner of the room. I looked at his face and at his watery eyes. I could have drowned in what felt like an ocean of silence. When it continued for what seemed like minutes, I felt my father's sadness welling up inside my own throat, where a hard, immovable lump had formed. It was as if his grief had become my grief. In that moment, I realized that I had carried that grief as a child, although it always eerily felt as if it were from beyond the borders of my own life experience. Now, as an adult, as a professional psychotherapist, I had come to understand that unmourned grief gets passed from one generation to the next. It does not go away but is carried, mysteriously, through the generations. It was my father's unwitting legacy to me: pain and loss left unmourned by the father inexplicably ends up in the son's life. And, as I looked at him, I thought of my own sons and the silence, melancholy, and grief that I might have already passed on to them in their young lives without even knowing it—all in the manner of things I could and could not talk about. I knew I had to interrupt the cycle at that very moment.

I gathered the courage—or was it the unmitigated nerve?—to ask my father again. But this time I had to try to mask the sorrow rising up from my throat to my eyes. "Why couldn't you ever tell us?" I finally asked.

My father paused and swallowed hard. "I have always felt guilty that she died and I survived," he said bravely, still holding his tears in check, "and that so many others died, and I didn't. I just don't understand why. It was all fate and luck. I didn't deserve it."

"Is that why you never grieved your mother's death?"

"How could I grieve?" my father shot back, his voice cracking into a whisper. "You need prayers to grieve, and I didn't have any prayers left. And you need faith in God. Maybe I didn't believe in God anymore—neither the God of the Christians nor the God of the Jews. After what happened, I would never set foot in a church again. For what my former countrymen did to my mother, they have morally bankrupted Christianity. And a Jewish God? I believe in the Jewish people, and that I am a Jew and not a Christian. But even if I believed in the God of the Jews, where would I get my prayers? Remember, I was a good Catholic for most of my life."

"Do you know," I said, "you have never talked about your mother with us? Do you still think about her?"

"I carry my tears for her every day of my life," my father said, with a great sorrow in his voice that I feared would implode his words. We both paused.

"If you ever were to say Kaddish for your mother," I finally asked, "do you think she would accept it?"

My father looked up at the ceiling for a second. "My father might," he said. "I don't know if my mother would. I don't think she would like knowing that I am a Jew."

It felt as if my eyes would burst open with torrents of sorrow. What could I say? How could I possibly respond—a mother murdered for being a Jew would be unwilling to accept her son's Jewish faith or Jewish prayers of grief? I couldn't and wouldn't believe it. I felt a surge of anger at my grandmother. But my sadness returned and was more enduring—for her and for my father. It had started as my father's sadness but now it was also my own. It was not new. It had always been there. I knew that now with complete certainty. But what would I do about it? In whose faith, and to what God, I asked myself, does one mourn a Christian who was murdered as a Jew—a Christian who might not accept her own son's Jewish prayers?

The answer became apparent to me: One grieves in one's own language of faith—even if that grief is not immediately one's own, even if it is not in a language that the bereaved would understand or appreciate. What else can one do, except to remain silent? That would just perpetuate the grief, and that was no longer acceptable.

"How would you feel," I asked my father as we sat together during that September weekend in 1992, "if I were to say Kaddish in your place for your mother? I would do it myself. I would go to services in synagogue every day for eleven months and say Kaddish for her. Could I do that? Would that be all right?" I was ready to do this, for my father and for his mother. I knew I had to, for the sake of surrendering his, mine, and our entire family's long-held sorrow—nearly fifty years after her terrible death.

My father listened to what I said. He put a hand up to his face and kept it there for a long time. Finally he put it down and looked at me sadly, nodding his head. "Okay if that's what you want to do. You can do that."

Then I would. I would mourn his mother, my grandmother.

✤

The morning minyan had just let out in the small Orthodox shul in the former Jewish ghetto of Budapest. I had begun saying Kaddish for my grandmother only a few weeks before, at home in Boston. Nearly our entire family was at the end of a weeklong journey we had taken to Hungary. My brother and sister and I had come with our spouses and children to accompany our parents back to their former homeland on the occasion of my father's eightieth birthday. There was a collective sense among us of returning from exile to a nation in which our family's life had almost ended.

The purpose of our trip was to discover the fabric of our parents' lives before it had been rent by the war. We all needed to risk reigniting sorrowful memories for the possibility of uncovering earlier moments of wholeness and happiness. Over the course of the week, my father seemed to experience a sense of renewal, allowing himself an expatriate's ambivalent longing for his birthplace. Taking comfort and strength from being surrounded by his family, this usually soft-spoken and somber man spoke his native language with utter self-possession and eloquence. Here, in Budapest, he recollected and recited the poetry of his youth and listened nostalgically to the music of his childhood and university days. Here, too, he and my mother finally spoke to us about their lives and the lives of their families, friends, and colleagues— sometimes about how they had suffered and perished, but mostly about how they had lived and how those lives had intersected with their own. Privately, I couldn't help but feel that we were tiptoeing through a minefield of sorrow and grief, and that someone needed to address our collective losses more directly and begin to lay them to rest. I instinctively felt that mourning must precede wholeness and happiness. As a result, my time in Hungary was spent in more solitary pursuits and reflection.

After the morning minyan, everyone quickly resumed his habits of daily life. By now I was no longer an unfamiliar presence in shul, having spent the week helping them be one person closer to completing a minyan. To them, I was an *Amerikai Zsidó* who had come to say Kaddish for a loved one. Although they became friendlier as the week progressed, I was secretly relieved that my rusty Hungarian helped me avoid making my own feelings, motives, and memories more visible. That I was saying Kaddish for a grandmother whose death during the Holocaust had not yet been mourned would certainly be more understandable to them that the fact that she was killed as a believing Christian by murderers who considered her more a Jew than she herself did. I had never relinquished a churning ambivalence about having come to Hungary—the need to draw near to and hallow those left behind pitted itself against the urge to flee and never look back, to forget forever, simply in order to be able to go on living. I could not escape the tension between the yearning to reclaim our family's stories and the ominous feeling that we did not belong here anymore and should not have come. Leaving the synagogue, I thanked the men and said good-bye.

As I left, ready to walk back to the hotel as I had done throughout the week, I gazed more carefully this last day at the modern city of Budapest, such as it was, in the already hazy daylight air sullied by the exhaust of cars, cabs, and trucks. It had a heavy, sickly odor that left a noxious taste on my tongue. I envisioned that, beneath the dirt and grime of years of neglect under the Soviets, the tarnished, once-stylish facades of formerly elegant buildings hinted of a more civilized time in the nation's history. But even before decades of Communist disregard had set in, more than just the exteriors of the city's structures had been tainted. I imagined it would take years of sandblasting to clean away the stain on a nation's soul for its widespread and all-too-eager collaboration in the persecution and liquidation of its Jewish population.

Here, it was unlike the anonymous rush-hour frenzy of New Yorkers or Bostonians; the passersby reflected a gray and hopeless mood. Even their hesitant gait mirrored the uncertain direction of their only recently found freedom from Soviet domination. If New Yorkers were one step ahead of depression and despair, then the less-than-frenetic inhabitants of Budapest were one step behind.

As I walked down the main thoroughfare, I departed from my usual route back to the hotel and walked down a side street. Directly ahead of me I saw the side of a huge church. I continued down the street to get in full view of it, and came upon a stately and open church square. This surely must be St. Stephen's Basilica, I told myself, the legendary place where my father and uncle had once played at being Christians. This imposing Renaissance structure, its surface blackened by the irreverent breath of modern society, was the place of family lore, the entryway for once nominally Jewish twin brothers to come into the presence of their Christian Savior. I shut my eyes for an instant and sighed deeply, as if I were approaching someone else's Holy of Holies, forbidden to me as a Jew. Hesitantly, I climbed the first tier of steps of the church and sat down as inconspicuously as I could along its edge, as worshipers and tourists were coming and going.

There I sat and pondered my family's story and wondered why I so urgently needed to return to this place of such painful ruptures and discontinuities. I asked myself some of the unspoken questions my family had carried since the end of the First World War. Now that the Iron Curtain had lifted, there still remained personal and private walls of self-imposed forgetfulness that we all needed to raze. I asked myself why, for so long, twin brothers of different faiths had barely spoken to each other and to us—to *me*—about their suffering and their healing, their sorrow and their disappointments? Why had my life and the life of our family become filled with the silence of unanswered and unasked questions, and entangled by the sadness and fear that became wrapped around those questions like so many cobwebs around discarded furniture in the basement of an abandoned house?

Sitting on the steps that the twins had first climbed so long ago, I knew that we had finally and truly begun to explore the silent and empty spaces that had kept all of us, my father's children, from knowing him more fully and, in turn, from knowing ourselves. And even while our lives felt fuller for our having come on this journey together, I realized that throughout our time in Hungary, we had all managed to conspire with one another to avoid places that would have provoked dangerously painful memories. Some of us, including my father's grandchildren, had occasionally asked why we would travel virtually all over the country but not visit my father's family's home in Szarvas. "There's nothing to see there anymore," my father had answered, his crusty irritation at the question loyally guarding the gates to his sorrow. We finally got the point.

❖ CHAPTER 21 ❖

Remembrance

Go, summon Abraham, Isaac, Jacob, and Moses. . . .
They know how to mourn.
Louis Ginzberg, "The Great Lament," in *Legends of the Jews*

For nearly a whole year, I said Kaddish at Temple Emanuel in Newton, Massachusetts, for the grandmother I had never known, who was killed as a Jew in Auschwitz but who died clutching a crucifix and uttering a prayer to Jesus Christ. At the very start, it was unnerving to pray for a Catholic family member. I felt like an interloper, having my Christian grandmother's name read among those Jews who had recently died or whose *yahrzeits*—memorial anniversaries—were being observed. Ironically, saying Kaddish for my grandmother made me feel more a Jew than all the religious practices I had previously learned. Now that I was to be counted among the mourners of Zion, the God of the Jews became for me a source of personal comfort and healing—a greater tangible reality than God as creator, lawgiver, or even redeemer of the world.

By mourning my grandmother, I wanted not only to help heal our collective sorrow but also to disentangle my father's grief from my own. Yet I also needed to come to know Gabriella as a person and as my grandmother. I realized she might have had mixed feelings about having a Jewish grandson, and that we might not have had much to say to each other. But I still needed to possess some knowledge of her, to acquire some memory of who she was. My prayers peculiarly helped me reclaim that memory, even if they were not my memories to reclaim. They were my father's.

It was all fairly natural. There were no new revelations about my grandmother's life on earth, no mystical insights into her spiritual destiny—just comfortable, matter-of-fact questions and answers between my father and me. If there was any mysterious effect of my prayers, it was that my father and I could now speak about Gabriella without lumps in our throats, without choking on our words.

It took a long time before I realized that saying Kaddish was more for my father's healing than for my own. And it was for the healing of our relationship, which had been characterized for so long by silence, remoteness, and unacknowledged though shared sadness. Only when the burden of his own sorrow was lightened could he begin to surrender that which had until then been unspeakable. In his having done so, he finally revealed the pain that lay at the root of his and his brother's mutual sadness. It had seemed so strange at first to realize that my father's silent grief had been passed on to me. Now it was even more peculiar to recognize that my mourning could help my father to heal, and in turn liberate his long-buried memories of his mother.

In the end, by saying Kaddish, my tears and our collective tears for the manner in which my grandmother died finally flowed into the river of Jewish grief. It finally enabled me to embrace my father's, my family's, and my people's history as my own.

But what about my grandmother? What spiritual benefits could she have received from my prayers? As a Jew, how could I honor her life as a Christian, rather than just as my grandmother? I did not begin this process because I believed my grandmother's soul needed to be saved. I had prayed with the assumption she had already found final rest long before I uttered my prayers for her. So why then pray for *her*, and not just for my father's or my own benefit? How could I penetrate the tangled sorrow of a devoutly Christian woman whose only claim to Jewish fate was her birth and death? Ignorant of her faith and barely able to imagine her physical and spiritual torment, I felt a terrible emptiness. There were no tears for my grandmother. I couldn't get at them. Through eleven months of praying, I had barely touched the surface of the well, yet I felt wrung dry. How could I begin to approach her life and faith as a Christian with greater reverence and awe? What further obligations fell to me? What prayer for *her* healing, and *to whom* should I pray?

❖

When I was in the fourth grade in Newark, a group of us who lived on Wainwright Street would walk home from school together. We would first cross and then go down Chancellor Avenue, past Unterman Field and Bernheim's Funeral Home, to the corner of Leslie Street, and walk further, down to Rubin Brothers' Drugstore, where we'd turn the corner onto Wainwright and head home.

A few times, near the second or third house from the corner, there was a van parked on the street with its side opened up, facing the sidewalk. A man stood inside. We were curious, maybe because we thought his truck resembled a circus sideshow. As soon as we came up to see what he was about, he started telling us stories, in a soft but clear voice, and drawing stick figures on a blackboard. The stories were about Jesus and how he had been sent by God to save the world. They were simple stories in language that little kids could understand, and we listened to him just long enough to know that he was trouble. He knew he had to talk fast, so he didn't wait until he was finished to hand out small volumes of the Christian Bible. When I got mine, my chest got tight and I clenched my hands into fists around the book.

Some of my more brazen friends tore up their Bibles in front of the guy. "We're Jewish, you idiot," one kid said. Of course the man knew that. He hadn't stumbled by accident into the most Jewish neighborhood in Newark. "And we're not going to bow down to Jesus Christ," said another.

"Jesus Christ!" still another kid yelled, with harsh, make-believe derision in his voice, the way grown-ups say the name to curse at something. "Are you crazy, mister?"

Then others joined in, "*Sh'ma Israel, Adonai eloheinu, Adonai echad,*" one after another. Then we walked away, unruffled and confident that we were all Jewish and that we'd never become anything else. "*A-do-nai, A-do-nai.* He's the only one we pray to. Now you say it, mister. *A-do-nai.*" What defiance and

scorn, I thought, from such cocky kids. I wished I could have said some of
those things myself. I wasn't sure why I couldn't or wouldn't. Maybe with my
uncle being a priest, I felt I had to be respectful of his religion. I was tied in
knots. I remember walking home, holding the Bible, trying to think of how to
throw it away or rip it up. But I couldn't. I didn't really know why.

"I see you are already well schooled in your defiance, you stiff-necked
Jews," I heard the guy call out as we all walked away.

The man was right. All my friends and I were well schooled to resist
threats to our religion, if that's in fact what he meant by our being stiff-
necked Jews. As I went on alone, I thought it had a nice ring to it, a certain
dignity, that I couldn't yet put into words.

✦

Now, in my forties, knowing more about my family's experiences in the war,
and about their religious twists and turns, I was coming to accept that some
members of my family could find comfort only in Jesus; that He was my
grandmother's Lord—even though I knew He would never be mine. If I were
truly interested in her eternal rest, I knew I would need to address this Christian Savior, if not with religious supplication, then with an openhearted personal appeal. He was the one to speak to. Maybe this was what was needed
for her to be at peace, and for there to be some peace in our family for her
having lived and died as a Christian but been killed for being a Jew.

Ever since my father refused to go to his hometown of Szarvas during our
family's visit to Hungary in 1992, I had harbored a wish that he could return
there one day and finally face the grief he carried for the death of his mother.
He was old, and I knew I was taking a chance. But it seemed like the right
thing to do, to urge my father to return with me to Hungary, not just to the
nation of his birth but to Szarvas, the site of his and his family's unredeemed
sorrow. And where more fitting, I thought, to search out my grandmother's
savior than in the homeland in which my family's life once briefly flourished
in the light of His love, even if, despite that love, they were torn forever from
one another and from their home?

I brought up the idea matter-of-factly with my father. I told him that I was
eager to visit some of the places of his childhood in Hungary that we had
missed during our previous visit. I mentioned almost in passing that I wanted
to go to Szarvas and maybe even try to find his parents' home and their graves.
About as nonchalantly, he agreed. I imagined he must have been flattered
that one of his children wanted to go to the trouble of learning more about
his past. I also wondered if, at eighty-four years old, he wanted to leave a

more complete legacy of himself to his children. Almost four years after our entire family had journeyed to Hungary, my father and I would return again. He would make the trip with me. And, perhaps, I secretly hoped, he would finally embrace and then let go of his sorrow.

We arrived in March at the end of a long winter. On our first morning in Budapest, I stole out of our hotel in Buda. I felt no joy or exhilaration in what I was about to do that morning, just a compelling sense of necessity. I never felt more alone than I was at that moment. As I exited the hotel into the cold morning air, I could see a noble-looking synagogue a few hundred yards away, facing the river. It actually looked more like a Greek temple than anything else, although I recognized the Hebrew letters below its Ionic frieze. Before I went off in the other direction, I walked close enough to the building to read the commercial sign posted on it and to realize that it had been turned into an office building.

As I drove in a rented car along the Danube, I looked across the frigid waters of the river at the imperial Parliament. It was wrapped in a dense gray mist that obscured its stately exterior. From a distance of thirty or forty yards, I could see puddles of water surrounding small, thawing patches of snow along the quays of the river. Winter was passing but spring was not yet in the air.

I was crossing over the Chain Bridge into Roosevelt Square in Pest. The place was familiar to me from our trip a few years before. Straight ahead was the government building that had once housed the formidable Hungarian Commercial Bank of Pest, where my father had worked before and even after the war. In the spring of 1938, he had stood at its third-floor window viewing the august procession of Christian dignitaries, including the Hungarian Roman Catholic prince primate, as well as the future Pope Pius XII, amid a densely packed crowd of pious celebrants. I imagined the pomp and celebration that day, during which speaker upon speaker heaped praises on Christ's gift to the world of His all-encompassing love. I glanced off into the distance at the leafless birches and acacia trees still visible on Margit's Island. They were quiet and still, eternally stretching their plaintive branches up toward the enveloping mist like thousands of twisted, skeletal fingers reaching toward heaven, their tops finally obscured by the ubiquitous ghostly mist. How much and how little had changed since descendants of Spanish Jews, fleeing the Inquisition, had settled here? Then I looked down at the Danube and couldn't help but realize how many innocent Jewish lives had found a wretched, watery grave there. There would always be a deep current of unredeemed sorrow to this place, which no amount of divine tears or all-encompassing love could ever heal.

There was no lack of human and divine tears in this city. But I hadn't come out this particular morning to add to it with my own weeping, nor to exact anyone else's. Instead, I was trying to find the city's and country's source of tears—its people's heart and soul, from which all their joy and sorrow emerge. In my mind, that place was the basilica, the colossal church built to honor the sainted King Stephen, who had brought the Christian Savior to his Magyar hordes a thousand years earlier and converted them into a Roman Catholic nation. It was just a few blocks away. I was there in less than a minute.

After parking in St. Stephen's Square, I walked over its cobblestone surface. Low-standing Communist-era office buildings flanking one side of the square made it appear infinitely smaller than it once must have seemed when six-year-old twin brothers stood here nearly a lifetime earlier.

Timidly I climbed the two tiers of granite stairs. By the time I got to the massive oak and bronze doors, my mouth was dry and my hands felt clammy. I had once gotten as far as these stairs, but now I was determined to go inside. "For what?" I knew my mother would say, and probably my father as well. I wasn't supposed to be doing this. I was a Jew, now and forever. This place was not my place.

As I entered the sanctuary, I was awestruck by the immense, otherworldly spectacle in front of me. I looked around and almost recognized the layout from the stories I had heard in my childhood—the four immense red marble columns supporting the central dome, the gilded arches and candelabra, the ornately painted friezes of angels and cherubs, and the lustrous statues of saints and kings.

The place was a quintessentially Christian palace of worship. I was respectful, even though the sanctity of the place belonged to others and there was nothing familiar about it to my Jewish sensibilities. I did not have to actively resist the magnificent visual spectacle. I had not been bidden here and, in truth, I did not feel welcome. I was not a mischievous and gawking six-year-old child whose heart and mind were still impressionable. I was a committed Jew and I needed to get on with why I had come.

I walked to the center aisle, where carved mahogany pews were cordoned off, preventing me from getting any nearer to the nave. From there, though, I could see the crucifix on the altar, as well as, off to my left, an immense oil painting of the crucified Christ being carried from Calvary. I looked at the painting and sighed, trying to exhale my tension. I looked again at His lifeless body and took another deep breath.

"I am a Jew," I began, "and I do not accept you as my Savior." I tried to measure my words and pace myself, as if I might receive a response. "But I recognize that you have known suffering, and that you must be a great soul to have willingly taken it on for the good of others. You must surely be an infinite spirit, for how else could you bear the anguish of so much evil that has been done on earth in your name, and the terrible crimes that were committed, or tolerated, despite the love that people professed for you. I'm certain that no finite being could bear that much grief and guilt. But I haven't come here to brazenly point my finger or shake my fist, to plead or to pray, or to be delivered from my imperfection.

"I have come to ask that you remember my grandmother's life and death. I have prayed to God for her heavenly rest. She died clutching the symbol of your redeeming death, and yet, even so, she is the grandmother and great-grandmother of Jewish children. We need to have a way by which she is remembered—by us and by you, her Lord. As Jews, we are redeemed only by memory. It is the only redemption we have known. If Christians can remember your passion, would you remember my grandmother's? Would you be for her, and become for all those who believe in you, not only a God of grace and salvation but a God who remembers what happens here on earth—a God who remembers human suffering? Maybe then my grandmother's suffering will be remembered by her Savior, and those who love you will learn to remember, as well."

✤

Tölgyfa Street had changed beyond recognition. My father's labored steps and his compromised eyesight kept me constantly by his side as we walked by landmarks from his childhood, ones we hadn't emphasized during our earlier family visit. I knew this old neighborhood was an important part of his life. But my father's memories no longer resided in the discolored gray facade of his childhood home or on the grimy streets where he must have played countless times with his twin brother. His memories were of the larger events and the spans of time rather than the places where they transpired—like the years of missing his father during the First World War, and waiting for him to return. The place spurred the memories but, ironically, in and of itself it did not look familiar to him. He was unmoved by it all. He might sooner have recollected his mother's manner from the smile that pulled at the brittle surface of his own stoical face when he conjured her nervous agitation at seeing him and George return home from a day's escapades in Pest, much sooner than by entering his family's apartment now inhabited by strangers. And he could remember his father, not from any clear recollection of walking down his old street but rather by simply touching the side of his own wizened, bald, and blemished pate and being reminded of the day that the "soldier man" returned home from war and lovingly caressed his son's wavy brown locks and smooth face. The street and buildings were bereft of clear memories. My father carried them, instead, in his mind and heart and on the surface of his skin.

It was similar in Báránd and on the way there, as we traveled over the Hungarian plain. To my father it represented a flat oblivion. To me it was the site of our family lore, and I looked for it wherever I could. I wanted to find the railway bridge over the Tisza River near Szolnok, to see the actual metal and wood frame, long ago rebuilt, that had once borne my uncle and grandmother on their way to Báránd. Its destruction by the Hungarian Red Army had disrupted my family's life for months. This was the same bridge over which my grandmother had crossed on her fateful exile, twenty-five years later, to Auschwitz. The thought may not have even crossed my father's mind. But to me this bridge finally anchored memory and myth to a place—a real place—and I felt that I could now possess the memories as my own.

This feeling continued as we passed the road sign for Püspökladány, on the near side of Báránd. I looked at the tree saplings along the railroad track running parallel to the roadway, and had trouble imagining that these could have been the makeshift gallows used by Tibor Szamuely to execute innocent Hungarian travelers during his brief reign of terror after the First World War. But I, nonetheless, remembered the glee with which Uncle George recalled the scoundrel's name after so many years and pronounced it with such precision when he recounted to me the story of the evils of godless communism. The road sign and the trees were markers—for me, if not for my father, and not even perhaps for memory but simply for *stories* that helped shape the people in our family. Photographs of these simple leafless trees, which had probably not even existed back then, would always help ground my family's story to this specific place and that distant time.

We walked through the narrow, unpaved streets of Báránd and looked at the stucco facades of the church, school, and town hall, all covered by a fresh coat of yellow wash. The family's house was now gone; there were buildings on either side of the empty field on which it had once stood. My father remembered the precise locations as well as the names of at least a dozen of the town's inhabitants, and their connection to his family, as if they were lifelong acquaintances. In that way, my father must have felt reassured that he was not inventing his childhood home as he gazed at the otherwise unfamiliar Hungarian village that had been his home nearly three quarters of a century ago. I looked inside the darkened sanctuary of the Catholic church and

tried to picture two young altar boys carrying a huge Bible up to the altar during Mass. I imagined one of them tripping over his cassock, colliding with his
Jewish origins in the self-consciousness and shame evoked by the giggles and
perceived taunts of the congregants.

I was also drawn by the town's Calvinist church. I self-consciously stood
in the rectory's garden for several minutes, not wanting my father to think
that this place meant more to me than it did to him. It was his home, never
mine. But there, amid the stone walkway, the surrounding brambles and
bushes, and the muddy flowerbed covered by the crushed, withered stems
and the brown, decayed heads of the last year's flowers, I imagined a six-year-
old boy playing alone. For five months, he hadn't seen his twin brother or his
sister, who were stranded in Budapest. His father had been abducted by Rumanian soldiers, and he was left with his bereft mother during dangerous
times. But the danger ended and young Gyuri was at last called from this garden to go to the train station to see his beloved brother and his nuisance of a
sister, whom he couldn't help but miss just as much after all those months.
This rectory garden was rife with bittersweet emotions that lay buried in the
earth, nearly forgotten, but for a story I once heard from my uncle. Having
found the place and unearthed the memory from the still cold, dank soil, I
felt connected to him and to the uncomplicated sweetness and longing that
once existed between him and my father. I had crossed the divide that religion had eventually put between them and found another primordial bridge
that reconnected twin brothers to each other.

As we drove from Báránd, the morning mist still hovered over the fields
along the southerly road to the county seat of Bihar. I realized it was the same
road over which my father had once traveled with his father in a horse-drawn
farm cart on their way to do the day's business. It may have been the only
time my father had ever traveled anywhere alone with his father. I remembered him telling me about it years earlier. It probably didn't occur to him
now as we drove. Perhaps that memory, too, had become nameless and no
longer to be distinguished from himself, simply part of who he was. I didn't
see any need to bring it up. It was probably more important to me as a nearly
forgotten relic of a father-son relationship of which I otherwise knew so little. I wondered if my father had become the person he was for having taken
that ride with his father, and maybe, especially, for having taken it only once.

What could they have talked about back then, on the road to the county
seat? Could their words have been the kind that pass between a father and
his young son, however inconsequential, that tell the son who his father is,
giving him clues about who he himself might be or might want to become?

As the two of us drove tediously slowly, behind a farmer in a horse-drawn cart taking bales of hay to feed his animals, I wondered how many times my father and I had taken such solitary rides together through the neighborhoods of Newark and Irvington, to and from Hebrew school or Little League games? How often had we talked about important things or entirely unimportant ones, or simply not talked at all? Perhaps, most fundamentally, these solitary conversations between a father and a son are meant to tell them nothing more than that they belong to each other.

By the time we got to Gyula in the early afternoon, my father was more animated than I was used to seeing him. The city was just a stopping-off point where my father and uncle had spent some of the happiest years of their lives together before their paths diverged. We entered the austere-looking Italian Renaissance building that had once been the orphanage where the brothers lived as schoolboys. It was now a technical high school run by the Order of Don Bosco. An administrator of the school was flattered to meet possibly the oldest surviving resident of that earlier era.

As my father looked around the building, he recognized very little. "The entire building has changed completely," he said. But memories flooded back to him all the same. He described the dormitory in which he and his brother slept, the library where they studied, and the chapel in which they prayed. As in Báránd, names of people whom he had not thought about in many decades came back to him—priests and sisters, mentors and students, companions and competitors. I could tell by his hesitations and silences, however, that he must have left certain memories undisturbed. I looked around the center hall of the school and studied the stairwell, its metal handrail, and the geometrically painted coffered ceiling. Fragments of stories superimposed themselves upon the scene. It was here at this landing that my uncle received news of the death of his only human love, and here in these halls that my father grew spiritually in the security of God's love.

The church that had been the parish of Father Baron Vilmos Apor, the future bishop of the city of Győr, was just down the street. It was a dignified structure with classical lines, and we peered inside its resplendently baroque interior. This was enough to remind my father of his occasional encounters with the humanitarian priest who had inspired his comfort in the Catholic Church so warmly that the adolescent had considered entering the priesthood. On the outside wall of the church we found a bronze memorial plaque with the portrait of Father Apor. Above the image of the gentle and noble priest with sad, inwardly turned eyes, there was the Star of David as a loving remembrance of one of the few Hungarian clergymen who fearlessly de-

fended the rights of Jews and the mandates of Christian charity in the face
of deportation and genocide. I felt grateful for this church's modest public
recognition of Apor's solicitude toward the Jews, in a nation where most
Christian clergymen had failed utterly to defend them and where former synagogues had now been turned into markets and bazaars bearing Communist-
era inscriptions acknowledging unnamed "victims" and "martyrs" of Nazism.
More than that, I felt deep personal gratitude to Father Apor, not only for his
singular efforts to save Jews but also for the inspiration he had given to my father and uncle to be good Christians—truly to become good people, sensitive
to the suffering of others. How strangely ironic that the priest who had so inspired my father's love of Christianity had become such a solitary voice in the
wilderness on behalf of the Jews.

Later that same day, my father and I began our journey to Szarvas. It had
been a forbidden destination for many years, the place where memories were
too bittersweet and events too cruel to justify our return. I still didn't understand why my uncle had once taken my father to task for avoiding this visit
for so long, but it couldn't have been an accident that George himself had
never managed to return there. Although my father said little as we left
Gyula, I was certain that he was feeling his own share of trepidation. I myself
felt a heaviness in my arms and in my throat.

"Don't upset your father," I heard a voice say in my head. Many years earlier, haunting me in an eerie reverie, my grandmother Gabriella had spoken
those words to me. Driving toward Szarvas, I heard them again. In a pained
and pleading voice, I thought she was saying, "Please leave him alone with
these things. It is too much." As we traversed the countryside of my father's
youth, I wondered whether I was proceeding without my grandmother's
blessing. Is some grief so great, I wondered, that it needs to be left alone, un-
buried and unredeemed? In their eternal care and solicitude toward us, are
the dead more aware than we are that we can't even draw near and pray for
them without our hearts breaking?

As I drove, my father gazed obliviously, almost sentimentally, at the surrounding farmlands around Kondoros, his family's home before they moved
just down the road to Szarvas. These were lands where his father once
tended to the farm animals, and where the farmers rarely gave much thought
to what his religion was. I suppose it was better that my father see this as a
sentimental journey guarded by benevolent forgetfulness, rather than as a
deliberate and too-poignant mission of remembrance and mourning thrust
upon him by his zealous son.

We arrived in town in the middle of the afternoon. The parish church was

right on the main street and we slowed down to look at it. It was little different from any other village church we had seen along the way—yet another
handsome pastel-colored legacy of the Counter-Reformation. But I knew
this was the place where my uncle had offered his first Mass and where my
grandmother had been escorted by gendarmes to pray as a Christian before
being deported as a Jew. I kept my thoughts to myself. They would not do my
father any good. I still had to navigate cautiously around his sensitivities. This
was my father's journey more than it was mine. It required more courage for
him than for me. Or did it?

We stopped just down the main street in the heart of the downtown to
have a late lunch in an elegant-looking corner building with patinated copper
spires and parapets. Surely it must have once been a distinctive landmark of
the area. During my father's youth there had been a distinguished town
square with Old World gardens and rows of hedges surrounding a circular
fountain—all pictured in a 1930s postcard I had once seen. Now there were
crowded, flat, bureaucratic-looking buildings from the Communist years.
There was a drab restaurant inside the corner building with a few idle-look-
ing young people drinking beer, smoking cigarettes, and killing time.

After lunch, with less than a few hours of daylight left, we continued to
drive through the area to get the lay of the land. We got to the far end of the
main street and then crossed a bridge over the Körös River, its banks covered
with withered and crushed grasses and softly arching, barren willows. The
river hugged the edge of the town, its waters only beginning to thaw at the
end of winter.

My father was quiet, with a look of perplexity on his face that was by now
familiar. He lowered his head, touching his brow with the tips of his fingers,
his elbow on the armrest of the car door. When I turned the car around to
cross back into town, I stopped for a few seconds and looked at him. "What
are you thinking?" I asked.

"I don't remember much here, either. It was all so long ago. My mind is
working, but a knot in my chest gets in the way. It makes me think that I don't
want to remember, not that I can't."

Perhaps he was telling me that the seat of his memory was his heart, not
his mind. My father's last experience in Szarvas was his father's funeral. Its
terrible aftermath, when the grave was desecrated, had probably compelled
him to want to forget the town forever. And then, so soon after that, the
knowledge of his mother's seizure, and deportation, and death, must have
propelled Szarvas into eternal oblivion. Why return to such a place and remember such things? I was beginning to sense the enormity of the emotions
at stake. Should we have come at all? Was it too dangerous, bringing an

eighty-four-year-old man back here? But we couldn't turn back, I told myself, not now. Something still beckoned.

It was dusk, at the end of a long day. We found a hotel in town. I went out alone, in what little daylight remained, and walked around the narrow side streets just to get a feel for the town. Although Szarvas was not a large place, it was much bigger than Báránd. It had rows and rows of identical-looking houses. I fancied maybe I would stumble upon my family's old neighborhood, not that I knew what it looked like, aside from its being next to an artesian well. I soon surrendered for the day and looked forward to the next one.

As I walked back to the hotel, there were still stragglers milling around the downtown area. I saw several teenagers, as well as a mother and child hurrying home. Then I saw an old man hobbling more casually down the street. I wondered how many of the people I passed knew of what happened in Szarvas some fifty years earlier, when Hungarian gendarmes and local police rounded up the town's more than six hundred Jews and took them to the train station. I felt sure that most people here were not well schooled in the Holocaust, especially after more than four decades of Communist repression. I wondered if such knowledge was passed down to them from their families, just as my family's sorrowful memories had been transmitted to me, sometimes even in the absence of words. But it is difficult enough for victims to tell their tales. How much more difficult would it be for perpetrators and bystanders, unless they wrap their guilt in helplessness and their hatred in heroics? Or had they learned a different version of history than I had? And did they resent people like my father and me, journeying all the way from America to act as subtle gadflies, reminding the community by our simple presence of its shameful past? As I walked through the darkened streets of my grandparents' town, I had to remind myself that we had not come back to question or accuse anyone. It was longing and grief, not outrage or vengeance, that brought us.

We spent the next morning hopelessly looking around for anything my father might remember from his life in Szarvas. I felt that our time was slowly running out.

"Dad," I finally said, "I'd like to go over to the city hall to see if there is any record of where your family lived. I'd very much like to find it before we leave." I didn't know why I mentioned the house or what I hoped we would find there. Maybe it was still my own fear and evasiveness about going more to the heart of the matter.

"Very well. I'll go with you," my father said, looking not in the least perturbed.

The city hall was a drab, Communist-era structure that had probably been in better repair seven years earlier, when the Soviets relinquished it. Wanting to find my family's home, I was hoping that someone there would have a record of it. I went in alone, confident that I could make myself understood in a language I had just had a week to polish up, even though I hadn't spoken it with any degree of fluency since I was sixteen years old. I approached an information window in the central hallway, behind which sat a middle-aged woman. She looked like a cheerless functionary from Communist days but was surprisingly pleasant.

"I am visiting Szarvas with my elderly father," I said. "His family lived here in the 1930s. He does not remember where. Do you have records?" The sentences were choppy. I was amazed the words were there.

The woman was respectful. She probably tried to hide what had become a familiar look among natives when I spoke Hungarian to them, that look of wondering whether I really was speaking their language or perhaps some distantly related Mongolian or Turkish dialect.

"Try the office on the second floor, halfway down the hall on the left," she said, with a wide smile, stifling a laugh with a fake cough.

Striding up the stairs, I opened the office door down the hall and asked the same question of the first person I saw. She said she wasn't sure that such records existed, but then pointed to a man on the other side of the room.

"He might be able to tell you," she said. Then she caught the man's attention. "This gentleman is looking for the house in which his grandparents lived in the 1930s. Can you help him?"

The man looked a little puzzled, as though he didn't have enough information. He was a stout and bald middle-aged man with a friendly manner.

"My grandfather was the town's animal doctor for fifteen years," I added.

"I'm not sure if we have records," he answered, "but I have always lived in Szarvas and so have my parents. My father is in his seventies and lives in town. Why don't I call him?"

I was delighted. As he began to usher me into his office, I hesitated and mentioned that my elderly father was waiting downstairs and would very much like to join us.

"Very well, then," he said. "Go get him. I'll wait."

After my father trekked up the stairs, introduced himself, and exchanged some pleasantries with our host, whose name was also Miklós, we sat down in his office, where he picked up the phone and immediately reached his father.

"Father, do you remember an animal doctor in Szarvas named Pogány?"

I was a few feet away and I could hear the answer at the other end of the phone. *"Hát persze"* was the excited reply. "Well, of course."

"Do you remember where they lived?" his son asked.

After listening to his father's reply, he told him that one of the doctor's sons and grandsons had come to visit and wanted to find the house.

"No, of course it's not the priest. The man came with his son. It must be the priest's brother." My father and I smiled at each other.

"Oh, twins," our host repeated, after a pause. "You remember a lot." I was thrilled. My father laughed.

After Miklós hung up the phone, he explained that his father had remembered our family. "The children were a few years older than he and one of them became a priest." My father looked as though he had been recognized by an old neighbor.

"He told me exactly where the house is. I'm happy to take you there."

Though I had only heard a few words of their conversation, the entire tone of the son's interaction with his father only confirmed my family's reports of the esteem in which my grandfather had been held by people in his community. This moment felt like the closest I had ever come to direct contact with anyone outside my family who knew my grandfather. It was the first time I ever felt that I actually had a grandfather. He had lived in this place, was known and liked. He was a real person.

"I remember this house," said my father as the three of us walked over to it from the car. "But it has changed so much. It doesn't look the same. I couldn't have found it myself, but I remember it." He paused. "But why does all this matter? It really doesn't," he said. His voice was matter-of-fact, even upbeat. I think he was still feeling so bolstered by the remarkable interaction we had witnessed between Miklós and his father. Seeing the house was anticlimactic.

There was one more task to fulfill, one last mission. To me, everything else was preparatory, prologue. As we drove Miklós back to the city hall, I turned to my father alongside me and said to him in English, "I'd like to ask him where the cemetery is, so we can find your parents' graves."

"Go ahead," he replied, barely making eye contact as he turned his head and stared out the window.

"If it's your grandparents' graves you want to visit," said Miklós, "I suppose you must want the older Catholic cemetery."

"I don't know," said my father. "I don't remember."

I remained quiet, feeling a little guilty that I didn't disabuse Miklós of the idea that we were Catholic. Of course, I knew the story was too complicated. But was this how my father felt during the war as a convert, at least until his cover was blown by the racist laws? How easy it must have been to fit in as a Catholic in a nation of Christians and feel safe.

"It probably is," said Miklós. "It's on the far end of town, on the other side of the main street." He pointed in that direction. "The newer one is exactly on the opposite end of town, on the side we have just been on. To get to the one you want, go down any of these cross streets and you'll come to it. But stay close to this side," he said, waving his hand across his chest. "There's a Protestant cemetery right next to it. Before you go there, if you want help finding the grave, you might stop off at the church and ask the parish priest. He has a register of burial places. I know he's at the church in the mornings, although he might still be there now."

We thanked Miklós for his kindness as he got out of the car and said good-bye.

"Let's go straight to the cemetery," said my father as soon as the car door slammed shut. "I'm sure we can find the grave. I don't want to stir anything up with the priest. There would be too much explaining to do. Let's just go."

By now it was after four o'clock and I knew we didn't have much daylight left. But I had a photograph of the gravestone and didn't suspect it would be a large cemetery. So off we went, arriving within minutes. We parked at the gate and walked in, stopping at the caretakers' house.

'Do you recognize this gravestone?" I asked the cemetery keeper, as I showed him a black-and-white photograph I had been carrying. "It's my grandparents' grave. They died in 1943 and '44."

Gazing at the picture, the man had a puzzled look on his face. "It's probably here, although I don't recognize it. My wife and I have worked here for twenty years, and your grandparents died long before that. In all those years, I just don't remember seeing it. But I'll help you look. My wife might be back in a few minutes. I'll ask her if she knows."

The caretaker walked toward the back and sides of the graveyard, past plots covered over with ivy and brush as though they hadn't been tended in some years. He and I explored nearly every corner of the cemetery. My weary father stayed behind at the caretakers' cottage, unable to help in the search. After half an hour, the man's wife appeared and joined in the search. But she didn't recognize the gravestone, either, or remember ever seeing it.

Throughout our search, an old, toothless peasant woman—possibly a Gypsy—dark-complected and dressed in rags, had been gathering water in plastic containers from a faucet next to some gravestones. Noticing our difficulty, she finally came over and asked to see the picture, as if she wanted to help. Gazing at the photograph, she glowed with a look of instant recognition. "I have seen this grave," she blurted out with a confident smile, baring her few stained teeth. "I have been here for many years and I have seen the grave. Look at the crucifix on it. There is no other like it. But listen to me," she pressed on. "It is not here, it's not in this cemetery. It's in the other one across the way." But instead of pointing in the direction of the other Catholic graveyard on the opposite side of town, she pointed down toward the furthermost tract of graves, on the opposite side of a fence from where we were standing.

"Woman, that can't be," said the caretaker. "You are pointing to the Protestant cemetery and these people were Catholic."

"I don't care what you say," said the Gypsy, scowling at the man. "I swear. Let my children be struck dead if that gravestone is not in the other cemetery."

I shuddered at the woman's reckless vow. But it may have succeeded in convincing the two caretakers that the search in their graveyard was hopeless.

"Look, it's just about dark," the wife suggested. "But there still may be time for you to spend a few minutes in the Catholic cemetery on the other side of town. Otherwise," she said, glaring back at the Gypsy, "you're wasting your time to look in the Protestant graveyard." She and her husband had apparently lost patience with the familiar old hag. "Or," she continued, "you can check with the parish priest in the morning. He would be able to help find it." Her husband nodded in agreement, but I felt no more comfortable with their suggestion than my father had earlier been with Miklós's. Time was running out.

My father had just about given up. Maybe he was quietly relieved; I didn't know. But I convinced him to come with me in what few minutes of daylight remained, to the second Catholic cemetery. He agreed, and as I hurriedly drove there I thought of the old woman—that unlikely angelic emissary—and hoped, at least for the sake of her children, that she was correct in guiding us elsewhere, even if she didn't recall precisely which direction.

Things then proceeded with eerie swiftness. We sped through town and headed, by chance, down exactly the correct side road that brought us to the gate of the cemetery. We left the car there and walked with blind instinct to the rear of the first row of graves we came to, without looking at any of them along the way. It was the final day of winter. Viscous and faintly redolent mud yielded under our feet as we trekked through the graveyard. The first crocuses were beginning to bloom, barely visible in the fading daylight.

When we got to the end of the row, I looked up and read my grandparents' names on the gravestone before even looking at its shape. I pointed to the stone. My father looked and tried to muffle a deep sigh. The air was damp and chilly as we stood before the common gravestone where my grandfather had been reburied and where endured an inscription and empty grave for my grandmother. We lowered our heads and stood for several moments in silence.

"Please say the Kaddish, Gene," said my father. He still could not pray in Hebrew.

I was startled, but responded immediately. *"Yit-ga-dol v'yit-ka-dash shmei rabba . . ."* (Exalted and sanctified be the name of God in this world of His creation.) I recited the Jewish prayer that glorifies God in the midst of death—partly in my father's stead but really for both of us, for the sake of his parents and my grandparents. *"Oseh shalom bim-ro-mav. Hu ya-a-seh shalom Aleinu ve al kol Israel. V'imru. Amen."* (May He who creates peace in the heavens create peace for us and for all Israel. And say amen.)

"Thank you," said my father. "Now they know."

"The Lord is my shepherd; I shall not want . . ." I continued, after a slight pause.

"That's a beautiful psalm," my father said. He then completed it in Hungarian. "I will never forget this," he said when he had finished, his voice cracking with emotion.

I thought my father felt relief that now, half a century later, he could finally make himself known as a Jew to his Christian parents and prayerfully mourn their deaths.

I thought of George, who had been gone for three years. Could his spirit have come to join us in this rural Hungarian cemetery, one to which even he could not bring himself to return while he was still alive? Might he have come back to his boyhood home on earth to bear witness to his twin brother finally praying at the graveside of his parents?

This is what had brought us back that March day, when the ice of the Körös River, caressing the edge of Szarvas in its cool embrace, was breaking and melting. It was my good-bye to grandparents who had become known to me only through my family's recollections. In being there that day, I felt I had begun to fulfill my obligations as the son and grandson of those who had suffered—in the name of the Father *and* the Son. When we were done, night had fallen and the formerly beclouded sky was rife with stars. My father and I walked slowly from the grave, saying nothing. We passed through the cemetery gate, as the earth was softening with the first thaw of spring.

NOTES

❖

CHAPTER 1

Descriptions of the social atmosphere of pre- and post-World War I Budapest were based on the work of Raphael Patai (*The Jews of Hungary: History, Culture, Psychology,* Wayne State University Press, 1996) and John Lukacs (*Budapest 1900: A Historical Portrait of a City and Its Culture,* Weidenfeld and Nicolson, 1988), as well as Randolph L. Braham, referenced below. The familial influences on my grandparents' marriage, including actual statements made by family members, as well as the character of individuals involved, were all based on personal reports by my father, uncle, and aunt.

CHAPTER 2

In light of my grandmother's steadfast devotion to Catholicism, it never appeared likely to me that she had converted for purely pragmatic reasons. My uncle had subtly hinted at a more personal and spiritual basis, one that he may have verbalized to others of his faith but certainly never discussed with members of my father's family. All three siblings mentioned the story of my grandmother's meeting with the rabbi in Budapest to inform him that she would be converting to Catholicism, each one differently coloring the reported events. Although some people love the religious faith into which they were born, I have come to accept that many are called by a still, small voice to another spiritual path. Roman Catholicism was my grandmother's calling, and in this chapter I combine my relatives' versions of this story into my own vision of the path she journeyed to arrive there.

The events of Gabriella and the children's baptism and Easter Sunday 1919 were reported to me primarily by George and elaborated by my father and aunt. It is George's enthusiasm that is reflected in my treatment of these occasions.

CHAPTER 3

The political and military background of the descriptions of the postwar period were based on Ivan Völgyes, ed., *Hungary in Revolution 1918–1919* (University of Nebraska

Press, 1971) and Jerome and Jean Tharaud, *When Israel Is King* (Robert M. McBride and Co., 1924). The dramatic events occurring to members of my family were based on the memories of my father and his siblings.

CHAPTERS 5 AND 6

Less than two years after George's death, on the second day of Passover in 1995—which coincided that year with Easter Sunday—my father finally shared his very private speculation about what had inspired his twin brother to seek his calling in the Church. Neither George's parents and sister nor anyone in succeeding generations of the family ever suspected the human drama that my father had always quietly believed was a major impetus in his brother's religious calling. My father's report is the basis for my own interpretation of the story.

CHAPTER 8

My father and uncle's reports provided the basis of the personal events that transpired at the Eucharistic Convention of 1938 in Budapest. Moshe Herczl's *Christianity and the Holocaust of Hungarian Jewry* (New York University Press, 1993), at times quoting from the *Nemzeti Ujsag* (*The National News*), the major Catholic newspaper in the country, supplied the details of events and quotations during that international three-day religious celebration.

CHAPTER 9

My uncle had spoken to me on more than one occasion of his friendship with Father Emil Kappler and his first meeting with Padre Pio. His comments about Father Kappler coincide with his remarks in the interview he gave to the Reverend C. Bernard Ruffin, which appeared in the epilogue of Ruffin's revised *Padre Pio: The True Story* (Our Sunday Visitor, Inc., 1991). As for his meetings with Padre Pio, George was often circumspect in his remarks, partly because he always modestly understated Padre Pio's mystical abilities, valuing instead the padre's religious piety. "Of course, the man was a saint," he would often state matter-of-factly, but he was also reluctant to jeopardize Padre Pio's cause for canonization by making any public pronouncements. Regarding his initial encounter with Padre Pio, George usually insisted that the padre invited him to remain in San Giovanni Rotondo for purely practical, health-related reasons, even while he acknowledged that the visionary Capuchin friar often knew more than he let on. Yet Mrs. Anna Zegna, George's friend and correspondent, helped me appreciate the urgency of Padre Pio's invitation to George in light of the impending dangers of war and the potential persecution of this Jewish-born Hungarian priest. Although others have similarly visited San Giovanni Rotondo and ended up spending the rest of their lives in devotion to Padre Pio, the geopolitical circumstances during my uncle's initial visit would support a supposition that he did not casually make an arduous journey by train across the breadth of Italy, in difficult and uncertain and soon-to-be dangerous times, merely on the whimsical suggestion of a friend. George surely sensed the mounting danger and may have been drawn to San Giovanni by the reasonable hope of finding sanctuary in an out-of-the-way corner of Italy. Likewise, it is not difficult to infer that Padre Pio instantly recognized my uncle not only as a refugee in need of safe harbor, but also as a spiritual and earnest priest whose presence—not to mention his linguistic abilities—he would value. Finally, Padre Joseph Pius Martin's suggestions helped me establish and clarify the setting and nature of my uncle's life-changing meeting with Padre Pio.

CHAPTER 11

Comments on the history of the Italian Jews during World War II were derived from the works of Susan Zuccotti (*The Italians and the Holocaust: Persecution, Rescue and Survival,* Basic Books, 1987), Ivo Herzer (ed., *The Italian Refuge: Rescue of Jews During the Holocaust,* The Catholic University of America Press, 1989), Meir Michaelis (*Mussolini and the Jews: German-Italian Relations and the Jewish Question in Italy 1922–1945,* Clarendon Press, 1978), and Sam Waagenaar (*The Pope's Jews,* Open Court Publishers, 1974). My uncle described life circumstances in San Giovanni Rotondo during that time, as well as his specific interactions with the carabiniere. General circumstances were further based on Ruffin's original edition of *Padre Pio: The True Story* (Our Sunday Visitor, Inc., 1982). Padre Pios Abresch also provided personal reports on this time period, as well as on postwar events. My uncle's later correspondence with Mr. and Mrs. Albino Zegna, of Biella, Italy, helped identify the time frame of George's dealings with the Italian state police.

My aunt Klari's 1984 visit from Australia supplied the major portions of the scene of my grandmother's deportation from her home in Szarvas. After the war, during her recuperation in a Budapest hospital from her own travail in a concentration camp, Klari met a Jewish neighbor from Szarvas who had been deported with my grandmother and who confirmed both the events in the Szarvas ghetto and the nature of my grandmother's final moments in Auschwitz—parallel to what was reported to my mother in Bergen-Belsen, as mentioned in Chapter 13. Professor Braham's exhaustive two-volume report, *The Politics of Genocide: The Holocaust in Hungary* (Columbia University Press, 1981), provided precise figures and dates.

CHAPTER 12

My mother recounted the stories in this chapter, as well as those in Chapter 13, countless times throughout my childhood. They were told in the spirit of a sassy, resourceful survivor, although they were never easy to listen to, partly because they never truly obscured my mother's underlying pain and desperation. But it was only much later, within two years of my completing this book, that my mother finally acknowledged what may have been the most painful episode of her life—her decision to be baptized in 1944. Afraid of the judgment of her children and grandchildren, she wished that I would withhold this account from my writing. While I could not faithfully promise to do so, my appreciation of the story and my reading of Braham and Herczl have heightened my sensitivity toward the desperate plight of Budapest's Jews in 1944 to avoid deportation. I can now also better grasp the sorrowful desperation of Spanish Jews during the Inquisition who underwent baptism under duress. I conclude that it is not for the children or grandchildren, much less for others, to stand in judgment of their forebears. We are more affirmed in our faith for these people having chosen life.

CHAPTER 13

Throughout my childhood, my mother often told stories of her experiences of victimization and survival. She still tells these stories, and each time she does it is as if she survives the experiences anew. The immigration official in Budapest who assists my mother in avoiding deportation for not being a native-born Hungarian is actually a condensation of two individuals, the other one being a flirtatious young physician who ultimately helped my mother secure higher benefits as the wife of a member of the Christian labor battalions. Similarly, the woman called Éva in Bergen-Belsen represents a number of characters whose names have been lost. I felt that giving them a name would help memorialize them. May they be of blessed memory.

Béla, the lawyer from Sopron, with whom my father was deported from Budapest to Bergen-Belsen, emigrated to Israel after serving two years for Zionist agitation in a Hungarian Soviet prison. He and I met frequently in Jerusalem in 1973–74, when I was a visiting student there. During that year, Béla served as an invaluable resource about events in Bergen-Belsen, as well as about the manner in which my father wrestled with his religious identity during their months of confinement.

The account of my father's experiences of liberation by the American Ninth Army from the train transport leaving Bergen-Belsen is a paraphrase of an essay he wrote in 1950, originally in Hungarian. His work was eventually published in the (Boston) *Jewish Advocate* on April 7, 1995 (Volume 185, Number 14), on the fiftieth anniversary of the liberation.

CHAPTER 15

George's conversation with Padre Pio regarding my father's return to Judaism is based in part on my conversation with Padre Pio Abresch in Rome. George's feelings regarding his brother's rejection of Christianity were known to the Abresch family and likely to Padre Pio and the fathers at the friary. In light of what has been described as George's characteristic religious orthodoxy, by which he opposed conciliation and permissiveness in the church, it seems highly unlikely that he would have withheld expressing his disappointment about his brother to those who knew him well. Padre Pio's response to my uncle is drawn from the padre's documented feelings about Judaism and his thoughts on the possibility of members of religions other than Catholicism achieving salvation. His comments about Jewish suffering in the Holocaust are inferences based on his knowledge by that time of the horrors of the death camps, of which my grandmother's death in Auschwitz may have been the instance most intimately known to him. Even while he referred to her as a Christian martyr, I find it impossible to believe that he would disregard the suffering and death of so many millions of Jews in the Nazi death camps. As to whether he blunted the tragedy by ascribing a higher religious significance to it, as other devout Christians have done, I do not know.

CHAPTER 18

Numerous discussions with Katharina Lamping about countless interactions she had with my uncle are the basis for the conversation between them regarding my father's reluctance to return to Szarvas on his visit to Hungary. Also, familiarizing myself with the content of many of his handwritten sermons helped me to re-create George's feelings about forgiveness and the institution of confession.

CHAPTER 21

Following hospitalization in Budapest after her return from deportation, my aunt Klari returned to Szarvas to find that the family's home and possessions had been eagerly plundered by townspeople. She also learned at that time that the man who was responsible for disinterring my grandfather's grave had been driven from Szarvas after the war by sympathetic townspeople. When my father and I returned there in 1996, we discovered that the man called Fekete in this book had returned years later and had been buried alongside his wife, only a few steps removed from my grandparents' gravestone.

10/00